Women Writers of
Ancient Greece and Rome

Women Writers of
Ancient Greece and Rome

AN ANTHOLOGY

Edited by
I. M. Plant

University of Oklahoma Press
Norman

Library of Congress Cataloging-in-Publication Data

Women writers of ancient Greece and Rome : an anthology / edited by I.M. Plant
    p. cm.
  Includes bibliographical references and indexes.
  ISBN 0-8061-3621-9 (cloth)
  ISBN 0-8061-3622-7 (pbk : alk. paper)
   1. Classical literature—Women authors—Translations into English. 2. Greek
literature—Women authors—Translations into English. 3. Latin literature—Women
authors—Translations into English. 4. Women—Greece—Literary collections. 5.
Women—Rome—Literary collections. I. Plant, I. M. (Ian Michael), 1963–

PA3621. W66 2004
880'.082'—dc22

2003063449

University of Oklahoma Press edition published by special arrangement with Equinox Publishing Ltd., Unit 6, The Village, 101 Amies Street, London, SW11 2JW (www.equinoxpub.com). Translations, introduction, and editorial apparatus © 2004 by Ian Plant.

1 2 3 4 5 6 7 8 9 10

Contents

List of Abbreviations

ad loc.	*on this passage*
ALG	Diehl, E., *Anthologia Lyrica Graeca*, I (Leipzig: Teubner, 1936)
Athen.	Athenaeus, *Scholars at Dinner*
Anth. Pal.	*Anthologia Palatina*
Anth. Plan.	*Anthologia Planudea*
Ap. Dysc.	Apollonius Dyscolus
Ap. Rhod.	Apollonius Rhodes
Ar.	Aristophanes
Arist.	Aristotle
c.	*circa* (about): used to indicate an approximate number
CAG	Berthelot, M., *Collection des Alchemistes Grecs* (Paris, 1888)
cf.	Compare *(confer)*
Chrysipp.	Chrysippus, *Negatives*
CIL	Borman, E. (ed.), *Corpus Inscriptionum Latinarum* (Berlin, 1863–1959)
CMG	Olivieri, A., *Aëtii Amideni libri medicales i–iv. Corpus Medicorum Graecorum* 8.2 (Berlin: Teubner, 1935)
Demmetr.	Demetrius, *On Style*
Dio Chrys.	Dio Chrysostomus, *Discourses*
Diog. L.	Diogenes Laertius, *Lives of the Philosophers*
Dion. Hal.	Dionysius of Halicarnassus, *On Literary Composition*
Epist. Gr.	Hercher, R. (ed.), *Epistolographi Graeci* (Paris: A. Firmin Didot, 1873)
Et. Gen.	Calame, C. (ed.), *Etymologicum genuinum: les citations de poètes lyriques* (Roma: Edizioni dell'Ateneo, 1970)
Et. Mag.	Lassere, F., and N. Livadaras (eds), *Etymologicum magnum genuinum* (Roma: Edizioni dell'Ateneo, 1976)
Eust.	Eustathius
FGrH	Jacoby, F. (ed.), *Die Fragmente der griechischen Historiker* (Berlin, 1923–57)
FHG	Muller, C. (ed.), *Fragmenta Historicorum Graecorum* (Paris, 1841–70)
fl.	*floruit* ('flourished'): the date at which someone reached a peak of achievement, usually cited when the exact dates of the person's birth are not known.
fr.	fragment
Gell.	Aulus Gellius, *The Attic Nights*
Hdn.	Herodian, *On Anomalous Words*
Heph.	Hephaestion, *Handbook of Metres*
Heph. *Poem.*	Hephaestion, *On Poems*
Hermog.	Hermogenes, *On Kinds of Style*
Himmer.	Himmerius, *Orations*
IG	*Inscriptiones Graecae* (Berlin, 1873–)
ILS	Dessau, H. (ed.), *Inscriptiones Latinae Selectae* (Berlin: Weidmann, 1892–1916)
Inscr. Eph.	Englemann, H. *et al.*, *Die Inschriften von Ephesos* (Bonn: Habelt, 1980)
L-P	Lobel, E., and Page, D.L., *Poetarum Lesbiorum Fragmenta* (Oxford: Clarendon Press, 1963)
Max. Tyr.	Maximus of Tyre, *Orations*

P. Amh.	Grenfell, B.P., and Hunt, A.S. (eds), *The Amherst Papyri*, II (London: Henry Frowde, 1901)
P. Haun.	Larsen, T. (ed.), *Papyri Graecae Haunienses*, I (Copenhagen: Munksgaard, 1942)
P. Berol.	*Papyri Berlinenses* in *Berliner Klassikertexte* (Berlin, 1904–96)
P. Oxy.	Grenfell, B.P., *et al.* (eds), *The Oxyrhynchus Papyri* (London: Egypt Exploration Fund, 1896–)
P. Fouad.	Bataille, A. *et al.*, *Les Papyrus fouad* (Cairo: Institut français d'archéologie orientale, 1939)
P. Mediol.	*Papiri Milanesi* (Milan, 1928–64)
PMG	Page, D.L., *Poetae Melici Graeci* (Oxford: Clarendon Press, 1962)
PSI	Vitelli, G. *et al.*, *Papiri della Societa Italiana* (1912–32)
Paus.	Pausanias, *Description of Greece*
Plin.	Pliny the Elder, *Natural History*
Plut.	Plutarch
s.v.	Under the word (*sub voce*)
Schol.	Scholiast (=Ancient Commentator)
Stob.	Stobaeus, *Anthology*
Strab.	Strabo, *Geography*
{Tib.}	In the Tibullus corpus, but not by Tibullus
Zos.	Zosimus

Introduction

Theano, when putting on her cloak, exposed her arm. A man said, 'Your arm is beautiful'. She said, 'But it is private'. Not just her arm, but also a virtuous woman's speech should be private; she should be modest and careful about saying anything in the hearing of people who aren't family, since this would be exposing herself. For in her speech, her feelings, character and temperament are revealed
(Plutarch, *Moralia* 142c-d).

This anthology provides a comprehensive collection of texts (in translation) by women from the Graeco-Roman world. Plutarch expresses a sentiment common in Graeco-Roman literature that women should keep their lives private. A virtuous woman, following this ideal, should not write anything that might be read by people outside her family, as this would expose her feelings, character and temperament to the world. Yet despite such prejudice, and the perception it produces that all literature was actually written by men, we find that from the seventh century BC through to the sixth century AD throughout the Graeco-Roman world women wrote on a wide variety of topics. However, the amount of work disseminated by women appears to have been relatively small and not all of it has survived.

The canon of Greek authors alone has some 3,200 entries,[1] but we have the names of only about one hundred Greek and Roman women writers.[2] Although they are a very small sample of the total corpus, they nevertheless span a surprising variety of genres. Poetry predominates, especially lyric poetry, but this was not all women wrote. We find works of history, philosophy, musical theory, grammar, literary criticism, astronomy, travel, medicine, sex, mathematics, drama, prophecy and alchemy attributed to women. This anthology brings together fifty-five of these women, the attested authors of virtually all extant works written by women and intended for dissemination outside their families.[3] The texts span a period of over a thousand years, and come from as far west as Galicia (Western Spain) and Aquitania (South-West France), as far south as Egypt and as far east as Asia Minor.

The identification of women authors is problematic. In the *Greek Anthology* there are two short lists of poets lauded by Meleager and Antipater,[4] and Tatian names Greek women who had been honoured with statues. Athenaeus, who lived in the late second to early third centuries AD, drew on a vast number of earlier writers whose works are now lost, including some women, in his *Scholars at Dinner* (*Deipnosophistae*).[5] The compiler of the *Suda,* a tenth-century Greek lexicon, provides a great deal of biographical information about earlier writers, including women. However, much of this is inaccurate, the result of later inferences or inventions. We can compile a list of women writers from references in these and other sources, but there is a suspicion that not all of the writers identified as women really were. In antiquity, it was recognised that some texts were pseudonymous. Aeschrion alleged a work on sex attributed to the famous prostitute Philaenis was a forgery and that it was really by Polycrates of Athens (*Anth. Pal.* 7.345).[6] A famous name might be used to characterise or add authority to a work, such as the pseudonymous philosophical letters written under the name of Theano, the wife of Pythagoras. An author might simply enjoy adopting a literary persona (as Ovid does in his fictitious letter from Sappho to Phaon). Such works might be rhetorical exercises or tributes to the original author, not intended to be mistaken for that author's own work.[7] The general perception that literature of quality was by men led to the modern denial that Erinna, one of the most famous female writers in antiquity, was a woman.[8] But the poetry of Sappho, which is among the earliest and finest lyric poetry we have, proves that high quality work was written by women too. The texts in this collection show that we cannot identify the work of women writers by the quality, subject matter or style of their work.

There are some pseudonymous works in this anthology: Theano's texts are a case in point. They are not by the wife of Pythagoras, but that does not mean that they were necessarily written by a man. Why would a male writer pretend to be a woman? Theano's texts are about what were considered women's issues—how to bring up children, how a woman should behave virtuously, how she should treat the servants—and the writer might have wanted an authoritative female voice to carry that perspective (as a dramatist might). The intended readers needed to accept the work as being by a woman for its didactic purpose to be effective. If the community could believe a text was by a woman, then it provides an example of what women were thought to be capable of knowing and writing.

The majority of attested women authors are poets. These include the personification of a poetic genre, Iambe, and legendary inventors of genres, Phantasia and Phanothea, who, along with the Muses, show the conceptual link between women and poetry.

Sappho's poetry stands out in the development of lyric poetry. It was musical, written for both solo and choral performance, and received by audiences of both men and women.[9] In writing unashamedly of her own emotions, Sappho created a personal perspective of the world, very different from that of earlier heroic poetry. Her impact on later poets was profound. She influenced and inspired Nossis, Erinna and Julia Balbilla, as well as such male poets as Catullus and Ovid. Philodemus suggests that in his day (some 500 years after Sappho) every educated Roman woman could sing Sappho's songs.[10]

Publication of poetry and prose in the Graeco-Roman world was initially by performance. Authors read, recited or sang their work to a suitable audience. This might be a small literary circle or a much larger audience at a public festival.[11] The ideal of the seclusion of citizen women in the Classical period (fifth and fourth centuries BC) limited their opportunities to perform in public. Nevertheless we do know of women writers, including Athenians, from this period.[12] Non-citizen women in Athens could and did perform poetry in public.[13] However, women were excluded from performing in drama, and this restricted them to other genres such as solo and choral lyric poetry, hymns and popular songs. A genre of poetry for which the author did not receive recognition in the ancient world was the oracle. The Pythia, the oracle of Apollo at Delphi, and some other oracles are recorded as giving verse responses, apparently composed on the spot but perhaps prepared earlier. Examples include the famous prophecies of the priestess Aristonice, given in the fifth century BC before the Persian wars.[14] Because we cannot be sure who composed such texts, I have not included them in this collection.

Aristocratic women in the Hellenistic period benefited from greater opportunities to receive a literary education. There are considerably more authors attested from this period. This is in part due to the development of a new genre of poetry intended for written publication, the creation of anthologies and the collection of books. The establishment of the Library and Museum in Alexandria promoted literary and scholarly work, creating a strong literary culture and discerning readers for women's poetry, and a means by which that poetry might be preserved.[15]

Surprisingly little poetry by Roman women remains from the first century BC and the first century AD (known as the Golden and Silver Ages of Latin literature). Occasional verse composed at Egyptian tourist sites and left there as graffiti by Julia Balbilla, Caecilia Trebulla and Terentia reinforces the impression gained elsewhere that wealthy Roman women received a good literary education and were in the habit of composing verse in Latin or in Greek.[16] It was not common for women to publish their verse, but this is not surprising in a community whose ideal woman was a shy listener to her husband's compositions, rather than an active participant in a literary circle.[17] Two women named Sulpicia prove the exception.[18] Though only two lines remain of the verse of the second Sulpicia, we have perhaps as many as eight elegies by the earlier Sulpicia, who lived in the reign of Augustus, and we have poems about her. She was part of a literary circle under the patronage of Marcus Valerius Messalla that included Ovid, Tibullus and Lygdamus. Membership of such a circle was necessary for the circulation and publication of poetry, and for it to be taken seriously by the wider literary community. Normally, women were not included in circles of professional poets; Sulpicia may have benefited from her personal relationship with Messalla (as his niece) to gain access.

Substantial works remain from much later, the fourth and fifth centuries AD, by Proba (in Latin) and the Empress Eudocia (in Greek). Taking whole and half lines from Virgil's works, Proba stitched together a Christian cento[19] of nearly 700 lines that tells the story of the creation of the world and the life of Christ. The Christian theme ensured that the work would be popular, widely read, and preserved in many different manuscripts. Her epic on Constantius' war against Magnentius (AD 350–52) has not survived. Eudocia, wife of the emperor Theodosius II, composed a Homeric Christian cento, along with other works. While long ignored by modern scholarship as a purely derivative genre, the skill with which cento writers could weave together a new creation has recently received more favourable attention.[20]

Although earlier writers were attested in antiquity,[21] we can date no extant prose works earlier than the Hellenistic period. The earliest fragments of a history may come from a work on Alexander the Great by Nicobule, who perhaps lived as early as the third century BC. Her date is conjectural, however, and the fragments are paraphrased rather than quoted directly.[22] Histiaea can be dated to around 200 BC; she wrote in Alexandria on grammar, history and topography, but none of her work has survived.[23] We know that Agrippina (mother of the Roman emperor Nero) wrote a history of her family cited by Tacitus,[24] but there are no extant fragments of her work. Political activity is attested in two fragments of a letter from Cornelia to her son Gaius Gracchus, which if genuine would date to 125 BC, but these fragments are probably not authentic.[25] In 42 BC Hortensia gave a speech that was praised by later critics, but the speech itself survives only in a Greek paraphrase by Appian. We do have fragments of the work of Pamphila, who lived in the first century AD and wrote expansively on a wide range of topics (specializing in epitomes of prose works), but these fragments are brief.

There are more extensive extant prose works in the field of philosophy. Hipparchia, the Cynic philosopher who lived in the fourth century BC, is one of the earliest attested female prose authors, though none of her work survives.[26] Another was the Epicurean philosopher

Leontion who lived at the end of the fourth and early third centuries BC. Her critique of Theophrastus (Aristotle's pupil) was praised for its good Attic style by Cicero; it too is not extant.[27] We do have substantial works attributed to Pythagoreans of the sixth century BC, including Pythagoras' wife, Theano, and daughters, Myia and Arignote. The attribution to Pythagoras' family members, however, cannot be correct. The texts should be dated to the third or second centuries BC (perhaps some of them slightly earlier).[28] Other Pythagorean authors with extant work are Aesara, Melissa, Perictione, and Phintys. Some of these texts are pseudonymous, but they may well be by women and are nevertheless interesting for the attitudes they convey regarding appropriate women's behaviour in the Pythagorean community. Ptolemaïs wrote on Greek musical theory. We know little about her. She lived in Cyrene and Alexandria some time between the fourth century BC and first century AD, perhaps around 250 BC.[29] Porphyry knew her work and quoted her three times. The most famous female Greek philosopher, Hypatia, was murdered by a mob in Alexandria in AD 415. The reasons for her death are not clear, but it is suggested that her fame as a philosopher and pagan made her the target of an anti-pagan faction.[30] She published on mathematics and astronomy, but none of her work is extant.[31]

An autobiographical prose work is attributed to Perpetua, a Christian martyr, put to death in Carthage during a persecution under Septimius Severus in AD 202–03. The account of her martyrdom includes a section in the first person, which purports to be Perpetua's own account of her trial and time in prison before her execution. If her authorship is accepted, this text gains particular significance as the earliest extant Christian literature written by a woman.[32] Perpetua's text was popular in the Christian community, and this in part accounts for its survival. Another Christian text in this anthology was not so widely read. It survived by chance in a single manuscript rediscovered late in the nineteenth century. This text, Egeria's *Journal,* is a diary of her pilgrimage to the Holy Land followed by an account of the liturgical year and liturgy in Jerusalem. The evidence suggests that Egeria was a wealthy member of a religious community in Galicia in western Spain, perhaps even an abbess, who composed the account of her pilgrimage for her fellow Religious—readers she addresses as 'Your Charity', 'revered ladies...my sisters'. The text was not intended for general publication, which may explain its rough and repetitive style.[33] Egeria's text is of great historical significance. Her description of the liturgy and religious observances in fifth-century Jerusalem is valuable. She also adds to our knowledge of biblical sites and religious buildings in her day. The testament of her faith, the religious objectives of her journeys, her faith in the physical reality of the Old and New Testament stories, provide insight into the beliefs and objectives of the Christian pilgrim.[34]

Medical texts form a significant portion of the extant prose by women. Women were an important part of the Graeco-Roman medical profession. While midwifery was a profession exclusive to women, inscriptions provide ample evidence that women regularly became physicians too.[35] Because social practice made it unacceptable for men to examine female patients, women used to examine and treat themselves under the guidance of a male physician, or be treated by an *obstetrix* (midwife)[36] or a *medica* (female physician). Female physicians did not treat women only, but women would have been their main concern, and so *medicae* and *obstetrices* provide examples of early specialisation in the medical profession.[37] Fragments of medical texts written by women remain; most are recipes for remedies reproduced in the texts of other medical writers.

Cleopatra and Fabulla provide examples of female physicians who recorded their remedies for use by fellow professionals. From Soranus (*Gynaecology* 1.3-4) we learn that a good midwife needed to be literate because her professional training included reading in theory; books of remedies, some written by midwives themselves, presuppose their literacy.[38] The midwives' work, and therefore their writings, necessarily focused on childbirth, but their knowledge was much wider.[39] They are cited by Pliny as general authorities on women's bodies.[40] We have too little biographical detail to know whether any of the extant female medical writers were freedwomen, but this is a distinct possibility. Inscriptional evidence from the first and second centuries suggests that physicians and (more often) midwives may have begun their careers as slaves. Roman epitaphs suggest medicine was profitable and that many slaves in this industry earned their freedom before they died.[41]

There is a third and perhaps surprising source of 'medical' literature from the Graeco-Roman world: prostitutes. Pliny (28.70) testifies to the existence of such work by *meretrices* (prostitutes) and two authors whom he names fall into this category: Laïs and Elephantis (see below). 'Prostitute' literature included pornography, read by men such as the emperor Tiberius (or so it was claimed)[42] and probably written for men (there is no evidence that it was read by women), and this erotic work was in all likelihood pseudonymous. Prostitute pseudonyms may have disguised work by male writers, but apparently it was accepted as the work of women. This reflects an assumption that women knew best the secrets of women's bodies and that prostitutes knew a great deal more than modest women. Perhaps it was felt that only such women were prepared to reveal this secret knowledge to men. But it was not just sexual secrets that were attributed to prostitutes; apparently, they also offered advice on cosmetics, revealed such 'women's' secrets as the magic power of menstrual fluid (Pliny 28.82) and how to cause abortions—a power that men did not like women to possess and seem to have feared (Pliny 28.81).[43]

The fragments we have from women medical writers come from the practical rather than the theoretical side of ancient medicine. There are instructions for the preparation and application of various remedies, and a comparative table of weights and measures. Some come from 'folk' medicine, offering traditional herbal remedies, some use supposed magical properties in their ingredients to effect the desired outcome, some are just magical words.[44] But not all are without a theoretical basis. The remedies of Cleopatra are cited by Galen, who proposed that bodily health is dependent on the balance of the four 'humours'; it is likely that Cleopatra supported her remedies with a similar theoretical framework, now lost.[45] Recent work has demonstrated that some ancient herbal remedies contained effective ingredients and may well have achieved their aim.[46]

Cleopatra and Maria were the names of two important early alchemists. Their work should be dated to between the first and third centuries AD. Some early alchemists used pseudonyms such as Isis the mother of Horus (an Egyptian god), but the belief that Cleopatra and Maria were respectively the famous queen and the sister of Moses may well have been a later invention. Cleopatra's alchemical work, *The Chrysopoeia* ('gold-manufacture'), survives only in a diagram.[47] Maria was an expert in the design of equipment, and her texts detail this as well as procedures for the creation of gold alloys and turning base metals a golden colour. Cited extensively by Zosimus, widely read by medieval alchemists and translated into Arabic, Maria's work now only survives in fragments.

The transmission of texts from the ancient world was problematic and a great many works by both men and women have been lost. One reason is that relatively few copies of most ancient works were made. Publication of a text (after its initial performance) was a private matter. Authors, or their patrons, or readers paid a high price for copies to be made. There were no copyright laws; anyone who owned a manuscript could make copies, for themselves, as gifts to friends, or to sell.[48] To survive, a work, had to be popular and in demand. Few works by women, it seems, were circulated widely, the greatest difficulty being the expectation in Graeco-Roman society that literary circles were for men. By the fourth century AD works on papyrus rolls needed to be copied on to less fragile parchment to survive the next four centuries when very few books were copied. Those not copied at this early date did not survive, save by chance. Even an author as popular in the ancient world as Sappho now survives only in fragments, for the most part quotations from her poems (sometimes as short as a single word) in other literary works from antiquity.[49] On the other hand, the Christian cento of Proba, popular in the fourth century AD and read in the seventh century, has survived complete. Her other, non-Christian work, however, has not survived.[50]

Only a few scraps of papyrus texts that circulated in antiquity have survived. Few texts have come to us directly from the author herself. These are the short epigrams from Egypt that were inscribed on the statue of Memnon and the pyramid of Cheops (originally) by Roman and Greek tourists, and a poem commemorating a set of public baths in Gadara that was found *in situ*.[51]

Where possible I have included in this anthology all the extant texts of an author. Few are complete, and some are reported rather than quoted verbatim. I have omitted some very short and essentially meaningless fragments of Corinna and Sappho. I have for reasons of economy provided only extracts of the longer texts of Egeria and Eudocia and a selection of the fragments of Maria.

The texts are arranged in chronological order to give the reader some sense of historical perspective, though uncertainty about the exact dates of many of the writers means that the sequence should not be taken as strictly definitive. Where the dates allow, texts of a similar genre are grouped together. The introduction to each author focuses on historical issues; for issues of literary interpretation, readers are for the most part directed towards relevant literary commentaries.[52] I have attempted to provide translations that do justice to the meaning of the original text; no attempt has been made to reproduce the Greek and Latin poetic verse. For consistency I have used Latinised forms of Greek names throughout. The chronological survey of women writers provides a further guide to their relative dates, along with the dates of some male writers mentioned in the text. I have also included a comprehensive glossary of people, places, texts, and Greek and Roman terms used in the text.

Notes

1. L. Berkowitz and K.A. Squiter, *Thesaurus Linguae Graecae: Canon of Greek Authors and Works* (New York: Oxford University Press, 1990); this canon does include the Byzantine period (AD 600–1453) too.
2. See my list of attested writers below. The list has more than one hundred entries, but includes legendary and fictional women, women who are referred to by more than one name, and women whose designation as 'author' is doubtful or conjectural.

3. I have not included private correspondence in this collection; for examples see A.K. Bowman and J.D. Thomas, *The Vindolanda Writing-Tablets* (London: British Museum Press, 1994), 257, 291, 292, 293, 294, and M.R. Lefkowitz and M.B. Fant, *Women's Life in Greece and Rome: A Source Book in Translation* (2nd edn; Baltimore: John Hopkins University Press, 1992), 102, 104, 105, 268, 269, 271, 272. I have included prose works by women in epistle form that have been preserved through publication: see below Cornelia and the Pythagorean writers Theano, Melissa and Myia.

4. *Anth. Pal.* 4.1; 9.26. For readers unfamiliar with people, places, texts or Graeco-Roman terms mentioned, I have provided a comprehensive glossary.

5. For more on Athenaeus, see the introduction to Hedyle below.

6. See also Dioscorides (*Anth. Pal.* 7.450).

7. We can compare the epigrams on Erinna, with the epigrams attributed to Erinna (see Erinna below).

8. See M.L. West, 'Erinna', *Zeitschrift für Papyrologie und Epigraphik* 25 (1977), 101-115.

9. Her poetry often addresses or refers to women (see poems 5, 16, 21, 30, 31, 33, 34, 84, 89 below and cf. Philostratus, *Life of Apollonius of Tyana* 1.30; Max. Tyr. 18.9), but also appears to have been acknowledged by her contemporary Alcaeus: Frg. 384.

10. *Anth. Pal.* 5.132.7.

11. See Plato, *Parmenides* 127c; Marcellinus, *Life of Thucydides* 54.

12. Charixena, Aspasia, Praxilla, Telesilla, Myrtis, Cleitagora and perhaps Corinna and Myia (see their texts below). For women's literacy, see S.G. Cole, 'Could Greek women read and write', in H.P. Foley (ed.), *Reflections of Women in Antiquity* (New York: Gordon and Breach Scientific Publishers, 1981), 219-45.

13. For the practice of a professional female musicians entertaining at men's drinking parties, see Xenophon, *Symposium* 2.1-2; Plato, *Symposium* 176e. Our evidence for the lives of women outside Athens is limited, and the same norms may not have applied. See S.B. Pomeroy, *Goddesses, Whores, Wives and Slaves: Women in Classical Antiquity* (New York: Schocken Books, 1975), and Lefkowitz and Fant, *Women's Life in Greece and Rome* (1992).

14. Herodotus 7.140, 141 cf. Plutarch 396e–397d. I have appended a list of attested verse oracles below.

15. For more on Hellenistic scholarship and the Library and Museum in Alexandria, see P. Green, *Alexander to Actium: The Hellenistic Age* (London: Thames and Hudson; Berkeley: University of California Press, 1993), especially pp. 79-91, 171-86. Further testimony to the existence and readership of women poets is the ridicule they attracted: see Lucian, *On Salaried Posts in Great Houses* 36; Persius, *Prologue* 13; Menander, *Synkrisis* 1.209-10, Frg 702 (Koch).

16. Cf. Sempronia (Sallust, *Conspiracy of Catiline* 25), Perilla (Ovid, *Tristia* 3.7), Cornificia (Jerome, *Chronicle*, Olympic Year 184.4), Cynthia or Hostia (Propertius, *Elegies* 2.3.21-22; Apuleius, *Apology* 10), Clodia (Cicero, *For Marcus Caelius* 64), Claudia Trophime (*Inscr. Eph.* 1062 G). See also Demo and Dionysia (below).

17. Just as Calpurnia listens behind a curtain to her husband, Pliny the Younger (Pliny, *Letters* 4.19); for poets' public recitals, see Pliny, *Letters* 1.13; 5.17; 7.17; 8.21 cf. 8.12.

18. There is also a later pseudonymous work: see Sulpicia II below.

19. A poem composed entirely of lines taken from another poet's work; Virgil and Homer were popular sources for such works.

20. M.D. Usher, *Homeric Stitchings: The Homeric Centos of the Empress Eudocia* (Lanham: Rauman and Littlefield, 1998).

21. These are pseudonymous philosophical works, see below, and a false claim that Thucydides' daughter wrote Book 8 of his history (Marcellinus, *Life of Thucydides* 43).

22. Athen. 10.434c and 12.537d

23. Strab. 13.599.

24. Tacitus, *Annals* 4.53; Plin. 7.46.
25. Some scholars accept them as genuine: see Cornelia below.
26. *Suda* s.v. Hipparchia; see also Perictione below.
27. Though he condemned her for daring to criticise Theophrastus: Cicero, *Nature of the Gods* 1.93. See also Diog. L. 10.4-7; 10.23; Athen. 13.588b; Plin. Preface 29 may refer to her.
28. See the introduction to each of the authors below for discussion of their dates.
29. A. Barker, *Greek Musical Theory* (Oxford: Clarendon Press, 1997), 230, 239.
30. J.McI. Snyder, *The Woman and the Lyre: Women Writers in Classical Greece and Rome* (Carbondale: Southern Illinois University Press, 1989), 113-20.
31. Socrates Scholasticus, *History of the Church* 7.15; *Suda* s.v. An extant commentary by her father Theon probably contains her revisions.
32. R. Radar, 'The Martyrdom of Perpetua: a protest account of third-century Christianity', in P. Wilson-Kastner *et al.* (eds), *A Lost Tradition: Women Writers of the Early Church* (Lanham: University Press of America, 1981), 1-32, 3.
33. The text has been much studied by philologists as an example of post-Classical Vulgar Latin. Its style has been defended by L. Spitzer, 'The epic style of the pilgrim Aetheria', *Comparative Literature* 1 (1949), 225-58.
34. On pilgrimages see R. Ousterhout (ed.), *The Blessings of Pilgrimage* (Urbana: The University of Illinois Press, 1990); E.D. Hunt, *Holy Land Pilgrimage in the Later Roman Empire AD 312–460* (Oxford: Clarendon Press, 1982); J. Wilkinson, *Jerusalem Pilgrims before the Crusades* (2nd edn, Warminster: Aris and Phillips, 1998)
35. For a collection of translated inscriptions, Lefkowitz and Fant, *Women's Life in Greece and Rome* (1st edn; Baltimore: John Hopkins University Press, 1982), 264-7, ns. 369-74.
36. Women preferred not to confide in a male (Hippocrates 8.126.5-15). Although Soranus (*Gynaecology* 4.7) shows a midwife working under a physician, Galen (14.641-7) tells of a physician being called in when a midwife is unable to effect a cure. In most cases the midwife no doubt acted alone.
37. For a good discussion of Graeco-Roman medicine, see R. Jackson, *Doctors and Diseases in the Roman Empire* (London: British Museum, 1988), 86; see also *Aufstieg und Niedergang der römischen Welt* II, 37.1 (Berlin: De Gruyter, 1990).
38. Our evidence comes from the first century AD and later. Pliny cites the writings of midwives generally (*Natural History* 28.67, 70, 255) as well as naming authors such as Salpe and Sotira (see below); see also Galen 13.840 cf. 13.837. Greeks dominated Graeco-Roman medicine, and most literature for physicians and midwives was in Greek rather than Latin.
39. Soranus tells us that the best midwives were trained in all areas of medicine, and would deal with cases that required treatment by diet, surgery and medicines (*Gynaecology* 1.4); and that these midwives were called in to deal with specific female ailments (*Gynaecology* 3.3).
40. Female bodies were very poorly understood by Greek philosophical medical writers, but some advances followed Hellenistic clinical studies, represented in the *Gynaecology* of Soranus. On this see L. Dean-Jones, 'The cultural construct of the female body in Classical Greek science', in S.B. Pomeroy (ed.), *Women's History and Ancient History* (Chapel Hill: University of North Carolina Press, 1991).
41. For translated Roman epitaphs, from the first and second centuries, see Lefkowitz and Fant, *Women's Life in Greece and Rome* (1982), 267, ns. 375-77. Soranus testifies to the opportunity for midwives to earn money (*Gynaecology* 1.4).
42. Suetonius, *Tiberius* 43: see Elephantis below.
43. For the fear of women using abortives, see Juvenal, *Satires* 6.592-601, Soranus, *Gynaecology* 1.4; for the male head of the family's right to decide the fate of the child in law, see the *Twelve Tables* IV (Lefkowitz and Fant, *Women's Life in Greece and Rome* [1982], 108, 95).

44. For magical chants, see Philinna and Syra.
45. For a discussion of 'high' and 'low' medicine, see J.M. Riddle, 'High medicine and low medicine in the Roman Empire', *Aufstieg und Niedergang der römischen Welt* II, 37.1 (Berlin: De Gruyter, 1990), 102-120.
46. J.M. Riddle, 'Oral contraceptives and early-term abortifacients during Classical Antiquity and the Middle Ages', *Past and Present* 132 (1991), 3-32.
47. For further discussion see J. Lindsay, *The Origins of Alchemy in Graeco-Roman Egypt* (London: Muller, 1970) and below.
48. For the circulation of books see Horace, *Epistles* 1.20.2; *Art of Poetry* 345. Pliny (the Younger) 4.7.2; 9.11.2; Catullus 14.17, 22; Cicero, *Letters* 12.17.2; *Letters to Atticus* 13.13.1; *Letters to Quintus* 3.4.5, 5.6.
49. We have only one complete poem by Sappho from the nine books of her work that existed in antiquity.
50. On the transmission of texts from antiquity, see L.D. Reynolds, *Scribes and Scholars: A Guide to the Transmission of Greek and Latin Literature* (Oxford: Clarendon Press, 1991) and *Texts and Transmission* (Oxford: Clarendon Press, 1983).
51. For inscriptions on the statue of Memnon, see Julia Balbilla, Caecilia Trebulla, Dionysia and Demo; Terentia's inscription was once on the pyramid of Cheops. Eudocia wrote the Gadara inscription.
52. For a very good introduction, see Snyder, *The Woman and the Lyre*.

1. Sappho (*born about 630 BC*)

Introduction

Sappho was by far the most famous woman writer in antiquity.[1] Plato called her the tenth Muse, Antipater said that she surpassed all other women poets, Strabo that no other woman came close to rivalling her as a poet.[2] She was honoured with portraits on coins from both Mytilene and Eresus (two cities on Lesbos which both claimed to be her birthplace)[3] and with a bronze statue outside the *prytaneion* (town hall) in Syracuse, where she also lived for a while.[4] Her early popularity in Athens is illustrated by an extant Athenian vase dated between 510–500 BC that shows her playing the lyre.[5]

The biographical details that have come down to us from antiquity are based on inferences drawn from her poetry, much of which is now lost to us, and later comedies in which she featured. She was thought to have been a contemporary of Pittacus (c. 645–570 BC) and Alcaeus (born about 620 BC) and King Alyattes of Lydia (c. 610–560 BC).[6] *Suda* says she was born or flourished (it is not clear) in the forty-second Olympiad (612–608 BC), while Eusebius dates her fame to 600/599 BC (Olympiad 45.1).[7] Her family held a high social position, as she indicates in reference to her brother Larichus.[8] She also spoke of her brother Charaxus in her poetry, criticising him for wasting money on a famous prostitute named Doricha or Rhodopis.[9] Sappho may have kept house for her brothers,[10] and apparently Ovid could infer from a poem (now lost) that one of her parents died when she was only six (*Heroides* 15.61-2).

Sappho went into exile in Sicily before 595/4.[11] The exile has been attributed to the tyranny of Pittacus at Mytilene; Sappho warns against friendship with the family into which he married (L-P 71).[12] In poem 36 Sappho apologises to her daughter for the lack of luxuries which their exile had brought. The same poem also referred to the sons of Cleanax, political enemies of Pittacus too, perhaps the faction to which Sappho's family was attached.[13]

An ancient biography tells us that Sappho's daughter was named Cleis after her mother, no doubt on the basis of something she said in her poetry, and indeed she refers to Cleis in two of the extant fragments.[14] The names of Sappho's father and husband are, however, less certain.[15] This is surprising, as it was normal Greek practice for a woman to identify herself using her father's name, or her husband's name after marriage. Sappho names herself, her mother and her daughter, but she apparently did not make her father's or her husband's names clear, a significant independent gesture.

The biographical tradition has also been muddied by the comedies written about her. We know of at least six comedies named *Sappho*.[16] These were probably responsible for the idea that Sappho was a prostitute and the invention of a second (less reputable) Sappho;[17] Hermesianax invented a love affair between her and the later poet Anacreon, Diphilus between her and Archilochus and then Hipponax.[18] Another story as early as the fourth century BC held that she threw herself from a cliff on Leucas, driven to suicide by unrequited love for Phaon.[19] This romantic tradition about Sappho was part of the fictitious biography that arose from misinterpretation of her poetry[20] along with comic invention. By the time of Ovid, Sappho had become a figure of legend to the extent that she appears as one of the legendary heroines for whom Ovid composed fictitious love-letters.

Sappho was criticised in antiquity for her frank expression of love for women in her poetry.[21] The passion found in some of the fragments that remain shows that her love should not be characterised as simply that of a teacher towards her pupils.[22] Recent criticism of her work has argued that her most homoerotic poem, poem 8 (L-P 31), is a wedding song. At Greek weddings the expectation was that the bride would be erotically appealing to all who saw her, both male and female, and this admiration was expressed in wedding songs. Such songs were sung by a chorus, and the homoerotic feelings expressed represented a form of public praise for the bride, rather than a personal sentiment on the part of the poet.[23] The biographical tradition that she married and had a daughter complicates the picture, and warns us of the difficulty of trying to create the poet from her poetry, particularly when so much of her work has been lost.[24]

A fragmentary commentary on Sappho states that she was a teacher, attracting students from noble families throughout Ionia. If true, this would be a remarkable example of literary and musical education for women. However, just as Nossis acknowledged her debt to Sappho and her work,[25] other female poets may have cited her and modelled their work on hers, leading to later misinterpretations of their relationship.[26] Damophyla, a Pamphylian, whose work was seen to be derivative of Sappho, was said to have spent time with her.[27] Sappho names some of her female companions, addressing songs to them.[28] Philostratus thought Sappho was the centre of a literary circle, and Maximus of Tyre (probably by inference from something in her poems) that Gorgo and Andromeda were the leaders of rival groups.[29] Her audience was not confined to a closed literary circle of women, though. She wrote wedding songs (*epithalamia*), and the widespread appreciation of her work by men shows that it was circulated widely. In a short fragment attributed to Alcaeus, her contemporary from her homeland of Lesbos, Sappho is named,[30] and one fragment of Sappho's, quoted by Aristotle, implies a poetic dialogue between her and Alcaeus.[31] There is some evidence that it was not just women who performed her work: an anecdote from Aelian describes a performance in Athens for another contemporary of hers, Solon, given by his nephew.[32]

Sappho's poetry was written to be sung accompanied by the lyre. An indication of the respect accorded her music is that she was deemed the inventor of the plectrum and a type of lyre called the *pectis*.[33] She was also regarded as the creator of an emotional style of music called the *mixolydian*, which was adopted by the tragedians.[34] As well as a lyre player (*psaltria*) Sappho was a singer.[35] It would have been by performance that her poetry originally was published, passed on from singer to singer.[36]

Sappho's songs were still alive more than five hundred years after she had composed them and entertained the leading Roman poets Catullus, Horace and Ovid.[37] Women were expected to be able to sing her songs.[38] Aullus Gellius tells us that in the second century BC her works were still performed, despite the difficulty caused by her Aeolian dialect.[39] In the third century BC Dioscorides called her songs her 'immortal daughters', but Tzetzes reported that by his day (the twelfth century) they had been lost.[40] Today, while we have more than two hundred fragments, we have only one complete poem, and it is only 28 lines.[41]

Sappho composed lyric poetry, for both solo and choral performance. Her subject matter included mythological narrative, but she was best known for her love poetry.[42] Poem 8, which was later imitated by Catullus (Catullus 51), is a fine example of her sensual poetry, of her ability to portray physical and emotional responses to love. She was also noted for writing hymns in the form of prayers (*klētikoi*).[43] In poem 1, the only complete poem we have, she calls on Aphrodite to help her once again in a campaign to win a lover. The goddess appears as an intimate of Sappho's, ready to fulfil her prayers.[44] Sappho's wedding songs (*epithalamia*) were probably written to be performed by a chorus; little of these, which were collected into Book 8, remain. She was also said to have written elegiacs, iambics and epigrams.[45] None are now extant, though three pseudonymous epigrams are attributed to her in the *Palatine Anthology* (poems 98-100 below).

I have included one hundred fragments in this anthology, omitting largely unintelligible and very short fragments (such as isolated words quoted by grammarians) and fragments which only give information about her poems. I have included the pseudonymous epigrams ascribed to her, though they date from the Hellenistic era. The division into nine books based on metre was also made in the Hellenistic era.[46]

Sappho

Book One
1.
Immortal Aphrodite on many-coloured throne,
child of Zeus, weaver of tricks, I beseech you:
don't tame my heart with pain and distress
my lady,

but come here, if ever before   5
you heard my voice from far away
and listened, left your father's golden home
and came

after yoking your chariot; beautiful swift sparrows
brought you over the black earth   10
whirling thick feathers down from heaven
through mid-air;

and suddenly arrived, and you, blessed one,
smiled with your immortal face
and asked what I had suffered again and why   15
I was calling her again

and what I most wanted to happen to me
in my maddened heart; 'Whom again am I to persuade
to be harnessed again to your love? Who
wrongs you, Sappho?   20

For if she flees, soon she'll chase;
if she doesn't accept your gifts, she'll give them instead;
if she doesn't love you, soon she will love
even against her will.'

Come to me now, too, and free me from   25
unbearable anxiety, and all that my heart longs to

be fulfilled, fulfil for me; and you yourself
be my ally.

2.
…here to me from Crete, to this
holy temple, where your lovely grove
of apple trees lies, and altars smoking
with frankincense.

In here cool water tinkles through   5
apple-branches, and with roses the whole place
is shaded, and while leaves flutter
deep-sleep descends.

In here a horse-grazing meadow blooms
with spring flowers, and winds   10
blow softly…
….

Here, Cypris, take garlands
and into golden cups gracefully
pour nectar-like wine mixed   15
with our festivities.

3.
O Cypris and Nereids, grant that
my brother arrives here unharmed
and all that he wants to happen
comes to pass,
…   5
and that he atones for all his past errors
and becomes a joy to all his friends,
a sorrow to his enemies, but may there be
no sorrow for us.

May he wish to honour his sister   10
…

4.
…
Cypris, and may Doricha find you more bitter
and may she not boast, saying this,
how she came for the second time
to a love she longed for.

5.
Some say the most beautiful thing upon black earth
is an army of horsemen, others infantry,
and others ships, but I say it is whatever
someone loves.

To make this understandable to all   5
is quite easy; for the woman far surpassing all

mortals in beauty, Helen, abandoned
her excellent husband

And sailing off she went to Troy, and did not
remember her child nor her dear parents   10
at all, but [Cypris] led her away...

...

... now reminds me of Anactoria   15
who is not here.

Her lovely walk and the bright shine
of her face I would rather look upon
than all the chariots of Lydia and fully armed
infantry.   20

6.[47]
May your lovely form appear near me,
Lady Hera, as I pray,
whom famous kings, the sons of Atreus,
entreated,

After accomplishing many labours   5
first at Ilium, then on the sea,
leaving for here, they could not
finish their journey,

Until they summoned you and Zeus,
and Thyone's lovely son.   10
But now help me too
as you did long ago

...
7.
...
...the night
and girls...
celebrate all night long...
singing of your loveliest songs   5
for the violet-bosomed bride.

But wake up and visit the unmarried
young men of your own age.
Let us see as much sleep
as the clear voiced nightingale.   10

8.
He seems to me to be equal to the gods
—whoever sits opposite you
and listens to you
talking sweetly

and laughing desirably, which makes   5
the heart in my breast fly;
for whenever I look upon you for an instant
I can no longer find a single word,

but my tongue is broken, and instantly
delicate fire runs beneath my skin,   10
and I see nothing with my eyes, my
hearing pounds,

a cold sweat covers me, trembling
grabs my all, I am paler than grass,
and I think I am little short   15
of dying.

But everything can be ventured
…

9.
[The Muses?] made me honoured when
they granted their works…

10.
O golden-crowned Aphrodite,
I wish that I might win this lot
…

11.
The stars around the lovely moon
hide away their shining form
whenever in its fullness it especially shines
upon the earth…

12.
Cyprus, or Paphos, or Panormos…

13.
I desire and I endeavour…

14.
…down my drops of pain…
…
May winds carry off the man who strikes at me,
and sorrows…

15.
…a sandal of many colours
was hiding her feet,
lovely Lydian work…

16.
My thoughts towards you beautiful women
cannot be changed...

Book Two

17.
Cyprus...
The herald came...,
Idaeus, swift messenger, ...[who said]

'... and of the rest of Asia immortal fame.
Hector and his companions bring a sparkly-eyed girl   5
from holy Thebes and fair-flowing Placia,
delicate Andromeda, in ships on the salty
sea; and many golden bracelets and purple
robes, many coloured delights,
countless silver cups and ivory.'   10

So he spoke. And quickly his dear father leapt up,
and the news came through the broad open city to his friends.
At once the Iliadae led mules to the smooth-running
chariots, and a whole throng of women and
of maidens made its way.,   15
and apart the daughters of Priam,
and the men brought the horses beneath the chariots
...bachelors...chariot drivers...
...
...   20
[*unknown number of verses missing*]

...like gods
...holy
...set out to Ilium...
and a sweet-singing aulos [and cithara] were mixed
and the sound of castanets...and then the maidens   25
sang a holy song, and the divine echo reached
the sky...
and through the streets everywhere...
wine mixing-bowls and cups...
myrrh and cassia and frankincense were mixed   30
and the women, all who were older, cried out
and all the men shouted a lovely loud cry,
calling upon Paean, the far-shooting, the well-lyred,
and sang of godlike Hector and Andromache.

18.
...
...to golden-haired Phoebus, whom the daughter of Coeus bore
after sleeping with the mighty-named son of Cronus.

And Artemis swore a great oath of the gods:
By your head, I will always be a virgin 5
…on the tops of the mountains
…grant me this favour.
The father of the blessed gods nodded his assent.
The gods called her the far-shooting huntress,
…a great name, 10
Eros never draws near…

19.
Eros shook out my heart
like a wind assaulting mountain oaks.

20.
You came and I sought you,
but you cooled down my heart burning with desire.

21.
While I loved you once, Atthis, long ago
…
You seemed to me a small and graceless child.

22.
While a beautiful man just looks beautiful,
a good man will therefore be beautiful too.

23.
I do not know what to do; I am of two minds…

24.
I do not expect to touch the sky with my poor arms.

Book Three
25.
Rosy-armed holy Graces, daughters of Zeus, come …

26.
… Eros
coming from heaven wearing a purple cloak…

27.
You will die and lie there, and there will be no memory of you
ever or desire for you later. For you have no
share in the Pierian roses, but unseen in Hades' home
you will fly off and you will wander among the obscure dead.

28.
Nor do I think there will be at any time again

a maiden who looks upon the light of sun
with wisdom as great as yours.

29.
What country-girl enchants your mind…
wearing her country dress…
not knowing how to draw her rags over her ankles?

Book Four

30.
…
O Dica, put round your hair lovely garlands
weaving together stems of anise with your tender hands.
For the blessed Graces too favour the well-flowered more
to look upon, but turn away from the ungarlanded.

31.
Mnasidika is more beautiful than delicate Gyrinno…

32.
…never having found any woman more annoying,
Irana, than you…

Book Five

33.
'…And honestly, I wish I were dead.'
She began to leave me, weeping

a great deal, and she said to me,
'O what terrible things we have suffered,
Sappho, truly I am leaving you unwillingly.'   5

And I replied to her,
'Go and farewell and remember
me, for you know how we cherished you.

But if you don't, I want
to remind you …   10
..and the beautiful things we enjoyed.

For many garlands of violets
and roses and crocuses…
together beside me did you put on,

and many plaited wreaths   15
of flowers around your tender
neck did you place,

and ..with much perfumed
royal myrrh …
you anointed…   20

and on a soft bed
…tender…
you satisfied your longing…

nor was there any…
nor any holy…   25
from which we were absent

nor grove, …nor dance
…the sound…
…

34.
…
Gongyla…

surely some sign…   5
for all especially…
Hermes entered…

I said, 'O master, …
for by the blessed goddess…
I do not enjoy when I am above the earth   10

and a desire to die holds me,
and to see the lotus-covered
dewy banks of Acheron…

35.
…Sardis…
often paying attention here

…she honoured you
like a goddess easily recognised,
and especially enjoyed your song.   5

But now she is conspicuous among
Lydian women as after the setting sun,
the rosy-fingered moon

surpassing all the stars; and its light
spreads out evenly over the salty sea   10
and the richly flowering fields.

And the dew pours out beautifully,
and roses flourish, and tender
chervil and flowery honey-lotus.

Often as she wanders she remembers   15
gentle Atthis with desire, and surely
her tender heart is eaten away because of your fate.

...

36.
(a)
...for my mother [said that]

in her youth if someone
had her tresses
bound in a purple hair-band,

this was a great adornment.   5
But the girl who has hair
more golden than a pine-torch

should wear garlands
of flowers in bloom.
Just now a hair-band   10

of many colours from Sardis
...cities...

(b)
But for you, Cleis, I do not
have a many-coloured hair-band
- where will one come from? But for the Mytilenean   15
...
...
these reminders of the exile
of the sons of Cleanax
for they wasted away badly...   20

37.
and covered her well with soft woolly cloth

Book Seven[48]
38.
Sweet mother, I really cannot weave my web,
as I am defeated by desire for a boy because of slender Aphrodite.

Book Eight

39.

[*A list of the first lines of ten poems*]

1.   For...address...
2.   [Sing of] the bride with beautiful feet...
3.   ...the violet-dressed daughter of Zeus...
4.   ..violet-dressed ..setting aside anger...
5.   ...holy Graces and Perian Muses...
6.   ...when songs... the heart...
7.   ...hearing a clear song...
8.   ...bridegroom, for angering companions...
9.   ...her tresses, setting down the lyre...
10. ...golden-sandalled Dawn...

Book Nine: Epithalamia

40.

(a)

Hesperus, you bring everything which shining Dawn scattered,
you bring the sheep, you bring the goat, you bring the child back to its mother.
...

(b)

[Hesperus] the most beautiful of all the stars...

41.

(a) [The bride]

Just like the sweet apple reddens on the high branch,
high on the highest branch, and the apple-pickers have forgotten it
—no they have not forgotten it, but they could not reach it.

(b)

It was Sappho who likened a girl to an apple...and equated the bridegroom with Achilles the hero in his achievements.

(c). [*The bride ?*]

Just as the hyacinth which in the mountains shepherds, men,
trample underfoot, but on the ground the purple flower...

42.

Superior, as when a Lesbian singer...foreigners...

43.

Do I still desire virginity?

44.

O beautiful woman, O graceful woman...

45.

We will give, the father says...

46.
The door-keeper has feet seven fathoms long,
and his sandals are made of five ox-hides,
and ten cobblers laboured hard to make them.

47.
Raise up the roof,
—Hymenaeus—
up high, carpenter men.
—Hymenaeus—
The bridegroom is coming, the equal of Ares,
bigger by far than a big man.

48.
Happy bridegroom, your marriage, as you prayed,
has been fulfilled, and you have the girl for whom you prayed,
And you, your appearance is graceful, and your eyes...
gentle, and love flows over your lovely face
... Aphrodite has greatly honoured you.

49.
For, bridegroom, there is no other girl like her.

50.
Virginity, virginity, where have you gone, abandoning me?
I will never again return to you, I will never again return.

51.
To what, dear bridegroom, am I to liken you best?
I liken you most to a slim sapling.

52.
Farewell bride, farewell honoured bridegroom...

53.
May you fare well, bride, and may the bridegroom fare well too.

Book Unknown

54.
Come then divine lyre, speak to me,
make your sound...

55.
But I am not someone with a bad temper,
but I have a gentle heart...

56.
But as you are my friend,
try to win a younger bed;
for I would not dare to live with you
as I am older.

57.
[Persephone] a very tender girl picking flowers...

58.
Golden-sandalled Dawn just now...

59.
And you yourself, Calliope...

60.
May you sleep on the bosom of your tender girlfriend.

61.
Come again here, Muses, leaving the golden...

62.
Now come, tender Graces and lovely-haired Muses...

63.
(a)   You have no memory of me
(b)   or you love some other man more than me.

64.
Again Love, the loosener of limbs, shakes me,
bitter-sweet, irresistible, reptile.

At this, thinking of me has become hateful
to you, and you fly off to Andromeda.

65.
I have a beautiful child, beloved Cleis,
who has a beauty resembling golden flowers,
for whom I would not [exchange] all Lydia not lovely [Lesbos]...

66.
While Andromeda has a fine atonement...
Sappho, why... Aphrodite rich in happiness...?

67.
I spoke with you in a dream, Cyprus-born.

68.
Why, Irana, does the swallow, daughter of Pandion...me?

69.
Lovely voiced nightingale, messenger of spring...

70.
[*A dialogue between Alcaeus and Sappho*]
'I want to say something to you, but shame
prevents me...'
'But if you desired good or virtue
and your tongue were not concocting something bad to say,
shame would not hold possess your eyes,   5
but you would be speaking about justice.'

71.
'Cytherea, pretty Adonis is dying.
What are we to do?'
'Girls, beat your breasts and tear
your dresses.'

72.
There a bowl of ambrosia
had been mixed,
and Hermes took a jug and poured wine for the gods.

Then they all
held their goblets
and poured libations, and prayed for all things good
for the bridegroom.

73.
Leto and Niobe were very dear friends...

74.
Golden chickpeas grew on the banks...

75.
...are completely fed up
with Gorgo...

76.
For me, neither the honey nor the bee.

77.
I say that someone, even a second person, will remember us...

78.
Wealth without virtue is a harmful neighbour...

79.
[Sappho, when she was dying, to her daughter]
For it is not right for there to be a funeral-song
in the house of servants of the Muses.
That would not become us.

80.
and the black sleep of night…the eyes…

81.
…mixed with colours of every kind…

82.
…a sweet-voiced girl.

83.
While the moon in its fullness began to appear,
around the altar stood the women…

84.
[To Gorgo or Andromeda]
I would like to wish a very good-day to the daughter of Polyanax…

85.
[a woman?]…more sweet-melodied than a harp by far…
more golden than gold…

86.
Lady Dawn…

87.
…when anger spreads within the breast
guard against an idly yelping tongue…

88.
…you [*Sappho*] and my servant Eros…

89.
Now will I sing them beautifully
to delight my women companions…

90.
Once, they say, Leda found a hyacinth
egg thickly covered…
…
…whiter than an egg by far…

91.
Alas for Adonis…
O for the Adonian…

92.
The moon has set
and the Pleiades; it is the middle
of the night, but the right time passes by,
and I sleep alone.

93.
...while embroidered is
the much-garlanded earth...

94.
Once the Cretan women danced so gracefully
on their tender feet around the lovely altar
...
softly stepping on the delicate flower of the grass.

95.
[Hecate] the golden-light servant of Aphrodite...

96.
As a child after its mother have I flown...

97.
My friend, learn the story of Admetus, love the good,
and keep away from the cowardly...

[Sappho] Epigrams

98.
Children, if anyone ask I reply although I am without voice,
as I set an untiring voice at my feet:
Arista, daughter of Hermoclides son of Saunaiadas, dedicated me
to Aethiopia, daughter of Leto,
your servant, mistress of women. And you, pleasing her,   5
willingly praise our family.

99.
These are the ashes of Timas, who died before marriage
and was received by the dark bridal-chamber of Persephone.
When she died all her friends her age took
the lovely hair from their heads with newly sharpened steel.

100.
Meniscus his father set on the tomb of Pelagon the fisherman
a fishing-basket and oar, memorials of his miserable life.

Notes

1. The testimonia have been collected and translated by D.A. Campbell, *Greek Lyric*, I. *Sappho and Alcaeus* (Cambridge, MA: Harvard University Press, 1990), 2-61.
2. *Anth. Pal.* 9.506; 7.15; Strab. 13.2.3.
3. See *P. Oxy.* 1800 fr. 1; *Suda* on Sappho; cf. Nossis 11.
4. Cicero, *Verres* 2.4.125-27.
5. For this and other portraits of Sappho from antiquity, see G.M.A. Richter, *The Portraits of the Greeks*, I (London: Phaidon, 1965), 70-72, and *The Portraits of the Greeks*, abridged (ed. R.R.R. Smith; Oxford: Phaidon, 1984), 194-96.
6. Strab. 13.2.3, Athen. 13.598 b-c.
7. Eusebius, *Chronicles*, Olympic Year 45.1.
8. Frg. 203=Athen. 10.425a.
9. See 4 below, and frg. 202=Herodotus 2.135; Strab. 17.1.33; Athen. 13.596bc; Photius and *Suda* s.v. Rhodopis' offering; *Appendix to the Proverbs* 4.51; Athen. 13.596cd.
10. Campbell Test. 14=*P. Oxy.* 2506 fr.48 col. iii vv. 36-48.
11. *Parian Marble* Ep. 36 = Campbell, *Greek Lyric* I, Test. 5, 8-9.
12. I have numbered my selection of Sappho's poems from 1-100; Sappho's poems are most widely known by the numbers allocated to them by E. Lobel and D.L. Page, *Poetarum Lesbiorum Fragmenta* (Oxford: Clarendon Press, 1963) (= L-P). I provide a complete table of comparative numeration with this edition in an appendix below.
13. The sons of Cleanax were members of the family of Myrsilus. For the aristocratic feuding on Lesbos, see Strab. 13.2.3, Arist., *Politics* 1285A, and the poetry of Alcaeus, a contemporary of Sappho from Mytilene, who was also forced into exile (eg. Alcaeus frg. 130B).
14. See below 36, 65 (=L-P 98b, 132); *P. Oxy.* 1800 fr.1= Campbell, *Greek Lyric* I, test. 1; also *Suda* s.v. Sappho; Ovid, *Heroides* 15.70.
15. Sappho's father is variously named as Simon, Eumenus, Eerigius, Ecrytus, Semus, Camon, Etarchus or Scamandronymus (*Suda* s.v. Sappho), Scamandronymus or Scamander (Herodotus 2.135; Aelian, *Historical Miscellanies* 12.19; *P. Oxy.* 1800 fr.1=Campbell, *Greek Lyric* I, test. 1). The name recorded for her husband, Cercylas of Andros (*Suda*), is a joke name, probably invented in one of the comedies about her (cf. Campbell, *Greek Lyric* I, 5 n. 4 and test. 25-26). Sappho names herself in 33 and 66 (L-P 94, 133).
16. These were by Antiphanes, Diphilus, Timocles, Ephippus, Ameipsias and Amphis (Campbell, *Greek Lyric* I, test. 25-26).
17. Aelian, *Historical Miscellanies* 12.19; Seneca the Younger, *Letters to Lucilius* 88.37; in antiquity, Lesbians had the reputation of being lascivious (Ar., *Frogs* 1308; *Wasps* 1346).
18. Athen. 13.598b-599d. Their approximate dates of birth are: Anacreon c. 570 BC; Archilochus c. 680 BC; Hipponax c. 580 BC.
19. Menander Fr. 258 (Koerte); Ovid, *Heroides* 15, Strab. 10.2.9; *Suda* s.v. Sappho (2) and fr. 211 (L-P). Ancient biography often reverses what an author professes, as well as building upon it: see M. Lefkowitz, *The Lives of the Greek Poets* (Baltimore: John Hopkins University Press, 1981), 36-37.
20. C.M. Bowra, *Greek Lyric Poetry* (2nd edn; Oxford: Clarendon Press, 1961), 212-14.
21. *Suda* s.v. Sappho; Ovid, *Heroides* 15.15-20, 200-1; *P. Oxy.* 1800 fr. 1.
22. U. von Wilamowitz-Moellendorff, *Sappho und Simonides* (Berlin: Weidmann, 1913), 56, cf. H.N. Parker, 'Sappho Schoolmistress', *Transactions and Proceedings of the American Philological Association* 123 (1993), 309-51.

23. A. Lardinois, 'Keening Sappho: Female speech and genres in Sappho's poetry', in A. Lardinois and L. McClure (eds), *Making Silence Speak* (Princeton: Princeton University Press, 2001), 75-92 (89-91).

24. On reactions to Sappho's sexuality in antiquity, see M. Williamson, *Sappho's Immortal Daughters* (Cambridge, MA: Harvard University Press, 1995), 5-33; for a modern lesbian reading of Sappho, see J.McI. Snyder, *Lesbian Desire in the Lyrics of Sappho* (New York: Columbia University Press, 1997). For the sexual experience that can be inferred from Sappho, see L.H. Wilson, *Sappho's Sweet Bitter Songs* (London and New York: Routledge, 1996), 68-86. For discussion of what to think about ancient sexuality, see H.N. Parker, 'The myth of the heterosexual: anthropology and sexuality for classicists' *Arethusa* 34 (2001), 313-62.

25. Nossis 11.

26. Anagora of Miletus, Gongyla of Colophon and Eunica of Salamis are named as her pupils (*Suda* s.v. Sappho); Gongyla was also a companion: 34 below (L-P 95) also L-P 22, and Campbell, *Greek Lyric* I, 213. See also the introduction to Corinna, for the association made between her, Myrtis and Pindar.

27. Philostratus, *Life of Apollonius of Tyana* 1.30.

28. Cf. Sappho 5, 16, 21, 30, 31, 33, 34, 84, 89 below.

29. Philostratus, *Life of Apollonius of Tyana*; Max. Tyr. 18.9.

30. Alcaeus frg. 384 (Campbell, *Greek Lyric* I); cf. J.McI. Snyder, *The Woman and the Lyre: Women Writers in Classical Greece and Rome* (Carbondale: Southern Illinois University Press, 1989), 4.

31. Poem 70 below: see Arist., *Rhetoric* 1367A.

32. Aelian in Stob., *Anthology* 3.29.58. Solon (c. 640–561/0 BC) was contemporary with Sappho. See also Aulus Gellius 19.9.3, Plut., *Moralia* 622c, 711d.

33. Menaechmus in Athen. 14.635b; *Suda* s.v. Sappho; cf. Horace, *Odes* 4.9.10-12; Himmerius, *Orations* 28.2; Ovid, *Heroides* 15.183-84.

34. Aristoxenus in Plut., *On Music* 16.1136c.

35. See 35, 54, 89 below (L-P 96, 118, 160); cf. Ovid, *Heroides* 15.43-44.

36. As Solon was said to have wanted to learn her songs: Aelian in Stob., *Anthology* 3.29.58.

37. Horace, *Odes* 4.9.10-12; Ovid, *Heroides* 15. Catullus 51 imitates Sappho poem 8 (L-P 31).

38. Philodemus, *Anth. Pal.* 5.132.7.

39. Gell., 19.9.3; Apuleius, *Apology* 9.

40. Dioscorides, *Anth. Pal.* 7.407; Tzetzes, *On the Metres of Pindar* 20-22.

41. A great deal of classical literature was lost between the sixth and eighth centuries, when the reading and copying of classical texts almost ceased. Particularly vulnerable were works not copied from papyrus rolls to the parchment codices that replaced them in the fourth century: see L.D. Reynolds, *Texts and Transmissions* (Oxford: Clarendon Press, 1983).

42. See Antipater, *Anth. Pal.* 7.14.3; Themistius, *Orations* 13.170d-171a; Himmerius, *Orations* 28.2; Ovid, *Tristia* 2.365.

43. Menander, *On Epideictic Oratory* 1.132, 135.

44. There is considerable scholarship on Sappho's poetry. For a good introductions see Snyder, *The Women and the Lyre*, 13-34, and E. Greene (ed.), *Re-Reading Sappho: Reception and Transmission* (Berkeley: University of California Press, 1996). See also Snyder, *Lesbian Desire in the Lyrics of Sappho*; Wilson, *Sappho's Sweet Bitter Songs*; J. Balmer, *Sappho: Poems and Fragments* (Newcastle: Bloodaxe Books, 1992).

45. *P. Oxy.* 1800 fr.1, *Suda* s.v. Sappho.

46. There is a table of comparative numeration with the Lobel-Page edition at the back of this volume.

47. The text of this poem is fragmentary; the translation includes restorations.

48. There are no extant fragments of Sappho that can be assigned to Book Six.

2. Cleobulina (fl. c. 600 BC)

Introduction

There remains doubt about the very existence of Cleobulina, although we have three short pieces of poetry attributed to her, numerous references to her life in a variety of ancient sources, and know of two plays named after her. Scholars have long suspected that she may have been invented to personify a female riddler.

Plutarch tells us that she was famous and greatly admired,[1] yet his anecdote about her in *The Seven Sages* (3) is clearly fictitious. He depicts her as a young girl in the company of Thales, a philosopher regarded by the Greeks as one of the seven wise men of antiquity (or 'Seven Sages'), who can be dated by his prediction of an eclipse that took place in 585 BC.[2] The stories about Cleobulina are not consistent, for elsewhere she is the mother of Thales.[3] There is even a problem with her name. Plutarch tells us that she was actually called by Cleobulus, her father (and another riddler), 'Eumetis', and that most people, apparently in error, referred to her by a female form of her father's name instead of her real name.[4] This information may be an invention of Plutarch or his source, as the name *Eumetis* means 'clever', and may be a personification. If Cleobulina is an invention used to characterise a poet of riddles, then the question arises why later Greek writers felt the need to create the character of a female riddler. One simple explanation could be the desire to complement a male riddler. Cleobulina and Cleobulus may both have been invented, as a pair, in an attempt to give historical authority to this genre of poetry.[5]

Despite the problems with her history, we should not lightly dismiss her as an historical figure and poet. Details of her life, like those of most ancient authors, were quickly forgotten. What remained was a reputation for wit, learning, sound political judgement, and philosophy arising from the works attributed to her. The association of Cleobulina with Thales would date her to the early sixth century BC. While such biographical detail is not to be trusted, we do know that she was already well known in the fifth century BC.[6] Athenaeus (10.448b) and Diogenes Laertius (1.89) agree that she came from the city of Lindus on Rhodes.

An otherwise unknown author, Diotimus of Olympene, wrote a discussion of Cleobulina's riddles, providing us with evidence that a corpus of work attributed to her existed in his day.[7] Only three riddles surviving from Classical Greece are specifically attributed to her, and the attribution of these poems has been questioned.[8] It is quite possible that anonymous riddles may, over the years, have been attributed to Cleobulina 'the riddler', in much the same way that anonymous epic verses were attributed to Homer. Perhaps she was a compiler rather than a composer of riddles. However, against the argument that she was merely a name we should note that the sources are quite specific at attributing authorship of only three extant riddles to her—and no others. She was not the only known composer of riddles.

The fragments we have may not indicate the quality and range of her work. Her corpus may have included slightly longer pieces too, though Greek riddles are not often longer than about six verses (three elegiac couplets); we have riddles of two and three couplets attributed to Cleobulus.[9] Aristotle discusses riddles in his work on poetry, giving an indication that scholars viewed them seriously as poetry as well as word-games. He argues that the essence of the riddle is to describe something that is real, but in such a way that it seems to be describing something impossible; the solution will have at its heart metaphoric use of language.[10] Cleobulina provides just such metaphoric riddles in her extant work.[11]

Riddles were a popular form of after-dinner entertainment. Athenaeus, in his description of a fictitious banquet, includes a lengthy section in which the guests discuss riddles. The penalty for those unable to solve the riddle was to drink a cup of wine mixed with salt-water without stopping to breathe.[12]

Both comedies named after her, one by Alexis and one by Cratinus, are lost.[13] Their titles are nevertheless intriguing. Both are called *The Cleobulinae*—that is, Cleobulina in the plural. Fifth century comedies were usually named after their chorus, and we can therefore be fairly sure that these plays featured a chorus of women called Cleobulina. Cleobulina was therefore well enough known, either as an archetype or an historical figure, to be caricatured on stage. Alexis and Cratinus lived a century apart, which attests to the longevity of her popularity. These plays may themselves have contributed to the creation of a fictitious Cleobulina. Cleobulina, the literary figure, was admired for her wit and learning, providing a positive image of a woman of intelligence and humour.

The answer to her first riddle is, 'A physician bleeding a patient into a bleeding-cup'. Greek physicians used to bleed their patients to help to restore the balance in the four 'humours' necessary for good health. When a patient was unwell there was thought to be an imbalance in the body's humours. If the body was unable to restore the balance itself, by expelling mixtures of unwanted humours through the nose, mouth, pores etc., then the physician could step in and bleed the patient. The bleeding cup, which was made of bronze, was warmed by a piece of lint placed in the bowl, and was applied to the body where a small incision had been made; the warmth helped to draw out the blood. This was a well-known riddle. It was quoted by Aristotle twice, Plutarch, Demetrius of Phalerum and Athenaeus. It provides an apparently impossible scenario which is explained by metaphor (in welding and sharing blood), a form of riddle approved by Aristotle. [14]

The commonly accepted answer to the second riddle is, 'A man stealing a dagger from a madman'.[15] The madness legitimises the theft of a weapon which the possessor could not be trusted to wield. This solution seems to be a little weak. There is no hint in the riddle of madness or a weapon. It is possible to offer an answer to many riddles by referring to a madman, the madness counteracting the puzzle and therefore the point of the riddle. This solution also fails to recognise any metaphor in the riddle.[16]

A better solution is to suggest that Cleobulina is referring to deception in art. The thief is an actor or figure in a work of art, the deception is in the relationship between the viewer and the art or performance as well as, or perhaps instead of, deception in the scene of a theft which is being described. The context in which this riddle was retold supports this interpretation. An anonymous philosophical writer, commenting on the relativity of the meanings of right and wrong, states that in tragedy and art, the best artist is the one who is most deceptive, the one who can make things appear to be most true. The philosopher quotes the riddle by Cleobulina to support this point.[17]

The third riddle refers to hearing a Phrygian flute. Greeks made flutes from bone. Plutarch tells us that while flute-makers used to use the bones of fawns to make their instruments, they had long since found that donkey bones gave a better sound. He quotes this riddle to illustrate his point and gives the solution (*Moralia* 150f). The *aulos* was actually a reed instrument and consisted of a pair of pipes equipped with finger holes, one pipe for each hand. In the 'Phrygian' *aulos* (perhaps so named because it was developed in Phrygia or was particularly popular there) the right-hand pipe was straight, while the left hand pipe was longer and ended in a flared bell shape. Plutarch has only preserved one verse of this riddle; it is quite probable that there was at least one more verse to it to complete the couplet. We have a glimpse here of the humour of Cleobulina: the image of a dead donkey assaulting your ears is startling, and the image is supported by the poem's alliteration.

Cleobulina

Riddles

1.

I saw a man with fire welding bronze to a man
so closely that he joined their blood together.

What did I see?

2.

I saw a man deceiving and stealing by force,
and this act of force was most rightly done.

What did I see?

3.

A dead donkey struck my ears with the bones of his shins.

What happened to me?

Notes

1. *Conjugal Precepts* 48.
2. Herodotus 1.74.2; cf. Herodotus 1.75.6, 170.3.
3. Diog. L., *Life of Thales* 1.22.
4. *The Seven Sages* 3; *Oracles at Delphi* 14.
5. In Greek literature the Sphinx was a female monster, known for her riddles (Apollodorus 3.5.7f.).
6. Cratinus, one of the greatest poets of Old Comedy, wrote a play named after her, first performed before 420 BC. Eusebius in the *Chronicle* tells us that in 451/50 BC (Olympiad 82.2) Cleobulina was especially renowned; perhaps this was the year in which Cratinus' play was performed.
7. Diotimus' work is not extant; see Athen. 10.448b.
8. Martin describes riddles 1 and 3 as 'staged': the subject matter, the flute and the cupping-glass are appropriate to the setting (i.e. the party and its guests) in which the riddles were told; R.P. Martin, 'Just like a woman: enigmas of the lyric voice', in A. Lardinois and L. McClure (eds), *Making Silence Speak* (Princeton: Princeton University Press, 2001), 55-75 (63).

9.   See Pamphila 4 (below) for one of Cleobulus' riddles.
10. *Poetics* 1458 A.22.
11. Aristotle quotes poem 1 by Cleobulina to illustrate his point, but does not assign an author to it.
12. Athen. 10.448b-10.459b; 10.458f-10.459b.
13. The dates for Cratinus are c. 475–c. 420 BC, for Alexis c. 375–c. 275 BC.
14. *Poetics* 1458 A.26-34; *Rhetoric* 1405 A.36; *Poetics* 1458 A.22; Plut., *Moralia* 154b; Demetrius of Phaleron, *On Style* 102; *On Greek Rhetoric* 6.200; 7.949; Athen. 10.452b.
15. As J.M. Edmonds, *Greek Elegy and Iambus*, I (Cambridge, MA: Harvard University Press, 1931, 1982), 165.
16. Metaphor, according to Aristotle, was the key feature of this genre (*Poetics* 1458 A.22).
17. See H. Diels and W. Kranz, *Die Fragmente der Vorsokratiker* (3rd edn; Berlin: Weidmann, 1952), 2.339.27.

3. Telesilla (*lived 6th–5th centuries BC*)

Introduction

Telesilla was a lyric poet who lived in Argos in the fifth century BC. She became famous for saving the city when it was attacked by the Spartans in 494 BC. In the story told by Pausanias, after the massacre of the Argive fighting men by the Spartans, Telesilla rallied all those left in the city able to bear arms, including the women, and drove off the invaders.[1] The story has been considered apocryphal, yet, although their role in the battle may have been exaggerated, there is nothing improbable in women joining in the last ditch defence of the city.[2] Plutarch tells us that even in his day the Argives still celebrated a festival on the day of this victory, during which women wore men's clothing and men women's clothing.[3] Telesilla's role in the battle, if not historical, may have been assumed later from something she wrote.[4] Eusebius dates her as late as Olympiad 82.2 (= 451/450 BC);[5] this, together with her role in the attack on her city in 494 suggests that she was long-lived, though Eusebius' date is for the time when she was 'famous' and so provides only an approximate indication of her lifetime.

Telesilla was admired in antiquity for her poetry. The Argives honoured her by erecting an engraved stele on which she was depicted in front of the temple of Aphrodite. Tatian tells us a statue of Telesilla was made by Niceratus (a sculptor of the first century BC) and Antipater of Thessalonica includes her in his canon of nine women poets, calling her 'glorious Telesilla'. Eusebius considered her as famous as the comic poet Crates and the lyric poet Bacchylides.[6] Yet of her poetry, only one fragment of more than one word has survived.

We may assume from her heroic reputation and the representation of her holding a helmet on the Argive stele that she wrote on martial subjects,[7] but the fragments of her work which remain are of a different nature. Five of the fragments concern Apollo, the most important god in Argos, or his sister Artemis, and suggest that religious themes were important to her. Fragment 1 addresses 'girls', and may have been written for choral performance. In Greece both boys and girls were trained in singing and dancing, and national songs about gods and heroes were popular.[8]

Telesilla was also remembered for the metrical innovation of her lyric poetry. Fragment 1 is an example of a Telesillean metre: a two and a half foot glyconic line which was named after her.[9] It is also the only fragment of her extant work that consists of more than one word. Fragments 2 and 6, 7 and 8 are single words only; fragments 3, 4, 5 and 9 are not direct quotations of her work.

Telesilla

1.
Now, girls, when Artemis
was fleeing from Alpheus…

2.
The song to Apollo is
the sun-lover[10]

3.
Telesilla says,
Pythaeus son of Apollo came first
to the Argives' land.[11]

4.
Telesilla remembers in her song,
on the peak of the mountain
is a temple of Artemis Coryphaea.

5.
According to Telesilla, ...
Amphion too was shot by Artemis and Apollo
and Amyclas and Meliboea were saved.[12]

6.
...the better women...

7.
...the round threshing-floor...

8.
... you curly-hair...

9.
Telesilla ... depicts both Virtue and Nobility as
a tall and beautiful woman ...[13]

Notes

1. Paus., 2.20.8-10; Plut., *Fine Deeds of Women* 4.245c-f. Herodotus describes the battle and the Spartan retreat, but mentions neither Telesilla nor the role of the women (6.77-83).
2. For women defending their city, see Thucydides 2.3.2; on the historicity of this story see R.A. Tomlinson, *Argos and the Argolid* (London: Routledge and Kegan Paul, 1972), 94; Snyder, J.McI., *The Woman and the Lyre: Women Writers in Classical Greece and Rome* (Carbondale: Southern Illinois University Press, 1989), 61-62.
3. Plut., *Fine Deeds of Women* 4.245c. The festival may have pre-dated the victory, which later provided a convenient aetiological explanation for it. Other festivals in which clothing exchange took place are attested: see J.G. Frazer, *Pausanias's Description of Greece*, III (New York: Macmillan, 1965), 197.
4. For the common practice of the invention of biography from an author's work see M. Lefkowitz, *The Lives of the Greek Poets* (Baltimore: John Hopkins University Press, 1981).
5. Eusebius, *Chronicle*, Olympic Year 82.2.

6. Paus., 2.20.8; Tatian, *Against the Greeks* 33; Antipater, *Anth. Pal.* 9.26.5; Eusebius, *Chronicle*, Olympic Year 82.2.
7. We might assume this too from the testimony of Maximus of Tyre, who states that the Argives were roused by the lyrics of Telesilla just as the Spartans were by Tyrtaeus (*Orations* 37.5).
8. Athenaeus 14.626e.
9. Hephaestion, *Handbook of Metres* 11.2. She was known for using particularly short lines: Censorius, *On Music* (H. Keil, *Grammatici Latini*, VI [Leipzig, 1857–80]).
10. The introduction is by Athenaeus, who quotes this one word fragment (14.619b).
11. Pausanias (2.35.2) reports Telesilla's words here and in fragment 4.
12. Apollodorus gives evidence for Telesilla's version of the myth of Niobe's children: two of whom are named here (Amyclas and Meliboea). Usually the children are slaughtered by Apollo and Artemis, but Amphion was her husband (*Library* 3.46).
13. From an anonymous commentator (scholiast) on Homer's *Odyssey* 13.289.

4. Myrtis (*fl. 5th century* BC)

Introduction

Myrtis was a lyric poet from Anthedon, a small coastal town in northern Boeotia (Plut., *Greek Questions* 40). Antipater calls her 'sweet-voiced' and places her amongst the best of women poets (*Anth. Pal.* 9.26.7s). She was famous enough to have a bronze statue made of her (Tatian, *Against the Greeks* 33). Two of the best Greek lyric poets, Corinna and Pindar, were both said to have been her pupils (*Suda* 3.157; 4.132) and she was even accused of daring to compete with Pindar himself (Corinna 7 above). Given this evidence of the high regard in which her work was held, it is a great pity that all her verse has been lost. Plutarch preserves a prose summary of one of her poems, and this is now all that remains of her work.

For the quality of Myrtis' poetry we have to rely on the ancient testimony. Ranking her alongside poets like Pindar and Corinna is high praise indeed, although few scholars trust the *Suda*'s claim that they were both her pupils.[1] Ancient biographers tended to link famous authors, but they seldom had any reliable evidence for the biography outside of the author's text itself (see the introduction to Corinna). Pindar was born in the 65th Olympiad (i.e. between 520 and 516 BC); the pupil/teacher relationship reveals that Myrtis and Pindar were later thought to have been near contemporaries, though it may have been the style of her work, its subject matter, or even a reference she made in her work to Pindar which led to the invention of a relationship between them. Corinna's criticism of Myrtis for entering into competition with Pindar (Corinna 7 above) should not be taken literally either—although the Greeks did hold musical competitions. For Corinna herself is said to have defeated Pindar five times in competitions, although they were probably never contemporaries (Aelian, *Historical Miscellanies* 13.25). Corinna's comment and the testimony linking them in the *Suda* are more likely to reflect a similarity of genre of poetry and perhaps also a similarity in style, language, imagery, range or even subject matter in their poetry.

Pindar made extensive use of Greek myths in his extant work, as did Corinna, and this provides a superficial point of comparison with the testimony we have in Plutarch of the work of Myrtis. In her one fragment, Myrtis tells a local aetiological myth which explained an obscure Tanagran custom. Lyric poets like Pindar and Corinna used myth, partly because the narratives were enjoyed by their audience, but also to illuminate and assess the present by means of contrast with the mythical past. The reputation that Myrtis had as the teacher of both Pindar and Corinna means that she may well have adopted a didactic style similar to them.

Greek lyric poetry was musical and written to be sung. There are hints that Myrtis was known particularly for the music she wrote; Corinna calls Myrtis 'clear-voiced' (poem 7 above) and Antipater of Thessalonica calls her 'sweet-voiced' (*Anth. Pal.* 9.26.7). Antipater thought that her poetry would be everlasting. Sadly he was wrong.

Myrtis

(Retold by Plutarch)[2]

Eunostus was the son of Elieus, the son of Cephisus, and Scias. His name, they say, came from the nymph Eunosta, who brought him up. He was as chaste and strict as he was handsome and just.

But they say that Ochna, one of the daughters of Colonus, who was his cousin, fell in love with him. When Eunostus rejected her attempts to seduce him and, after scolding her, went away to her brothers to bring an accusation against her, the girl managed to get in first with an accusation against him, and, claiming that Eunostus had raped her, urged her brothers, Echemus, Leon and Bucolus, to kill him. So they ambushed the young man and killed him, and Elieus imprisoned them.

Ochna, now repenting and stricken with worry and fear, wanting to free herself from her grief for her love and at the same time feeling pity for her brothers, told Elieus the whole truth, and he told Colonus. Colonus passed judgement and Ochna's brothers went into exile, while she threw herself from a cliff. This is the story that Myrtis, the lyric poet of Anthedon, has told.

Notes

1. See *Suda* on Pindar (4.132) and on Corinna (3.157).
2. Plut., *Greek Questions* 40, = *Moralia* 300d-f. Plutarch sets himself the question, 'Who was the hero Eunostus in Tanagra and why are women not allowed to enter his grove'. He then cites Myrtis to answer his question.

5. Praxilla (*mid-5th century* BC)

Introduction

Praxilla was a versatile lyric poet from Sicyon. A contemporary of Telesilla, she lived in the mid-fifth century BC.[1] Antipater of Thessalonica lists her first among his canon of nine 'immortal-tongued' women poets (*Anth. Pal.* 9.26.3), and Lysippus, a famous fourth century sculptor, also from Sicyon, made a bronze statue of her, evidence of the high esteem in which she was held. She was clearly popular in her own day: a vase dated to around 450 BC has been found with the first four words from one of her poems on it (fragment 5 below).[2] Further evidence for the reception of her work in the fifth century BC comes from the comic playwright Aristophanes, who parodied lines from her poetry both in the *Wasps* (1238) and the *Thesmophoriazusae* (528). Not only did he know her work, but his parody implies that he expected his Athenian audience to recognise it too.[3]

Eight fragments of her work have survived, but in only five of them are any of her words quoted. Nevertheless these fragments exemplify the range of her poetry. She wrote drinking songs (*scolia*), hymns and dithyrambs (choral odes performed at festivals of Dionysus). In addition, she was remembered for a dactylic metre she invented (or at least made famous) which was named the Praxilleion after her.[4]

Drinking songs were a popular form of entertainment amongst the participants at aristocratic *symposia*. Praxilla's drinking songs were well known and enjoyed into the second century AD.[5] Three of the surviving fragments are *scolia*. That Praxilla wrote poetry of this type, intended to be sung at parties from which respectable women would be excluded, has led to speculation that she may have been a *hetaera*, or courtesan, as women of this class did attend such parties.[6] Such a conclusion is dangerous when we have no testimony on Praxilla's life, but it does raise the issue of the place of women writers in fifth century Greek society and expose how little we know about the process of publication. Praxilla may have been a wealthy aristocrat (and could pay to publish her own work), but *scolia* would seem an unlikely genre for such a woman to choose. It seems more likely that she was a professional musician, offering original compositions to paying audiences at *symposia,* probably, initially at least, performing them herself.[7] Dithyramb competitions were held at festivals of Dionysus at Athens and elsewhere, attracting entries from poets like Pindar and Bacchylides. Such competitions may have provided the opportunity for a poet like Praxilla to become well known too.[8]

Later reception of her work is not all favourable. Tatian (*Against the Greeks* 33) states that she said nothing useful in her poetry, but his criticism is of little value to us, as the moral Christian standpoint he adopts causes him to criticise all Greek works of art. What he does demonstrate is that her poetry was still known and read in his day (mid-second century AD). Zenobius, who also lived in the second century AD, records that 'sillier than Praxilla's Adonis' had become proverbial (*Proverbs* 4.21), and he cites fragment 1 (below) to illustrate his point. This is not a criticism of Praxilla, as it has been taken to be,[9] but of a character in one of her poems. Given the light-hearted nature of the image in this fragment, we should not assume that Adonis is meant to be taken seriously. An apparent pun in line three between cucumber (in Greek *sicyos)* and the name of Praxilla's own city suggests we can read more than one level of meaning into Adonis' lines. The bathos here is effective.[10]

The fifth fragment has attracted various interpretations, but the most straightforward one is that it is about a prostitute. Prostitutes are often characterised in Greek poetry as 'looking out' for their customers—unlike respectable women, who stay secluded. Fragments 6-8 are references to her work which do not quote her words directly.

Praxilla

1. Hymn to Adonis
The most beautiful thing I leave is the light of the sun,
second are the shinning stars and the face of the moon,
and cucumbers, and apples and pears too.

2. Achilles
But I never persuaded the anger in your heart.

3. Scolion
Learn the story of Admetus, my friend, love good people,
and keep clear of cowards, knowing the cowards' thanks is very small.

4. Scolion
My friend, watch out for a scorpion under every stone.

5. Scolion (Praxilleion)
Through the window you look so beautifully,
you virgin (your head), you bride (down below).

6.
But Praxilla of Sicyon says that Chrysippus was carried off by Zeus.

7.
Praxilla wrote that Carneius was the son of Europa and Zeus, and Apollo and Leto raised him.

8.
The Carneia: Praxilla says that it was named after Carnus, the son of Zeus and Europa, who was Apollo's eromenos.[11]

Notes

1.   Eusebius dates her to Olympiad 82.2: 451/450 BC. (*Chronicles* 82.2). For a modern edition of the testimonia see D.A. Campbell, *Greek Lyric*, IV (Cambridge, MA: Harvard University Press, 1992), 370-73.
2.   Cited by Campbell, *Greek Lyric* IV, 380-81.
3.   For the parody, see scholiast on *Wasps* 1238 and *Thesmophoriazusae* 528 (in D.L. Page, *Poetae Melici Graeci* [Oxford: Clarendon Press, 1962], 388). Eustathius also knew of her (*Iliad* 326.43).

4.   Hephaestion, *Handbook on Metres* 7.8.

5.   Athen. 15.694a.

6.   See J.McI. Snyder, *The Woman and the Lyre: Women Writers in Classical Greece and Rome* (Carbondale: Southern Illinois University Press, 1989), 56; for the segregation of women in Greece, see Cornelius Nepos, *Lives* preface, 6.

7.   For the practice of a professional female musician entertaining at drinking parties, see Xenophon, *Symposium* 2.1-2; Plato, *Symposium* 176e.

8.   Corinna and Myrtis were thought to have entered competitions, suggesting that women could compete too.

9.   For the view that this is a form of criticism of the poet, see J. Balmer, *Classical Women Poets* (Newcastle: Bloodaxe Books, 1996), 53.

10. The fragment has also been interpreted aetiologically, the myth referring here to vegetables used in the Adonia festival: ibid, 55; or to show Adonis not as a fool, but an 'exuberant youth who cannot really decide what he misses most': Snyder, *The Woman and the Lyre*, 57-58.

11. The *eromenos* was the younger partner in male homosexual relationships which were pederastic.

6. Aspasia (fl. 450 BC)

Introduction

Aspasia is one of the most famous women of classical Greece, yet little is known of her life, and most of what was written about her in her own day is dubious. As the partner of Pericles, Athens' leading statesman in the mid-fifth century BC, Aspasia moved in the highest aristocratic circles and attracted the attention of comic and serious writers. She inspired literary personae which in turn led to the creation of pseudonymous works in her name.

Aristophanes refers to her as a keeper of prostitutes, implies that she has the power to influence both Pericles' and Athens' politics, and that she sent Athens to war to avenge the theft of two of her girls (*Acharnians* 516-39).[1] Later writers embellished the tradition, establishing her as prostitute and sexual expert, who used her sexuality as a means to gain political influence. She was depicted as a teacher of both Pericles and Socrates, an expert in rhetoric, and a keen philosopher (Plut., *Pericles* 24.5). According to Plutarch she came from Miletus and became Pericles' partner after he divorced his wife. As a resident alien in Athens (i.e. a non-Athenian Greek resident), she would not have been eligible to marry Pericles.[2] As she could not marry him, her status as his partner would be that of a concubine (*pallake*). However, in an extraordinary gesture, the Athenians did recognise their union as a marriage, granting citizenship to Aspasia's son, who was named Pericles after his father.[3] After Pericles' death in 429 BC, she is said to have become the partner of Lysicles, another Athenian politician, who died the following year (Plut., *Pericles* 24).[4]

Plato, who may have met Aspasia, composed a speech which he attributed to her (*Menexenos* 236d-249e). By giving Aspasia this *epitaphios* (funeral oration), Plato distances the ideas from himself; the irony of a woman and an outsider praising the ideals of an Athenian male citizen produces a parody of the funeral oration genre. Xenophon uses her as an authority on male-female relationships (*Memorabilia* 2.6.36; *Economics* 3.14).

Herodicus, a Greek from Babylon who worked around 125 BC, wrote a work called *Against the Lover of Socrates*, directed against the image of Socrates established by Plato. He used Aspasia as a character in his work to discredit Socrates. Socrates is overcome by his desire for Alcibiades and needs the guidance of an expert on passion. The real author of the two poems which Herodicus cited is unknown, though Düring suggests that Herodicus wrote them himself.[5] This work, however, may not have been pseudonymous originally. Athenaeus, who has preserved these fragments (5.219c, 220e), provides a context for the poetry. A narrative about Socrates hunting Alcibiades but being unsuccessful in his suit reverses the better attested story that the young Alcibiades tried to seduce the much older Socrates (a humorous switching of the normal roles of *erastes* and *eromenos*)[6] found in Plato (*Protagoras* 309a; *Symposium* 214-22b). In both passages Aspasia is speaking, and perhaps it is this dramatic context which led to later readers attributing the poetry to her rather than to the text's (now unknown) author.

Aspasia

1.

Socrates, I can see your heart has been bitten by desire
for the son of Deinomache and Cleinias. But listen,
if you want to do well with your little darling. Don't
disobey my message, but obey it, and you will do much better.
When I heard, my body was covered with a perspiration of joy,
and welcome tears fell from my eyelids.
Equip yourself, and fill your heart with the inspired Muse
with whom you will conquer him, implant her in his yearning ears,
for she is the start of love for you both. With her you will possess him,
offering his ears a bridegroom's gifts of the heart.

2.

Why do you cry, dear Socrates? Does a thunderbolt
dwelling in your chest stir you up, desire smashed
by the eyes of the unconquered boy, whom I promised
to tame for you?

Notes

1. Hermippus the comic poet also made fun of her (the best interpretation of Plut., *Life of Pericles* 32.1), as apparently did Eupolis and Cratinus, fragments 110, 192, 267, and 246-68 respectively, in R. Kassel and C. Austin (eds), *Poetae Comici Graeci* (Berlin: De Gruyter, 1983).
2. Pericles himself is credited with proposing the law passed in 451/0 BC which restricted Athenian citizenship to children with two Athenian parents, and so discouraged Athenians from marrying non-citizens (Ar., *Athenian Constitution* 26.4, Plut., *Life of Pericles* 37.2-3). At some later stage a law forbidding an Athenian to marry a non-Athenian was enacted (Demosthenes, *Against Neaera* 59.17).
3. Plut., *Life of Pericles* 26.4.
4. For a full discussion of her biography and the sources for it, see M.M. Henry, *Prisoner of History: Aspasia and her Biographical Tradition* (Oxford: Oxford University Press, 1995). For speculation on her family and descendants, see P.J. Bicknell, 'Axiochos Alkibiadou, Aspasia and Aspasios', *L' Antiquité Classique* 51 (1982), 240-50.
5. I. Düring, *Herodicus the Cratetean: A Study in Anti-Platonic Tradition* (Stockholm: Wellström and Widstrand, 1941), 63-64.
6. In homosexual relationships, the *erastes* was normally the older partner who pursued a much younger male (the *eromenos*).

7. Eurydice (born c. 410 BC)

Introduction

Eurydice was born about 410 BC, the granddaughter of Arrhabaeus, king of the Lyncestae, and the daughter of Sirras (Strab. 7.7.8). She was the mother of three sons, each of whom became king of Macedonia, and grandmother of Alexander the Great. Plutarch praises Eurydice for the example she set to mothers by learning to read and write so that she could teach her sons properly, and he reproduces an epigram which she wrote, the only extant work we have by her.[1]

Despite his praise, Plutarch nevertheless belittles Eurydice (to Greek sensibilities) by calling her a non-Greek, an Illyrian, and 'thrice-barbarous' (*Moralia* 14b-c). The kings of Lyncestae, however, were Greek-speaking, and claimed descent from the Bacchiadae, an important Corinthian aristocratic family. The slander derives from the rhetoric published in the fourth century BC in Athens, which sought to discredit her third son, Philip. Eurydice's reputation suffered from this propaganda which claimed that she had an affair with Ptolemy Alorites, arranged to marry her daughter to him, and then plotted to murder her husband and hand Ptolemy the throne. She was even blamed for the deaths of two of her sons, Alexander and Perdiccas.[2] While this sensational account is fictional and rightly dismissed as 'poppycock',[3] Macedonian queens did take active roles in political affairs[4] and Eurydice may have done so too.

The facts known about her are few: she married the Macedonian king Amyntas III, probably around 393 or 391 BC, and bore three sons who were to rule Macedonia in turn: Alexander II, Perdiccas III and Philip II (father of Alexander the Great). She also had a daughter named Eurynome. She was long-lived: excavations at the village of Vergina, site of the Macedonian city of Aegeae, have uncovered the bases of two statues dedicated by Eurydice which date to the second half of the fourth century BC. A magnificent tomb found at Vergina has been tentatively identified as hers.[5]

The text is a fine example of a dedicatory epigram and useful as a point of comparison with the later epigrams of the Hellenistic period. The poem was written to be inscribed on a statue base. We do not know what the statue was, though Hammond suggests that it may have been of Hermes as patron of letters,[6] though it may have been of the Muses themselves.

The text is also useful for the light cast on literacy at this period, and in Plutarch's own day. Eurydice was proud to announce to the world that she had learnt to read and write. Even amongst the aristocracy in the early fourth century, this was something worth noting, and she is proud rather than ashamed that her learning was accomplished relatively late in life (apparently after the birth of her children). While the evidence comes from Macedonia, we should not assume that the Macedonian aristocracy was 'backward'.[7] Her pride would not have been so great if it were not a notable achievement by the standards of the Greek world. Plutarch presents Eurydice as a model for mothers, incorrectly inferring from her poem that she learnt to read and write to teach her sons. The text does not suggest this, but writing from the perspective of the second century AD, Plutarch saw home education as one of the roles for a mother, and that a woman's education was important for the future education of her sons. Eurydice however speaks only of the benefits of the learning for herself: her hard work opened up written knowledge, her soul's desire.

Eurydice

Eurydice daughter of Sirras[8] presented this
to the Muses when she filled the longing for knowledge in her soul.
For the delighted mother of thriving sons laboured
to learn letters, the record of speech.

Notes

1. The epigram was probably seen and recorded by Theopompus, who was read by Plutarch: as N.G.L. Hammond, *Philip of Macedon*, II (London: Duckworth, 1994), 17.
2. Justin (7.4.7–7.5.8) and the scholia to Aeschines 2.29.
3. N.G.L. Hammond and G.T. Griffith, *A History of Macedonia*, II (Oxford: Clarendon Press, 1979), 183.
4. See J.G.E. Whitehorne, *Cleopatras* (London and New York: Routledge, 1994).
5. M.A. Andronikos, *Vergina: The Royal Tombs and the Ancient City* (Athens: Ekdotike Athenon S.A., 1984), 24, 50-51. The statue bases bear the same inscription: 'Eurydice daughter of Sirra, to Eucleia'. The statues are lost, see M.A. Andronikos, 'Vergina', *Ergon* (1982), 19 and (1990), 83.
6. Hammond, *Philip of Macedon*, 17.
7. Euripides, the Athenian tragedian worked at the Macedonian court at the end of the fifth century (Hyginus, *Fabula* 219) and Eurydice's grandson Alexander learnt his work off-by-heart (see Nicobule 2). We may compare Eurydice's achievement with evidence from the end of the fourth century and later for higher levels of literacy among women in the Hellenistic world: see S.B. Pomeroy, *Women in Hellenistic Egypt: From Alexander to Cleopatra* (New York: Schocken Books, 1984), 59-72. See also S.G. Cole, 'Could Greek women read and write', in H.P. Foley (ed.), *Reflections of Women in Antiquity* (New York: Gordon and Breach Science Publishers, 1981), 219-45.
8. Sirras should be preferred to Irras (in the manuscript) on the strength of the Vergina inscriptions. On the text see U. von Wilamowitz-Moellendorff, 'Lesefrüchte CLXIX', *Hermes* 54 (1919), 71-72.

8. Philaenis (*fl. 4th century* BC)

Introduction

Philaenis was well known in antiquity as the author of pornography. The first mention of her is by Timaeus of Tauromenium who lived in the fourth and third centuries BC.[1] Chrysippus in the fifth and seventh books of his *On Pleasure and the Good* referred to Philaenis' erotic manual; Clearchus mentioned her in his work *On Proverbs*; and she appears in fiction to epitomise a prostitute, where her mother, Gyllis, is also named.[2] Three pieces of a papyrus fragment of Philaenis' book have been found (*P. Oxy.* 2891). The fragment names the author, identifies her as a Samian, and the daughter of Ocymenes.[3]

Despite this testimony, scholars generally believe that 'Philaenis' was a pseudonym disguising the identity of the true author, who may well have been a man.[4] There is some ancient evidence for this: Aeschrion of Samos, in an epitaph for Philaenis, claimed that the work attributed to her was a forgery, alleging that it was really by Polycrates of Athens (*Anth. Pal.* 7.345). Dioscorides also defends her reputation in an epigram written in the voice of Philaenis, in which she claims that she did not compose the work attributed to her (*Anth. Pal.* 7.450). Such defences of well known figures (e.g. Helen of Troy) were composed as rhetorical exercises. Polycrates was criticised by Isocrates for the triviality of his work, and the reputation he consequently suffered may have led to him being associated with Philaenis' pornography.[5]

Pornography was often attributed to prostitutes and Philaenis appears to have been perhaps the best known of these.[6] Samos was notorious for the poor moral standards of its women and for a high number of prostitutes, and it is not surprising to find Philaenis linked to that island.[7] By using her name, the author characterised the text and assigned authority to it. For her name, a feminine diminutive of the Greek word for love, was regularly used by prostitutes.[8] By concealing his or her own name, the author went one step further than Lucian, Alciphron and Herodas, who wrote dialogues of courtesans but under their own names. Nevertheless, 'Philaenis' existed as a female literary figure, reinforcing one of the typical images of women in the Classical world: the prostitute.[9]

The Oxyrhynchus scraps contain text from the beginning of Philaenis' pornographic book. The book had been thought to deal with sexual positions, but the papyrus demonstrates that it was a more general work on the art of lovemaking, with subject headings suggesting a systematic approach to the subject.[10] The style is brief and matter of fact, with a few words in the Ionic dialect, but no real attempt has been made to write in Philaenis' native language.[11] The text is extremely fragmentary: I have used Tsantsanoglou's text, along with the readings he suggests.[12] The papyrus provides three fragments of Philaenis' book, though fragment 2 is not legible (only about five letters can be identified) and fragments 1 and 3 both have illegible sections. The extant text provides an introduction, a section on seduction (with heading), a section on flattery (for which the heading is missing) and the heading for a section on kissing.

The introduction provides a clue as to the nature of the work as a whole: parody. Behind a veneer of seriousness lies witty reference to well known prose *topoi*. The introduction bears a strong resemblance to serious works such as the histories of Herodotus and Thucydides. It parodies their emphasis on the 'scientific' nature of their work, and the considerable labour which the author has undertaken to provide a useful work, wittily transferring the context from history to the art of love.[13]

The section on seduction continues the playful tone of the opening. Contrary to normal practice, men are advised not to present themselves well, but rather the opposite, when attempting a seduction. The section on flattery advises men to liken their paramours to a deity. 'Rhea' here is a reading suggested by Tsantsanoglou as a suitable ironic compliment for an older woman; elsewhere this elderly goddess was ridiculed for having a passion for a young man named Attis.[14]

Philaenis

Philaenis the Samian, daughter of Ocymenes, composed this book
for those who wish to lead their life with knowledge gained scientifically,
not unprofessionally. She toiled ...

On Seductions
Now, the seducer must come untidy and uncombed,
so that he does not seem to the woman
to be a man who takes too much trouble ...

...

{*On Flattery*}
...with the intention...,
while he says that
she ... is equal to a goddess,
that she who is ugly is as lovely as Aphrodite
and that she who is older is as Rhea.

On Kissing
...

Notes

1. Timaeus is in turn cited by Polybius (12.13.1 = *FGrHist* 566 F 35).
2. Athen. 8.335b-e;10.457e (= *FHG* ii 317); 220F; Herodas, *Mime* 1.
3. Athenaeus calls her a Leucadian, rather than Samian, either in error, or because of a rival tradition (Athen. 5.220f.).
4. M.L. West, 'Erinna', *Zeitschrift für Papyrologie und Epigraphik* 25 (1977), 95-118 (118); K. Tsantsanoglou, 'The memoirs of a lady from Samos', *Zeitschrift für Papyrologie und Epigraphik* 12 (1973), 183-95 (192-94).
5. Polycrates was a fourth century BC Athenian author on rhetoric, Dioscorides and Aeschrion poets of the third century BC.
6. Pornographic works were also attributed to Astyanassa, Elephantis (or Elephantine), and

Pamphila (*Suda*, s.v.); Flora, identified as a prostitute, was cited as a source on why women found Pompey the Great attractive (Plut., *Life of Pompey* 53); the historian Fenestella repeated a prostitute's anecdote about Crassus (Plut., *Life of Crassus* 5).

7.   As Tsantsanoglou, 'The memoirs of a lady from Samos', who gives examples on p. 193.

8.   *Anth. Pal.* 5.4, 121, 186, 202; 6.206, 207, 284; 7.198, 477, 486, 487; 8.254; 9.18; Lucian, *Dialogues of Prostitutes* 6.1; Martial 7.67, 70.

9.   See A. Richlin (ed.), *Pornography and Representation in Greece and Rome* (Oxford: Oxford University Press, 1992); S.B. Pomeroy, *Goddesses, Whores, Wives and Slaves: Women in Classical Antiquity* (New York: Schocken Books, 1975).

10. As E. Lobel, *Oxyrhynchus Papyri* 39 (London: Egypt Exploration Society, 1972), 51.

11. Tsantsanoglou, 'The memoirs of a lady from Samos', 194-95.

12. For further discussion on the text see H.N. Parker, 'Another go at the text of Philaenis' (*P. Oxy.* 2891), *Zeitschrift für Papyrologie und Epigraphik* 79 (1989), 49-50.

13. As Tsantsanoglou, 'The memoirs of a lady from Samos', 192.

14. Ibid, 190; cf. Lucian, *Dialogues of the Gods* 12.1; Lucillius, *Anth. Pal.* 9.69. Rhea was the mother of the older Olympian gods, Hestia, Demeter, Hera, Hades, Poseidon and Zeus.

9. Erinna (fl. c. 350 BC)

Introduction

Erinna was celebrated in antiquity for her poem *The Distaff*, a lament for her childhood friend, Baucis. In the *Greek Anthology* Asclepiades, an anonymous poet, and Leonidas sing her praises. Meleager honoured her with a place in his 'Garland' of poets, likening her work to a sweet, maidenly coloured crocus.[1] Antipater of Sidon says that although she wrote few verses, her work was inspired by the Muses, and she would always be remembered (*Anth. Pal.* 7.713). Her great work was lost, however, except for a short quotation, until 1928 when a papyrus text was found with about 54 lines of the 300 line poem partly intact. Even though the text is fragmentary, the high opinion of her as a poet in antiquity has been proven to have been fully justified by the excellence of this work.

Biographical details about her are few and most probably derived from *The Distaff*. The *Suda* puts together some of the speculation about her that had accumulated by the tenth century AD: it records that she was believed to be a contemporary of Sappho and to have come from Lesbos, or possibly Teos, Telos or even Rhodes,[2] and to have died a virgin at the age of 19. The *Suda* is better on the poem itself, noting that *The Distaff* was written in a mixed Aeolian and Doric dialect and 300 lines long. The tribute poems to her in the *Greek Anthology* were sources for the *Suda* and we can see in them the accumulation of details as an Erinna romance is invented. An anonymous poem (*Anth. Pal.* 9.190) states that she was only 19 when she wrote her 300 line hexameter poem, a detail which Erinna seems to have recorded herself. Her work is compared favourably both with Homer and Sappho, introducing a link between Erinna and more famous poets. Erinna's poem is about the death of her childhood friend, and this may have inspired the romantic tradition to play on the irony of her early death too; such was her sorrow at her friend's death, Erinna may have indicated in her poem that she wanted or expected such a fate too.[3]

Eusebius states that Erinna lived around 353/2 BC. This date is generally accepted, but it is not without problems. Tatian claimed that the sculptor Naucydes made a statue of her. Naucydes lived in the fifth century BC, so Tatian must have been mistaken.[4] Her dialect is interesting. Hexameter poetry was traditionally written in Ionic, even by non-Ionians, but Erinna wrote in a mixed Aeolian and Doric dialect. Only Sappho and Alcman had previously written hexameters in a non-Ionic dialect. In using her own Doric dialect she made the sentiments in her poem—the grief for her friend—seem more personal and heartfelt. The Aeolian element, West argues, echoes Sappho's dialect. It is a literary allusion which emphasises the female sex of the writer.[5] The Aeolian link with Sappho will have added to the later confusion over her homeland.

In *The Distaff* Erinna plays upon the theme of weaving as she constructs a personal lament for her childhood friend. Weaving is a metaphor for writing poetry and alludes to the thread of life spun by the Fates,[6] as well as referring to a traditional female activity. Erinna recalls her childhood and the games they used to play[7]—the recollection of a shared past is a theme found also in Sappho (e.g. fragment 33). Erinna's mourning seems to have been for the loss of her friend to marriage as well as her death. These two themes, death and marriage, are united as early as the myth of Persephone.[8] Erinna's poem has also been judged important for the glimpse it gives us of a girl's view of her relationship with her mother.[9]

Erinna was perhaps the most famous female Greek poet in the ancient world after Sappho. As she is one of the few female poets whose work has, at least in part, survived, it is ironic that West has argued that the excellence of her poetry makes it impossible for her to have been a woman. He argues that *The Distaff* was a clever literary ruse, written by a man in the guise of a young woman. He finds the persona of the poet—an unsophisticated 19-year-old girl pouring out her heart in poetry on the death of her friend—at odds with the polished hexameter poetry.[10] However, there is ample evidence for the education of women in the fourth century, including evidence from Teos, one of the possible birthplaces of Erinna. While it is true that there were literary forgeries in the fourth century BC, these works were pseudonymous and were attributed to famous people.[11] Texts were not invented for unknown female authors. So only when Erinna became famous was there a context for the invention of other works in her name, particularly ones which echo the theme of her great poem on the death of Baucis: hence we have later pseudonymous epitaphs for Baucis by authors purporting to be Erinna.[12]

There are three extant epigrams attributed to Erinna. Two of these poems (5 and 6 below) are epitaphs for Baucis and focus on death and marriage, a popular theme in Hellenistic poetry. West argues against their authenticity, pointing out that they are derivative and only contain information that was in *The Distaff* itself. He sees them as fictions inspired by Erinna's work. They seem never to have been intended for inscription, though this in itself does not mean that they were not written by Erinna.[13] The epigram on Agatharchis is of a quite different tone, and is similar to the poems of Nossis. West argues on this basis that the poem should be attributed to Nossis,[14] but it is possible that Erinna wrote on more than one theme. Nevertheless, the epigrams were included in the *Greek Anthology* under Erinna's name, and it is clear that in antiquity readers could accept them as her work.[15] The dialect, vocabulary and subject matter of the epigrams are reminiscent of the works of earlier Hellenistic poets like Asclepiades, Theocritus and Anyte.

The comic poet Herodas alluded to a link between Nossis and Erinna, and this may have been because of some similarity in the subject matter of Erinna's epigram. It is perhaps more likely to have arisen from a comic prejudice against women who published poetry. Nossis likened her work to Sappho's, and was the subject of dildo jokes in Herodas (6.20-34 and 7.57)—prompted by a comic association of erotic poetry and women with excess sexual appetite. As a fellow female poet, Erinna is included in the joke, referred to as Nossis' 'mother' at 6.20, while Baucis is also alluded to at 7.58. Erinna appears to have represented herself as a 'mother' figure in the *Distaff* in the child's game which she recollected.

Fragments 2–3 below are from *The Distaff* preserved in quotations by Stobaeus and Athenaeus; fragment 1 is a translation of column two of the three columns in *The Distaff* manuscript—very little can be made of the other columns.[16] Bowra tentatively ascribes another papyrus fragment (7 below) to *The Distaff*, though the manuscript does not name the author.[17] West identifies in the dialect of this fragment a mixture of Doric and Aeolian along with Arcadian, which Erinna would not have used. He suggests that the poem may have been by Anyte (who was an Arcadian), but this is unlikely as she does not use this dialect in the epigrams attributed to her.

Erinna

The Distaff

1.

…virgins

…tortoise

…moon

…tortoise…

…into the deep wave   5
you jumped from the white horses with a crazy step.
'I've got you', I cried, 'my friend'. And when you were the tortoise
jumping out you ran through the great hall's court.

Unhappy Baucis, these are my laments as I cry for you deeply,
these are your footprints resting in my heart, dear girl,   10
still warm; but what we once loved is now already ashes.

Young girls, we held our dolls in our bedrooms
like new wives, hearts unbroken. Near dawn your mother,
who handed out wool to her workers in attendance,
came in and called you to help with salted meat.   15

What terror the monster Mormo brought when we were both little girls:
on her head were massive ears and she walked
on four legs and kept changing her face.

But when you went to the bed of a man
you forgot all you heard from your mother while still a child,   20
my dear Baucis. Aphrodite filled your thoughts with forgetting.

As I weep for you now I desert your last rites,
for my feet may not leave the house and become unclean
nor is it right for me to look upon your corpse,
nor cry with my hair uncovered; but a red shame
divides me...   25
…
Nineteen…Erinna…the distaff…

2.

From here an empty echo reaches into Hades.
But there is silence amongst the dead, and darkness closes their eyes.

3.

Pompilus, escort-fish, you send sailors a fair passage,
from the stern please escort my dear friend.

Epigrams

4.

This portrait was made with delicate hands: Prometheus my good friend,
there are people with skill equal to yours too.
Anyway, if whoever drew this girl so-true-to-life,
had added speech, Agatharchis would be complete.

5.

My gravestone, my Sirens, and mourning urn,
who holds Hades' meagre ashes,
say to those who pass by my tomb 'farewell',
both those from my town, and those from other states.
Also, that this grave holds me, a bride. Say also this,   5
that my father called me Baucis, and that my family
was from Tenos, so that they may know, and that my friend
Erinna engraved this epitaph on my tomb.

6.

I am the tomb of Baucis, a young bride, and as you pass
the much lamented grave-stone you may say to Hades:
'Hades, you are malicious'. When you look, the beautiful letters
will tell of the most cruel fate of Baucis,
how her father-in-law lit the girl's funeral pyre   5
with the pine-torches over which Hymen sang.
And you, Hymen, changed the tuneful song of weddings
into the mournful sound of lamentations.

A Hexameter[18]

7.

We came to mighty Demeter, nine
young girls, all wearing our beautiful clothes,
wearing our beautiful clothes, and even bright necklaces
sawn from ivory, just like the light of the sun...

Notes

1. *Anth. Pal.* 7.11-13; 4.1.12.
2. The Doric dialect which she used makes Telos or Rhodes more likely than the Ionian city of Teos
    or the Aeolian island of Lesbos.
3. Asclepiades, who lived about 270 BC, may have introduced the idea of her early death (*Anth. Pal.*
    7.11); cf. *Anth. Pal.* 7.13 (Leonidas or Meleager). See also *Anth. Pal.* 7.12. On this see M.L.
    West, 'Erinna', *Zeitschrift für Papyrologie und Epigraphik* 25 (1977), 95-119 (96).
4. Eusebius, *Chronicle*, Olympic Year 106.4 or 107.1; Tatian, *Against the Greeks* 34.10.
5. West, 'Erinna', 117.
6. On Fate and the distaff, see *Anth. Pal.* 7.12 (on Erinna) and 7.14 (on Sappho).

7. For the association of the tortoise with the lyre and with weaving, as well as with Aphrodite and marriage, see S.B. Pomeroy, 'Supplementary notes on Erinna', *Zeitschrift für Papyrologie und Epigraphik* 32 (1978), 18-19.

8. See the Homeric *Hymn to Demeter*.

9. E. Stehle, 'The good daughter: mothers' tutelage in Erinna's *Distaff* and fourth-century epitaphs', in A. Lardinois and L. McClure (eds), *Making Silence Speak* (Princeton: Princeton University Press, 2001), 179-200.

10. West, 'Erinna', 115-19; Pomeroy, 'Supplementary notes on Erinna', 19-21, argues against West's thesis.

11. Examples include Aspasia, Theano and the famous courtesan Philaenis.

12. S.B. Pomeroy, '*Technikai kai mousikai*: the education of women in the fourth century and in the Hellenistic Period', *American Journal of History* 2 (1977), 51-68, and 'Supplementary notes on Erinna', 19.

13. West, 'Erinna', 114-15; Pomeroy, 'Supplementary notes on Erinna', 21, argues that they may nevertheless have been inscribed. There is some evidence for the later publication of Erinna's work. Asclepiades wrote an introductory poem to preface her work (*Anth. Pal.* 7.11). Leonidas or Meleager quoted a phrase from one of Erinna's epigrams (*Anth. Pal.* 7.13.4 cf. poem 6 line 3 below), attributing it to Erinna, though it is possible that the phrase came originally from a lost part of *The Distaff*.

13. C.M. Bowra, *Greek Poetry and Life: Essays Presented to Gilbert Murray* (Oxford: Clarendon Press, 1936).

14. West, 'Erinna', 116.

15. Athenaeus expresses some doubt about the attribution of *The Distaff* to Erinna, preferring an unknown male writer (Athen. 7.283d). He does not give any reasons.

16. For a possible reconstruction of the 54 verses partly preserved in the manuscript, see West, 'Erinna', 94-113.

17. Bowra, *Greek Poetry and Life*, 160.

18. The attribution of this fragment to Erinna is doubtful: see discussion above.

10. Hedyle (*fl. c. 310 BC*)

Introduction

The only information we have for the poet Hedyle, and the only extant fragment of her work, comes in a discussion of different types of fish in a fictitious dialogue by Athenaeus called the *Scholars at Dinner* (*Deipnosophistai*). Although at first sight this may seem an unpropitious context for poetry, in fact Athenaeus was extremely well read, compiling quotations from a wide range of Greek poets, and he uses his fictitious after-dinner dialogues as a vehicle to display this knowledge. He gives the titles of more than one thousand plays, cites 1,250 authors and more than 10,000 lines of poetry—a remarkable achievement at a time when manuscripts would have been difficult to come by and were never indexed![1] The fragment of Hedyle's poem *Scylla* has survived in his collection through a reference in it to *Glaucus*, a word which denoted both a type of fish and a character in Greek mythology.

Athenaeus tells us that Hedyle was the daughter of the Attic poet Moschine (7.297a-b). There is a tendency in ancient commentators, when biographical details are lost, to link known writers together.[2] This, however, is the only reference we have to Moschine, none of her poetry is extant, and there is no evidence upon which to question Athenaeus' knowledge. Comparison with Nossis may be profitable here. Nossis gives the names of both her mother and her grandmother in a poem about her artistic forebears (poem 3); perhaps Hedyle mentioned her mother in a work now lost (or, of course, Moschine may have mentioned her daughter in one of her poems). Hedyle was one of the earlier Hellenistic poets and probably lived in the second half of the fourth century BC.

Athenaeus also tells us that Hedyle was the mother of Hedylus, another poet.[3] The similarity of their names, professions and dates of birth may have invited the invention of such a link, but we should not rule out this relationship without any contrary evidence. For a son to be named after his mother would be unusual. However, mother and son could both be named after Hedyle's father (or another maternal male relative); perhaps Hedyle's fame allowed her to name a son after herself—a son who was to continue the family's love of poetry. Athenaeus does not tell us where Hedyle lived, but he does tell us that her mother was from Athens making that city her probable home too. Athenaeus is unsure whether Hedylus was from Athens or Samos.

Athenaeus quotes just over two and a half couplets of Hedyle's mythological poem *Scylla*. The elegiac couplet, with its epic rhythm, is well suited to a subject known to us from epic. Yet Hedyle's Scylla is something original, not the twelve-footed, six-headed (each with three rows of teeth) man-eating monster of Homer. She is an object of love, not fear and loathing, and is called a 'nymph' (line 3), a word with connotations of youth, beauty and virginity, and used to denote a class of female nature-deities, along with its other sense of 'bride'. The Siren is also not the alluring monster of epic, but a sympathetic character, and is depicted as a young maiden (line 4).

Hedyle describes the visit of the merman Glaucus to the cave of Scylla. He brings a gift from the sea, as a merman should, and kingfisher chicks, to try to win her love. We do not meet Scylla herself, the subject of the poem,[4] in this short passage. In art and in later versions of the myth there was an evolution of her form from monster to human, beast to beauty. Hedyle leads this change in the extant literature, offering a fresh interpretation of Scylla. Ovid's later version of the myth draws on the new interpretation of Scylla, but also allows for the authority of Homer in mythology. In his version of the story Scylla begins life as a woman, but is changed into a monster by the jealous witch Circe,[5] and it is possible that Hedyle's poem included a similar transformation.

Hedyle's description of Scylla as a *nymphē* is ambiguous: in its sense 'bride', it indicates what Glaucus hopes she will be, not what she actually is. Other versions of the myth tell us that Glaucus was to be disappointed in love, and Hedyle pictures him, even at the moment when he offers his gifts of love, already 'without hope', prepared for his failure. The sorrow that this will bring him is inevitable and the Siren can already see this for us (line 4). Her response directs the reader to pity him too. The change in focus from the narrative is used effectively by the poet to amplify the key emotion in the scene.

Athenaeus tells us that Hedylus wrote a poem on Glaucus too—an unusual example of the son following his mother's lead. In his version of the myth, Glaucus commits suicide, throwing himself into the sea because of his love of Melicertes (Athen. 7.297a). Athenaeus implies that in Hedyle's poem Glaucus commits suicide after rejection by Scylla. His second love gift, the young kingfishers, foreshadows this fate. For, according to another Greek myth, Alcyone threw herself into the sea after the death of her lover, Ceryx, and they were both transformed into birds, she into the *halcyōn* or kingfisher. The kingfisher chicks are described as 'wingless', emphasising their powerlessness, while their inability to fly provides another point of comparison with Glaucus who will shortly, we anticipate, fall to his death.

The Siren is interesting for the new perspective she offers for the reader, but also as a character in her own right. Indeed, it is unusual to find a Siren on her own. Sirens usually appear in a group of more than one: in Homer there are two Sirens, in other writers there are three or more, Plato finds eight.[6] Hedyle has made her Siren an individual, and like Scylla she is depicted as a young woman—implicit in the Greek *parthenos*, 'virgin'. Again rather than playing the Siren's traditional role in myth, that of destroying men by luring them to her, she plays a different, opposite role, pitying hopeless love rather than inducing it. She swims away, showing sympathy for Glaucus. This conception of the Siren as a creature of the sea could well be an innovation of Hedyle's.[7] The action of swimming likens her physically to Glaucus (a merman), complementing her concern for him, yet her leaving contrasts with the closeness implicit in 'neighbour' (line 4).

However, the 'she' in line 5 is ambiguous and could refer to Scylla herself. This reading would highlight Glaucus' love, as he enters the home after she has departed. The absence of the bride thus suggested is confirmed by the shift of narrative view to the Siren. If indeed she were the swimmer then Hedyle has made her a suitable bride for a merman and pathos for him is increased. The ambiguity is no doubt caused by the fragmentary nature of the text and is not a deliberate device of the poet. The poetry of Hedyle is thus rich in images, innovation in plot and character, and pathos. Reinterpreting Homer, she can make a monster into the heroine of her poem. Even in such a brief fragment as this, the quality of her poetry is clear.

Hedyle

Scylla

Glaucus, in love with Scylla, entered her cave, carrying[8]

gifts, cockleshells from Erythraean rock,
or the children of kingfishers still wingless,
baubles for the bride, without hope though he was.
Even Siren, virgin neighbour, pitied his tear;
for she was swimming away, to that shore and the land   5
close by Etna...

Notes

1. See Athenaeus in S. Hornblower and A. Spawforth (eds), *Oxford Classical Dictionary* (Oxford:
    Oxford University Press, 1996). The most accessible edition of Athenaeus is C.B. Gulik,
    Athenaeus, 'The Deipnosophists' (Cambridge, MA: Harvard University Press, 1927–43).
2. See discussions on Corinna and Myrtis.
3. For the fragments of the work of Hedylus that remain, see A.S.F. Gow and D.L. Page (eds), *The
    Greek Anthology: Hellenistic Epigrams* (Cambridge: Cambridge University Press, 1965).
4. As the title of the poem indicates.
5. Ovid, *Metamorphoses* 13.730-37, 898-968, 14.1-74.
6. Homer, *Odyssey* 12.39-54, 158-200; Apollonius of Rhodes, *Argonautica* 4.891-919; Plato,
    Republic 6176.
7. The Sirens were normally portrayed as bird-like in some way rather than aquatic. For illus-
    trations of the Sirens in art, see H.C. Ackermann *et al.* (eds), *Lexicon Iconographicum Mythologiae
    Classicae*, VI.1 (Zurich: Artemis Verlag, 1992), 962 ff.
8. The introduction is by Athenaeus.

11. Anyte (fl. 300 BC)

Introduction

Anyte was admired in antiquity by Meleager who mentions her 'lilies' first in his catalogue of women poets.[1] In the *Greek Anthology* there are 25 epigrams attributed to her, but either Planudes or the Palatine editor (or both) were unsure about the authorship of six of them; today only 21 of the epigrams are generally considered genuine (numbers 1-21 in this edition). She is credited with working in other poetic genres too. In antiquity she was called 'Anyte the lyric poet', and Pausanias refers to her epic poetry, but no lyric or epic poetry by her has survived.[2]

Some of her poetry places Anyte as a contemporary of the earlier Hellenistic poets, such as Moero and Nossis, and so her work is generally dated between about 310 and 290 BC.[3] However, poem 23 is an epitaph to three young women of Miletus who committed suicide to escape invading Gauls. The Gaulish invasion of Asia Minor began in 278 BC (after attacks on Thrace, Illyria, Macedonia and Greece in 280–279 BC) and led to their eventual settlement in Phrygia. They terrorised the region, intermittently for almost 50 years, but particularly in 277 BC. This poem is thought by D.L. Page (amongst others) to be incorrectly attributed to Anyte in an ancient manuscript.[4] Indeed the historical event described does postdate the generally accepted dating of Anyte amongst the earlier Hellenistic epigrammatists, though this dating is by no means secure. It is possible for her career to have spanned the period 310 to 275 BC.

Pollux tells us that she came from Tegea, a Dorian city in the central Peloponnese (5.48). He may well have inferred this from her mention of Tegea in poem 2,[5] though we cannot assume that Pollux had only the poems now extant on which to form his opinion. In the *Greek Anthology* she is once identified as 'Anyte the Mitylenaean' (see poem 23, *Anth. Pal.* 7.492), but as Gow and Page point out, this is an invention: she is given a Lesbian homeland to link her as a female poet with Sappho.[6]

One anecdote about Anyte has been preserved. Pausanias tells us that Ascelpius, the healing god at Epidaurus, sent Anyte a message to go to Naupactus and cure the eye disease of Phalysius (a rich local who built a shrine to Ascelpius there). He gave her a sealed tablet, and she took it to Phalysius, whose eyes were cured as he read the tablet. Written on the tablet was Anyte's fee for this service (2,000 gold pieces).[7] Levi speculates that Anyte may have written a prose account of this miracle which was engraved in stone and seen by Pausanias, but it is more likely that the story was invented from a dedicatory poem by a storyteller eager to find autobiography in Anyte's poetry.[8]

Anyte's epigrams take the form of inscriptions. The subject matter of some of her poems along with the literary allusiveness of her work has led to a suspicion that all her poems were epideictic, rather than inscriptional. While the content itself is not decisive, the very preservation of her poems implies the publication of a collection by the author herself and an underlying epideictic purpose to her work.

Anyte exploited the conventional epigrammatic genres, dedicatory (poems 1-3) and funereal (poems 4-12, 20-21), with both men and women (who are named in the poems but are otherwise unknown) as her subjects.[9] In addition, she introduced new epigrammatic genres with her descriptive (poems 13-15) and bucolic epigrams (poems 3, 16-19). She also developed the funereal genre in composing epitaphs for animals and insects (poems 9-12, 20). Pastoral landscapes and animal epitaphs became common subjects in Hellenistic poetry, and Anyte was at the forefront of the development of these genres.[10] Her poems are learned, with varied and complex use of Homeric allusion.[11] She wrote in a mixed artificial literary dialect of Doric and Epic/Ionic, with even the occasional Atticism too, adding variety to the sound of her poetry, which is rich in alliteration, assonance and rhyme.[12] The allusive nature of her work is a quintessential feature of Hellenistic poetry.

Anyte

1.

Rest here, my murderous spear, and no longer
from your bronze claw drip dark blood of enemies.
But sitting in the high marble hall of Athena,
announce the bravery of Echekratidas the Cretan.

2.

A cauldron for an ox, dedicated by Eriaspidas' son
Cleobotus. His fatherland is broad Tegea.
The gift is to Athena. Aristoteles of
Cleitor made it - he has the same name as his father.

3.

To hair-standing Pan and to the grotto nymphs
lonely Theudotus set this gift beneath the mountain peak,
for they ended his great suffering beneath the fragrant summer heat,
offering honey-sweet water in their hands.

4.

Youth buried you, captain, and like children of their mother,
Pheidias, you put youth into dark sorrow when you died.
But this stone above you sings a fine story,
how you died fighting for your dear fatherland.

5.

Again and again Cleina weeps upon the tomb of her girl,
a mother crying out for her dear short-lived child,
calling to the soul of Philaenis, who before her wedding
made her way across the pale stream of the river Acheron.

6.

I mourn for Antibia, a virgin.
Eager for her, many bridegrooms came to her father's house
on account of her beauty and the fame of her wisdom.
But Fate, the destroyer, tossed away the hopes of all.

7.
Throwing both arms around her dear father
sheding pale tears Erato spoke these, her final words,
'Father, I live no longer, and as I die
dark black death now conceals my eyes'.

8.
Instead of a sacred wedding and a lovely bedded bridal-chamber
your mother presents you with this statue for your tomb,
a young virgin girl with your height and with your beauty,
Thersis, so you exist when we speak to you although you are dead.

9.
Damis set up this memorial for his horse, steadfast
in battle, when Ares struck its blood-red
chest, and black blood bubbled up through the leather shield
of its skin, and soaked the soil with grievous slaughter.

10.
You too once perished by a many-rooted bush,
Locrian, swiftest of the puppies, who love to bark;
into your nimble paw such cruel poison
sank the speckle-throated viper.

11.
You will no longer get me up out of bed as before
rising at dawn and rowing with your compact wings.
For Sinis sneaked up on you while you slept
and killed you, swiftly digging his claw into your throat.

12.
No longer exalting in the swimming seas
will I toss up my neck, rising from the depths,
nor will I blow around the fine prow of a ship
leaping and enjoying the figure-head.
But the sea's blue wetness threw me up on dry land
and I lie on this narrow strip of beach.

13.
The children put purple reins on you, Mr Billy-Goat,
and a bridle on your bearded throat,
and teach you horse-racing round the god's temple
so he may watch them having fun as children do.

14.
Look upon the horny goat of Bromius, how haughtily
he looks down upon his flowing beard
exulting because often in the mountains
a Naiad took the rough hair around his cheeks in her rosy hand.

15.
This is the home of Cypris, since she loves to watch
always the shining sea from the land,
to make the sailors' voyage happy; and all around the sea
trembles as it stares at her anointed statue.

16.
Sit, all, beneath the beautiful plentiful leaves of this laurel,
and draw a sweet drink from the lovely spring,
so your dear limbs panting with the work of summer
may rest, beaten by Zephyr's blow.

17.
I, Hermes, stand here by the windy row of trees
in the crossroads, near the white-edged beach,
with rest for people exhausted by their road;
and the spring murmurs cold and clear.

18.
Stranger, rest your tired legs beneath this elm;
hear the sweet breeze in the green leaves;
drink a cold drink from the fountain;
for to travellers in the heat of summer this resting place is dear.

19.
Why, country Pan, sit in this dark lonesome wood
and play on your sweet-singing pipe?
So my calves may graze in these dewy mountains
harvesting the long-haired ears of corn.

20.[13]
For her grasshopper, nightingale of the field, and her tree-dwelling
cicada, Myro built a common tomb,
a girl who shed a virgin's tear. For pitiless
Hades left with both her toys.

21.[14]
This Lydian ground holds Amyntor, son of Philip,
who many a time fought iron battle with his arms.
No painful illness drove him to the home of Night,
but he died with the circle of his shield covering his comrade.

22.
I am not the Magnesian tomb of Themistocles, but I was made
as a memorial of the Greeks' jealous misjudgement

23.
We depart, Miletus, dear to my father, renouncing
the lawless violence of the unholy Gauls,

three virgins, your fellow citizens, whom Ares,
the mighty Celt, directed to this fate.
For we did not wait for unholy blood, no Hymen's
bridal song, but found our guardian Hades.

24.
Alive this man was Manes the slave, but now
dead, he is as powerful as Darius the Great.

25.[15]
No longer, sharp-voiced locust, will the sun look on you
as you sing in the wealthy house of Alcis,
for already you have flown to the fields of Clymenus
and dewy flowers of golden Persephone.

Notes

1.   *Anth. Pal.* 4.1.5. Other ancient readers of Anyte were Pollux (5.48), Antipater (*Anth. Pal.* 9.26), Paus. (10.38.13), Tatian (*Speech to the Greeks* 33), and Stephanus Byzantius (s.v. Tegea).
2.   *Anth. Pal.* 7.215, 208; Paus. 10.38.7.
3.   D.L. Page, *Epigrammata Graeca* (Oxford: Clarendon Press, 1975), x.
4.   Ibid, 66.
5.   D. Geoghegan (ed.), *The Epigrams: Anyte* (Rome: Edizioni dell'Atenco and Bizzarri, 1979), 37.
6.   See also Erinna and Melinno; A.S.F. Gow and D.L. Page (eds), *The Greek Anthology: Hellenistic Epigrams* (Cambridge: Cambridge University Press, 1965).
7.   Paus. 10.38.7.
8.   P. Levi, *Pausanias: Guide to Greece*, I (Harmondsworth: Penguin, 1979), 513 n. 270; cf. J.McI. Snyder, *The Woman and the Lyre: Women Writers in Classical Greece and Rome* (Carbondale: Southern Illinois University Press, 1989), 68.
9.   Poem 20 refers to a young woman named Myro. Myro was an alternative spelling of Moero, the name of another Hellenistic poet. Moero wrote accomplished poetry while still very young (*Anth. Pal.* 2.410) and may be alluded to here.
10. G. Luck, 'Die Dichterinnen der griechischen Anthologie', *Museum Helveticum* 11 (1954), 170-87 (181). Her work may be compared with the earlier poets Simonides and Anacreon (sixth century BC), as well as with the Hellenistic poets Callimachus and Asclepiades.
11. For identification of these allusions and a more detailed literary commentary on Anyte see Geoghegan, *The Epigrams, passim*.
12. Geoghegan, *The Epigrams*, 14.
13. Attributed to Anyte or Leonidas in the manuscripts. Myro may well refer to the poet Moero.
14. 21 and 22 attributed to Anyte by Planudes; the *Anth. Pal.* attributes them to Antipater.
15. Attributed to Anyte by Planudes; the *Anth. Pal.* attributes it to Aristodicus.

12. Moero (fl. 300 BC)

Introduction

There are around a dozen references to Moero or to her work in ancient literature, though only three short fragments of her poetry have survived in quotation. Two forms of her name were used: Meleager and Athenaeus call her Moero, while Pausanias, Tatian and *Suda* call her Myro. Some biographical details have been preserved, probably based on inferences from her poetry. She was remembered as the wife of Andromachus, a learned etymologist, and as either the daughter of the tragic poet Homerus (*Suda* on Myro) or his mother (*Suda* on Homerus), and to have come from Byzantium.[1] Her poetry dates her to around 300 BC.[2] The *Suda* tells us also that she was the author of epic poetry (i.e. hexameter verse), elegiacs and lyric poetry, and Christodorus notes that she wrote accomplished heroic poetry while still very young.

The three fragments which remain preserve part of an epic poem and two short epigrams. The epic was called *Memory,* and included the story of Zeus' childhood.[3] We know a little about the content of other works. Pausanias tells us that she told a story about Amphion, a mythical king of Thebes; Parthenius paraphrases the plot of a narrative poem she wrote called *The Curse*; and Eustathius refers to a hymn to Poseidon which she composed.[4] Her contemporary Anyte (poem 20: *Anth. Pal.* 7.190) and the Augustan poet Marcus Argentarius (*Anth. Pal.* 7.364) referred to Myro in two epigrams on the theme of the death of a cicada and grasshopper; they may both be reworking a poem by Moero herself.

Meleager had a high opinion of her work, calling her poems 'lilies', and we are told that she was honoured in antiquity with a statue.[5] Snyder argues that the three extant poems do not justify this opinion.[6] We should not be too harsh in our criticism of her as a poet on the basis of the remaining scraps of what Meleager implies (*Greek Anthology* 4.1.5) was once an extensive corpus.

Moero

1.
You lie in the golden hall of Aphrodite,
grapes, full of Dionysus' juice.
Your mother no longer throws her loving branch around you
to give birth to the nectar-filled leaves above your head.

2.
Hamadryad nymphs, daughters of river, women
of ambrosia who ever tread these forest depths with rosy feet,
greetings; and please preserve Cleonymus, who set up
beneath the pines these beautiful statues to you, goddesses.

3. Memory

Now mighty Zeus was raised in Crete, and not one
of the blessed gods knew about him. In every limb he grew strong,
while doves looked after him in a holy cave
bringing ambrosia from Ocean's streams,
a mighty eagle, ever drawing nectar from a rock,   5
in its beak carried a drink for wise Zeus.
After defeating his father Cronus, wide-seeing Zeus
made the eagle immortal and settled it in heaven.
Just so did he bestow honour on the trembling doves
who are the messengers of summer and winter.   10

Notes

1. Her poems are in *Anth. Pal.* 6.119, 6.189, and Athen. 9.491b. The references to her are: Christodorus of Thebes, *Anth. Pal.* 2.410; Meleager's introduction to the *Anth. Pal.* 4.1.5; Parthenius, *On Alcinoe* 27; Eustathius, ad B, 711, 247; Paus. 9.5.4; *Suda* (s.v. Myro and Homerus).
2. A.S.F. Gow and D.L. Page (eds), *The Greek Anthology: Hellenistic Epigrams*, II (Cambridge: Cambridge University Press, 1965), 414.
3. Zeus' brothers and sisters were all eaten by their father, Cronus. Zeus' mother, Rhea, smuggled Zeus away and he later returned to defeat his father, thereby becoming king of the gods. See Corinna 1.
4. Paus. 9.5.4; Parthenius, *On Alcinoe* 27; Eustathius, ad B, 711, 247.
5. *Anth. Pal.* 4.1.5; Tatian, *Against the Greeks* 33.
6. J. McI. Snyder, *The Woman and the Lyre: Women Writers in Classical Greece and Rome* (Carbondale: Southern Illinois University Press, 1989), 86; see ibid, 84-86 for a commentary on the poetry.

13. Nossis (fl. c. 300 BC)

Introduction

Nossis was a Greek poet who lived around 300 BC.[1] In her extant poetry she tells the reader a little about herself, although only a small portion of her published work has survived. She says that her home city was Locri (poem 11, see also poem 3), a Dorian colony in southern Italy founded in the seventh century BC, and her pride in her home city is evident in poem 2 (despite the poem's light touch).[2] She identifies herself as a member of the aristocracy in poem 3, and her command of poetic forms and evident knowledge of Greek literature, such as the poetry of Sappho and the work of Rhinthon, reveal that her family was able to give her a literary education. In poem 3 she acknowledges the roles her mother and grandmother played in passing on their knowledge to her, a testament to a girl's upbringing, which is so poorly documented in surviving literature.[3]

Eleven or twelve poems by Nossis survive, all of them epigrams.[4] In Greek, *epigramma* means 'inscription', and originally the genre was reserved for short verses intended for tombstones, votive offerings or perhaps signposts. Nossis was at the forefront of a Hellenistic development of this genre, which transformed the epigram into a form intended for literary publication. Poems 1 and 11 have been identified as the preface and epilogue of a published volume of work. This fact and the nature of the surviving poems reveal that Nossis had primarily a literary rather than epigraphic purpose for her work. For while Nossis appears to follow the traditional epigraphic purposes for epigrams, identifying and celebrating dedications to a god (poems 2, 3, 4, 5, 6), as an epitaph (poems 10 and 11), or short prayer (poem 12), some of these works (poems 2, 10 and 11) were never meant for actual inscription. She also uses epigrams to describe plastic art forms (poems 6, 7, 8, 9); this *ekphrasis* was a development of the dedicatory epigram. Nossis defends non-traditional literary forms (poem 10) and compares her work with the poetry of Sappho, both through literary allusion as well as more explicit comparison (especially poems 1 and 11). She was a confident and serious writer who looked to a female authority and a female tradition of poetry.[5]

The comparison with Sappho is not a superficial one. Some of her poems suggest a female reader and reflect a specifically female perspective, but she did not write just for women. Even in the small extant corpus of her work we find a wider readership anticipated (see for example poem 10).[6] Her poems nevertheless reflect a consciously female world, centred around the worship of female deities, Hera and Aphrodite (and perhaps also Artemis). In poem 8 she observes that it is good for a girl to resemble her mother, changing the emphasis of a common Greek idea that it is good for the son to resemble his father.[7] Only two of her twelve surviving poems focus on males. Like Sappho, Nossis personalises her poetry, creating the vivid authorial persona of a woman who delights in sex. Greek literature generally creates two images of women: the modest, retiring virgin or wife, and the lascivious *hetaera* (courtesan), with comedy blurring the distinction between the two. Nossis reverses this perception, offering a respectable woman's voice which publicly honours sex, yet is not the voice of a *hetaera*. And while male writers would ridicule *hetaerae* for their love of sex and way of life, Nossis, praises them for their feminine qualities and their piety towards Aphrodite.

The frankness of her erotic poetry, especially poem 1, recalls Sappho too, but it is not mere literary allusion. It reveals a confident voice speaking for women in the male-dominated public world.

We have some indication of her reception by the ancient literary world. Meleager in the first century BC included some of her work in his collection of epigrams, entitled the *Garland*. Meleager tells us that in his anthology he 'wove in at random the myrrh-breathing, well-blooming iris of Nossis, for whose [writing-]tablets Eros melted the wax'.[8] He saw her as a love poet, her work as sensual and erotic, and poem 1 attests to the veracity of his judgement. The rest of her extant corpus is not principally erotic in tone, suggesting that the work which Meleager thought best characterised her has been largely lost.[9] Two sketches by the comic Herodas refer to Nossis too. Both associate her with sex, showing us that his intended audience were expected to be familiar with her work and understand his satire of the sexual persona she adopted in it. Herodas pictures her with or even as a leather dildo (6.20-36; 7.57-58). In part, this is a familiar misogynistic joke about what women get up to in private (i.e. when the men are not there), and any woman could suffer this charge in Greek comedy.[10]

We can be sure that Nossis was read and appreciated as a poet. Antipater of Thessalonica includes her in a brief survey of female writers. He uses an unusual word to describes her: *thelyglossos*, 'with a woman's tongue'. This is the only extant use of this epithet, and it was probably invented by Antipater for Nossis. The meaning, that she 'spoke like a woman', has been criticised as 'not very descriptive' for a female writer.[11] Yet the epithet succinctly captures the distinctly female persona which dominates her work, which was not adopted by all women writers.[12] Hellenistic poetry is characterised by its cleverness, the poet's enjoyment of the succinct but telling observation, weighted with subtle (or less than subtle) literary allusion. Nossis is a fine exponent of this style, imbuing her poetry with a light touch. Indeed, she should be recognised as one of the inventors of the Hellenistic style.

Nossis

1.
Nothing is sweeter than love—all riches are second—
even honey I spat from my mouth.
Nossis says this: whom Cypris did not kiss,
does not know what sort of roses her flowers are.

2.
The armour the Bruttian men threw from their doomed shoulders,
when struck by the swift-fighting Locrians with their hands,
lies in the palace of the gods singing to their courage
not longing for the forearms of the cowards they abandoned.

3.
Honoured Hera, you who often leave heaven
and watch over your sweet-scented Lacinian temple,
receive this linen cloak which, with her noble daughter
Nossis, Theuphilis daughter of Cleocha wove for you.

4.

Let's go to her temple and look at Aphrodite's
image– how cleverly it is made with gold.
Polyarchis set it up, enjoying the benefits of very great
wealth from her own body's beauty.

5.

It is right for Aphrodite to receive this votive gift with great pleasure,
a net from the hair of Samytha,
for it is cleverly made and scented sweetly of nectar;
with this she too anoints handsome Adonis.

6.

Callo has dedicated a picture in the house of fair-haired Aphrodite,
a portrait painted as a close likeness.
How gently she stands; look how well her loveliness blossoms.
May she fare well, for her life is without reproach.

7.

The picture holds the beauty of Thaumareta; so well
did it create her pride and the fairest youth of her gentle look.
If she saw you the watchdog puppy too would wag her tail,
believing she was looking upon the mistress of her mansion.

8.

Melinna herself has been recreated; see how gentle her face is.
She seems to look at us kindly.
How the daughter actually looks like her mother in every respect;
indeed it is good when children come to be like their parents.

9.

Even from far away this picture is seen to be
by its beauty and majesty Sebaithis'.
Admire! From here I think I see her understanding
and kindness. I hope you are delighted, blessed lady.

10.

Laughing out loud pass by and say a friendly
word to me. I am Rhinthon of Syracuse,
a tiny nightingale of the Muses, but from my tragic
farces I plucked my own ivy.

11.

Stranger, if you sail to Mytilene, land of lovely dances,
to set yourself on fire with the flower of Sappho's graces,
say that the land of Locri bore me dear to the Muses
and to her; and upon learning that my name is Nossis, go on.

12.
Artemis, you who keep Delos and lovely Ortygia,
put away your sacred bow and arrows into the bosom of the Graces.
Wash your pure skin in the Inopos, come to the house
to free Alcetis from her grievous labour pains.

Notes

1.   For more on her dates see the commentary by A.S.F. Gow and D.L. Page (eds), *The Greek Anthology: Hellenistic Epigrams* (Cambridge: Cambridge University Press, 1965), 434-5.
2.   The full name of the city was Locri Epizephyrii; Polybius tells us something about the city (12.5-6).
3.   For a collection of sources see M.R. Lefkowitz, and M.B. Fant, *Women's Life in Greece and Rome: A Source Book in Translation* (2nd edn; Baltimore: John Hopkins University Press, 1992), 166.
4.   Although it is written in her style, the attribution of poem 12 to her is not secure, see discussion of that poem below. *The Greek Anthology* preserves the poem with a heading which may mean either 'in the style of Nossis', or 'allegedly by Nossis': see Gow and Page, *The Greek Anthology*, 443; M.B. Skinner, 'Sapphic Nossis', *Arethusa* 22 (1989), 5-18 (5 n. 1). Stylistically and metrically the poem cannot be distinguished from her genuine work, which does not prove that it is hers, but at least it reassures us that it is a fair sample of the sort of work she was capable of producing: M. Gigante, 'Nosside', *La Parola del Passato* 29 (1974), 22-39 (29-30).
5.   Compare with J.McI. Snyder, *The Woman and the Lyre: Women Writers in Classical Greece and Rome* (Carbondale: Southern Illinois University Press, 1989), 77; M.B. Skinner, 'Nossis *Thelyglossos*: the private text and the public book', in S.B. Pomeroy (ed.), *Women's History and Ancient History* (Chapel Hill: University of North Carolina Press, 1991), 20-47 (20-21).
6.   See Skinner, 'Nossis *Thelyglossos*', 29.
7.   Cf. the Pythagorean Phintys. See also Lefkowitz and Fant, *Women's Life in Greece and Rome*, 302 n. 430.
8.   Gow and Page, *The Greek Anthology*, I; Meleager 1.934-5. The Greeks used wooden tablets which had a wax surface for writing upon. This translation from Skinner, 'Nossis *Thelyglossos*', 35, who discusses more fully Meleager's assessment of Nossis.
9.   Skinner, 'Nossis *Thelyglossos*', suggests that the reference to Eros indicates that Nossis displays desire towards the subjects of her poetry (p. 35). This is a possible reading of Meleager, but is not one which the extant corpus supports.
10. See Ar., *Thesmophoriazusae* for a Greek comic view of what women get up to in private. For Aristophanes' view of women's love of the dildo, see *Lysistrata* 23-4, 107-10, and Fragment 592, 16-28. Skinner argues that Herodas' *Mime* 4 is a parody of Nossis' ekphrastic epigrams, and a satire of women writers in general ('Ladies' day at the Art Institute: Theocritus, Herodas, and the gendered gaze', in A. Lardinois and L. McClure [eds], *Making Silence Speak* [Princeton: Princeton University Press, 2001], 201-222 [216-21]).
11. A.S.F. Gow and D.L. Page (eds), *Garland of Philip and Some Contemporary Epigrams* (Cambridge: Cambridge University Press, 1968), 37.
12. See Skinner, 'Nossis *Thelyglossos*', for a fuller treatment of this topic.

14. Nicobule (fl. c. 300 BC)

Introduction

No biographical details of Nicobule have been preserved. We know of her from two fragments of a work on Alexander the Great, cited by Athenaeus (10.434c and 12.537d). Her name is Greek, and we can only tentatively place her as most probably writing at the time when Hellenistic scholarship took a great interest in Alexander: the third to first centuries AD. Athenaeus voiced some doubts about the attribution of this work to her, though he does not explain why. Perhaps the prejudice against women as historians, exemplified in the testimonia to Pamphila, likewise created doubts about Nicobule's abilities as a serious writer. Athenaeus appears to paraphrase, rather than quote her work directly. Nicobule was not the only writer to comment on Alexander's excessive drinking.[1]

Nicobule

(Retold by Athenaeus)
1.

And Nicobule, or the man who compiled her history for her, says that when Alexander was dinning with Medeius the Thessalian, he drank a toast to every man at the dinner (and there were twenty), and he accepted the same number back from them all. He left the party and very soon passed out.

2.

Nicobule says that during dinner, every actor strove to entertain the king, and that at his final dinner Alexander himself performed a scene from Euripides' *Andromeda* from memory, and eagerly offered toasts with unmixed wine and forced everyone else to do so too.

Notes

1. Athenaeus cites other writers who reported Alexander's excessive drinking (10.434a-435a) as well as that of his father (10.435a-d).

15. Theano (*lived 6th century* BC; *texts late 4th–3rd centuries* BC *and later*)

Introduction

In antiquity Theano was thought to have been one of the early Pythagoreans (of the sixth century BC), and various texts were in circulation under her name. However, there is serious doubt about the authenticity of the extant texts attributed to her. Philological study has determined that they were written by at least two different hands from at least two different periods.[1] Moreover, the biographical details preserved from antiquity about Theano are confused and conflicting, suggesting later invention. The extant works attributed to her—and other Pythagoreans, male and female (including Aesara, Phintys and Perictione)—have been generally considered to be forgeries, perhaps dating from as late as the first–second centuries AD.[2] Consequently the collection of these works has been labelled the *Pseudoepigrapha Pythagorica*.

While Theano was remembered as an early Pythagorean, her exact relationship to Pythagoras was the subject of some speculation. She is variously described as a pupil, a daughter or the wife of Pythagoras, and the mother of his children, Telauges, Mnesarchus, Myia and Arignote (who were also Pythagoreans). She is also said to have been the wife of another Pythagorean, Brontinus of Croton (or Metapontum). She came from Metapontum, Thuria, Cressa or Croton, and her father was Leophron or Pythonax or Brontinus.[3] Iamblichus adds a little more to her biography, telling us that she married Aristaeus after Pythagoras' death. Aristaeus thus succeeded Pythagoras as head of his school, educator of his children and husband of his wife.[4]

We cannot reconcile these conflicting accounts and some details must be wrong. They may be based on inferences from various pseudonymous texts published in her name. We should not discard Theano as an historical figure entirely. There may even have been two (or more) Pythagoreans named Theano, and the details of the women may have become confused. Iamblichus distinguishes the wife of Brontinus from the wife of Pythagoras (*Life of Pythagoras* 265 cf. 267, 132[5]), and Theano was not an uncommon name (there is a Theano in Homer).[6]

The attribution of both lost and extant works to Theano is another problem. Were the texts by Theano (wife of Pythagoras), Theano (wife of Brontinus), other women named Theano, anonymous authors (male or female) who attributed them to Theano to associate them with Pythagoras' famous wife, or a variety of these possibilities? In antiquity Theano was a credible historical and philosophical figure with a reputation as an ideal wife and mother. She provided an example of the application of Pythagorean philosophy in a woman's life and was therefore an attractive subject for pseudonymous writers. The ancient testimony that Theano was a student of Pythagoras and wrote philosophical works is (as most ancient biography) a later fiction—at any rate, the extant texts attributed to her are not that old.

Thesleff has demonstrated that some of Theano's apophthegms should be dated, on the basis of their dialect, to some time in the fourth/third centuries BC; the rest of this work (in

Attic and Attic Koine) is much later.[7] The authenticity of the fragments and letters attributed to Theano (and other women philosophers) has nevertheless been defended by Waithe,[8] who distinguishes the wife of Pythagoras, Theano I, from another later Theano II. She attributes fragments 1-8 to the former and fragments 9, 12 and 13 to the latter. Fragments 10, 11, 14-16, she suggests, were eponymous—each by a Theano—arguing that it is only the attribution to Theano, wife of Pythagoras (which the letters do not explicitly claim) which is spurious. However, the dialect of 1-8 makes them unlikely to have been by Pythagoras' wife. It also seems unlikely that the letters are by various women who happened to have been named Theano, for their publication (and hence preservation) was a deliberate literary act. Each author would have to take care to distinguish herself clearly from the historical Theano. There was an acceptance of pseudonymous work as a literary genre in the ancient world. Pseudonymy does not imply that the texts should not be taken as serious expressions of the application of Pythagorean philosophy in a woman's life, nor that the texts were written by men.[9]

The works attributed to Theano were: *Pythagorean Apophthegms*, *Female Advice*, *On Virtue*, *On Piety*, *On Pythagoras*, *Philosophical Commentaries* and *Letters*.[10] In the extant fragment of *On Piety*, Theano argues that Pythagoras drew an analogy between numbers and objects, offering commentary on a Pythagorean doctrine interpreted differently by Aristotle (*Metaphysics* 1090 A.22). The apophthegms may have been published as a collection under her name: they consist of sayings that were thought to have been appropriate to her. Philosophical letters have been preserved in her name, and may have been published under the title of *Philosophical Commentaries* or *Female Advice*.[11] They treat three key concerns of a wife: the way she should bring up her children, how she should treat the servants, and how she should behave virtuously towards her husband.

In the letter to Euboule, the author is critical of luxurious treatment of children, arguing that the mother's role is to prevent children from falling into self-indulgent habits, and to foster their virtue through moderation—a typical Pythagorean sentiment.[12] In the letter to Nicostrate she discusses the correct way for a wife to behave when her husband takes up with a prostitute. She argues that the wife should win back the husband through her virtue. Criticising his behaviour and behaving dishonourably herself are shown to only further hurt her. In contrast, by setting an example of the correct behaviour, the wife distinguishes herself from the courtesan and will restore the husband's true love for her, forcing him to repent of his immoral behaviour. Her virtuous behaviour, she argues, will make him act virtuously. Harmony in the family can only be achieved by the honourable behaviour of the wife. She can provide a role model for her husband and thereby control his behaviour; thus can a woman's honour exceed that of a man. The letter to Eurydice offers an explanation for a husband's infidelity to this wife, excusing his behaviour with a superficial analogy to music; it offers a very different argument to the one used in the letter to Nicostrate, which deals with essentially the same subject.[13] The third philosophical letter, addressed to Callisto, advises moderation in the treatment of the household servants. Here the important principle—the right measure—is shown to give the best results.

The letter to Eucleides adopts a more humorous tone. Theano ironically expresses concern for the doctor who failed to come to treat a friend of hers because of his own illness. The letter to Rhodope reads more like a genuine letter, but was clearly not by the historical Theano;[14] it offers evidence for the literacy of women and the sharing of books.

Theano

On Piety
1.

I have discovered that while many Greeks think that Pythagoras said that everything is produced by number, this theory itself is problematic: how can what does not exist be thought to create? But he did not say everything comes from number, but happens according to number, because primary order is in number. By sharing in this in counting, something is assigned to be first, and second, and the rest sequentially.

Apophthegms
2.

For many writers confirm that a woman is able to give birth in the seventh month, including Theano the Pythagorean....

3.

Theano, the wife of Pythagoras, when asked how she would be held in high honour, said, 'By plying my loom and resisting my bed'.

4.

Theano, when putting on her halation, exposed her arm. A man said, 'Your arm is beautiful'. She said, 'But it is not public'.[15]

5.

Theano, when she was asked how many days it was after sex with a man that a woman becomes pure, said, 'With her own husband, at once, but with another man, never'.[16]

6.

Theano, the Pythagorean philosopher, when asked what the duty of a woman was, said 'To please her husband'.

7.

There are no writings by Telauges, but there are some by his mother Theano. And they say that when she was asked how many days it was after sex with a man that a woman becomes pure, she said, 'With her own husband, at once, but with another man, never'. And she advised a woman who was about to go to her husband to cast off her shame with her clothes, and to pick it up with her clothes when she got up again. Asked what that was, she replied, 'That which defines me as a woman'.

Philosophical Commentaries (?)
8.

Theano writes: Life would be feast to the wicked, who, after doing evil, then died; if the soul were not immortal, death would be a blessing.

Female Advice or Letters (?)
9. Letter to Euboule

Theano to Euboule: greetings.

I hear that you are bringing up your children in luxury. The mark of a good mother is not concern for her children's enjoyment, but training towards moderation. So watch you do not do the work of an indulgent mother rather than a loving one. When pleasure and children are brought up together, it makes them undisciplined. For what is sweeter to the young than accustomed pleasure? So, my friend, it is necessary that the raising of children is not their downfall. And luxury is the downfall of natural character whenever they become lovers of pleasure in their souls, and sweet sensations in their bodies, their souls shunning work, their bodies becoming softer.

(2) It is also necessary to exercise the children you are raising in what they fear, even if this inflicts pain and distress; so that they do not become slaves of what they experience, eager for pleasure and reluctant to face pain, but honour what is good above all, holding back from pleasure and standing up to pain. Don't let them become completely full of food nor have their every pleasure gratified, nor be undisciplined in their childhood, nor allow them to say everything and try everything, especially if you are worried if they cry and take pride if they laugh, and laugh if they strike their nurse or abuse you, and if you provide coolness in summer and warmth in winter and every luxury. Poor children sample none of these things and they are raised well enough, and do not grew any less and become stronger by far.

(3) But you nurse your children like the offspring of Sardanapalus, weakening his masculine nature with pleasure. For what would one do with a child who cries if he does not eat sooner, and if he eats seeks the delights of treats, and if he is hot wilts, and if he is cold collapses, and if someone criticises him responds by fighting, and if someone does not serve his pleasure he is upset, and if he is not chewing is unhappy, and wastes his time on mischief for the pleasure of it, and wanders around to no good purpose.

(4) Be careful, my friend, knowing that children who live with no restraint, when they grow up into men become slaves, and keep such pleasures from them. Make their food plain not sumptuous, and allow them to bear hunger and thirst, and even cold and heat, and feel ashamed among their peers or supervisors. For this is how it comes about that they are ennobled in spirit, whether they are being uplifted or downtrodden. For, my friend, labours are a hardening up process for children, during which virtue is perfected; those who have been sufficiently dipped in this process bear the bath of virtue as something which is natural to them. So look out, my friend, lest, just as vines which have been badly looked after produce little fruit, because of luxury your children produce the evil of hubris and complete worthlessness. Farewell.

10. Letter to Eucleides
Theano to Eucleides the doctor.
Yesterday someone had dislocated his leg and the man sent to summon you came to you (and I myself was present—for the injured man was a friend) but returned immediately in a hurry, saying that the doctor was poorly and physically unwell. And I dismissed the pain of that friend (I swear by the gods) and turned my attention to the doctor and prayed to Panacea and Apollo, the famous archer, that nothing incurable had happened to the doctor. Although I am despondent I write this letter to you, dearly wanting to learn how you are, lest your gastric orifice is bad, your liver has been weakened by fever, or some organic harm has come upon you. So with no thought for the many limbs of my friends, I welcome your own dear health, my good doctor.

11. Letter to Eurydice
Theano to the wonderful Eurydice.
What grief is hanging on to your soul? You are upset by nothing other than that the man with whom you live has gone to a prostitute and takes his physical pleasure with her. But you should not be like this, you paragon among women. Do you not see that when the hearing has become sated with

pleasure from an instrument, it is filled with musical song, but when it has become sated with this, loves again the flute and enjoys listening to the reed-pipe? And what sort of fellowship is there between the flute, musical song and the wonderful echo of the instrument made most sweet for music? It is just the same for the prostitute with whom your husband is living as it is for you. For your husband thinks of you in his habits and nature and thought, but whenever he has too much, he will go and live with the prostitute for the time being. There is a certain love of foods which are not good in those in whom a corrupting humour lies.

12. Letter to Callisto
Theano to Callisto.
Authority to rule the household is granted by the law to you younger women as soon as you are married, but instruction is needed in everything about household management from older women, who always offer advice. For it is good to learn in advance what you do not know, and to consider the advice of older women as best. For in these matters a young soul must be raised from its girlhood. And the primary area of authority in the house for women is over the servants. And, my friend, the most important thing is good will on the part of the slaves. For this is not purchased as a possession along with their bodies. but intelligent mistresses create it in the fullness of time.

(2) Just use is responsible for this, ensuring that they are neither exhausted by work nor made unable to work through lack of food. For they are human by nature. Some women think profitable what is the most unprofitable, treating their servants badly, weighing them down with work, while taking away what they need. Then after making a profit of an obol, they pay the cost of enormous damages: hatred and the most evil plots. In your case, provide an amount of food in proportion to the amount of wool-working done in the day.

(3) This will do for their diet, but for disorderly behaviour, what must serve is what is right for you, not what is advantageous for them. For it is necessary to value your servants at what they are worth. While cruelty will not bring any grace to your soul, reasoning provides control no less than hatred of evil. If there is an excess of vice in the servants which cannot be overcome, they must be sent to market to be sold. Let what is foreign to the needs be estranged from the mistress too. Let your judgement of this be proper. Thus you will balance the truth of the wrongdoing with the justice of the condemnation, and the magnitude of the wrongdoing with the appropriate magnitude of the penalty.

(4) A mistress' forgiveness and grace towards those who have done wrong will release them from the penalty, and in this way too you will maintain a proper and appropriate way of life. For some women, my friend, through cruelty even whip the bodies of their servants, dehumanised through jealousy or anger, as if they are inscribing a memorial with the excess of their bitterness. Some slaves in time are tired out by work and can do no more; others make their way to safety by running away; and some cease living, making the transition to death with their own hands, and in the end, the isolation of the mistress, who weeps for her own lack of good counsel, provides an empty change of heart.

(5) But, my friend, imitate musical instruments and think over what sounds they make when they are loosened too much, and how they break when they are over-tightened. For it is just the same with your servants. Excessive slackness creates dissonance in respect for authority, but a tightening always causes a natural break. You must think on this: the right amount is best in everything.
Farewell.

13. Letter to Nicostrate
Theano to Nicostrate: greetings.

I heard about the madness of your husband—that he has a prostitute, and that you are jealous of him. I, my friend, have known many men with the same disease. For they are hunted out by these women, it seems, caught and loose their minds. But you are upset by night and by day, and troubled and plot something against him. My friend, do not do it. For the virtue of a wife is not in watching over her husband, but bearing things in common with him. And bearing things in common with him is to bear his madness. If he mixes with a prostitute for his pleasure, he does so with his wife for his advantage. It is an advantage not to mix evils with evils, nor to add madness to madness.

(2) Some errors, my friend, are made worse when they are condemned, but cease when kept silent—as they say, fire puts itself out when left in peace. In addition, although you seem to want to escape notice, if you condemn him you lift the veil from your own feelings. And clearly you will be making a mistake. You believe the love of your husband is the behaviour of a gentleman. For this is the grace of fellowship. So believe that when he goes to the prostitute he is insincere, but he stays with you to live a shared life, and he loves you in thoughtful reflection, but her in passion.

(3) The moment of time for this madness is short. For it exists at the same time as its satisfaction, and begins and ceases very quickly. For a man who is not thoroughly bad, the time with a prostitute is very brief. For what is more empty than desire that enjoys what is wrong? So he will eventually realise that he is diminishing his own life and slandering his own good reputation—no one keeps up a self-induced injury when he reflects on it. So, summoned to you by what is just, and seeing the diminution of his own life, he will notice you, and soon repent, unable to bear the shame of his condemnation.

(4) But, my friend, live, not responding to prostitutes but remaining aloof from them by your proper conduct towards your husband, by your care for the house, by your compassion for those who work for you, and by your deep love for your children. There is no need for you to be envious of that woman (although it is a fine thing to envy virtuous women), but you should prepare yourself for reconciliation. For a fine character brings high regard even from enemies, my friend, and honour is the outcome of a true nobility. Through this it is possible for a woman's authority to exceed a man's, and for her to be honoured even more, rather than serve her enemy.

(5) So he will be more ashamed if he has been fostered by you, and he will be willing to reconcile more quickly. He will love you deeply, as you will be easier to sympathise with, when he has recognised the wrongs he has committed against you, noticing your care for his livelihood and testing your love for him. And just as physical sufferings make their cessation sweeter, so disagreements between friends make their reconciliation more significant.

(6) In addition, avoid plans that arise from your suffering. For he has a disease and urges you to catch this painful disease too. In harming his own good name he urges you to harm your appropriate behaviour, and in destroying his own life he urges you to destroy what is beneficial for you. By this you will seem to have set yourself against him and in punishing him you punish yourself. And if you separate from him and leave, you will change your former husband only to find another, and if he errs in the same way, yet another (for not having one is not bearable for young women), or you will stay alone without a husband like a spinster.

(7) Or will you neglect the house and destroy your husband? Then you will live with the harm of a painful life. Or will you seek to fight back against the prostitute? She will be on her guard and will get around you, and if she fights back against you, a woman who does not blush is a champion in battle. But is it good day after day to fight against your husband? And what more? For while the fights and reproaches will not stop his licentiousness, as they increase they will increase the

disagreements. What then are you planning against him? Do not do it, my friend. Tragic drama taught us to defeat envy, in the meaning of the outcome of Medea's unlawful actions. But just as your hands must not touch your infected eyes, so too you must separate your actions from your suffering. By steadfastly enduring it, you will sooner quench your suffering.

14. Letter to Rhodope
Theano to Rhodope the philosopher.
Are you upset? I am upset myself too. Are you sad because I have not yet sent you Plato's book, the one called *Ideas or Parmenides*? But I am most deeply aggrieved myself too, because no one has yet met with me to discuss Cleon. I will not send you the book until someone comes here and clarifies the issues concerning this man. For I love his soul too much, because it is the soul of a philosopher: one keen to do good, one who fears the gods beneath the earth. And do not think that the story is other than what has been said. For I am half-mortal and can not bear to look upon this star which lights the day.

15. Letter to Timareta (in Pollux)
…'the master-of-the-house' and 'the mistress-of-the-house'… *I found both of these words in a letter of Theano, the wife of Pythagoras, written to Timareta.*

16. Letter to Timonides
Theano to Timonides.
What fellowship is there for you and me? Why do you always slander us? Or do you not know that we praise you before everyone, even if you do the opposite? But, again, understand that even if we do praise there is no one who believes, and even if you do slander, there is no one who listens. And I am happy because of this: a god sees it like this and the truth especially judges it so.

Notes

1. H. Thesleff, 'An introduction to the Pythagorean writings of the Hellenistic Period', *Acta Academiae Aboensis, Humaniora* 24.3 (Abo: To akademi, 1961).
2. As E. Zeller, *Philosophie der Griechen*, III.2 (Leipzig: D.R. Reisland, 1903), 97-126.
3. Iamblichus, *Life of Pythagoras* 267, 132; *Suda* s.v. Theano 1, Theano 2, Pythagoras; Diog. L. 8.42; Porphyry, *Life of Pythagoras* 4, 19; Anonymous in Photius 438b.31; Hermesianax in Athen. 13.599a; Schol. in Plato, *Republic* 600b: sources (in Greek) collected by H. Thesleff, 'Pythagorean texts of the Hellenistic Period', *Acta Academiae Aboensis, Humaniora* A, 30.1 (Abo: To akademi, 1965), 193-4.
4. *Life of Pythagoras* 265.
5. At *Life of Pythagoras* 132, Brontinus' wife is called Deino (with Scaliger's emendation of the text, which is corrupt); Theano is a better reading.
6. B. Nagy, 'The naming of Athenian girls', *Classical Journal* 74 (1979), 360-64.
7. Thesleff, An Introduction to the Pythagorean Writings', 113-5.
8. M.E. Waithe, *A History of Women Philosophers*, I (Dordrecht: M. Nijhoff, 1987), 12-15, 41-55.
9. The collection of letters published by R. Hercher, *Epistolographi Graeci* (Paris: A. Firmin Didot, 1873; Amsterdam 1965), is testimony to this literary genre.
10. Thesleff, 'Pythagorean texts of the Hellenistic Period', 193-95; there are two vague references to poems attributed to her: Didymus in Clement of Alexandria (*Stromata* 1.80.4), and *Suda* (s.v. Theano 2); Thesleff, 'An introduction to the Pythagorean writings', 22-23.

11. The attribution of fragments to known titles can only be tentative.
12. See Myia on childcare too.
13. See also Melissa, Phintys and Perictione above.
14. The text refers to Plato's *Parmenides*, which was published in about 370 BC.
15. This fragment is cited by Plut. (*Moralia* 142c-d) (translated on p. 1 of this volume), Stobaeus (585.1) and Clement of Alexandria (*Stromata* 4.19).
16. Stobaeus (586.20), Clement of Alexandria (*Stromata* 4.19), and Diogenes Laertius (see fragment 7 below) cite this fragment.

16. Perictione (texts date late 4th–3rd centuries BC, and 3rd–2nd centuries BC)

Introduction

Two works attributed to Perictione have survived in fragments: *On the Harmony of Women* and *On Wisdom*. Differences in language suggest that they were written by two different people. Allen and Waithe identify them as Perictione I and Perictione II.[1] Plato's mother was named Perictione, and Waithe argues that she should be identified as the earlier Perictione, suggesting that similarities between Plato's *Republic* and *On the Harmony of Women* may not be the result of Perictione reading Plato, but the opposite—the son learning philosophy from his mother.[2] *On the Harmony of Women*, however, is written in Ionic prose with occasional Doric forms. This mixed dialect dates the work to the late fourth or third centuries BC.[3] The reference in *On the Harmony of Women* to women ruling suggests the Hellenistic monarchies of the third century BC or later. *On Wisdom* is written in Doric and is partly identical with a work by Archytas of the same name. This work should be dated later, to the third or second centuries BC.[4] Both the dates of the works and their dialects mean Perictione the mother of Plato could not have written them.

We have then two Pythagorean texts, attributed to otherwise unknown women named Perictione who should be dated perhaps one hundred years apart. The texts themselves are very different in content. *On the Harmony of Women* is directed to women, and reiterates the important Pythagorean principal of moderation. It discusses the duty of a woman to her husband and marriage,[5] and to her parents, providing a practical expression of Pythagoreanism. The link she makes between chastity and proper dress, criticising women for dressing up, has a long history.[6] As Perictione describes the luxury clothes, cosmetics and jewellery that women should not wear, we gain an impression of what was fashionable at the time. *On Wisdom* is more theoretical. It offers a philosophical definition of wisdom, and is not directed towards women.

Perictione I

On the Harmony of Women

1.

It is necessary to consider the harmonious woman full of intelligence and moderation. For it is necessary for a soul to be extremely perceptive regarding virtue to be just and brave and intelligent and well decorated with self-sufficiency and hating baseless opinion. For from this there comes great benefit for a woman, for herself as well as her husband and children and her house, often too for her city, if such a woman rules cities and peoples, as we see in kingdoms. So when she rules over her desires and passions, she becomes righteous and harmonious, so unlawful lusts will not pursue her, but she will keep hold of her love for her husband and children and entire house. For all women who end up lovers of other men's beds become enemies of everyone in the house, both free and servant. She fabricates lies and deceptions for her husband, and invents false stories about everything for him, so she alone may seem to provide good will and rule the house although she loves laziness. From this there comes disaster for everyone, and it falls upon her as well as her husband. This is enough said about this.

But one must also lead the body to natural amounts of food and clothing and washing and anointing and hairstyles and jewellery made of gold and stones. For all women who eat and drink and dress in everything expensive and wear the things women wear, they are ready for the error of every sin, both of the bed and of the other types of criminal activity. The only necessity is to satisfy hunger and thirst, even if this is done meagrely, and the cold, even if this is done with a goat-skin or rags. It is a great sin to wear clothing from far away and purchased at great cost or from eminent people. It is a great foolishness to wear cloaks excessively and elaborately dyed by sea-baths of shellfish or some other expensive colour. For the body wants neither to shiver nor to be naked (for the sake of decency), and needs nothing else. But human opinion, with its ignorance, rushes into what is empty and excessive. So she will not wear gold nor Indian stone nor any from elsewhere, nor will she plait her hair with great skills, nor anoint herself with Arabian perfumes, nor will she paint her face, whitening or rouging it, nor blacken her eyebrows and eyelashes and treating her grey hair with dyes, nor will she bathe too often. For a woman who seeks these things seeks an admirer of feminine weakness. For beauty from intelligence, and not from these things, pleases women who are well-born. She should not believe that noble birth and wealth and coming from a great city are all that is necessary, nor reputation and the friendship of eminent and royal men. If this is the case, it does no harm, but if not, longing for it does not create it. For thinking about things other than these does not keep a woman from living her life. And even if these things have been allotted to her, do not let her soul chase after great and wonderful things, but let it walk away from them. For they drag her into misfortune and harm rather than help her. With them lie plotting and hatred and torture, so a woman of this kind would not be untroubled.

It is also necessary to revere the gods, confident in happiness, obeying ancestral laws and customs. After them I say honour and revere your ancestors. For they exist and for their offspring act upon everything equally with the gods. With respect to her husband, it is necessary for a woman to live lawfully and honourably, not thinking of her private concerns, but keeping and guarding her marriage. For everything depends on this. She must put up with everything from her husband, even if he is unlucky, if he errs through ignorance or sickness or drunkenness, or lives with other women. For while this error is forgiven in men, it is never forgiven in women, and revenge is taken. So while a wife must keep the law and not be jealous, nor bear any anger, meanness, criticism, jealousy, badness or anything else that is a part of his character. She should be prudent and arrange everything just as he likes it. For when a woman is dear to her husband and acts honourably towards him, harmony rules and loves the whole house and makes outsiders well disposed towards the house. But when a woman is not dear to her husband, she does not want to see her house safe, nor her children, nor the servants, nor any of the property, but she calls and prays for complete ruin, as if she were an enemy, and prays for her husband to die as if he were an enemy, so that she may mix with other men, and she hates whoever pleases him.

I think this is how a woman is harmonious: if she is full of intelligence and prudence. For she will benefit not just her husband, but also her children and relatives and slaves and her whole house, and the possessions in it, and friends from her city and foreign friends. And she will keep their house without over-elaborate skill, speaking and hearing good things, and following her husband in the unity of their shared life, serving the friends and relatives whom he praises, and considering sweet and bitter the same things as her husband, so that she is not out of harmony with the whole.

2.

You must not speak ill of your parents nor do them any ill, but obey them in important and minor matters. And in everything that happens to the body and soul both from without and from within, and in war and peace, in sickness and in health, in poverty and wealth, in bad and good repute, in private and public affairs, you must stay with them and never run away, and obey them even in madness. For those of due reverence, this is appropriate and honourable. But if someone should despise her parents, planning an evil of some sort, she is charged with a sin by the gods, whether she is alive or dead, and she is hated by people, and through her evils she finds a place beneath the earth with the irreverent, in their domain for eternity, put there by the hands of justice and the gods of the underworld, who are appointed as overseers of these acts.

For the sight of your parents is beautiful and divine, and the honouring and care of them too, more so even than the sight of the sun and all the stars, which the heavens wear and revolve, and anything else which someone might think greater through observation. But I think that the gods are not unhappy when they see this happen. And so one must revere parents, whether they are alive or departed and never speak against them, but even if they act irrationally through illness or mistake one must urge them and teach them, and in no way hate them. For there could not be any greater sin and injustice for humans than irreverence of one's parents.

Perictione II

On Wisdom

1.

Mankind has come into being and exists to contemplate the theory of the nature of the whole. To possess this very thing is the function of wisdom, and to contemplate the purpose of existence.

2.

So geometry and arithmetic and other theoretical things and sciences study what exists, but wisdom is concerned with every type of thing that exists. For thus wisdom is concerned with everything that exists, as sight is concerned with everything that can be seen, and hearing with everything that can be heard. But with respect to what has occurred to attributes of all things, some things have happened to everything, some to most things, and some to each thing individually. So while what has happened to everything is in the provenance of wisdom to see and to contemplate, what has happened to most things is in the provenance of science, and what has happened to each thing individually is in the provenance of sciences for each separate thing. And because of this wisdom discovers the principles of all things that exist, natural science for the principles of things that occur in nature, geometry and arithmetic, and music for the principles of quantity and harmony.

So whoever is able to analyse every type of thing by one and the same principle, and in turn from this principle to synthesise and enumerate, this person seems to be wisest and truest, and moreover, to have discovered a beautiful look-out from which he will be able to look out upon god and everything separated from him and arranged in rank and file.

Notes

1. M.E. Waithe, *A History of Women Philosophers*, I (Dodrecht; M. Nijhoff, 1987), 32.
2. Ibid, 86-71.
3. H. Thesleff, 'An introduction to the Pythagorean writings of the Hellenistic Period', *Acta Academiae Aboensis, Humaniora* 24.3 (Abo: To akademi, 1961), 17, 113-15.
4. Ibid, 17, 113-15.
5. On this see also Theano 11 (*Letter to Eurydice*) and 13 (*Letter to Nicostrate*).
6. See also the Pythagoreans Melissa, and Phintys; for the tradition of criticising women for using cosmetics see the discussion on Cleopatra, and see Xenophon (*Economics* 10.5-13) and Juvenal (*Satires* 6.457-73, 486-510).

17. Myia (lived c. 500 BC: text written 3rd century BC)

Introduction

Myia was remembered as one of the daughters of Theano and Pythagoras. She married Milo of Croton, a famous athlete who was also a Pythagorean.[1] As a girl she was a choir leader, as a wife she was noted for her exemplary religious behaviour (Iamblichus, *Life* 30; Timaeus in Porphyry, *Life* 4). Writings attributed to her (and Pythagoras' other children Telauges and Arignote)[2] were extant in Porphyry's day,[3] and one philosophical treatise in her name survives today.

This treatise, in the form of a letter, cannot be by Pythagoras' daughter. The dialect dates it to the third or second centuries BC, and Pythagoras lived in the sixth century BC. The earliest reference we have to her comes in a fragment of Timaeus written in the first quarter of the third century BC[4] (shortly before this letter was composed) and it is possible that his representation (or even invention) of Pythagoras' daughter as an ideal Pythagorean woman led to the creation of pseudonymous work in her name.

While we should not believe that Myia's letter to Phyllis is by the daughter of Pythagoras it may well have been written by a woman.[5] It was composed during the renaissance of Pythagorean philosophy around the third century BC, possibly to serve as a philosophical textbook for practical use.[6] It has been suggested that the work was not written by a woman.[7] While men did write on breastfeeding and childcare,[8] the subject matter makes a female author likely; in any event, for the advice to be taken seriously as coming from a woman, it had to be believable that a woman could have written it. The letter is addressed to a new mother named Phyllis and offers woman-to-woman advice on the treatment of her baby. It is sensible, advocating moderation and balance in all things—key Pythagorean concepts. The treatise ends with reference to further work on childcare, and it may have been part of a series of short articles on this topic, designed to introduce Pythagorean philosophy into daily life. Advice on childcare was also attributed to Theano.[9]

Myia

Letter to Phyllis

Myia to Phyllis: Greetings.

I am giving you this advice on children, as you have become a mother. Choose a nurse who is most friendly and clean, and moreover modest and not disposed to sleep nor drunkenness. For a woman of this kind would best judge how to raise free-born children, if she has nutritious milk and is not easily won over to her husband's bed. For the nurse has an important role in raising the child well, laying the foundations for its whole life. For at the appropriate time she will do everything well. She should offer the nipple, the breast and nourishment not on the spur of the moment but after some forethought, for thus she will put the baby into good health. She should not give in whenever she wants to sleep, but when the newborn wants a rest. She will provide no small help to the child. Let the nurse not be prone to anger, not talkative nor indifferent in the taking of food, but organised and sensible and, when it is not impossible, not foreign but Greek. It is best, if the newborn is put to sleep suitably filled with milk. For in this way rest is sweet to the young and such nourishment is most easily digested. It is necessary to give simple food, if any other is given. Refrain from wine completely, as it is too strong, or add it sparingly in a mixture to the evening milk. Do not bath the child continually; for using baths rarely and at a moderate temperature is best. Moreover, the air should have a suitable balance of warmth and coldness, and the house should be neither too drafty nor too shut up. In addition the water should be neither hard nor soft, and the bedding should not be rough, but well designed for touching the skin. In all these things nature desires what is appropriate, not what is extravagant.

It seems useful to write these things to you for the present, my hopes stemming from nursing according to guidelines. With the assistance of god, I will provide appropriate and suitable reminders about the child's upbringing at another time.

Notes

1. Clement of Alexandria, *Stromata* 4.19; *Suda* s.v. Myia and Theano; Iamblichus, *Life of Pythagoras* 30, 36; Porphyry, *Life of Pythagoras* 4.
2. See Aesara for the tradition that she was another daughter of Pythagoras.
3. The late third–early fourth centuries AD, *Life* 4.
4. Porphyry, *Life* 4.
5. Contrast M.E. Waithe, *A History of Women Philosophers*, I (Dodrecht: M. Nijhoff, 1987), 15.
6. H. Thesleff, 'An introduction to the Pythagorean writings of the Hellenistic Period', *Acta Academiae Aboensis, Humaniora* 24.3 (Abo: To akademi, 1961), 72.
7. As M.R. Lefkowitz, and M.B. Fant, *Women's Life in Greece and Rome: A Source Book in Translation* (2nd edn; Baltimore: John Hopkins University Press, 1992), 163.
8. E.g. Favorinus in Aulus Gellius, *The Attic Nights* 12.1; Soranus, *Gynaecology* 2.18-20.
9. See Theano 9: Letter to Euboule.

18. Aesara (*fl. 3rd century* BC)

Introduction

Aesara of Lucania is a shadowy figure. She is only known to us from Stobaeus, who names her as the author of a philosophical work *On Human Nature*, some of which he quotes (1.49.27). Thesleff casts some doubt on the name of the author of this fragment, arguing that 'Aesara' is an emendation of a Doric 'Aresa' based on a tradition that Pythagoras and Theano had a daughter so named, and he follows Heeren in correcting the text.[1] With a further emendation Thesleff attributes the work to Aresas, a male writer from Lucania, known to us from Iamblichus' *Life of Pythagoras* 266. However, it is unnecessary to emend the text: there is only very weak textual support for a tradition that Pythagoras had a daughter named Aesara.[2] The Doric prose of Aesara can be dated to the third century BC.[3]

There is some debate about whether any of the Pythagorean texts attributed to women were by women. We should not assume that a text like this was not by a woman. It must at least have been credible to the intended readers that it was written by a women: hence it provides us with evidence for female scholarship in the Pythagorean community.[4] Aesara's work *On Human Nature* argues that contemplation of our own nature, particularly the nature of the human soul, reveals the philosophic basis for human law and morality. Aesara divides the soul into three component parts; the mind, the spirit, and desire. All three need to work together in appropriate balance for each specific task. There are thus rational, mathematical and functional principles at work in the soul, with god providing a divine principle to order the whole.[5] Like Perictione *On Wisdom* and unlike the extant philosophical tracts attributed to other Pythagorean women, Aesara's treatise is neither directed to nor exclusively about women.[6]

Aesara

On Human Nature

I think human nature provides a common standard of law and justice for both the family and the city. Whoever follows the paths within him and searches will discover; for within him is law and justice, which is the proper arrangement of the soul. For as it is naturally threefold in form, it is formed for three functions: the mind performs judgement and thought, the spirit courage and strength, and desire love and friendliness. Each of these is so drawn up that the best part leads them, the worse part is ruled and the part in between takes the middle ground and both rules and is ruled. God brought about these things in this way through reflection on both the outline and completion of the human home, because he planned humankind alone to become the recipient of law and justice, and none of the other mortal animals. Nor could a composite whole of fellowship arise from one thing nor from many that are alike (for it is necessary since things are different, the parts of our souls are also different, as the organs of sight and hearing and taste and smell are for the body; for all these do not have the same connection with everything), nor from many dissimilar things coming together by chance, but things made for the fulfilment and arrangement and connection of the whole composition. Not only is the body made complete from many dissimilar things, but also these are not arranged by chance nor at random, but with some law and sensible understanding. For if they carried an equal share of power and honour, though they are unlike and some worse, some better and some in between, the fellowship throughout the soul of the parts could not have been constructed. If they had an unequal share, and the worse rather than the best carried the greater share, there would be much thoughtlessness and disorder in the soul. But if the better had the greater share, and the worse the lesser, but each one not according to some rationale, there could not be unity and friendship and justice in the soul; since when each one has been drawn up with a balanced rationale, this is the sort of thing I call the most just.

And indeed, a certain unity and unanimity accompanies such an arrangement. Such a thing would justly be called good order of the soul, which would add to the strength of virtue, from the better part ruling and the worse being ruled. And friendship and love and friendliness, both within the same tribe and the same family, will sprout from these parts. For the examining mind persuades, desire loves and spirit is filled with strength, boiling with hate it becomes friendly to desire. For the mind combines the sweet with the painful, mixing up the intense and the excessive with the light and relaxed part of the soul. And each part is distributed with respect to the consideration of the tribe and family of each thing: the mind examining and tracking things, the spirit adding eagerness and strength to the examination, and desire being a relation of affection, changes the mind, making the sweet its own and adding thoughtfulness to the thoughtful part of the soul. Because of these things, I think that life for humans is best whenever the sweet is mixed with the earnest, and pleasure with virtue. The mind is able to attach these things to itself, becoming lovely through education and virtue.

Notes

1. H. Thesleff, 'Pythagorean texts of the Hellenistic Period', *Acta Academiae Aboensis, Humaniora* A, 30.1 (Abo: To akademi, 1965), 48-50.
2. Evidence for such a 'tradition' exists only in an emendation: Photius (438b) cites an anonymous biography that names Pythagoras' daughters as Myia and Sara. 'Sara' has been variously emended to both Aesara and Arignote: ibid, 237. See work attributed to Myia, and to Pythagoras' wife Theano.
3. H. Thesleff, 'An introduction to the Pythagorean writings of the Hellenistic Period', *Acta Academiae Aboensis, Humaniora* 24.3 (Abo: To akademi, 1961), 113-15.
4. For prejudice against female philosophers, see Phintys, *On the Chastity of Women* 1, cf. Cicero, *Nature of the Gods* 1.93.
5. For a more detailed commentary on Aesara, see M.E. Waithe, *A History of Women Philosophers*, I (Dodrecht: M. Nijhoff, 1987), 19-26.
6. For other Pythagorean writers in this collection, see Melissa, Myia, Perictione, Phintys and Theano.

19. Melissa (*fl. 3rd century* BC)

Introduction

Melissa is known from the one extant work attributed to her—a philosophical treatise in the form of a letter to another woman, named Cleareta. The treatise is on the conduct of women and is preserved in a manuscript now in Paris.[1] The Pythagorean text is written in Doric Greek and dated by the dialect to about the third century BC.[2]

Melissa's text is on the qualities of a virtuous woman, and treats the way in which she should dress and her duties towards her husband. In particular it stresses that she should carry out her husband's wishes. This has lead to a suspicion that the treatise was written pseudonymously by a man intent on providing an example of female behaviour in a woman's voice. Such sentiments were not new: in the fifth century BC Xenophon advises women to behave in a similar modest and dutiful fashion (*Economics* 7–10). Pythagorean texts discussing a woman's virtue and her duty to her husband were also written by (or at least attributed to) other women writers: Phintys, Perictione and Theano.

Melissa

Letter to Cleareta

You seem to me inherently full of virtues. For your enthusiastic desire to hear about good conduct for women provides the virtuous hope that you are going to become old and grey virtuously. So a free and sensible woman must be attached to a man according to the law, and beautify her face moderately, but not by using excessive skill, and she should be clad in white, neat and simple clothes, not extravagant and expensive ones. She must avoid clothes that are translucent and decorated with gold and purple, for they are used by courtesans for hunting the greater number of men, while when a woman is pleasing to her one man, her way of life is her adornment, and not her dresses. For it is comely for a free woman to be seen by her husband, but not by her neighbours. And you should have a blush on your face as a sign of a sense of honour instead of rouge, and respectability and decency and moderation instead of gold and emeralds. For a woman who desires moderation must not love extravagance in clothes, but the economy of her household. And this woman delights her husband when she accomplishes this wish. For the wishes of a man should be the unwritten law for a moderate woman, for which she should live her life. And she should believe that she brought with her as her dowry a discipline of the very best kind. She should trust the beauty and richness of her soul rather than that of her appearance and wealth; for envy and illness remove the latter, but the former extend right up to her death.

Notes

1. R. Hercher, *Epistolographi Graeci* (Paris: A. Firmin Didot, 1873; Amsterdam, 1965).
2. H. Thesleff, 'An introduction to the Pythagorean writings of the Hellenistic Period', *Acta Academiae Aboensis, Humaniora* 24.3 (Abo: To akademi, 1961), 113-15.

20. Phintys (*3rd century* BC)

Introduction

Scholars disagree widely on the historicity of Phintys, and the authenticity of the extant work in her name: two extracts from a treatise on the correct behaviour of women. Waithe accepts she was a fifth century Spartan and that her work is authentic, whereas Lefkowitz and Fant doubt whether her work is original or was even written by a woman.[1] Her Doric dialect could date her work to the fourth century BC; odd archaisms in the text, however, suggest a deliberate attempt to compose a work that would appear earlier than it really was, and a third century date is more likely.[2] Stobaeus (4.23.11) accepts that she was real, and tells us that Phintys was the daughter of Callicrates, who is otherwise unknown. Thesleff suggests that we read 'Callicratidas' for Stobaeus' 'Callicrates'. This emendation gives her father the name of a famous Spartan admiral who died in the battle of Arginusae in 406 BC.[3] Phintys would thereby become a Spartan born towards the end of the fifth century BC, and writing in the fourth century BC. This identification and dating of Phintys, based as it is on a revision of the text and a near-coincidence of names, is fanciful. Iamblichus provides a possible reference to Phintys. He lists a 'Philtys' in his catalogue of female Pythagoreans (*Life of Pythagoras* 267), noting that she came from Croton. Philtys is a possible Doric form of Phintys. While Croton is a more likely birthplace for a Pythagorean like Phintys, Iamblichus states that Philtys was the daughter of Theophrius, further distinguishing her from Stobaeus' Phintys. We should accept that the little existing information records there were two similarly named Pythagorean philosophers, Phintys (daughter of Callicrates) and Philtys (daughter of Theophrius). Phintys was most probably a member of the Pythagorean community who lived in Italy in the third and second centuries BC.

Phintys expounds on the differences between men and women, focusing on a woman's particular virtue: chastity. This places her philosophy squarely within the bounds of contemporary morality. She offers a defence of chastity, and explains why it is necessary. Her view that a woman's greatest honour is to bear children resembling their father is well attested elsewhere, and offers a counterpoise to Nossis (poem 8) who points out that it is good for girls to resemble their mothers. Her advice on moderation, particularly with respect to a woman's dress and appearance, is also well attested.[4] Phintys follows a traditional argument on women's chastity and the division of activities between the sexes, with women taking a domestic role, but she defends the appropriateness of a woman engaging in philosophy. She argues that, unlike some other activities, philosophy is not just for men, and can be shared by both sexes.

Phintys

On the Chastity of Women

1.

On the whole a woman must be good and orderly; and one could not become such a woman as this without virtue. For each virtue is appropriate to a different thing and improves what is receptive to it:

virtue of the eyes the eyes, the virtue of the hearing the hearing, the virtue of a horse the horse, and the virtue of a man a man. Thus too the virtue appropriate to a woman improves a woman. And a woman's greatest virtue is chastity. For because of this virtue she is able to love and honour her own husband.

While many people perhaps think that it is not appropriate for a woman to philosophise, just as it is not appropriate for her to ride horses nor to speak in public, I think that some activities are peculiar to men, some to women, and that some are common to women and men, some are more appropriate for men than women, and some are more appropriate for women than men. And while generalship and political activity and public speaking are peculiar to men, keeping house, staying indoors, receiving and looking after her husband are activities peculiar to women. But I say that courage and justice and intelligence are common to both. For virtues of the body are suitable for both a man and woman, as are similarly those of the soul. And for both men and women it is as beneficial for the soul to be healthy as it is for body. The virtues of the body are health, strength, good perception and beauty. Some of these are more natural for a man to have and foster, and some are more natural for a woman. For while courage and intelligence are more for a man because of the constitution of his body and strength of his soul, chastity is for a woman.

Because of this it is necessary for a woman, while she is being educated, to learn about chastity: from what kinds and numbers of things this good comes to a woman. And in fact I say it comes from five things: first from her piety and reverence of her marriage bed; secondly from the orderliness of her body; thirdly from the occasions when she goes out from her own house; fourthly from her not participating in secret and Cybeline rituals; fifthly in her being devout and fair in her sacrificing to the divine. But of these, the most important cause of chastity, and its most important preserver, is incorruptibility with respect to the marriage bed and not mixing with men outside the family. For firstly, a woman who breaks this law wrongs the gods of her family, and provides her family and race with bastards, not legitimate offspring. She wrongs the gods of nature, with respect to whom she swore, along with her ancestors and family, to share in a common life and produce children according to the law. And moreover she wrongs her fatherland if she does not abide by the laws which have been established. Then, she sins beyond those things for which the greatest penalty, death, is laid down, because of the magnitude of her crime: sin and hubris for the sake of pleasure is outside natural law and most unforgivable. The outcome of all hubris is destruction.

2.

She must consider this too, that she will find no purification from this sin so that she can approach the shrines and altars of the gods as a chaste woman loved by the gods. For with this crime particularly the divine is unforgiving. The most beautiful adornment of a free-woman and her greatest honour is to testify to her chastity towards her husband through her children, if they bear the stamp of likeness to the father whose seed produced them. This is my view on the marriage bed.

This is my view on adornment of her body. She must be dressed in white, simply, and without anything fancy. She will be like this if she does not wear clothes that are transparent or embroidered or silk, but moderate and white. For thus she will avoid being too well dressed and luxurious and ostentatious, and arousing unpleasant envy in other women. She should on no account wear gold or emeralds, for it would be an extravagant and arrogant gesture with respect to the local women. For a well governed city, the whole city arranged for benefit of the whole city, must be sympathetic and in agreement, and the craftsmen who make such jewellery must be excluded from the city. She should not embellish her appearance with imported and foreign colour, but by the natural colour of her body, by washing with water, and adorn herself instead with modesty. She will also bring honour to herself and to the man with whom she shares her life.

Women of high status must leave the house to make sacrifices to the founding god of the city on behalf of themselves, their husbands, and their whole households. They do not leave the house when it is dark, nor in the evening, for some festival or to buy something for the house, but when the market is running and it is light, accompanied decorously by one female servant or at the most two.

She should offer prayers of sacrifice to the gods, as is within her power, but refrain from secret and Cybeline rituals at home. For the city's common law prevents women from celebrating these rites, because, amongst other reasons, these forms of ritual lead to drunkenness and ecstasy. The mistress of the house must be chaste and untouched with respect to everything, even when supervising at home.

Notes

1. M.E. Waithe, *A History of Women Philosophers*, I (Dodrecht: M. Nijhoff, 1987), 26; M.R. Lefkowitz and M.B. Fant, *Women's Life in Greece and Rome: A Source Book in Translation* (2nd edn; Baltimore: John Hopkins University Press, 1992), 163.
2. H. Thesleff, 'An introduction to the Pythagorean writings of the Hellenistic Period', *Acta Academiae Aboensis, Humaniora* 24.3 (Abo: To akademi, 1961), 113-15.
3. Xenophon, *Hellenica* 1.6.1-34; Diodorus 13.76-9, 97-100.
4. See for example Melissa, Perictione I and Cleopatra; for the tradition of criticising women for using cosmetics, see Juvenal (*Satires* 6.457-73, 486-510) and Xenophon (*Economics* 10.5-13).

21. Ptolemaïs (perhaps 250 BC)

Introduction

Ptolemaïs is known to us through reference to her work by Porphyry in his *Commentary on the Harmonics of Ptolemy*. He tells us that she came from Cyrene and gives the title of her work, *The Pythagorean Principles of Music*, which he quotes. She is the only known female musical theorist from antiquity. Her dates cannot be known for sure. She clearly preceded Porphyry, who was born about AD 232; Didymus, who is also quoted by Porphyry, knew Ptolemaïs' work and may even have been Porphyry's source for it. This Didymus is probably the one who lived in the time of Nero, giving us a date for Ptolemaïs of the first century AD or earlier.[1] Ptolemaïs cites the work of Aristoxenus, a philosopher and musical theorist of the fourth century BC, and so her work must post-date his. Her name suggests that she may have been related to Ptolemaeus of Cyrene, a sceptical philosopher of about 100 BC.[2]

One of the problems in dealing with this text is that it is in quotation. Porphyry does not clearly distinguish between the text he quotes from Ptolemaïs and his own discussion of the issues raised. He introduces the quoted passages clearly enough (I have provided his introductions in italics), but he does not indicate where the quotation ends. Barker suggests, for example, that the second paragraph of fragment 2 may be Porphyry's own words.[3] A second issue is the problem of the accuracy of the quotation. Porphyry says in the introduction to fragment 4 that he has altered a few things in the quotation for the sake of brevity. We should not assume that this is the only quotation to have suffered from editing. On the other hand, where he quotes the same passage twice (fragment 3 is repeated almost verbatim in fragment 4) his consistency is encouraging.

Ptolemaïs' extant work is a catechism, written as a series of questions and answers. She discusses different schools of thought on harmonic theory, distinguishing between the degree to which they gave importance to theory and perception. Her text prefers the approach of Aristoxenus to that of the Pythagoreans, thus she should not be thought a Pythagorean, despite the title of her work.

Ptolemaïs

1.
Ptolemaïs of Cyrene also writes about canonics in her Pythagorean Principles of Music, *as follows:*

The study of canonics—with whom is it more strongly identified?
Generally with the Pythagoreans. For what we now call 'harmonics', they used to name 'canonics'.

From what do we get the term 'canonics'?[4]
Not from the musical instrument called the canon, as some people think, but from straightness, as through this study reason finds what is correct and the regular marks of what is in-tune

They also call 'canonics' the study of pan-pipes and flutes and other musical instruments, although these are not actually 'canonic', but they say these are canonic too because the ratios and theorems apply to them. So, rather, the instrument was called the canon from the study of canonics. Generally, a 'canonicus' is a harmonic-theorist who makes calculations about what is in-tune. Musici and canonici are different. For they call harmonic theorists who begin from perceptions 'musici', but Pythagorean harmonic theorists are called 'canonici'. But generically they are both musical theorists.

2.

She adds to this, again by question and answer:

From what principles has the theory to do with the canon been constructed?
From those principles postulated by the musici and those taken up by the mathematici.

The principles postulated by the musici are all those which the canonici take up from perceptions, such as the existence of harmonious and discordant intervals and the octave being a compound of the fourth and fifth, and that a tone is the excess of the fifth over the fourth, and things like that. The principles taken up by the mathematici are all those which the canonici study theoretically in their own way, only starting their study from the starting points that come from perceptions, such as that the intervals are in ratios of numbers, and that a sound is from numbers of collisions, and other principles of that kind. So one could define the postulates of canonics as existing within the science of music and within the science of numbers and geometry.

3.

Ptolemaïs writes about these things in the introduction mentioned above, as follows:

Pythagoras and his successors want to adopt perception as a guide for reason at the beginning, as if to provide a spark for it, but to treat reason, when it has started off from such a beginning, as separating from perception and working by itself. So if the composite whole is found in a study by reason to be no longer in accord with perception, they do not turn back, but make their own accusations, saying that the perception is mistaken, and that reason by itself finds what is correct and refutes perception.

Some of the musici who follow Aristoxenus hold a contrary position. They adopt theory based upon thought, but advance through expertise on musical instruments. For they regarded perception as authoritative, and reason as accompanying it, and for necessity only. According to them it is quite reasonable for the rational postulates of the canon to be not always in harmony with the perceptions.

4.

Ptolemaïs of Cyrene wrote about these things briefly in her introduction, and Didymus the musical theorist went into them at greater length in his On the Difference Between the Aristoxenians and the Pythagoreans. *We shall write out what they both say, changing a few things for the sake of brevity. Ptolemaïs writes as follows:*

What is the distinction between those who are eminent in the field of music?
Some preferred reason itself, some perception, and others a combination of both together. On the one hand, all those of the Pythagoreans who enjoyed disputing with the musici preferred reason, saying that perception should be dismissed entirely, and reason brought in as an autonomous criterion by itself. But they are entirely refuted by their adoption of something perceivable in the beginning and their forgetting of this fact. On the other hand, the instrumentalists preferred perception. They gave no thought at all (or very little thought) to theory.

What is the distinction between those who preferred a combination of both?
While some adopted both perception and reason in the same way, as being of equal importance, others took one as the leader and the other as a follower. Aristoxenus of Tarentum adopted them both in the same way. For neither can what is perceived be composed by itself without reason, nor is reason

strong enough to establish something if it does not take its starting points from perception, and the conclusion of the theorising does not agree again with the perception.

In what way does he want perception to be in advance of theory?
In order, but not in importance. For he says when what is perceptible whatever it is, is grasped, then we must promote reason for the theoretical study of it.

Who treats both together?
Pythagoras and his successors. For they want to adopt perception as a guide for reason at the beginning, as if to provide a spark for it, but to treat reason, when it has started off from such a beginning, as separating from perception and working by itself. So if the composite whole is found in a study by reason to be no longer in accord with perception, they do not turn back, but make their own accusations, saying that the perception is mistaken, and that reason by itself finds what is correct and refutes perception.

Who holds a contrary position to this?
Some of the musici who follow Aristoxenus. They adopt theory based upon thought, but advance through expertise on musical instruments. For they regarded perception as authoritative, and reason as accompanying it, and for necessity only.

Notes

1. See A. Barker (ed.), *Greek Musical Writings*, II (Oxford: Clarendon Press, 1997), 240.
2. Diog. L. 9.115.
3. Barker, *Greek Musical Writings* II, 240.
4. A canon was originally a ruler for measuring length and straightness, and canonics meant 'regular' before taking on a more technical meaning in musical theory. Ptolemaïs also refers to a monochord musical instrument that was called a canon. On this, see ibid, 239.

22. Boeo (*fl. 3rd century* BC)

Introduction

Boeo and a short fragment of her work are known to us from a reference in Pausanias' discussion of early stories about the prophetic oracle of Apollo at Delphi. He believed that Boeo was a 'local' woman who wrote a hymn for Delphi (10.5.8). She was also known to Philochorus, though he does not seem to know her work well, as he confuses her with a male writer named Boeus (Athen. 9.393e). Boeo's obscurity, and her confusion with a similarly little-known Boeus, has led to a suspicion that she never existed, her hymn a Hellenistic composition complementing forgeries or attributions of early hymns to Olen in that age, and her name an invention to characterise the author as a woman from central Greece (Boeotia) who could be a credible authority on Delphi. Clement of Alexandra tells us that there was a prophet named Boeo,[1] and this too has been seen to cast some doubt upon the existence of the writer. A Boeo is also named as the mother of Palaephatus, a legendary Athenian epic poet (*Suda* s.v. Palaephatus), and a link with a figure of legend weakens the case for her own existence.

Nevertheless, Boeo was accepted by Pausanias and Philochorus as a credible woman writer, and texts were attributed to her. Moreover, there would be no practical benefit for a male writer to pose as the female author of this hymn unless there was a strong tradition of women writers in this genre. Yet ancient hymns were normally attributed to males (Homer, Olen, Hesiod), so the attribution of this work to a woman is unusual and should not be dismissed as without some foundation. An author may have written under the name of Boeo from Delphi, whether or not that was her real name and home.

The subject of her hymn was the foundation of the famous oracle at Delphi, which Boeo attributed to Olen and Hyperboreans (remote legendary people from the north).[2] She also said that Olen was the first Delphic prophet and invented the hexameter. Olen was not a Hellenistic invention—he had been regarded as the author of ancient hymns at least as early as the fifth century BC (Herodotus 4.35)—but Boeo adds to his story by linking him to Delphi and the hexameter prophecy. She goes against the much stronger tradition that a woman, Phemonoe, was the first prophet, that she invented the hexameter, and that the prophets were always women (as Pausanias points out 10.5.7, 6.7). Elsewhere Olen is associated with hymns about another important Greek religious site, Delos. The Hyperboreans were also traditionally associated with the rites at Delos (Herodotus 4.33-35). Boeo's hymn, therefore, appears to have been innovative in transferring elements of a tradition associated with Delos to Delphi, from one sanctuary of Apollo to another. This perhaps reflects a local tradition, but is more likely a Hellenistic fancy.

Boeo

1.

Where Pagasus and godlike Aguieus, sons of the Hyperboreans,
founded the well-remembering oracle

...

2.

She lists other Hyperboreans, and at the end of the hymn names Olen.[3]

And Olen, who became the first prophet of Phoebus,
and the first who fashioned a song of ancient verses.

Notes

1. Clement of Alexandria (*Stromata* 1.399P).
2. For the Delphic oracle see J.E. Fontenrose, *The Delphic Oracle: Its Responses and Operations, with a Catalogue of Responses* (Berkeley: University of California Press, 1981); H.W. Parke and D.E. Wormell, *The Delphic Oracle* (Oxford: Blackwell, 1956).
3. The italics indicate Pausanias' words.

23. Corinna (*fl. 3rd century* BC)

Introduction

Corinna was a lyric poet from Tanagra in Boeotia. The *Suda* (3.157) tells us that she was the daughter of Acheloodorus and Procatia, the pupil of Myrtis, and that her nickname was Myia ('Fly').[1] Her excellence as a lyric poet is well attested: she is said to have defeated Pindar five times in poetic competition. It is recorded that she wrote five books of lyric poetry, which were called 'Tales', as well as epigrams (two hexameters survive) and lyric nomes (narrative poems). Perhaps as many as 42 fragments of her work survive, though no complete poem is extant, and some fragments are only single words.

In antiquity Corinna was thought to have lived in the middle of the fifth century BC as a contemporary and rival of Pindar, the most famous lyric poet of the day. Plutarch tells a story of Corinna first advising Pindar to include more myths in his poetry, and then laughing at him for mixing in too many (*On the Glory of Athens* 4.347f-348a). Pausanias describes a painting of her in the gymnasium at Tanagra in which she was shown tying back her hair to mark her victory over Pindar (9.22.3). In Aelian's anecdote, Corinna defeated Pindar five time in public competitions (*Historical Miscellanies* 13.25). These are, however, relatively late sources.[2] Corinna and her work are not alluded to in any ancient source until as late as the first century BC,[3] and both her spelling and the metre of her poetry indicate that it was written in the third rather than fifth century BC. This is decisive, and so we should date her to around 200 BC, rather than to the fifth century. [4] It is not likely that later (i.e. third century) copyists tried to modernise her spelling, nor should we be concerned with the historicity of the anecdotes about her. Ancient biographers liked to invent personal relationships between poets, and references by Corinna to both Pindar and Myrtis (fragment 7 below) would have promoted such an idea.[5] Tatian does mention that there was a statue to her, made by the fourth-century Athenian sculptor Silanion (*Against the Greeks* 52b). Tatian, however, was not a reliable critic of Greek art, and we cannot trust his identification of subject or sculptor.[6]

Corinna's main subject seems to have been Boeotian myths and legends.[7] She wrote in an Aeolian dialect—the dialect spoken in Boeotia. Pausanias concludes this would have made her particularly popular in her homeland, more popular even than Pindar, who, though a Boeotian, wrote in a literary Doric dialect. She was so popular in Tanagra, that a tomb was erected to her there in a conspicuous part of the city.[8] Pausanias tells us that, judging from her portrait, she was the most beautiful woman of her day (9.22.3).

Substantial fragments of three of her poems have been preserved on papyrus which has survived from the second century AD from Hermopolis and Oxyrhynchus in Egypt. Other short fragments come typically from grammarians who commented on features of her dialect. Corinna states that she sings of 'the honours of heroes and heroines' (fragment 8), and this is reflected in the extant fragments.

Corinna's lyric songs were *Partheneia*, songs composed for public performance by choirs of young girls. Consequently her poetry does not have the intimate and personal qualities of Sappho, but rather celebrates the community's collective knowledge through the retelling of its myths and legends. Fragments 4 and 7 are perhaps exceptions to this, suggesting some personal reflection. However, juding from other *partheneia*, such as Alcman, *Partheneion* 1, and Pindar *Partheneion*, poets working in this genre gave the chorus a persona of its own, and even created individual personae for chorus members. So we must be careful in our assessment of a fragment that has been preserved without context, like fragment 7 below, where the poet may be speaking through a character, and not in her own voice.[9]

Despite the difficulties posed by her dialect,[10] Corinna's songs were well known and liked in antiquity. She was read by the Roman poets Statius (and his father), Propertius and Ovid.[11] Commentaries were written on her work,[12] and she was included in canons of women poets that were compiled by Antipater of Thessaloniki, Clement of Alexandria and Eustathius. Her subject matter—the ancient myths—was one reason for her popularity. It is what Antipater uses to define her work, and when Propertius calls her 'ancient Corinna', he is referring to the subject matter of her poetry rather than the antiquity of Corinna herself.[13]

Corinna's text in the papyrus is often difficult and illegible portions have been reconstructed. Where there is a well accepted reconstruction, I use it without signalling so in the translation; only where the reconstruction is more tentative do I indicate this by the use of square brackets. Gaps in the text are indicated by '…'. Of the 42 fragments attributed to her I have included in this collection 11 fragments which offer something worthwhile in translation to the non-Greek reader.[14]

Corinna

The Contest of Helicon and Cithaeron[15]

1.
'…the Curetes
hid the sacred child of the goddess
in a cave, a secret unknown
to the twisted-scheming Cronus,
when blessed Rhea stole him away   5

and seized great honour among
the immortals'. And this was his song.
At once the Muses told the blessed gods
to cast their secret votes
in the golden-glowing urns   10
and together they all rose up.

Cithaeron took the majority
and at once Hermes shouted out and proclaimed
that he had taken the victory he so desired,
and the blessed gods crowned him   15
with a victor's garland of fir,
and his mind was full of joy.

But Helicon was seized
by bitter pains and

ripped out a shinning rock   20
and the mountain shook. In pain
he cried and from above he smashed it down
into ten thousand pieces of stone.

…

[so sang] the daughters of Zeus and Mnemonsyne.

The Daughters of Asopus[16]
2.
Enjoying the gifts of the Muses
I tell my story in song…

…

Zeus, giver of good things
took from her father Asopus
his daughter Aegina   5
and Thebe and Plataea,
but Corcyra and Salamis

father Poseidon stole
and beautiful Euboea,
while Leto's son holds on   10
to Sinope and Thespia,
and Hermes Tanagra.

…

'Father Zeus, king of all
has three of your daughters,
while Poseidon lord of the seas   15
married three, and for two
Phoebus rules their beds,

for one the good son of Maia,
Hermes. For so did Eros
and Cypris persuade them,   20
so did they steal into your house
and take your nine daughters.

In time they shall bear
a race of half-god heroes,
and they will have many children   25
and never be old. This was I told
before the tripod of the oracle.

This prize I have mastered,
I of fifty mighty brothers,
highest prophet of the   30
holy sanctuary that
never lies, I Acraephen.

Now first the son of Leto
gave Euonymus the power
to speak oracles from his tripods,   35
but Hyrieus threw him from the land
and held the honour second,

a son of Poseidon; and then
Orion my own father
after he inherited the land;   40
I too, while he is up in the heavens,
gained this honour myself.

So I know well the truth
in oracles, and I speak it.
Give in to the immortals and   45
end the grief in your heart,
for you are father-in-law to gods'.

Just so spoke the most reverend prophet.
Asopus full of joy
took his right hand   50
and pouring tears from his eyes
he made this answer:

…

(—or Ares) Tales, Book I (?)

3.
Terpsichore calls me
to sing lovely tales
to white-dressed girls of Tanagra,
and the city is filled with joy
at my sweetly-voiced gossipy songs.   5
For whatever great [deeds were done]
[still greater] lies [decorate]
the wide-dancing earth;
and legends from our fathers' time
I adorn with my own words   10
for our girls and begin.

Many times I adorned
Cephisus ancient ancestor
with my words,

and many times great Orion   15
and the almighty fifty
sons whom he fathered
sleeping with nymphs,
and lovely Libya
... [I shall sing of]   20
the girl...lovely to see...the earth whom [she] bore...fathered...

Tales, Book 5
4.
Are you sleeping for ever? In the past, Corinna,
you were not [a slug-a-bed].

Voyage Home
5.
The almighty Orion
defeated him and named
after himself all the land
...

Voyage Home
6.
For the envious man
does not punish you...

(7-11, titles uncertain)

7.
Well I for one criticise sweet-voiced
Myrtis because she although a woman
once went into competition with Pindar.

8.
But I [sing of] the honours of heroes
and of heroines...

9.
Thespia, mother of beautiful children, lover of strangers, loved by the Muses...

10.
murderer...
his heart said kill...
but he hid...
and he gave gifts...
they burnt with a fire...
[sailing] on swift-running [ships].

Orestes

11.
As Dawn leaves ocean's
seas, she drags from heaven
the holy light of the moon,
while the Seasons take life from ambrosial Zeus
among the flowers of spring,   5
and the choir enjoys its weary
steps in the city of the seven gates.[17]

Notes

1. There may be some confusion here, as Myia is attested as a Spartan poet elsewhere in the *Suda* and by Clement of Alexandria (*Stromata* 4.19.122.4). The *Suda* also lists a Corinna from Thespia or Corinth and a younger Corinna from Thebes; these are further confusions, perhaps caused by references to these places in Corinna's poetry.

2. From the second (Plutarch and Pausanias) and third (Aelian) centuries AD. The evidence for her life and work is collected by D.A. Campbell, *Greek Lyric*, IV (Cambridge, MA: Harvard University Press, 1992), 18-35.

3. Antipater of Thessalonica (*Anth. Pal.* 9.26).

4. See E. Lobel, 'Corinna', *Hermes* 65 (1930), 356-65; Campbell, *Greek Lyric* IV, 1-3; for arguments for and against the earlier date, see J.McI. Snyder, *The Woman and the Lyre* (Carbondale: Southern Illinois University Press, 1989), 165 n. 14, and D.L. Page, *Corinna* (London: Society for the Promotion of Hellenic Studies, 1953), 65-84.

5. As a further example compare the invention of a relationship between Homer and Hesiod and the idea that they competed with each other (Schol. Pindar, *Nemean Odes* 2.1). On the fictional nature of ancient biographies see M.R. Lefkowitz, *The Lives of the Greek Poets* (Baltimore: John Hopkins University Press, 1981). For the misinterpretation of the insult 'Boeotian sow' as a reference by Pindar (*Olympian Odes* 6.89 f.) to Corinna (Aelian, *Historical Miscellanies* 13.25): see Campbell, *Greek Lyric* IV, 2.

6. Tatian's credibility as an art historian is discredited by A. Kalkmann, 'Tatians Nachrichten über Kunstwerke', *Rheinisches Museum* 42 (1887), 489-524. In the Musée Vivnel, Compiègne there is a marble statuette of Corinna, thought to be a copy of the statue referred to by Tatian. This statuette is not indicative of the work of a great master: G.M.A. Richter, *The Portraits of the Greeks* (Oxford, 1984), 156 and fig. 116.

7. The subject of the one fragment we have of Myrtis is a Boeotian myth from Tanagra.

8. Indeed, there is a modern statue to Corinna in Tanagra today.

9. For criticism of Corinna, see M.B. Skinner, 'Corinna of Tanagra and her Audience', *Tulsa Studies in Women's Literature* 2.1 (1983), 9-20.

10. Statius refers to her 'arcana' (mysteries) (*Silvae* 5.3.158), and many of her extant fragments are the result of scholarly discussion of her Boeotian orthography.

11. Statius, *Silvae* 5.3.16-18; Propertius, *Elegies* 2.3.19-22; Ovid named Corinna of his *Amores* after her.

12. Melampus or Diomedes on Dionysus of Thrace: Campbell, *Greek Lyric* IV, 25 n. 7.

13. Corinna probably only predated him by 150 years or so.

14. For a complete collection of her fragments, see ibid, 18-69; for earlier scholarship on the fragments, see D.L. Page, *Corinna*.

15. Two mountains thought sacred to the Muses, Cithaeron and Helicon are competing in a song contest. The fragment begins with the end of Cithaeron's song. The infant rescued is the god Zeus. Moero also retold this myth.

16. The first 50 lines or so of the poem are poorly preserved, with only a few (mostly incomplete) words extant. I adopt some of Campbell's suggestions to supplement the fragmentary text here and elsewhere.

17. Thebes.

24. Melinno (*fl. c. 200–150 BC*)

Introduction

The fate of the poetry of Melinno is fairly typical of that of many women authors from antiquity. Stobaeus, a Greek writing in the fifth century AD, quotes one short poem by her. This is the only reference we have both to Melinno and to her work. Consequently, our appreciation of her as a poet must be limited to the mere glimpse which this poem can offer.[1]

Stobaeus describes her as being from Lesbos, a Greek island more famous as the birthplace of Sappho, and this is all he says about her. Even this little information has been rejected by scholars, who assume that Stobaeus has inferred this detail from the metrical form—the Sapphic strophe—which this poem takes. The fame of Sappho tempted ancient biographers to associate other women writers with Lesbos; Melinno may have fostered such an association out of respect for Sappho.[2]

It has proved difficult to assign a date to Melinno and her work. Suggestions range from as early as 340 BC to as late as the second century AD. The content of the poem can help us. The subject, praise for the power of Dea Roma (Rome personified as a goddess), suggests a date early in the second century BC, a time when Rome had extended its power throughout the Mediterranean world. A cult to this goddess became established and was popular in the Greek cities of the Roman empire.[3] The general style of the poem is also consistent with Greek poetry of this period. The worship of Dea Roma seems to have been less popular in the Greek world after the middle of the second century BC and a post-Republican date should be ruled out as the poem makes no reference to an emperor (a necessity in a poem about Rome's power in the imperial period). We should therefore date the poem at 200–150 BC.

The poem is a hymn in honour of Roma, lauding the power of Rome. In Greek *Rhōmē* means both 'strength' and 'Rome'. Stobaeus quotes this poem in a collection of passages about strength (*Eclogues* 3.7.12), indicating that this play on words may have been a deliberate poetic device on the part of the poet. That a Greek female poet would write such a work in honour of Rome raises the question of the context for the composition and performance of the poem. The poem addresses Dea Roma, and so, it has been suggested, it may have been composed to be performed at a ritual in honour of the goddess. However, we should not assume that women only wrote poetry for ritual purposes, and indeed there is nothing in the content of the poem itself to tie it to any specific ritual acts, though a festival in honour of Roma does provide a possible context for performance. At a time when Roman power was paramount in the Mediterranean, there was every reason for the wealthy, both Roman and Greek, to commission a poem to be sung in honour of Rome. We know so little about Greek female poets that we cannot rule out the possibility that women poets of talent could be commissioned to compose works, as male poets were.

What we can say about Melinno is that she was well educated. She masters the artificial dialect of Greek choral poetry, and the Sapphic metre (a lyric metre little used after Sappho), and builds her poetry from well attested poetic images—the mark of an Alexandrian poet. She has been criticised for not achieving the melody of Sappho and Alcaeus in her hymn.

However, her more weighty adjectives, the certain stiffness found in her rhythm, and even the breaks she imposes between stanzas suit the image of power and authority which Melinno seeks to create. The image of Roma as a mighty warrior queen, driving a chariot from which she controls the world, provides a well conceived and memorable tribute to the power of Rome.

Melinno

I welcome you, Roma, daughter of Ares,
war-loving queen crowned in gold,
you who live in holy and eternally strong Olympus
on earth.

To you alone, most reverend, Fate has given   5
royal glory of invulnerable rule,
so that holding sovereign power
you may lead.

Beneath your yoke of powerful straps
the chests of the earth and the white sea   10
are bound-tight; and you safely steer
the cities of your peoples.

While the greatest eternity defeats all
and reshapes life, sometimes in this way, sometimes in that,
for you alone a fair wind of rule   15
does not change.

In truth, you alone of all bear the most powerful
great spear-carrying men
making them spring up like Demeter's plentiful fruits
from men.   20

Notes

1. My discussion draws upon C.M. Bowra, 'Melinno's Hymn to Rome', *Journal of Roman Studies* 47 (1957), 21-28, the most important work on Melinno to date.
2. Erinna and Anyte were other poets later attached to Lesbos.
3. See R. Mellor, *Thea Roma: The Worship of the Goddess Roma in the Greek World* (Göttingen: Vanden-hoeck and Ruprecht, 1975).

25. Cornelia (*fl. mid-2nd century* BC)

Introduction

Cornelia is one of the most famous women from late Republican Rome. She was the daughter of Publius Scipio Africanus, and married another leading politician, Tiberius Sempronius Gracchus. She was the mother of twelve children, the most famous of whom were Tiberius and Gaius Gracchus (the 'Gracchi').[1] She was greatly admired in antiquity for her nobility and as a model wife and mother. She took charge of her husband's estate after his death in 154 BC, and refused all offers to remarry, including one from the king of Egypt, Ptolemy VI Philometor (Plut., *Life of Tiberius* 1). Her nobility was particularly admired, according to Plutarch, for the way in which she bore the misfortune of the deaths of her sons (*Life of Gaius* 19). Anecdotes about her include one in which she takes great pride in her sons, calling them her jewels (Valerius Maximus, *Memorable Deeds and Sayings* 4.4). She reputedly told stories of her sons with great pride after their deaths, and was responsible for the education of her sons (Plut., *Life of Tiberius* 1, Tacitus, *Dialogue on Oratory* 28). She is also remembered for the excellence of the prose in her letters (Cicero, *Brutus* 211; Quintilian, *Institutes of Oratory* 1.1.6). A statue of her was erected in Rome (Pliny, 34.31) in the Augustan period, an extraordinary honour. She served as an idealized example for the female aristocracy of a well educated woman who devoted herself to the proper education of her sons.[2]

Two fragments of a letter attributed to Cornelia have been preserved in some of the manuscripts of Cornelius Nepos. These purport to be extracts of a letter from Cornelia to her son Gaius. The fragments are particularly significant in the history of women's writing—indeed, it has been claimed that they are the earliest extant prose in any language by a woman.[3] However, the authenticity of the fragments has long been disputed. Evidence from Cicero (*Brutus* 211) and later Plutarch (*Life of Gaius* 13) shows that a corpus of letters attributed to Cornelia existed and the style of the letter dates it correctly to the late second century BC. The content, however, is difficult to balance against the historical record. In the fragments Cornelia is strongly critical of her sons. She vehemently opposes Gaius' plan to stand for the tribunate and warns him not to continue the revolutionary policies of his brother, as this will bring disgrace on the family and disaster upon him. Yet in the historical record she strongly supports her sons, pushing them forward (Plut., *Life of Tiberius* 8), giving advice to Gaius and recruiting mercenaries for him (Plut., *Life of Gaius* 4, 13). She is even suspected of murdering her son-in-law (in league with her daughter) as he was her son's political opponent (Appian, *Civil Wars* 1.20).[4]

On the other hand, there were some sources known to Plutarch which maintained that Cornelia disapproved of the revolutionary policy of her sons (*Life of Gaius* 13). He tells one anecdote in which she persuaded Gaius to adopt a moderate policy in the treatment of one of his brother's political opponents. But this incident was apparently described by Gaius himself, used by him to justify the course of action he took and to emphasise the more moderate policy he had chosen to pursue (*Life of Gaius* 4). The weight of evidence finds Cornelia a strong supporter of her sons. It is unlikely that the historical record could have remembered her as such—even after the later re-evaluation of the Gracchi—if she had published documents opposing their politics. Such a document as this, ostensibly a private letter from mother to son, could not have been published by accident and it would not have suited either party, Gaius or Cornelia, to have published the letter themselves. In the letter, Cornelia tells us that she wants to avoid any public disgrace to her family while the very publication of such a letter draws attention to this fear. The writing and publication of this document was a strongly political act. By the use of condemnatory vocabulary from a later assessment of the policies of the Gracchi, and in anticipating Gaius' fate, the author reveals that the text was written with hindsight, perhaps even by Cornelius Nepos himself.[5]

Nevertheless, the letter was written to be accepted as the work of Cornelia. It contains a powerful rhetoric, and has been compared in tone and expression to Cicero.[6] As such, it provides testimony to the acceptance of Cornelia as a very capable writer. In particular, there is nothing that marks the letter as the work of a woman, demonstrating that female written work was not stylistically distinguished from male. We do know that women did correspond regularly, both with female friends and with men, but little of this correspondence has been preserved.[7]

Cornelia

Letter to Gaius Gracchus

1.

You will say that it is a beautiful thing to get revenge on your enemies. This seems neither greater nor more beautiful to anyone than it does to me, but only if it is possible both to follow these aims and maintain the security of the state. But in as much as that is not possible, our enemies will not perish for a long time and for many reasons, and they will be as they are now rather than the state be ruined and perish.

2.

I would be bold enough to swear a solemn oath that except for those who killed Tiberius Gracchus, no enemy has given me as much difficulty and trouble as you have because of this affair. You should have shouldered the responsibilities of all of those children whom I once had and made sure that I had as little to worry about as possible in my old age, and that whatever you did, you should want to please me most greatly, and you should consider it sacrilegious to do anything significant which was against my wishes, especially as I have only a small part of my life left.

Can that span of time, brief as it is, not help, so you do not oppose me and ruin our state? Finally, what end will there be? When will our family cease from its madness? When will it be possible to have moderation in things? When will we cease insisting on causing and suffering troubles? When will we be ashamed of confusing and disturbing the state? But if this is completely impossible, seek the tribunate when I am dead. As far as I am concerned, do what you like, when I will not be aware of it. When I am dead, you will sacrifice to me as your parent and call upon the god of your parent. At that time will you not be ashamed to seek the intercession of those gods whom you deserted and abandoned when they were alive and present? May Jupiter not allow you to persist in this nor allow such madness to enter your mind. And if you persist, I fear that through your own fault you will receive so much trouble for your whole life that at no time will you be able to feel content.

Notes

1. Sempronia was the only other one of her children to survive to adulthood (Plut., *Life of Tiberius* 1).
2. E.A. Hemelrijk, *Matrona Docta: Educated Women in the Roman Élite from Cornelia to Julia Domna* (London and New York: Routledge, 1999), 64-68.
3. A.S. Gratwick, 'Prose Literature', in E.J. Kenney and W.V. Clausen (eds), *The Cambridge History of Classical Literature*, II. *Latin Literature* (Cambridge: Cambridge University Press, 1982), 145-46.
4. See also Dio 24.83.
5. Cf. H.U. Instinsky, 'Zur Echtheitsfrage der Brieffragmente der Cornelia', *Chiron* 1 (1971), 177-89 (186-89); N. Horsfall, 'The "Letter of Cornelia": yet more problems', *Athenaeum* 65 (1987), 231-34 (233-34). For a thorough discussion of the arguments for and against authenticity, see Hemelrijk, *Matrona Docta*, 193-97. For the political context, see R.A. Bauman, *Women and Politics in Ancient Rome* (London and New York: Routledge, 1992), 42-45.
6. Hemelrijk, *Matrona Docta*, 196.
7. On the reasons for the loss of nearly all letters written by women, see ibid, 203-6. Other letters by women that have been preserved through publication: Paula and Eustochium (Jerome, *Letters* 46), Plotina Augusta (*IG* II^2 1099; *ILS* 7784), Julia Domna (*Inscr. Eph.* 212), and various Pythagorean texts. Some private correspondence has been preserved from Vindolanda; see A.K. Bowman and J.D. Thomas, *The Vindolanda Writing-Tablets* (London: British Museum Press, 1994), 257 (Valatta), 291, 292, 293 (Claudia Severa), 294 (Paterna?). Many letters from women have survived on Greek papyri: see for example Diogenis, Ptolema, Herais, Senesis, Syra and Dionysarion in M.R. Lefkowitz and M.B. Fant, *Women's Life in Greece and Rome: A Source Book in Translation* (2nd edn; Baltimore: John Hopkins University Press, 1992), 102, 104, 105, 268, 269, 271, 272.

26. Hortensia (*fl. 42 BC*)

Introduction

In 43 BC three political and military leaders, the triumvirs, Mark Antony, Lepidus and Octavian (who later adopted the name Augustus), seized what amounted to absolute power in Rome. The following year the wealthy women of Rome marched to the Forum in the centre of Rome where Hortensia made a speech to the triumvirs, demanding that they change their plans to impose a tax on the richest 1400 Roman women. Not only was the speech successful in persuading the triumvirs to reduce the imposition to only the richest 400 women, but it was long remembered and admired in antiquity for the excellence of Hortensia's oratory.

Public speaking by women was extremely rare in Rome, so Hortensia's speech was unusual and memorable in itself. Political action by women was almost unheard of. The only precedent was over 150 years earlier, when there was a demonstration by women who demanded that a law which limited their luxuries be repealed.[1] Hortensia's speech was a particularly brave act too, as the triumvirs had embarked upon a reign of terror, eliminating their political opponents.

Hortensia begins by apologising for her inappropriate behaviour in addressing the public tribunal, noting that she and the other women had previously tried to get Antony's wife Fulvia to intercede on their behalf. The anecdote provides evidence for women's political action (despite not having any formal position) and for the political role that the wife of a leading politician might be expected to play in private.[2]

A copy of her speech (or what purported to be her speech) must have been published as it was cited by Valerius Maximus (*Memorable Deeds and Sayings* 8.3) and read by Quintilian (*Institutes of Oratory* 1.1.6) in the first century AD, both of whom admired it. Hortensia's eloquence was favourably compared with that of her father, Quintus Hortensius Hortalus, a famous orator (114–50 BC, consul in 69 BC). Neither Quintilian nor Valerius question the authenticity of the speeches they read, and while it is possible they were genuine copies, it is more likely that they were the product of later rhetorical exercises. The copy we have of the speech comes from Appian and is, at best, his Greek translation and paraphrase of the original Latin. Even if Appian did have a copy of the original speech, his rewriting means that little more than the general gist of Hortensia's words remains. The balance of probability is that Appian wrote the speech himself to suit his context. The speech is used by Appian to promote sympathy for the victims of the triumvirate.

Hortensia
(Retold by Appian)

Speech to the Triumvirs

As befitted women like us addressing a petition to you, we fled to your women. But after we were treated as did not befit us by Fulvia, we were driven by her to the Forum.

You have robbed us of our fathers and our sons and our husbands and our brothers, claiming that they have wronged you. But if you rob us of our property too, you will be putting us into a position unworthy of our family, our manners, and our female sex. If, on the one hand, you claim you have been wronged by us as you were by our men, proscribe us as you did them. But if, on the other hand, we women did not vote that any of you were public enemies, nor demolished your houses, nor destroyed your army, nor led another army against you, nor prevented you from gaining public office nor from gaining honour, why do we share the penalties when we did not participate in the crimes?

Why should we pay taxes when we do not participate in public offices nor honours nor commands, nor the whole government, fought over by you to such a terrible outcome? Because, you say, it is war? And when have there not been wars? When have women paid taxes? Women's sex absolves them among all mankind. Long ago, superior to their sex, our mothers once paid tax, when you were in danger, your entire government and the city itself, when the Carthaginians were at war with you. Then the women paid tax willingly, not from their land or fields or dowry or households, without which it is impossible for free women to live, but only from their own jewellery, and not with a set value for this nor threatened by informers or accusers nor by force or violence, but only as much as the women wanted to pay. What fear is there now for the government or fatherland? Let a war with the Celts come, or the Parthians, and we will not be inferior to our mothers in respect to the fatherland's salvation. But we will never pay taxes for civil wars, nor join you in acting against each other. For we did not pay taxes to Caesar nor to Pompey; neither Marius nor Cinna forced us to pay, nor Sulla, who ruled the fatherland as a tyrant. And you say that you are re-establishing the republic!

Notes

1. In 195 BC: Livy, *History of Rome* 34.1.
2. See further R.A. Bauman, *Women and Politics in Ancient Rome* (London and New York: Routledge, 1992), esp. 81-83.

27. Sulpicia *(late first century BC)*

Introduction

Sulpicia's elegies are the only extant lyric poems in Latin by a woman. What we know about Sulpicia is extrapolated from biographical information she gives in the poems themselves. In poem 4 she gives her own name and names her father as Servius, thereby identifying herself as a member of one of Rome's leading aristocratic families and asserting her own high status. In poem 2 she reveals that she was related to and, it seems, the ward of, Messalla. We know from Jerome that Messalla's sister, Valeria Messalla, married a Servius and did not remarry when she was widowed (*Adversus Iovinianum* 1.46), so we can conclude that Valeria was Sulpicia's mother, Messalla her uncle. By a Roman convention, the daughter always took her father's name (*nomen*), and so we can identify her father as Servius Sulpicius Rufus, which makes her grandfather the Roman orator (and friend of Cicero) of the same name.

Marcus Valerius Messalla Corvinus (64 BC–AD 8), her uncle, was an important military and political figure in Rome, commanding armies under Brutus, Antony and Octavian. He was also an important literary patron, sponsoring a circle that included Ovid and Tibullus, and presumably Sulpicia too.[1]

Sulpicia's poems were preserved in a collection divided into three or four books and attributed to the elegiac poet Tibullus.[2] However, only the first two books are thought to have been written by Tibullus himself. Eleven elegies in Book Three of the Tibullan corpus concern Sulpicia, and six are generally agreed to have been written by Sulpicia herself (poems 1-6 below).[3] The five poems which precede them in the Tibullan corpus (poems 7-11)[4] are about Sulpicia, but have been attributed since the nineteenth century to another unknown author and called the 'Garland of Sulpicia'.[5] Three of these poems describe Sulpicia in the third person, the narrator thereby distancing himself (or herself). However, in two of the 'Garland' poems the narrator speaks in the first person, in the persona of Sulpicia. A good case has been made for the restoration of these two poems to Sulpicia. Holt Parker demonstrates that in Roman subjective lyric love poetry, the reader expects the named speaker to be the poet unless given specific reading clues to think otherwise. We should therefore include [Tibullus] 3.9 (4.3) and 3.11 (4.5) (poems 7-8 below) in the corpus of her work.[6]

Sulpicia's poems are addressed to a young man whom she calls Cerinthus. The literary pseudonym is a convention and disguises the real name of her love-interest who cannot be identified.[7] We do Sulpicia an injustice if we read her poems as if they are the naïve autobiography of a young girl. Latin elegy exploited certain conventional situations to explore the fluctuating emotions produced by a love affair. In using such conventional themes for depictions of her own romance, Sulpicia displays her grasp of the genre and distances her poetic life from her real one, as did her contemporary elegists, Ovid, Propertius and Tibullus. Adopting another convention, Sulpicia disguises the name of her lover, but asserts her own name. While this follows the common practice of male elegists, the flouting of public morality by a woman in declaring her secret passions is extraordinary.[8] Some modern readers have suspected that Sulpicia's poems are pseudonymous, pointing to a lack of anything distinctly feminine in these texts, and the juxtaposition of the anonymous poems about Sulpicia in the corpus of Tibullus. However, the family details the author gives about herself in her work make this unlikely.

Sulpicia's poetry shows that she was both intelligent and independent. She complains about the lack of control over her own life. While revealing her passion for her lover, she reserves a proper concern about propriety and a pride in her status. Unlike male elegists, she does not engage in sexual conduct with her lover, and she complains about his uncaring or inappropriate treatment of her. Her style is colloquial and even convoluted. This distinguishes it from the elegies of her contemporaries, but this youthful spontaneity seems well suited to the persona of the character she develops and to the occasions she describes.[9]

Sulpicia

1.
Love has come at last—a kind that it would be more of a scandal
for me to cover up through modesty, than to bare to anyone.
Cytherea won over by my Muses dropped him
in my heart and left him there.
Venus has fulfilled her promises: let them talk about my delights,   5
as they will, if they do not have any of their own.
I would not want to entrust anything to sealed tablets
so that no one could read it before my lover,
but to err is fun, to maintain appearances because of the scandal
a bore; may I assert that I a worthy woman am with a worthy man.   10

2.
A hateful birthday is here, that will have to be spent sadly
in the dreadful countryside and without Cerinthus.
What is sweeter than the city? Would a country villa
and a freezing river in Arrentine fields be suitable for a girl?
Now, my over-zealous Messalla, please take a rest;   5
journeys are often made at the wrong time, uncle.
Here I leave my heart and my feelings if I'm carried off:
force does not allow me to make my own decision.

3.
Do you know a journey has been removed from the sad heart of a girl?
Now I can be at Rome for my birthday.
The birthday may be celebrated by us all
which now by chance to your surprise is on its way to you.

4.
I'm pleased that carefree you now allow yourself such license with me,
that I won't all of a sudden fall, a very silly woman.
You can have your love of the slut and prostitute laid out
with her wool-basket instead of Sulpicia, daughter of Servius:
there are men who worry about me, who worry greatly   5
that I might yield to some vulgar bed.

5.

Cerinthus, haven't you got any true love for your girl,
because now a fever troubles my tired body?
Oh—I wouldn't wish to recover from my sad illness
unless I thought you wanted it too.
But what would be the use of recovering from illness,   5
if you can bear my ills with heart unfeeling.

6.

May I never be such a burning desire for you, my light,
as I seem to have been a few days ago,
if I have ever done anything more foolish in the whole of my life
of which I should confess to being more ashamed
than that I left you alone last night,   5
longing to hide my passion.

7.

Spare my young man, you who live in the good pastures of the plain
or out of the way places of the shadowy mountain, wild boar,
nor sharpen your hard tusks for battle.
May Love as guardian protect him for me.

But through love of hunting Delia leads him far away.   5
O may the woods die and the hounds desert!
What madness it is. What sense is there in wanting to
harm tender hands surrounding densely clad hills in a hunt?
What use is there in stealthily entering the hiding places of wild animals
and marking your white legs with hooked brambles?   10

But yet, Cerinthus, if I could wander with you
I myself would carry the twisty nets for you through the mountains,
I myself would search for the footprints of the fleet deer
and loose the swift hound from its iron chains.
Then, then the woods would please me, if, my light,   15
I were accused of lying with you beside the very traps.
Then a boar could approach the snare and leave unharmed,
so it would not disturb the joy of desirous Venus.

Now without me may there not be any Venus, but by the law of Diana,
chaste boy, touch your nets with chaste hand,   20
and may any woman who sneaks up stealthily on my love
meet with wild animals and be ripped apart.

But you leave love of hunting for your father
and swiftly run back yourself to my embrace.

8.

The day which gave me you, Cerinthus, must always be
sacred for me and kept as a festival.

When you were born, the Parcae sang a new slavery
for girls and gave you haughty monarchy.
I burn before other girls; but I am happy that I burn, Cerinthus,   5
if in you there is any reciprocal fire that comes from me.
May there be reciprocal love, I ask, by your sweetest thefts,
and by your eyes, and by your very spirit.

Good spirit, take this incense willingly and favour my prayers,
if only he warms when he thinks of me.   10
But if he by chance should already sigh for other loves
then, I pray, Holy One, leave this unfaithful altarfire.

And don't you be unjust, Venus. Either let both serve you,
equally chained, or make my chains lighter.
But rather may we both be bound by a strong fetter,   15
which no day after can break.
The young man prays for the same thing as I, but he prays secretly.
For he is ashamed to speak here openly.

But Birthday, as a god you know everything,
nod assent. What does it matter if he asks openly or secretly?   20

Garland of Sulpicia[10]
9.
Sulpicia is dressed for you, great Mars, on your Calends.[11]
Come from the sky to see her yourself, if you are wise.
Venus will overlook this. But impetuous as you are, be careful
you don't drop your weapons in shameful amazement.

When he wants to burn the gods, from her eyes   5
fierce Love lights twin torches.
Whatever she does, wherever she places her footprints,
beauty follows and composes her stealthily.
If she undoes her hair, flowing locks suit her;
if she styles her hair, she has to be admired for her hair-style.   10
She burns, if she wants to go out in a Syrian dress;
she burns, if she comes in a dress of snowy white,
just as lucky Vertumnus on eternal Olympus
has a thousand adornments, and a thousand suit him.

She alone of girls is worthy to be given by Tyre   15
soft wools soaked twice in precious dyes,
and to possess whatever the rich Arab tiller reaps
of the fragrant crop in his sweet-smelling fields,
and whatever gems the dark Indian, neighbour
of Dawn's waters, gathers on the red seashore.   20

Pierides, sing of her on the Calends holiday,
and Phoebus, proud of your lyre of tortoiseshell.

May she celebrate this holy festival for many years;
no girl deserves your choir more.

10.
Come here and drive away the illness of a tender girl.
Come here, Phoebus, proud of your hair uncut.
Believe me, hurry, and you will not be sorry
to lay healing hands on beauty.
Make sure utter thinness does not possess the pale body   5
nor ugly colour mark the fair limbs.
And whatever is wrong and whatever sadness we fear,
may the river's rushing water carry out to sea.

Holy One, come and bring with you whatever delicacies,
and whatever spells lighten a tired body.   10
Don't torture a young man who fears for the fate of his girl
and makes vows for his mistress, impossible to count.
Sometimes he prays, sometimes, as she weakens,
he speaks hard words on the eternal gods.

Put aside fear, Cerinthus. God does not harm lovers.   15
But love always; your girl is safe.
There is no work for weeping; it would be better to use your tears
if and when she is more ill-tempered with you.
But now she is completely yours. She thinks fairly only of you
and in vain the trusting crowd sit by her.   20

Favour us, Phoebus. Great praise will be bestowed on you,
giving back two lives by saving one body.
You will be famous, you will be joyful too, when both repay
their debts in joyful competition at your holy altar fire.
Then the holy crowd of gods will call you fortunate,   25
and each one of them will wish for your skills.

11.
Birthday Juno, take these holy heaps of incense
which a learned girl gives you with her tender hand.
For you today she bathed, for you she styled herself most gladly
to stand before your altar fire to be seen and admired.
She says in truth she dressed up to adorn you,   5
but secretly there is someone she wants to please.

But, Holy One, favour us and don't let anyone tear lovers apart,
but, I pray, prepare reciprocal chains for the young man.
Thus will you settle things well. He does not deserve to be
the slave to another girl, nor she to another man.   10
Nor let the vigilant chaperone catch their desires,
but let love serve up a thousand ways to deceive.

Nod assent and come, shining in purple robe.
Three times you have cake, chaste goddess, and three times wine too.

She prays and the devoted mother tells her daughter what to ask for.   15
She, now her own woman, asks silently for something else.
She burns as the swift flames burn on the altar,
nor, although she could be cured, would she want to be.
May she please her young man and, when the next year arrives,
may this same love through her prayers then be long-standing.   20

Notes

1. For scholarship on the identification of Sulpicia see H.N. Parker, 'Sulpicia, the *Auctor de Sulpicia*, and the authorship of 3.9 and 3.11 of the *Corpus Tibullianum*', *Helios* 21.1 (1994), 39-62, 55 n. 2.
2. Editors divide the Tibullan corpus into either three or four books. Sulpicia's poems are still traditionally referred to by reference to this corpus and under the name of Tibullus (with square brackets to indicate that Tibullus is not actually considered the author: i.e. '[Tibullus]').
3. [Tibullus] 3.13-18 (4.7-12).
4. [Tibullus] 3.8-12 (4.2-6).
5. Ibid, 40. I include the rest of the *Garland of Sulpicia* in this collection too (poems 9-11 below).
6. Ibid, 39-62.
7. Tibullus addresses a young man (recently married) called Marcus Caecilius Cornutus (Tibullus 2.2, 2.3) and there is speculation dating back to the Renaissance that he was Cerinthus, based upon a pun in his name (Greek 'ceras' and Latin 'cornu' both meaning 'horn') and his association with the circle of Tibullus. A Cerinthus also appears in Horace, *Satires* 1.2.81-2.
8. Cf. the sentiment attributed by Plutarch to Theano (Plut., *Moralia* 142c-d) (translated on p. 1 of this volume).
9. For literary appreciation of Sulpicia's poetry see J.McI. Snyder, *The Woman and the Lyre: Women Writers in Classical Greece and Rome* (Carbondale: Southern Illinois University Press, 1989), 130-36; M. Santirocco, 'Sulpicia reconsidered', *Classical Journal* 74 (1979), 229-39; N.J. Lowe, 'Sulpicia's syntax', *Classical Quarterly* 38 (1988), 193-205; J.R. Bradley, 'The Elegies of Sulpicia: an introduction and commentary', *New England Classical Newsletter* 22.4 (1994–5), 159-64.
10. Poems about Sulpicia, preserved with Sulpicia's poems in the corpus of Tibullus as [Tib.] 3.8, 10, 12. Poems 7-8 above ([Tib.] 3.9, 11) are usually included in the *Garland of Sulpicia* rather than attributed to Sulpicia herself.
11. The first of March, the date of the Matronalia, a women's festival.

28. Philinna (*1st century* BC *or earlier*)

Introduction

Philinna is named as the author of a incantation to cure a headache. Her short poem is in hexameters, and has been preserved with the incantation of a Syrian woman (whose name has been lost) and at least one other incantation in a papyrus from Graeco-Roman Egypt. The papyrus has been dated to the first century BC, but the date of the charms themselves can only be broadly defined from the poetry as Hellenistic.[1]

In Greece, witches were usually thought of as foreign, and Thessaly was apparently far enough away from civilisation to be a suitable location for a witch (Ar., *Clouds* 749). Philinna was a typical woman's name (*Clouds* 684). Hence we cannot be sure that Philinna the Thessalian is not a pseudonym, invented to reassure the reader that the spell comes from an authentic witch. Magic was used in the Graeco-Roman world to create love potions, for prophecy, and to curse as well as to heal. Healing charms were used at least as early as Homer: the sons of Autolycus apply firstaid to Odysseus (who has been injured by a boar) with an incantation to stop the bleeding (*Odyssey* 19.457). As a later example, Marcus Porcius Cato offers a magical cure for a fracture (*Agriculture* 160). The command for illness to flee is common in charms.[2]

Philinna

Incantation of Philinna the Thessalian for a headache:

Flee, pain of the head, flee and perish beneath a rock.
Wolves flee, hoofed horses flee, hurrying
beneath the blows of my perfect incantation.

Notes

1. See B.P. Grenfell and A.S. Hunt (eds), *The Amherst Papyri*, II (London: Henry Frowde, 1901); P. Maas, 'The Philinna Papyrus', *Journal of Hellenic Studies* 62 (1942), 33-38; A. Henrichs, 'Zum Text einiger Zauberpapyri', *Zeitschrift für Papyrologie und Epigraphik* 6 (1970), 204-209; R.H. Pack, *The Greek and Latin Literary Texts from Greco-Roman Egypt* (Ann Arbor: University of Michigan Press, 1965). For the Syrian woman's text, see Syra below.
2. See Maas, 'The Philinna Papyrus', 38. Theocritus, *Idyll* 2 and Horace, *Epode* 5 provide good examples of the love-spell as a literary subject; see also Xenophon, *Memorabilia* 3.11.16-17. For examples of curses, see M.R. Lefkowitz and M.B. Fant, *Women's Life in Greece and Rome: A Source Book in Translation* (2nd edn; Baltimore: John Hopkins University Press, 1992), 296-98. For further examples in this collection, see Syra, and Eudocia's *Martyrdom of St Cyprian and St Justa*. For further reading on magic see H.D. Betz, *The Greek Magical Papyri in Translation*, I (Chicago:

University of Chicago Press, 1986); C.A. Faraone and D. Obbink (eds), *Magika Hiera: Ancient Greek Magic and Religion* (Oxford: Oxford University Press, 1991); G. Luck, *Arcana Mundi: Magic and the Occult in the Greek and Roman Worlds* (Baltimore: John Hopkins University Press, 1985); and M. Dickie, *Magic and Magicans in the Greco-Roman World* (London and New York: Routledge, 2001).

29. Syra (The Syrian Woman) (*1st century BC or earlier*)

Introduction

On the same Egyptian papyrus as the incantation by Philinna of Thessaly is an incantation attributed to a Syrian woman ('Syra') whose name has been lost from the damaged manuscript. Syria was seen as the sort of foreign place that a witch might come from (Theocritus, *Idyll* 2.162) and so would have been attractive to a writer who wanted to invent a convincing persona for the author of this charm.

This incantation is for fever. The papyrus has been dated to the first century BC,[1] and includes the ending of another incantation, as well as those by Philinna and the Syrian. It is interesting that incantations attributed to (at least) two different women are reproduced in this manuscript. Each author may have published work elsewhere which was drawn upon by the compiler of this text, for there is evidence for wider distribution of this charm. Maas has published a different version of this incantation, discovered in a papyrus from Oxyrhynchus dated to the fourth century AD. This later text also provides evidence for the longevity of the Syrian woman's charm in Hellenistic Egypt.[2] The incantation tells a short narrative in which a fever is miraculously cured. The number seven is prominent, as are animals and virgin girls. The story appears to be an historiola, a mythical story in which the actions of the seven maidens in putting out a great fire are analogous to the purpose of the charm in curing a fever.[3] There is, however, no known Greek myth in which seven maidens quench a fire.

Syra

Incantation of [...] the Syrian woman from Gadara, for every fever
A child initiated in the mysteries of the most holy goddess was burnt with fever,
and was burnt with fever on the highest mountain; and the fire gobbled up
the springs of seven wolves, of seven bears, of seven lions.
And seven dark-eyed virgins drew water
to their dark bosoms and carried away the unquenchable fire.

Notes

1. See B.P. Grenfell and A.S. Hunt (eds), *The Amherst Papyri*, II (London: Henry Frowde, 1901); P. Maas, 'The Philinna Papyrus', *Journal of Hellenic Studies* 62 (1942), 33-38; A. Henrichs, 'Zum Text einiger Zauberpapyri', *Zeitschrift für Papyrologie und Epigraphik* 6 (1970), 204-209; R.H. Pack, *The Greek and Latin Literary Texts from Greco-Roman Egypt* (Ann Arbor: University of Michigan Press, 1965).
2. A discovery made by Lobel: see Maas, 'The Philinna Papyrus', 36.
3. Ibid, 37, claims this is the earliest example of a historiola in Greek or Latin charms.

30. Salpe (before AD 79)

Introduction

Pliny the Elder is perhaps more famous for his nephew's account of his death in AD 79 during the eruption of Vesuvius than for his own work. Yet his *Natural History* provides a remarkable testimony to both learned knowledge and some of the popular beliefs of the Romans about their natural world. He describes medicines that were used for a wide range of ailments, from the common cold to witchcraft, and he quotes from various medical texts that were available to him. One of these was by Salpe. Pliny describes her as an *obstetrix* or midwife. Her name is Greek (it was the name of a fish, Athen. 7.321d-322a). All we have of her work is Pliny's paraphrase of six remedies.

Athenaeus tells us that a Salpe who came from Lesbos was the writer of *paignia* or 'frivolous works' (Athen. 7.322a). It is possible that the *obstetrix* and this Salpe were one and the same. However, as these *paignia* were, evidently, similar to the work of a certain Botrys whose work was elsewhere deemed similar to the pornographic work of Philaenis,[1] we should distinguish them from the medical works here and so also distinguish Salpe the *obstetrix* from her namesake.[2]

The scope of work goes beyond what we might expect of a treatise by a midwife. The fragments we have include remedies for sunburn, stiffness, dog bites and sore eyes, as well as an aphrodisiac, a depilatory cream and a way to stop a dog barking. The mix in Salpe's work of herbal cure and belief in the magical potency of certain substances is typical of Graeco-Roman folk medicine.[3]

The fragments of her work in Pliny are indirect: the original is reported rather than quoted directly, and would have been in Greek, rather than Pliny's Latin. Pliny introduces each remedy with 'Salpe tells us that...' or words to that effect, which I have omitted from the translations below. The same is true of the citations of the other medical writers in Pliny: Olympias, Sotira, Laïs and Elephantis. I have added the headings from the context Pliny supplies.

Saliva is the key ingredient in the first remedy. Pliny tells us that human saliva was particularly potent and could be used against both natural and unnatural attacks. It could safeguard against snakes and ward off witchcraft and the bad luck which occurs upon meeting someone who is lame in the right leg (Pliny 28.35-39). Spitting into the bosom was also practised as an act of contrition to ask forgiveness of the gods for expressing a hope or wish that was too presumptuous (Pliny 28.35-36).

Urine is the second key ingredient. Like saliva, it was believed that urine had both natural and supernatural powers. The urine of eunuchs, for example, could counteract infertility spells (Pliny 28.65). Urine was also used to treat babies' sores, gout, skin irritations and dog bites, amongst other things (Pliny 28. 67). Scribes used it to take out ink blots (Pliny 28.66). It is acid and has some antiseptic qualities.

Both Laïs and Salpe agreed on the third remedy, which harnessed one of the magic powers in menstrual fluid (see Pliny 28.77-86). Ordinary medicines, Pliny notes, were useless against malaria, in both its forms, the milder ('quartana': onset after intervals of two days) and the more severe ('tertiana': onset every other day), and so magic remedies and amulets were recommended (see Pliny 30.98-104).

The fourth recipe is for an aphrodisiac: let us hope the donkey was no longer attached at the time! Pliny reports other aphrodisiacs which include the application or drinking of fluids from horses, asses, bulls or boars, in particular, the fluids produced during or after the animals have copulated. Powdered testes from these animals were also considered efficacious. The relative size of the animals, especially their genitalia, inspired such recipes; a mouse's dung could be used as an antaphrodisiac (Pliny 28.262).

Pliny also gives us Salpe's recipe for a depilation cream, and he tells us that she used it to smarten up boys for the slave market. The Greeks and Romans generally found body hair unattractive and considered the clean-shaven look a sign of civilisation, as well as youth and beauty. While depilation was normal for women, it was not unknown among men, though it could bring accusations of effeminacy. Depilation was particularly seen as way to increase sexual attractiveness. Salpe's advice was probably for the preparation and presentation of boys to be sold into prostitution.

Salpe

1. The Efficacy of Saliva
Stiffness is removed from any numbed limb if you spit into your bosom or if the upper eyelids are touched with saliva.

2. The Efficacy of Urine
Bathe the eyes with urine to strengthen them. Apply mixed with an egg-white to sun-burn for two hours; an ostrich egg works best.

3. The Efficacy of Menstrual Fluid (also attributed to Laïs)
The bite of a mad dog, and a tertian and a quartan malaria, are cured by menstrual fluid on wool from a black ram enclosed in a silver bracelet.

4. An Aphrodisiac
Dunk a donkey's genital organ into hot oil seven times; the appropriate parts of your body should then be anointed with the oil.

5. Depilation
A depilation cream is: the blood, gall and liver of a tunny fish, either fresh or preserved (even the liver), ground up and mixed with cedar oil, and kept in a lead box.

6. Dogs that Bark
Dogs who have a live frog put in with their meat do not bark.

Notes

1.   Polybius 12.13 = Timaeus *FGH* 566 T2.
2.   See D. Bain, 'Salpe's *ΠΑΙΓΝΙΑ*: Athenaeus 322A and Plin. H.N. 28.38', *Classical Quarterly* 48.2

(1997), 262-68. For the opposite view, see J.N. Davidson, 'Don't try this at home: Pliny's Salpe, Salpe's *Paignia* and magic', *Classical Quarterly* 45 (1995), 590-92.

3.   See W.G. Spencer (ed.), *Celsus De Medicina*, II (Cambridge: Harvard University Press, MA, 1977), xiii-xiv, for a brief outline of Graeco-Roman folk medicine. For comments on the therapeutic nature of some Graeco-Roman remedies in Pliny see J. Stannard, 'Medical Plants and folk remedies in Pliny, *'Historia Naturalis'*, *History and Philosophy of the Life Sciences* 4 (1982), 3-23.

31. Elephantis (fl. late 1st century BC)

Introduction

Elephantis was also known as Elephantine. She was the author of erotica popular at the end of the first century BC. Martial suggests that she wrote some sort of licentious sex manual in verse (12.43.4)[1], and according to Suetonius, the emperor Tiberius was a fan of her work (*Tiberius* 43.2). Along with the subject of sex, work attributed to her included other women's business: cosmetics (Galen 12.416) and abortives (Pliny 28.81). It is likely that other writers used her name to publish pseudonymously works thought to be within the provenance of a woman who wrote about sex.[2] Her name may reflect the name of the place this literary figure claimed to have come from: Elephantine, a town on an island below the first cataract of the Nile.

This medicine is based upon the belief in the magic powers of menstrual fluid. The reasons for menstruation were not known and there was a great deal of speculation about it. It was accorded great power, including the ability to drive away storms, but often the effects of it were thought to be harmful (Pliny 28.77-86; 7.64). Ancient remedies could, as Pliny finds, be contradictory. Elephantis suggests here that menstrual fluid could cause sterility and act as an abortive, against the view of Laïs (see also Sotira 1).

Elephantis

The Efficacy of Menstrual Fluid[3]
Laïs and Elephantis give contrary opinions about abortives: burning coal from the root of the cabbage, myrtle or tamarisk, put out by menstrual blood, and that donkeys do not conceive for as many years as grains of barley they have eaten contaminated with menstrual blood, and in the other monstrous and strange things which they pronounce in contradiction to each other, the former says that fertility is caused by the same things that the latter says causes sterility.

Notes

1. See also *Suda* s.v. Astyanassa.
2. For further discussion of erotica, see Philaenis. For prostitutes in antiquity see S.B. Pomeroy, *Goddesses, Whores, Wives and Slaves: Women in Classical Antiquity* (New York: Schocken Books, 1975), and A. Richlin (ed.), *Pornography and Representation in Greece and Rome* (Oxford: Oxford University Press, 1992).
3. This fragment is the same text as Laïs 1. For further discussion of this type of remedy, see Salpe.

32. Laïs (before AD 79)

Introduction

Laïs was the name of one of the most famous prostitutes of the ancient world. She was a native of Hyccara in Sicily. In 416 BC when she was still a girl, the Athenians sacked her city, captured her and sold her into slavery in Corinth (Plut., *Nicias* 15.4).[1] She became renowned, and was alluded to in later Greek poetry as a personification of a beautiful woman and object of love.[2] In an anecdote told by Athenaeus, Laïs appears as a clever philosopher in the company of the tragedian Euripides. She challenges Euripides on the concept of moral relativism, using a sophistic argument that turns on the meaning of the Greek word *aischropoios* (which could mean 'evildoer' or 'fellatrix/fellator') quoting words from two of his own plays back at him to make her point.[3]

Pliny had access to a work attributed to a Laïs and refers to it twice. We have too little evidence to judge its authenticity or even its main subject, but it is as likely to be by someone purporting to be Laïs as by Laïs herself (there is no record of the original Laïs writing anything). The name however gives a clue as to the content: Laïs was such a famous prostitute, that a work attributed to someone with that name would have implied that it was the work of a prostitute. Pliny makes a comparison between her opinion and the opinion of Elephantis, a woman well known as an author of erotica. Perhaps the works were of a similar nature.[4]

The two passages from her work which Pliny read for us both deal with the power of menstrual fluid, one with a dispute about whether menstrual fluid acts as an abortive or an aid to fertility. Laïs apparently viewed it as a power for fertility and a magic cure for malaria and rabies. The reasons for menstruation were not known and there was a great deal of speculation about it. It was accorded great power, including the ability to drive away storms, but often the effects of it were thought to be harmful (Pliny 28.77-86, 7.64). Laïs suggests that menstrual fluid could be beneficial in medicine (see also Sotira 1). Ancient remedies could, as Pliny finds, be contradictory.[5]

Laïs

1. The Efficacy of Menstrual Fluid[6]
Laïs and Elephantis give contrary opinions about abortives: burning coal from the root of the cabbage, myrtle or tamarisk, put out by menstrual blood, and that donkeys do not conceive for as many years as grains of barley they have eaten contaminated with menstrual blood, and in the other monstrous and strange things which they pronounce in contradiction to each other, the former says that fertility is caused by the same things that the latter says causes sterility.

2. The Efficacy of Menstrual Fluid[7]
The bite of a mad dog, and a tertian and a quartan malaria, are cured by menstrual fluid on wool from a black ram enclosed in a silver bracelet.

Notes

1. She is included in the *Suda*'s list of famous *hetaerae* (s.v. *hetaerae*). Many anecdotes were written about her in Greek comedy: see Athenaeus 13.570b-e, 574e, 582c-d, 586e, 587d-e, 588c-589b, 592d, 599b. Her daughter Timandra was also a famous *hetaera*; see Plut., *Alcibiades* 39.4.
2. See *Anth. Pal.* 6.1, 18, 19, 71, 7.218, 219, 222, 229, 9.260.
3. Athenaeus 582c-d; on this see D.M. O'Higgins, 'Women's cultic joking and mockery: some perspectives', in A. Lardinois and L. McClure (eds), *Making Silence Speak* (Princeton: Princeton University Press, 2002), 158-59. For the prostitute as philosopher, see Aspasia and cf. Gnathaena (Athenaeus 13.58b).
4. See Elephantis and Philaenis.
5. For a discussion of remedies in Pliny, see Salpe.
6. This fragment is also attributed to Elephantis.
7. This remedy was also attributed to Salpe: see Salpe 3 and discussion there.

33. Olympias (before AD 79)

Introduction

Olympias of Thebes was an important source for Pliny's *Natural History*, books 20–28,[1] though he cites her opinions explicitly only three times.[2] His use of her work for this section of his *Natural History* indicates she published many medicines from plant and animal products. Olympias' concern with birth and the treatment of women probably marks her out as an *obstetrix* (midwife). Pliny credits Olympias with an addition to an established remedy. His testimony shows how the name of the creator of a remedy was important, giving the reader an authority on which to judge the quality and effectiveness of the treatment. Recent research has demonstrated that Graeco-Roman herbal medicine could provide women with effective contraceptives and abortifacients,[3] but the treatments which were available were of variable quality.

Olympias

1. An improved remedy
Women's purgings are helped by bull's gall applied on natural wool. Olympias of Thebes added oesypum and sodium.[4]

2. A fertility ointment
It is certain that sterility may result from suffering at childbirth. This is cured by the area being anointed before intercourse with bull's gall and snakes' fat and copper-rust and honey.

3. An abortive
Mallows with goose fat cause abortion.

Notes

1. See Pliny 1.20-28.
2. Pliny 28.246, 28.253, 20.226. For a general discussion of Pliny's use of texts by midwives, see Salpe.
3. See J.M. Riddle, 'Oral contraceptives and early term abortifacients during Classical Antiquity and the Middle Ages', *Past and Present* 132 (1992), 3-32; and *Contraception and Abortion from the Ancient World to the Renaissance* (Cambridge, MA: Harvard University Press, 1992).
4. Oesypum (sometimes called suint) was the greasy, sweaty wool from the parts of a sheep's forelegs or flanks that were not exposed to the sun. It would have contained extra lanolin. For its preparation and effectiveness, see Pliny 29.35-37.

34. Sotira (before AD 79)

Introduction

Sotira is identified by Pliny the Elder as a midwife (*obstetrix*), but she is otherwise unknown.[1] Her name is Greek and so presumably was she. 'Sotira' means a 'saviour'; she may have adopted this as a professional name. She evidently published magic cures for malaria and epilepsy which relied on the medicinal power of menstrual fluid. The text includes instruction for the application of the remedy. The magical properties of the menstrual fluid extended beyond the fluid itself—the menstruating woman was thought to increase the potency of this medicine if she applied it herself. Salpe and Laïs also offered a cure for malaria using menstrual fluid (see Salpe 3). The use of similar ingredients in these remedies (and others) suggests that midwives had access to a common body of traditional and published knowledge thought reliable, which led to some consistency in treatment.[2]

Sotira

The Efficacy of Menstrual Fluid
To anoint the soles of the patient's feet with menstrual fluid is a most efficacious cure for tertian and quartan malaria;[3] it is much more effective if it is done by the woman herself without the patient's knowledge. The same remedy also awakens an epileptic.

Notes

1. Pliny 28.83.
2. For a discussion of medical texts in Pliny, see Salpe.
3. I.e. malaria with onset after intervals of one or two days respectively.

35. Timaris (before AD 79)

Introduction

All of the poetry of Timaris has been lost. We know of her and her work from Pliny the Elder, who calls her a queen (*regina*). There were many Greek monarchies in the Hellenistic world, and she probably belonged to one of those (as Julia Balbilla could claim to). Pliny tells us she wrote on *paneros,* a Greek word meaning 'all-love' (*Natural History* 37.178). Timaris' lyric poetry or song (Pliny calls it a *carmen*) was no doubt in Greek and, appropriately for this subject, was addressed to the goddess of love—probably the Greek Aphrodite rather than the Roman Venus. The chance reference to her work shows that a scholar like Pliny, writing in the first century AD, knew a great deal of published literature which is now lost, some of which had been written by women.[1]

Timaris (*reported by Pliny*)

Hymn to Venus (Aphrodite?)
Meterodorus does not state what the nature of paneros is, but a song of queen Timaris on it, addressed to Venus, puts it elegantly, leading us to understand that it is an aid to fertility.

Notes

1. For the ridicule of women poets—further testimony to their existence—see Lucian, *On Salaried Posts in Great Houses* 36; Persius, *Prologue* 13.

36. Sulpicia II (*1st century* AD)

Introduction

The modern impression of Sulpicia II's poetry is largely derived from her appearance in two epigrams by her contemporary Martial. He characterises her work as a celebration of both chastity and sexual love, an unusual combination. Her erotic verse, he tells us, was directed towards her love of her husband Calenus (*Satires* 10.35, 38), and the one fragment of her poetry which remains appears to support this observation. Other testimonia demonstrate her popularity and readership: Ausonius ranked her alongside Plato and Juvenal (*Wedding Cento* 139.5-6); Sidonius Apollinaris noted her wit (*Songs* 9.261-2), and Fulgentius that she was shameless (*Myth* 1.4). She was sufficiently well known and respected in the fourth and fifth centuries for a pseudonymous poem to be written in her name. This poem, the *Sulpicia conquestio*, is a denunciation of the rule of Domitian.[1] It provides testimony to the respectability of the authorial persona created by Sulpicia in her poetry.

The two line fragment of her poetry which remains was quoted by Probus, a scholiast on Juvenal, in a manuscript which is now lost, but was in turn quoted by Giorgio Valla of Piacenza (about 1430–99).[2] The fragment comes with no context, but the expression of eroticism is clear, as is the boldness of the celebration of sexual satisfaction—a motif found in male writers of this era, but surprising in a female writer living at a time when women were expected to be more modest.[3]

The anonymous satire which purports to be by Sulpicia cannot be by her. Some of the vocabulary postdates Sulpicia, and the poem is critical of Domitian, unlike literature in his day. The poet benefits from hindsight to predict the end of Domitian's reign. The poem appears to have been written by someone who knew Sulpicia's work, and as such provides evidence for what is now lost; it contains motifs which enable her work to be recognised (such as Calenus, Numa and Egeria[4]) and details the poetic metres she used.[5] It is best dated to the end of the fourth or beginning of the fifth centuries AD, the date of the Bobbio collection in which it was found.[6]

Sulpicia II

1.

...

if, after the bed-straps for my mattress have been replaced,
[it] might reveal me naked lying in bed with Calenus

2. {SULPICIA II}

'O Muse, in the metre in which you celebrate heroes and arms,
Allow me to weave my story in few words.
For I have withdrawn to you, with you revising my inmost
plan. So I neither run with Phalaecus' song,

nor with Iambic trimeter, nor that same metre with its broken foot   5
which with its guide from Clazomenae learnt to be very angry.
Indeed all other gentle metres I have played
(and I first taught Roman women to compete with the Greeks
and offer variety with new wit), I uniformly abandon,
and I approach you, most eloquent leader, in what you are   10
well-versed: come down and hear your dependant's prayer.

Tell me, Calliope, what does *the* father of the gods
have in mind? Does he transform the earth to his father's age
and snatch away as we die the arts he once gave?
Does he order us, silent and now lacking reason,   15
just as when at first we arose from the soil,
to sink down again for acorns and the pure spring water?
Or does he look after all other lands and cities as a friend,
but expel the race of Ausonia and the foster-children of Romulus?
Why? Let us think: there are two ways by which Rome   20
raised its mighty head: courage in war and wisdom in peace.
But courage was set in motion at home and sprang with allies'
arms into the straits of Sicily and the citadels of Carthage,
and carried away all other empires as well and the whole world.
Then just as the victor, alone on an Achaean racing track,   25
is weary and with courage unmoved little by little becomes exhausted,
just so does the Roman force, when it ceased struggling
and bridled peace with long reins,
and revising at home the laws and Greek discoveries,
it began to rule every prize gained in war   30
by land and sea with policy and gentle reason.
By this it stood (nor could it have continued to stand without it);
or Jupiter would have been proved deceitful and to have said
once to Venus in vain, 'I have given them empire without end'.
Therefore now, the man who rules among the Romans as king,   35
falling forward onto his back, not his beam, and white in his maw,
has he ordered all studies and the wise name and race of men
to go outside and leave the city?
What villainy! We sought the cities of Greece and Ionia
so that Roman youth would be better taught by these teachers.   40
Now just as the Gauls abandoned their wealth and scales and fled
when Capitoline Camillus threw them into a panic,
so our old men are forced to wander off and
carry away their own books like some deadly burden.
Therefore, Scipio Numantius and Libycus erred, in that   45
he thrived moulded by a Rhodian teacher?
And that other force in the second war, which was fluent in speech?
Among whom the divine opinion of Priscus Cato
held it to be of great importance to know whether Roman
offspring would stand better through prosperity or adversity.   50
By adversity, no doubt! For when love of their homeland
urges them to protect

themselves with arms, and their wife is captured, along with the Penates,
(just like when a beehive on the top of Matinus is disturbed by wasps
and a fierce swarm rushes together protecting the king
with the bristling stings along their golden bodies);
but when a safe situation returns, forgetting their labour   55
the common people and the fathers pass away together in a fat sleep.
Therefore a long and venerable peace has been the ruin
of the offspring of Romulus.

Here the story ends. Henceforth, most kind Muse,
without whom I have no enjoyment in living, please warn them
that as once when Smyrna was destroyed by the Lydians,   60
now again is it pleasing to you to emigrate? Or anything else
you want to demand, goddess: only, turn Calenus from the walls
of Rome and equally from Sabine pleasures.'

That is what I said; then the goddess deigns to address
me briefly and begins,
'Put aside your cruel fears, my attendant. See, the greatest of   65
hatreds are upon the tyrant and he is going to perish to our glory.
For we inhabit the laurel trees of Numa and the same springs
and with Egeria as our companion we laugh at all empty undertakings.
Live on! Farewell! Its fame awaits this beautiful grief;
the chorus of Muses promises, and Roman Apollo.'   70

Notes

1.   *Epigrammata Bobiensia* 70: see A. Giordano-Rampioni (ed.), *Sulpiciae Conquestio* (Bologna: Pàtron, 1982).
2.   H.N. Parker, 'Other remarks on the other Sulpicia', *Classical World* 86.2 (1992), 89.
3.   For condemnation of a woman who demonstrated male vices, see Sallust, *Conspiracy of Catiline* 25 on Sempronia. On the oddity of a woman working in this genre in Rome at this time, see A. Richlin, 'Sulpicia the satirist', *Classical World* 86.2 (1992), 125-39 (137-39). For Sulpicia's 'feminist gesture', see J.P. Hallet, 'Martial's Sulpicia and Propertius' Cynthia', *Classical World* 86.2 (1992), 99-123 (121), and further, 'Martial's Sulpicia and Propertius' Cynthia', in M. DeForest (ed.), *Woman's Power, Man's Game: Essays in Honour of Joy King* (Chicago, 1993), 322-52.
4.   Cf. Martial 10.35.13.
5.   See Richlin, 'Sulpicia the satirist', 132-34.
6.   H.E. Butler, *Post-Augustan Poetry: From Seneca to Juvenal* (Oxford: Clarendon Press, 1909), 178-79, defends the genuineness of Sulpicia's satire, as does J.L. Butrica, 'Sulpicia's complaint: on the state of the nation and the age of Domitian', *Diotima* (2000): http://www.stoa.org/diotima/ anthology/complaint.shtml. Butrica also discusses problems with the manuscript and offers some different readings (with a translation).

37. Pamphila (*fl. mid-1st century* AD)

Introduction

Eleven fragments of Pamphila's *Historical Commentaries* were paraphrased by other authors in antiquity (Diogenes Laertius, Aulus Gellius and Photius) and these are now all that remain of the original 33 books. Nothing remains of an epitome of Ctesias' work in three books, other historical epitomes and the many other prose works which she is believed to have written. Her attested work includes a collection of apophthegms, lectures, debates and discussions of poetry.[1] According to the *Suda* a work on sex was also attributed to her.

Pamphila lived in the first century AD, and Photius suggests that she was a mature woman during the reign of Nero (AD 54–68). Photius also notes that her family came from Egypt, a centre for learning in the Hellenistic world, though the *Suda* states that both she and her father Soterides were Epidaurian. Pamphila was a polymath, specialising in epitomes of prose works. She must have had access to a substantial library, though she evidently attributed her learning to her husband Socratides (fragment 11). It may have been a misreading of this prologue, along with the widespread misogynistic view of women writers in Greek society, that led to the attribution of her work by some ancient commentators to her father or husband.

Photius offers an evaluation of her prose style, deeming it simple and thus appropriate to her sex. The fragments that remain offer no opportunity for us to judge her words for ourselves, as they have been filtered through the media in which they are reported. She characterised her work as *poikilia*, a tapestry, weaving together many different genres and not adopting a single source, particularly in her descriptions of the more distant past. She defends this approach to prose in the prologue to her *Historical Commentaries* (fragment 11), arguing that it makes her work more enjoyable to read, anticipating criticism (or perhaps replying to criticism of an earlier work) of her style. In this respect her work appears to have been similar to the *Attic Nights* of Aulus Gellius. The content which remains reveals an interest in the history of philosophy and biography. Fragments 1 to 6, 8 and 10 offer biographical notes on famous Greek philosophers,[2] fragment 7 biographical notes on early Greek historians, and fragment 9 an anecdote about an infamous Athenian politician, Alcibiades.

Pamphila

Historical Commentaries (Retold)

1.

Pamphila says that Thales, after learning geometry from the Egyptians, was the first man to inscribe a right-angled triangle inside a circle, and that he then sacrificed an ox.

2.

Chilon said to his brother, who was unhappy that he had not been made ephor although Chilon had, 'I know how to act when wronged, but you do not'. Chilon became ephor in the 55th Olympiad; Pamphila, however, says that it was in the 56th Olympiad.

3.

In the second book of her *Commentaries* Pamphila says that a bronze-smith attacked Pittacus' son Tyrraeus with an axe while he was sitting in a barber's shop in Cumae and killed him. But when the people of Cumae sent the murderer to Pittacus and he learned what had happened, he set him free and said, 'Forgiveness is better than repentance.'

4.

In the *Commentaries* of Pamphila is this riddle of Cleobulus:
There is one father, twelve sons. Each one
has twice thirty daughters, who have two different looks,
some are white to see, yet others are black;
although they are immortal, they all die too.

The answer is: the year.

5.

Sotion, Heraclides, and Pamphila in Book 5 of her *Commentaries* say that there were two Perianders, one the tyrant, while the other was the sage, and he was Ambracian. Neanthes of Cyzicus agrees with this, and adds that they were related to each other. Aristotle says that the sage was the Corinthian, but Plato denies this.

6.

Socrates was independent and dignified. Pamphila says in Book 7 of her *Commentaries* that once, when Alcibiades gave him a large block of land to build a house on, he said, 'If I needed shoes and you gave me a whole hide to make my shoes with, if I took it I would look ridiculous'.

7.

Hellanicus, Herodotus and Thucydides, writers of history, flourished to great acclaim at almost the same time, and were very close in age. For Hellanicus appears to have been 65 years old at the start of the Peloponnesian war, Herodotus 53, and Thucydides 40. This is recorded in Book 11 of Pamphila.

8.

Pamphila, in Book 25 of her *Commentaries*, says that the Arcadians and Thebans, when founding the city of Megalopolis, invited Plato to draw up their laws, but that he refused when he learnt that they were not willing to have equality.

9.

When he was a boy, Alcibiades the Athenian was trained in the liberal arts and sciences in the house of his uncle, Pericles. Pericles ordered Antigenides, a flute-player, to be summoned, to teach Alcibiades to play the flute, which at that time was considered a most honourable pursuit. But when he was given the flute, put it to his lips and blew, Alcibiades was embarrassed by the distortion of his face and threw it away, breaking it. When news of this event had spread, by agreement of all Athenians of that time, the art of playing the flute was given up for good. This story is written in Book 29 of Pamphila's *Commentaries*.

10.

Theophrastus was a man of remarkable intelligence and industry, and, as Pamphila says in Book 32 of her *Commentaries*, he taught the comic poet Menander.

11.

Pamphila lived with her husband, as she herself noted carefully in the preface to her *Commentaries*. She says that she began this historical work after living with him from childhood for thirteen years, and that she wrote what she learnt from her husband, not leaving his side for a day nor even an hour, staying with him without break for thirteen years. She also wrote what she happened to hear from any of his visitors (for many people came to learn from him, as he had a very good name for his teaching) and in addition what she collected from books. She combined as much of this material into her *Commentaries* as she thought worthy of note and preservation, not dividing up each piece along the lines of its original design, but writing up each one at random, as she came across it. This was not, as she says, because she found it difficult to divide the material according to genre, but because she considered a mixture, an embroidery, more delightful and more enjoyable than material of only one genre.

Notes

1. See Photius, *Library* cod. 175, 119; Bekk., *Suda* s.v. Pamphila: C. Müller, *Fragmenta Historicorum Graecorum*, III (Paris: A. Firmin Didot, 1849), 520.
2. For the seven Greek 'Sages', see, for example, Plut., *Moralia* 146b-64d. Cleobulus (fragment 4) was the father of Cleobulina who was also remembered for her riddles (see above).

38. Maria (*fl. 1st century AD or earlier*)

Introduction

Maria is one of the most famous alchemists. Post-Medieval alchemy treated her work with great respect. She was regarded by some as the sister of Moses—a title she is given in a Latin text (see 6 below)—though this legend was questioned as early as 1617 by Meier.[1] Her work survives in fragments. She was quoted extensively by Zosimus of Panopolis, who probably lived in Alexandria in the third or fourth centuries AD. He regarded Maria as the first of the ancient authors, and so she probably lived no later than the first century AD. Fragment 5 below shows that she revealed her Jewishness in her writing. Zosimus believed that Jews had special knowledge of alchemy, a belief perhaps derived from her work which he treats with great respect. She is also cited by Olympiodorus, an Alexandrian historian and alchemist who wrote in the early fifth century. Arab alchemists used her work too, translating the Hellenistic Greek sources.[2]

Maria is particularly remembered for her practical writing on apparatus. She described many different types of ovens and equipment made of clay, metal and glass for heating and distilling, including types of still, such as the *kerotakis* and the *tribikos*. Her most famous piece of apparatus is the bain-marie, which was named after her.[3] It has been argued that she did not actually invent the bain-marie—perhaps she described it or improved the design—but nevertheless her work on apparatus was authoritative and linked her name for ever to this water-bath heater.[4]

The manufacture of gold alloy, called by the Greek alchemists a *doubling* (*diplōsis*), is referred to in fragment 2. This gold-copper alloy, perhaps with a small quantity of zinc and arsenic, would produce a quite acceptable gold alloy, just as we use 9-18 carat gold alloys today. Other formulae sought to produce gold-coloured metals, such as brass-like alloys of copper, tin, lead, zinc and other metals. Though cheaper to produce, the results would be less satisfactory in weight and colour. The alloy processes described are complicated, revealing the chemistry involved was not understood. Lack of pure ingredients complicated the process and made results less certain. Zinc was important to the gold alloy as it provided the yellow colour, but was unknown to Greek alchemists and had to be produced through cadmia, an impure zinc oxide found in the flues of smelting furnaces.[5]

Fragment 1 gives a glimpse of the philosophy which underpinned her work. Maria takes it for granted that all substances are basically the one, an alchemical doctrine apparently favoured by Alexandrian alchemists including Cleopatra.[6] Maria claims that her knowledge of the mysteries of alchemy was revealed to her by God (e.g. fragment 4).

One piece of apparatus used to unify separate bodies and so create the desired substance (e.g. gold or silver), or at least its colour in a metal, was the *kerotakis*, a type of still. Originally the word referred to an artist's palette, which had to be kept warm over a pot of charcoal as artists painted with a mixture of pigment and wax. Maria would warm base metals, copper, silver or even gold with pigments in compounds and other substances to change the colour of the base metal. A substance such as a sulphur or sulphurated arsenic would be vaporised in a vessel below the metal in the *kerotakis*, while an inverted bowl above would condensed the vapour into a liquid. Maria would heat the metal to de-sulphurise it and then smelt it, and repeat the process with different compounds including cadmia. The process could produce golden coloured alloys. Figure 2 below is an illustration of the simple *kerotakis* from a Greek alchemical manuscript. A more complicated still called the *tribikos* was attributed to Maria: it is described in fragment 8 and illustrated in figure 1. In the fullest account of one of Maria's alchemical processes, she uses a small white herb as a key ingredient; this may be the Moonwort, which was thought to have many healing and magical qualities.[7]

Zosimus used Maria's work extensively. Indeed, it is often not clear where the fragments of her work which he quotes end and his own words begin. I have provided only a small sample of these many fragments.[8]

Maria

1.
If the two do not become one, that is, if the volatile materials do not combine with the non-volatile, there will be nothing of what is expected—unless it is whitened, and the two become three with the white sulphur, which whitens it. Whenever it is yellowed, the three become four—for it is yellowed through the yellow sulphur. But whenever it is made violet—the all becomes one.

2.
Taking water of sulphur and a little gum put them in the ash-bath. For thus they say the water is fixed. …Taking one part of our copper, one part of gold, make a flat sheet of the metals melted together and put it on the sulphur suspension and leave for three days and nights, until it is hardened.

3.
You will find five parts less one part, clearly because of the [sulphur] evaporating. Likewise (she says) in the process of reduction, and in smelting, at the end of its treatment, copper loses a third of its weight.

4.
Copper heated with sulphur and treated with an emulsion of soda and oil and shaken, after receiving this treatment many times, becomes a superior gold, without shadow….
God said this, 'Everyone knows from experience that burning copper before the sulphur does nothing; but if you burn the sulphur (first), then not only does it make the copper shadowless, but it also comes close to gold.
… And God graciously revealed this to me: first copper is burned with sulphur, then with the body of magnesia; and you insufflate it until the sulphurous materials escape from it with the shadow. And the copper becomes shadowless.

5.
Do not touch the philosopher's stone with your hands; you are not of the race of Abraham. And if you are not of our race…

6.
Excerpts from the dialogue of Maria the Prophetess (the sister of Moses and Aaron) which she held with a certain philosopher named Aros on her most excellent work for three hours.

Take white and red gum, which is the Kybric of the philosophers, and their gold, and marry the gum with the gum, in a true marriage, that is: make it just like running water, and vitrify this divine water, manufactured from two Zaybechs over a fixed body, and liquefy it by the secret of nature in the vessel of philosophy. Keep the fume and be careful that none of it escapes. Ensure that in its capacity the size of your fire is just the same as the heat of the sun in the months of June and July. Stay near the vessel and observe its interior—how it goes black and white and red in less than three hours of the day, and the fume will penetrate the body, and the spirit will be condensed and they will become waxy like milk, both liquefying and penetrating. And this is a closely guarded secret.

Take again the brilliant, honoured, best white herb, which exists on small mountains, and grind it fresh (just as it is at the hour of its birth), and it is the true fixed body which does not disappear when subjected to fire. Indeed, people in their haste do not know of this rule. Next burn or vitrify that Kybric and Zaybech over it, because these are two fumes which complete the two luminaries and project over it the complementary tincture. Grind it all and put it on the fire, and you will see amazing things from it. The rule consists of the timing of the fire. O how amazing the way it is moved from colour to colour in less than the hour I stated! And when it comes to the change to white and red, then extinguish the fire and allow it to cool, and when it becomes cool and is opened, you will find that body pearl-like, brilliant, in the colour of a forest poppy mixed with white, and that it is also waxy, liquefying and penetrating. And its golden colour sets over one thousand thousands and two-hundred thousands.

Take again that brilliant body which grows on small mountains, which does not take putrification or movement, and grind it with the gum Elzarog and with two the two fumes. Because the gum Elzarog is a body which holds, grind it all and it will all liquefy. If you project it over the same fume, it will become like distilling water and when she strikes it will be hardened in air and be one body.

The roots of this work are the two fumes mentioned and humid lime. But the body is fixed from the heart of Saturn which holds the tincture. And its compare is the brilliant white body of the small mountains. The vessel of Hermes which the Philosophers have hidden is not the vessel of the necromancers, but is the capacity of your fire.

7.

The divine water will be taken away for those who do not know, as has been written, what will be sent up through the pan and the tube to the top. But this is the custom, to call water the sooty vapour of sulphur, both pure and with arsenic; for which you sneered at me, because in the one chapter I have spoken to you about such a great mystery.

This water of sulphur becomes white (whitened through whitening materials), and becomes yellow (yellowed through yellowing materials), and becomes black (blackened through copperas and gallnut), for the blackening of silver and our lead-copper (I have spoken to you previously about lead-copper under the subject of the silver of our forefathers). So the water is blackened and takes hold of our lead-copper and colours it a permanent black, which, although it is nothing, all the initiates long to know greatly. The same water which takes such a process and colours with permanent colour, with the oil and honey removed.

8.

Make three tubes of ductile copper, with the beaten metal the thickness of a pastry-cook's copper frying-pan, but a little thicker, and with a length of one and a half cubits. Make three tubes of this type, and also make a wide tube, one hand wide, with an opening equal to that of the copper vessel. The three tubes should have an opening like the neck of a light flask (or small nail), so that there are a thumb and two fingers attached from either side. Near the bottom of the copper vessel, three holes designed to fit the three tubes, and glued on when fitted, one, unlike the others, above the vapour. After placing the copper vessel on the earthenware pan that holds the sulphur, and smearing joints with a dough-paste, put glass flasks at the end of the tubes, stout, so that they will not break from the heat which comes from the water in the centre. Here is the diagram:

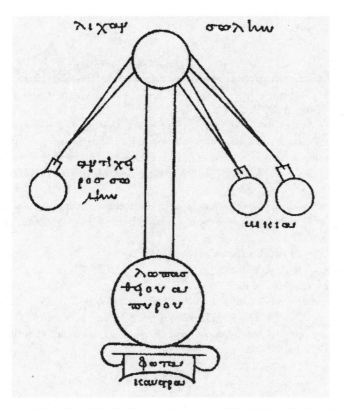

Figure 1. Maria's triple-still (*tribikos*). Venetus Marcianus 299 (*CAG*, 139, fig. 15).

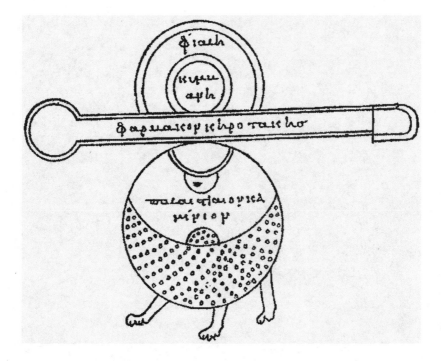

Figure 2. The *kerotakis*. ms. Saint-Marc fol. 195 verso (*CAG* I, 146, fig. 22).

Notes

1. See R. Patai, 'Maria the Jewess: founding mother of alchemy', *Ambix* 29 (1982), 177-97 (190); F.S. Taylor, 'A survey of Greek alchemy', *Journal of Hellenic Studies* 50 (1930), 109-39, and 'The origins of Greek alchemy', *Ambix* 1 (1937–8), 30-47; J. Lindsay, *The Origins of Alchemy in Graeco-Roman Egypt* (London: Muller, 1970), 240-52.

2. For the Arab sources see Patai, 'Maria the Jewess', 184-86. Other female alchemists were Cleopatra (see below), Theosebeia, who collaborated with her brother Zosimus in composing a 28 book encyclopaedia of alchemy (*Suda*), and perhaps Isis, whose female pseudonym indicates she was most likely a woman: *CAG* II.28-33, cf. Lindsay, *The Origins of Alchemy in Graeco-Roman Egypt*, 194-211.

3. Though the term *balneum Mariae* is not attested until the fourteenth century: ibid, 244.

4. See F.S. Taylor, 'The evolution of the still', *Annals of Science* 5:3 (1945); Patai, 'Maria the Jewess', 179.

5. Taylor, 'A survey of Greek alchemy', 128-29, 185-202

6. Patai, 'Maria the Jewess', 182-83.

7. The *Botrychium Lunaria*: see ibid, 189-92.

8. For further reading see *CAG* II.93, 102-103, 146, 149, 151-52, 157-58, 172-73, 182-83, 192-3, 196-97, 198, 200-201, 236-38, 351-52, 356-57, 382, 404. L. Abraham, *Dictionary of Alchemical Imagery* (Cambridge: Cambridge University Press, 1998) is a useful reference work for some of the obscure alchemical terms.

39. Cleopatra (*fl. after* AD 64)

Introduction

Six fragments of Greek prose by Cleopatra survive in the corpus of medical writings that have come down to us from antiquity. Four are said to be from a work called *Cosmetics* and are cited by Galen. The other two fragments, one quoted by Aëtius and the other by Paulus of Aegina, probably came from *Cosmetics* too. Aëtius claims that the author he is quoting is queen Cleopatra, that is, Cleopatra VII Philopator Philopatris. The last and best known of the Macedonian Ptolemy dynasty which ruled Egypt from 323–30 BC, she was renowned for her success at seducing both Julius Caesar and Mark Antony and for her wealth and extravagance.[1] It is this reputation which has caused her name to become attached to a treatise which dealt, amongst other things, with expensive soap. The work also discusses cures for baldness and different weights and measures. It seems unlikely that the queen Cleopatra, a busy political and religious leader, bothered with such matters (even though Julius Caesar was troubled by baldness!). Conclusively, the weight standard which Cleopatra uses dates to AD 64 or later, whereas the famous queen took her own life in 30 BC.[2]

Cleopatra was not an uncommon Greek name. As ancient testimony consistently cites a Cleopatra as the author of *Cosmetics*, we should accept that the author identified herself by that name. The link with queen Cleopatra may have been a late invention; it is made by Aëtius and Tzetes,[3] but not by Galen (even though he discusses the death of the queen Cleopatra elsewhere [14.235-7]), and may not have been claimed by the author herself. Galen implies that she was a physician (12.393, 446). She should be thus identified as Cleopatra the physician to distinguish her from the queen.[4]

Cleopatra wrote *Cosmetics* as a professional manual.[5] She offers advice on the preparation and application of remedies, and gives some instructions for the patient (Cleopatra 2 i, iii). We have enough of Cleopatra's *Cosmetics* to hint at a structure to the work. It appears to have been organised topically, and to offer a number of remedies for each illness (see Cleopatra 3 i-iv), though this organisation may be due to Galen. The remedies were of differing strengths, and it was up to the physician to choose the remedy of the strength appropriate for the severity of the illness (cf. Galen 12.405).

Cleopatra's treatments would have been prefaced by a direction to purge or bleed the patient to provide equilibrium in the four humours. Alopecia and baldness, like other illnesses, were thought to be caused by an imbalance in humours; Galen (12.381) and Paulus (3.1.1) provide discussions (Paulus takes his largely from Galen). Humour theory linked the four 'elements' with four 'humours' in the body: air-blood, water-phlegm, fire-yellow bile, earth-black bile. Drugs were warming or cooling, drying or moistening (in one of four degrees of intensity) and so worked to balance humours in disequilibrium: dryness relating to earth and fire, wetness to air and water, coldness to earth and water, warmness to air and fire. Descriptions of the qualities of the ingredients used in medicines were compiled, establishing the degree to which they dry or moisten, cool or heat, providing a theoretical framework to support the manufacture of remedies.[6] Her topical remedies include antiseptics such as realgar, pitch, turpentine and rose oil.

Testimony to the effectiveness of her remedies is the longevity of her work: the *Cosmetics* was cited by Crito (about the end of the first century); Galen in the early third century; Aëtius of Amida in Alexandria in the mid-sixth century; by Paulus of Aegina in the mid-seventh century, and was known to John Tzetes in the twelfth century.

Cleopatra

Cosmetics

1. For Hair-disease
(i) Take realgar and pound it fine with oak mistletoe. First clean the area as thoroughly as possible with soda, plaster a linen cloth with the mixture and then apply. I also mix soda scum into the aforementioned ingredients and it works very well.
(ii) Another remedy: One drachma of squill, one drachma of white hellebore. Add vinegar and grind until smooth. Smear on after shaving and cleaning the area with soda.
(iii) Another remedy: One drachma of mustard, one drachma of nose-smart. Add vinegar and grind until smooth. Apply after shaving and cleaning the area with soda. It is better if the area is lacerated.
(iv) Another mixture: Four drachmae of reed bark, four drachmae of soda scum. Use with liquid pitch. Shave the area immediately and again as soon as the hair starts to grow, and in addition rub the area with a linen cloth.
(v) Another mixture: Pound up together the heads of mice and rub on.
(vi) Another mixture: Smear on ground-up mouse droppings, after making the area red by rubbing with a cloth.
(vii) Another mixture: Roast bitter almonds along with their shells. Grind together with vinegar and honey. Smear on after making the area red by rubbing. Do this at once and shave the area, and again as soon as the hair comes up.
(viii) Another mixture: This mixture is more powerful than any of the others. Use for hair which is falling out, with olive oil or myrrh added, and it is amazing both for those just starting to lose their hair or for those who have a bald crown. One portion of roasted domestic mice, one portion of roasted vine pannicula, one portion of roasted horse teeth, one portion of bear fat, one portion of marrow from a stag, one portion of reed bark. Grind up the dry ingredients mixed with sufficient honey until you have the consistency of honey. Rub in the fat and the marrow after melting it down and mix. Place the medicine in a bronze box, and apply to the hair-disease, until the hair begins to grow again. Anoint the hair daily in a similar fashion when it comes up.

2. For generating hair on the head
(i) After beating the roots of tender reeds, mix the juice with dried flies in a porridge. Blend bear fat and cedar oil and add to the mixture. Hand over for anointing. To blunt the smell, mix in wine or grape-juice.
(ii) For growing hair: Dry linseed with fine flax, blend with sesame oil and anoint.
(iii) For hair that is sprouting: wet the thickest Cimolian earth with rough wine and as much mulberry juice as you can drink, and add to an oxybaphum of ground henbane. Make the medicine into a round ball and dry in the shade, then place in a new clay vessel. For its use, give instructions to soak in water and anoint. Then when it has dried, wash it off on the fifth day. Do the same thing again. Use it also for skin problems on the face and neck.
(iv) For quickly increasing thickening and darkening hair: blend ladanum with olive oil and sweet wine, and after mixing until thick wash the area and then anoint.
(v) For hair loss without illness: Dried cabbage, ground, with water, and plaster on, or clover root prepared in the same way.

3. *For Dandruff*

(i) Take fine, boiled fenugreek, soaked in the juice of black beet. Wash the head either with the decoction of beet or with Cimolian earth soaked in these things and dissolved. Or anoint the head with ground myrtle and wine mixed with oil, and put beet leaves on the top.

(ii) For the badly ulcerated: 2 drachmae of dried white lead, 2 drachmae of male frankincense, 1 drachma of brimstone. Grind these up and anoint with olive oil.

(iii) For dandruff: 1 drachma each of soda and garden ranunculus. Grind up, pour on olive oil and anoint.

(iv) Also for dandruff: Myrrh and green leaves of white myrtle ground up. Grind them up in olive oil and anoint. Or anoint with dried Cimolian earth mixed with black wine. Or equal parts of white lead and molybdaena; grind up with myrtle and anoint. Or six drachmae of brimstone, 1 drachma of coarse frankincense, 1 drachma each of stone-alum, stavesacre, rocket, and soda scum, 1 drachma of garden ranunculus, and 3 twigs of rue. Grind and add equal measures of vinegar and bay oil, or myrtle oil, or saffron oil or aged olive oil, and make an oily mixture and anoint, after first scrubbing with this soap:

(v) A soap: Take one choinix of hyssop, 2 choinikes of lupine, 1 choinix of barley gruel, 1 choinix of bruised corn, 4 drachmae of wild cucumber root. Grind these up and mix; give it to be smeared on. Make this also for other skin disease and facial pimples.

4. (?) *A Perfumed Soap*

One uncia each of kostos, troglitis myrrh, iris, spikenard, cardamon, dog Mercury, cassia, and rush flower; four librae of myrobalanoi; two librae of soda; chop the ingredients, and sift before using. Apply to the whole body.

5. *To curl and dye the hair*

(i) First shave the head, then anoint the hair with cow-parsnip root in undiluted wine.

(ii) Another mixture: Shave the head and scrub it. Take a new pine-cone and burn it until it becomes ashes. Place it in a mortar and pulverize it, adding myrtle ointment until it becomes the consistency of honey, then anoint the head with it.

(iii) Another mixture: Myrtle and beet in equal quantities; use with oil.

(iv) Another mixture: Grind up twenty galls and 2 drachmae of maiden-hair with sea-water until the consistency of honey. Rub the hair with urine or ashes and wash it with warm water, then anoint with the mixture for two days. On the third day clean it and after shaving anoint with myrtle oil. This makes hair smooth and curly and black, but it will be curlier if you use it after shaving.

6. *About weights and measures*

I. *Weights*

(i) The mina is the name of a weight. It weighs 16 unciae, 128 drachmae, 384 grammata, 768 oboli, 1152 thermi, 2,304 ceratia and 6,144 chalci.

The 'Attic' mina weighs 12 ½ unciae, 100 drachmae, 300 grammata, 600 oboli, 900 thermi, 1,800 ceratia, 4,800 chalci.

The Ptolemaic mina weighs 18 unciae, 144 drachmae, 432 grammata, 864 oboli, 1296 thermi, 2592 ceratia and 6,912 chalci.

(ii) The libra weighs 12 unciae, 96 drachmae, 288 grammata, 576 oboli, 864 thermi, 1728 ceratia, 4,608 chalci.

(iii) The uncia weighs 8 drachmae, 24 grammata, 48 oboli, 72 thermi, 144 ceratia, 384 chalci. The uncia is called the Italian tetrassaron.

(iv) The drachma weighs 3 grammata, 6 oboli, 9 thermi, 18 ceratia and 48 chalci.

(v) The Italian denarius weighs 1 drachma.

(vi) There is another drachma, called the Egyptian drachma, which is one sixth of an Attic drachma, and weighs an obol.

(vii) The gramma weighs 2 oboli, 3 thermi, 6 ceratia and 16 chalci.

(viii) The obolus weighs 1 $^1/_2$ thermi, 3 ceratia, 8 chalci.

(ix) The hemiobolon weighs 1 $^1/_2$ ceratium and 4 chalci.

(x) The thermus weighs 2 ceratia, 5 $^1/_3$ chalcoi.

(xi) The Attic hemiobolon weighs $^4/_5$ of the other hemiobolos.

(xii) The ceratium weighs 2 $^2/_3$ Attic chalci.

(xiii) A chalcus weighs $^1/_4$ of a hemiobolon, so that four chalci weigh one hemiobolon.

(xiv) The stater weighs 4 drachmae, and they call it a tetradrachmon.

(xv) The dupondium also weighs 4 drachmae

(xvi) The royal caryum also weighs 4 drachmae.

(xvii) The large cheme weighs 3 drachmae and the small cheme 2.

(xviii) The assarios weighs 2 drachmae.

(xix) The cochlearium weighs 1 drachma.

II. *Measures*

(xx) The cyathus weighs 10 drachmae or 1 $^1/_4$ unciae, 30 grammata, 60 oboli, 90 thermi, 180 ceratia, 480 chalci. The cyathus is $^1/_6$ of a cotyle.

(xxi) The cotyle is 6 cyathi in size, and weighs 60 drachmae, 7 $^1/_2$ unciae, 180 grammata, 360 oboli, 540 thermi, 1080 ceratia and 2880 chalci.

(xxii) The tryblion is the same size as the cotyle, for it too is the size of 6 cyathi, and is 60 drachmae in weight.

(xxiii) The xestes is 2 cotylae in size, and weighs 120 drachmae, and it is called by the Egyptians the inion.

(xxiv) The oxybaphum is $^1/_4$ of a cotyle in size, 1 $^1/_2$ cyathi, and weighs 15 drachmae.

(xxv) The large konche holds the same amount as the oxybaphum, for it is 1 $^1/_2$ cyathi in size, and 15 drachmae in weight. The smaller konche is the size of a hemikyathos, 5 drachmae.

(xxvi) The large mystrum is $^1/_{16}$ of a cotyle in size, and so weighs 3 $^3/_4$ drachmae. The smaller mystrum is $^1/_{22}$ of a cotyle, and so weighs 2 drachmae plus 2 grammata plus 1 $^1/_{11}$ ceratia.

(xxvii) The chous is 12 Attic cotylae in size, 6 xestes, 4 choinikes, and in weight 720 drachmae.

(xxviii) The choinix is 3 Attic cotylae in size and 180 drachmae in weight.

(xxix) But in farming I found that the cotyle is $^3/_4$ of a xestes, that the chous is 9 xestes, and 12 cotylae, that the amphora is 36 xestes, 48 cotylae, that the metretes is 72 xestes, 96 cotylae, and that the medimnus is 102 xestes, 136 cotylae.

(xxx) For the Syrians the metretes is 6 xestes, for others 90, and for the Italians 120.

(xxxi) The tryblion and the oxybaphum are the same at $^1/_4$ of a cotyle. The cyathus is $^1/_6$ of a cotyle.

Additional Notes

Due to the technical nature of this text, I have included these additional notes.

1. This fragment comes from Galen (12.403-5) and I include his title. By 'hair-disease' I render the Greek *alopecia* (or 'fox-mange'), a disease in which there was scalp irritation and the hair fell out (said to have been suffered frequently by foxes). It is often translated as 'mange' but this seems unsuitable, as it is word we tend to use only for hair-loss in animals. Celsus has an account of the disease (6.4); see also Pliny (28.164), Aëtius (6.65), Paulus of Aegina (3.1.1-2).

(i) Realgar is red sulphide of arsenic; it is caustic (i.e. warming), and if oxidised becomes poisonous white arsenic. Dioscorides recommends it for alopecia, as well as mixed with honey for a sore throat, or with dry pitch for asthmatics (v.121): it does have antiseptic qualities. Oak mistletoe (*Hozanthus europeaus*) was also used by Fabulla (see below). Pliny gives a lengthy description of what 'soda' ('nitrum') is and where it is found at 31.106-15; Jones identifies it as probably a mixture of sodium carbonate, calcium carbonate and various chlorides.[7] For 'soda scum' cf. Sappho 165; it was a sodium carbonate or nitrate, or perhaps a mixture of soda and potash (saltpetre), coloured by copper and iron oxides. It was used in soaps. (ii) For the unit of measure, the drachma, see Cleopatra 6; it was a weight, equivalent to about 4.32g. Squill was used to denote a shrimp or prawn (*Urginea maritima*; Jones identifies it as a species of *Palaemon* [prawn] and *Crangon* [shrimp]). White hellebore is *Yeratrum album*. Cleopatra adds a personal recommendation for this remedy which suggests that she regularly tried it on her patients. For soda, see (i) above. Pliny found that preparation of the head by shaving was recommended for the treatment of hair-disease, and remedies which he cites use some of the same ingredients as these recipes of Cleopatra (such as mice bodies and dung, pitch, reed, honey, nuts, mustard in vinegar and hellebore). He may have read her work, but he does not cite her—it is better to take this as evidence of some consistency of treatment (29.106-10). (iii) Nose-smart is a cress (*Lepidium sativum*), and was classified as caustic; mustard was caustic and desiccative. (iv) Liquid pitch is tar; it has antiseptic qualities. (v) Mice were evidently a common ingredient in remedies for hair-disease and appear in alternative recipes cited by Pliny (29.106-7) as well as (vi, and viii below). (viii) This is Cleopatra's most powerful medicine for hair-disease. Some thought is given to the storage of the medicine. Cleopatra does not use the Greek weight system she uses elsewhere (1ii-iv, 2iii, 3 ii-v, cf. 4), preferring relative quantities (the quantities in i, v-vii do not seem to matter); perhaps she took this remedy from another source. Stag marrow was the most highly valued marrow used in ancient medicines. It was considered a good emollient; for its preparation and storage see Pliny 28.145 and Dioscorides 2.95.

2. A series of five separate fragments from the *Cosmetics* quoted by Galen at 13.432-34. I have reproduced the fragments in the order that Galen gives them (adding numbers for clarity). Galen gives short notes to the titles of each of these fragments to indicate their relative placement in the original work he is quoting. He tells us that ii came shortly before i, that iii followed i, and that v followed shortly after iv. Galen indicates that he is reading from a longer work, picking out medicines from here and there, and not keeping to the order of the original.

   Fragments i and iii reveal instructions for preparing and giving the remedy to the patient, indicating that the work was meant for a doctor, rather than the patient. (i) Dried flies appear in remedies for hair-disease described by Pliny (29.106-7). (iii) Cimolian earth was a white clay. The oxybaphum was a Greek measure of liquid volume (see Cleopatra 6 (xxiv) above); it was the equivalent of about 67.5ml.

3. Another fragment from Galen (12.492-3); again he gives the title, probably from Cleopatra's text. There are four remedies in this section (with variations in {iv}) and a soap, and it may be one connected passage, indicating the way Cleopatra structured her work. (i) For Cimolian earth, see 2 (iii) above. (ii) Frankincense is well known from the gift of the magus to the Christ, and comes from a tree (*Boswellia Carterii*); brimstone is a naturally occurring sulphur. (iv) Cleopatra offers a series of different recipes for this remedy; coarse or 'male' frankincense was considered the best kind; stavesacre is *Delphinium staphisagria*; rocket is *Eruca sativa*; rue is *Ruta graveolens*. (v) Hyssop is *Origanum hirtum*; lupine is *Lupinus albus*. The choinix was a Greek measure of capacity, used for dry goods, see Cleopatra 6 (xxviii) above; it was the equivalent of about 1.08 litres.

4. The fragment comes from Aëtius, 8.6. He introduces it as '*another soap: an expensive fragrant soap of Cleopatra the queen*'. If it is by Cleopatra, we can presume that it came from *Cosmetics* too, as this is her only named work. It is not a remedy, but her work was not limited to medicine as fragment 5 demonstrates. It is possible, however, that the name of the queen has been spuriously attached to this luxury product, and it may not be the work of Cleopatra the physician. The quantities in this recipe are given in librae and unciae, the Roman system of weights, unlike the other extracts from Cleopatra's work, which use Greek weights and measures, where any are given (1ii-iv; 2iii; 3 ii-v; cf. 1viii). Although she was familiar with Roman weights (as fragment 6 shows) she seems to have used the Greek system in the *Cosmetics*. So although the text is quoted in Greek, it has either been 'Latinised' by an editor, or falsely attributed to Cleopatra.

Kostos was a root used as a spice (*Saussurea lappa*). Troglitis was a type of myrrh; cardamon was probably nepard cardamon (*Amomum sublatum*); phyllon could mean leaf, plant (in general) or dog mercury (*Mercurialis perennis*), fruit of silphium, or even white thistle (*Tyrimnus leucographus*); cassia is *Cinnamomum iners*: See Sappho 17 for its use at a wedding. Rush flower was the flower of *Scirpus holosi-hoenus*, or club rush, a rush used in wicker work; myrobalanoi is *Balanites aegyptiaca*, which has a fruit similar to an acorn; soda (sodium carbonate) was often mixed with oil to make a soap (see 1 (i) above).

5. This fragment comes from Paulus of Aegina, who wrote an epitome of medicine in the mid-seventh century AD. He relied heavily on early works, which he knew well, including Galen, and when he quotes a passage from Cleopatra on curling and dying hair (3.2.1) we have no reason to doubt that it was from her work (cf. 2 iv above).

Juvenal poked fun at women who dyed their hair or used cosmetics (*Satires* 6.457-73, 486-510), part of a tradition of criticising women for using beauty-products that is found in earlier Greek literature too (Xenophon, *Economics* 10.5-13). The argument that women likened themselves to prostitutes in using cosmetics was out of date by the time of Augustus (if not long before[8]) as they were already in widespread use amongst the aristocracy of Classical Athens; yet cosmetics continued to be regarded as casting doubt on the virtue of a woman: for a Pythagorean opinion, see Perictione 1 (1), Phintys (2) and Melissa in this collection. Galen (a near contemporary of Juvenal) notes that aristocratic women demanded cosmetics from their physician, and he admits to providing them, though he does so with some embarrassment (12.434-35), and prefers to summarise and cite the *Cosmetics* by Crito than to provide his own formulae. There were other works on cosmetics by Elephantis and male medical writers known to Galen (12.416). It was their expertise with plant products which led physicians into such a role.

6. Galen gives the title of the work from which this fragment comes as *Cosmetics* (plural) whereas elsewhere he refers to the work as the *Cosmetic* (singular). While it is possible that they were from two different works, it is more likely that we simply have an inconsistency in the citation of the title. This fragment is from book 19 of Galen (19.767-71), which is considered to be written by a different author to book 12 (source of fragments 1-3 above) and this may account for the inconsistency in reference to the work's title.

In the Hellenistic world, many different weight standards were in use: the traditional two Greek systems, Aeginetic and Euboic/Attic (which had largely replaced it), along with the Ptolemaic, Egyptian or Alexandrian system, one which is called 'Attic' but was based on a Roman coin/weight, as well as the Roman system with its own name for its weights and standards.[9] The names of weights were used to define weights of silver and hence to name coins; coins were also sometimes used as weights.

Cleopatra offers a description of the different units within the Greek and Roman weight systems, as well as a comparison between the different standards. Such a work would have been invaluable for anyone working in a field that needed precise weights and measures, particularly if the scope of the work went beyond the local community and the local system of measures. We find this work of Cleopatra's preserved in both Galen's medical corpus, and in the corpus of alchemical writers, two areas that relied on precise measures, and for whom the literature was international. Cleopatra's *Cosmetics* was apparently a medical work written as a manual for physicians; that it included a comprehensive description of weights and measures in use throughout the Mediterranean world suggests that the intended readership was international rather than local.[10]

(i) Cleopatra begins with three Greek weight standards,[11] but the bases from which Cleopatra works are Roman: the uncia (Roman ounce), and the 'Attic' drachma (actually a Roman weight, based on the weight of the Roman denarius). She describes the weight of each mina in Roman unicae, then she works out the number of 'Attic' drachma that would be needed to make up that weight, followed by the number of each of the smaller weights within the 'Attic' weight-system. The ratio between the units within the Greek system was constant and can be tabulated as follows:

	Talent	Min.	Drach.	Gram.	Obol.	Therm.	Cerat.	Weight[*]
Talent	1							20.25 kg
Mina	60	1						337.5g
Drachma	6000	100	1					3.375g
Gramma	18000	300	3	1				1.125g
Obolus	36000	600	6	2	1			562.5mg
Thermus	54000	900	9	3	1.5	1		375mg
Ceratim	108000	1800	18	6	3	2	1	187.5mg
Chalcos	288000	4800	48	16	8	5.33	2.66	70.3mg

[*] The weight given is for the 'Attic' standard (which Cleopatra used) based on a mina of 337.5g.

The first mina Cleopatra describes is on the Attic/Euboic standard, still apparently used by medical writers in her day. This mina weighed about 433g, with the drachma weighing about 4.33g. The second, the 'Attic' mina, was a weight derived from the Roman denarius, which had once weighed about the same as the Attic/Euboic drachma. In AD 64, however, Nero reduced the weight of the denarius to 3.375g[12]; thus the 'Attic' mina then only weighed 337.5g—or 12 ½ unciae—and there were 8 'Attic' drachmae to the Roman uncia. This gives us the earliest date for the composition of this work—indeed we can speculate that perhaps it was the new weight of the 'Attic' mina that prompted Cleopatra to compile this work. The Ptolemaic mina weighed about 490g, or 18 unciae. Cleopatra does not mention the talent, a weight of 60 minae—perhaps she never needed to use such a large weight in her work.

(ii) Cleopatra then describes the Roman weight system. The Latin unit was the 'libra'(or pound),[13] made up of 12 'unciae' (or 'ounces'). The libra weighed about 325g, the uncia about 27g. Cleopatra uses the Greek names for the Roman units, which I have preserved (though I have used the Latinised spellings, as elsewhere). The Roman equivalents for the subunits of the drachma Cleopatra uses are the 'scrupulus' (= gramma), 'lupinus' (= thermus), 'siliqua' (= ceratium) and 'aereus'(= chalcus). The Greek talent was reckoned to be the same weight as 80 Roman librae.[14]
A table of the Roman weights is as follows:

	Libra	Uncia	Scrupulus	Lupinus	Siliqua	Weight[*]
Libra	1					325g
Uncia	12	1				27.08g
Scrupulus	288	24	1			1.285g
Lupinus	864	72	3	1		376.15mg
Siliqua	1728	144	6	2	1	188.07mg
Aereus	4608	384	16	5.33	2.66	70.529mg

[*] Weight is based upon a libra = 325g

(iii-xv) Cleopatra describes the ratios of the smaller units of weight. Notice that she equates the denarius with the drachma (v). The 'Egyptian drachma' is a misnamed obolus. The tetradrachma (xiv) was issued in Alexandria by Tiberius, after a break of 50 years or so. It was the main coin issued in Alexandria under Nero.[15] The dupondium and the as (xviii) were Roman coins.

(xvi-xix) This section has been misplaced or is a later interpolation. The text lists four small Greek measures along with a Roman weight/coin (the as). The Greek measures are defined by weight not capacity and their relation to other measures of capacity is not given (cf. xx-xxx below). The royal caryum, large and small cheme would be better placed before the mystra (xxvi), the cochlearium following them; the as (xviii) may be placed with the dupondium (xv) (both Roman weights). The as was a copper coin, originally weighing one libra, but successively reduced in weight (here it weighs only 1/48th of a libra).

(xx-xxx) Cleopatra describes Greek measures of capacity. Most were used to measure both liquid and dry measures, though the chous was only used for liquids while medimnus and choinix were restricted to dry goods (such as grains). The measures were named after the vessels which nominally accommodated them (eg. amphora, chous = pitcher, cotyle = cup, cyathus = ladle, cochliarium = spoon). Below is a table showing comparative sizes of the liquid measures based on Cleopatra's text,[16] with estimates of size in litres and millilitres (based on a cotyle at 270ml).

	chous	xestes	cotyle	oxyb.	cyath.	small con.	large myst.	capacity
Chous	1							3.24 l
Xestes	6	1						540ml
Cotyle	12	2	1					270ml
Oxybaph. and Large conche	48	8	4	1				67.5ml
Cyathus	72	12	6	1.5	1			45 ml
Small conche	144	24	12	3	2	1		22.5ml
Large mystrum	192	32	16	4	2.66	.75	1	16.9ml
Small mystrum	264	44	22	5.5	3.66	2.75	.73	12.2ml

Cleopatra uses the cotyle as a standard to compare other measures. She also gives a weight for each measure, probably the weight of water of that volume. A cotyle is normally given at the weight of 80 'Attic' drachmas; Cleopatra gives the weight as 60 'Attic' drachmas, i.e. ³/₄ of the regular size.

After dealing with the liquid measures, she describes the dry measures, choinix and medimnus (xxvii-xix). The standard ratios are tabulated below; Cleopatra varies from these, giving a smaller choinix (and so medimnus). The regular ratios were:

	medimnus	choinix	capacity
Medimnus	1		51.84 l
Choinix	48	1	1.08 l
Cotyle	192	4	270ml

There were normally two cotylae to the xestes, and four to the choinix, but it is clear that the ratios were not universal. Cleopatra notes that the farming community used different ratios (xxix), and that the Syrians, Italians and 'others' all give different sizes for the metretes (xxx). The figures she gives for measures used by the farming community are as follows (I have added an approximate capacity in litres):

	medimnus	*metretes*	*amphoreus*	*chous*	*xestes*	*capacity*
Medimnus	1					36.72 l
Metretes	1.416	1				25.92 l
Amphora	2.833	2	1			12.96 l
Chous	11.33	8	4	1		3.24 l
Xestes	102	72	36	9	1	360ml
Cotyle	136	96	48	12	1.33	270ml

Notes

1. For an example of her reputation for wealth (which was probably justified), extravagance and perfume, see Plut., *Mark Antony* 25–29. Cleopatra the Queen bore a son to Caesar (Caesarion) and three children to Antony (Plut., *Mark Antony* 38, 53, 71, 87).

2. Plut., *Mark Antony* 85–86.

3. Tzetes: Introduction to C. Matranga (ed.), *Allegory of Iliad* V.7, *Anecdota Graeca* (Leipzig: Teubner, 1850), 1. Cleopatra is not identified as the queen Cleopatra by Paulus of Aegina 3.2.1 nor by the Byzantine commentator in J.A. Cramer (ed.), *Anecdota Graeca e Codd. Manuscriptis Bibliothecarum Oxoniensum*, III (Oxford: Clarendon Press, 1836), 164.15-16. Queen Cleopatra is rightly dismissed by scholars as the author of this work, see B. Grillet, *Les Femmes et les Fards dans l'Antiquité Grecque* (Lyon: Centre national de la recherche scientifiques, 1975), 26; and I. Becher, *Das Bild der Kleopatra in der Griechischen und Lateinischen Literatur* (Berlin: Akademie Verlag, 1966). We should not assume that the author of this work meant to imply that the queen Cleopatra was its author, though this is possible.

4. She should also be distinguished from the author of alchemical works, cited by Olympiodorus and Zosimus (see following chapter).

5. As it apparently was: e.g. Cleopatra was read by Titus Statilius Crito, and summarized in his *Cosmetics* (now only extant in fragments) in about AD 100 (Galen 12.446).

6. Dioscorides wrote *De Materia Medica* in about AD 60, the most authoritative ancient description the medicinal properties of plants (and some minerals and animal products). See also Paulus of Aegina, book 7. W.G. Spencer (ed.), *Celsus De Medicina*, II (Cambridge, MA: Harvard University Press, 1977), xv-lv, offers a useful summary of the plants generally used and their properties.

7. See W.H.S. Jones, *Pliny, Natural History* (Cambridge, MA: Harvard University Press, 1963), 567-68, for both soda and soda scum.

8. Xenophon was not a typical husband. Cosmetics were in general use by those who could afford them: the husband in Lysias' *On the Murder of Eratosthenes* (Lysias 1.14, written about 400 BC) considered his wife the best of women and the most chaste woman in the city, although she wore cosmetics. Criticism of the use of cosmetics reveals their widespread use (cf. Seneca the Younger, *On Consolation* 16). For more on cosmetics, see Grillet, *Les Femmes et les Fards dans l'Antiquité Grecque*.

9. Other standards included the Babylonian, Tyrian, Rhodian, Syrian, and Cilician: see R. Hussey, *An Essay on Ancient Weights and Money and the Roman and Greek Liquid Measures* (Oxford: Clarendon Press, 1836).

10. For the text, with a commentary (in Latin), see the edition of F. Hultsch, *Metrologicorum Scriptorum Reliquae*, I (Leipzig: Teubner, 1864; repr. 1971), 233-36.

11. The names of weights and measures provide some problems for the translator, as English names are sometimes used for some of the weights (such as 'pound' and 'ounce' for the Latin 'libra' and 'uncia'), but this can be misleading as we are dealing with a different weight standard; also,

Cleopatra gives Greek names for Roman weights, rather than the Latin names themselves. To avoid confusion, I have used Latinised forms of the Greek names Cleopatra uses (the practice I have followed with proper names).

12. From about 211 BC to 155 BC the Roman denarius, or 'Attic drachma' weighed 4 scruples, or $^1/_6$ of an uncia; in 155 BC the weight was reduced to $^1/_7$ of an unci, and in 64 it was reduced again to $^1/_8$ of an uncia, i.e. 3 scruples, or about 3.375g. See F. Hultsch, *Griechische und Römische Metrologie* (Berlin: Weidmann, 1887); and W.F. Richardson, *Numbering and Measuring in the Classical World* (Auckland: St Leonards Publications, 1985).

13. The libra was used in the phrase 'libra pondo', or just 'pondo', from which 'pound' is derived; 'ounce' is derived from uncia.

14. Polybius 21.42.19.

15. J.G. Milne, *A Catalogue of Alexandrian Coins* (Oxford: Clarendon Press, 1933), xvii.

16. Elsewhere the small mystrum is described as being $^1/_{12}$ or $^1/_{24}$ of a cotyle: see Hultsch, *Metrologicorum Scriptorum Reliquae*, 91, 222, 99, 229.

40. Cleopatra the Alchemist (fl. between 1st and 3rd centuries AD)

Introduction

Alchemists often published under pseudonyms, and one name used by more than one author was the name of Cleopatra the queen. The true identity of any alchemist working under this name is unknown, but as the author attributed the work to a woman, she was probably female too. Cleopatra was among the earliest alchemical writers, but her date cannot be fixed more precisely than between the first and the third centuries AD.[1] We should distinguish her from the physician, though the treatise on weights and measures from the *Cosmetics* is sometimes attributed to Cleopatra the alchemist.[2] Her alchemical work, *The Chrysopoeia* ('gold-manufacture') survives only in a diagram.[3]

The diagram is complex, despite the brief annotations in Greek. The heading reads, '*The Chrysopoeia* of Cleopatra'. Top left there is a double circle, surrounding symbols for gold, silver (with a tail added) and mercury. The inner circle text reads, 'The serpent is one, who has the poison with two symbols'. The outer circle reads, ' The all is one and the all is through it and the all is into it and if the all does not contain the all it is nothing'. The circle has a tail which suggests the symbol of the mystical serpent Ouroboros, which denoted the idea of the alchemical process being an eternal one, in a closed system, all metals coming ultimately from the same substance. Ouroborus (also spelt Uroboros) is depicted below, with the axiom, 'The all is one'.[4] Between them are illustrations of the *kerotakis*, a piece of apparatus used for heating metals and other substances, and condensing the vapours to produce alloys that could be passed off as gold or silver.[5] The meaning of the incomplete circle symbols to the right is doubtful, but they may represent the transformation of lead to silver.[6] The apparatus at the bottom right is a still, with two condensing arms, a lower and upper bowls (the top one labelled 'phial', the bottom one 'matrass'). The word 'fire' is written on the representation of the heater that sits beneath the still.[7]

The diagram illustrates the blending of magical and supernatural reverence with knowledge of specific processes that marked ancient alchemy. The statement that 'the all is one' was an axiom central to the doctrine of Maria, whose works survives in fragments.[8] It appears to be derived from the belief that all substances in nature were one, and that the alchemist's purpose was to find the method of unifying various separate materials, typically by breaking down their physical bodies by heating, and then recombining them by condensing.

Cleopatra

The Chrysopoeia

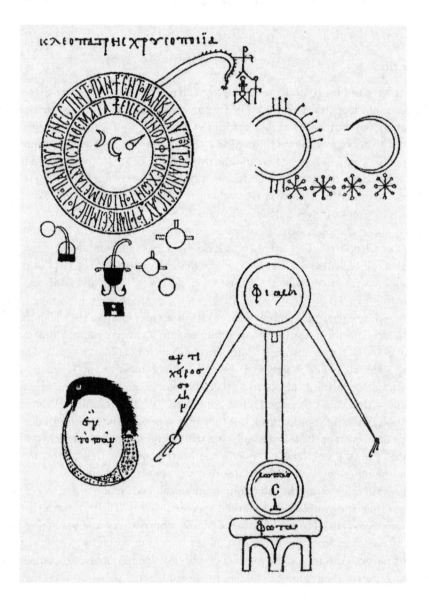

Figure 3.　Cleopatra's *Chrysopoeia*. ms. Saint-Marc fol. 188 verso (*CAG*, 132, fig. 11).

Notes

1.　F.S. Taylor, 'A survey of Greek alchemy', *Journal of Hellenic Studies* 50 (1930), 109-39 (113).
2.　Cf. ibid, 116.

3. A fictitious dialogue between Cleopatra and Comarius or philosophers cannot be attributed to her, though her responses in it may be based on a reading of her lost work: *CAG* II.289-90; see also J. Lindsay, *The Origins of Alchemy in Graeco-Roman Egypt* (London: Muller, 1970), ch. 12.

4. For Ouroborus, the mystical serpent, and other alchemical imagery, see L. Abraham, *Dictionary of Alchemical Imagery* (Cambridge and New York: Cambridge University Press, 1998).

5. See Taylor, 'A survey of Greek alchemy', 125-38. For the *kerotakis*, see chapter on Maria who was regarded as its inventor.

6. *CAG*, 133.

7. On the still, see F.S. Taylor, 'The evolution of the still', *Annals of Science* 5:3 (1945), 185-202.

8. For further discussion on alchemy, see chapter on Maria.

41. Dionysia (*fl. AD 122*)

Introduction

On the statue of Memnon at Thebes there is one short epigram by Dionysia, who is otherwise unknown. The text was inscribed by the same person as two other inscriptions, one of which is dated to 5 September AD 122, giving us a good indication of the date of Dionysia's visit to Thebes.[1] Dionysia may well have travelled to the site in company with the authors of these other (prose) inscriptions, Julia Saturnina, Lucius Funisulanus Charisius and his wife Fulvia.[2] Funisulanus was a Roman official in Egypt, *strategos* of the *nomoi* of Hermonthis and Latopolis. Dionysia (whose name tells us she was Greek) was mixing in respectable Roman company, if not the elevated circle of Julia Balbilla. The inscription adds to our evidence for tourism in Roman Egypt.

Dionysia's short epigram forms an iambic trimetre (preceded by the author's name). Greek and Roman visitors to the site believed that noises made by the stone of the statue as it was warmed by the morning sun came from Memnon himself. Dionysia offers her text as an act of worship, promising to listen to the god many times—and, perhaps a little presumptuously, anticipating that the hero will respond.[3]

Dionysia

Dionysia's worship.
Many a time
will she hear.

Notes

1. A. Bernard and E. Bernard, *Les Inscriptions Grecques et Latines du Colosse de Memnon* (Cairo: Institut français d'archéologie orientale, 1960), 18 and 65; the date of her visit is discussed on p. 158. For more on the statue of Memnon, see Julia Balbilla (below). For other inscriptions by women on the statue, see Demo and Caecilia Trebulla.
2. Ibid, 65, 18 and 19.
3. As ibid, 158. For the singing statue of Memnon, see Julia Balbilla.

42. Caecilia Trebulla (*fl. c. AD 130*)

Introduction

The statue of Memnon near Thebes in Egypt was famous in antiquity for the noise made by the stone as it was warmed by the morning sun.[1] Caecilia Trebulla composed three epigrams on her visit to the statue of Memnon, proudly placing her name above her verses.[2] She is otherwise unknown. The first poem seems to have been inscribed on Memnon's left leg before the visit of Julia Balbilla, whose first poem was inscribed immediately below it.[3] This juxtaposition suggests she visited Memnon not long before Julia Balbilla in AD 130.

Caecilia Trebulla has an appealing simplicity. She displays some learning in her iambic poetry—referring to the history of the statue and echoing sentiments that go back to Plato[4]—along with warmth in her desire for her mother and her affection for Memnon. Her command of literary Greek is typical of the well educated Roman aristocracy. She empathises with the statue, hearing its voice both as a personal greeting and as a lament for Memnon's fate. The popular belief was that Memnon 'sang' to his mother, Eos (Dawn); Caecilia is reminded by Memnon of her own mother whom she includes in her prayers.

Caecilia Trebulla

1.
By Trebulla.

When I heard the holy voice of Memnon,
I longed for you, mother, and I prayed for you to hear it too.

2.
Caecilia Trebulla,
upon hearing Memnon for the second time.

Before we heard only his voice,
Today he greeted us as friends and intimates,
Memnon, son of Eos and Tithon.
Did Nature, creator of all,
Give perception and voice to stone?

3.
I, Caecilia Trebulla,
Wrote after hearing Memnon here.
Cambyses smashed me, this stone,
Made as a likeness of an Eastern king.
My voice of old was a lament, groaning
For Memnon's suffering, which Cambyses stole.
Today I cry sounds inarticulate and unintelligible
Remains of my former fate.

Notes

1. For further discussion of Memnon and his 'singing', see Julia Balbilla.
2. For further discussion of the inscriptions on Memnon, see Julia Balbilla and Demo (below), Dionysia (above) and A. Bernard and E. Bernard, *Les Inscriptions Grecques et Latines du Colosse de Memnon* (Cairo: Institut français d'archéologie orientale, 1960), 92-94, 187-191.
3. Ibid, 187.
4. Poem 2, line 8 is compared by ibid on p. 189 to *Gorgias* 508a and *Lysis* 214b.

43. Julia Balbilla (*fl.* AD 130)

Introduction

Julia Balbilla is another poet we know only from four poems inscribed on the (misnamed) colossal statue of Memnon near Thebes in Egypt. She accompanied the Roman emperor Hadrian and his wife Sabina to this tourist attraction in AD 130, celebrating the visit in verses which she had inscribed on the statue itself. She was a member of the Roman aristocracy, on intimate terms with the imperial family, and had royal ancestry of her own (on both the maternal and paternal sides of her family), all of which she proudly announces in her poetry. [1]

Her work has been referred to as 'graffiti', and it is true that she has contributed to the 107 Greek and Latin inscriptions scratched into the feet and legs of the statue, a practice which Roman tourists seem to have begun about 20 BC.[2] This graffiti, however, was no doubt approved by the emperor: it is a public inscription not a private scribble. It honours Hadrian and Sabina, while also paying respect to the Greek hero, Memnon. In addition, Julia Balbilla takes the opportunity to boast of her own royal blood, her position in the imperial retinue, and the power of her poetry.

The statue, which Julia Balbilla wanted to preserve with her poetry, was in a poor state of repair in her day. It was one of a pair which once stood before the mortuary temple of the Egyptian king Amenhotep III.[3] The temple was intended for the worship of the king after his death, along with the Egyptian god Amun. The Greeks came to associate this Egyptian king with their mythological hero Memnon. The statute had been deliberately damaged by Cambyses, the Persian king, and may also have suffered damage from an earthquake.[4] Ironically, it was the damage which led to the statue's fame in antiquity. For the cracked stone, under certain temperatures, hummed or 'sang', and it was this phenomenon which attracted the tourists. Those lucky enough to hear the statue singing explained the phenomenon as contact with the hero himself, and liked to celebrate by adding their names to the stones, both in simple prose inscriptions or more learned epigrams, like those of Julia Balbilla.[5]

I have reproduced the poems in the order they appear on the colossus. Poems 1-3 were put on the left leg, poem 4 lower down on the left foot, with simple prose inscriptions to Sabina and another companion, Lucius Flavianus Philippus.[6] The poems describe visits to the statue on two consecutive days and at least one other day (though it is not clear how many times the party visited the site). The poems describe each visit, recording carefully Memnon's response, but the visits are not inscribed in chronological order. The poem in praise of Hadrian was placed first, no doubt out of respect for his superior status, although it describes the second visit.[7]

The poems are generally seen as spontaneous compositions, and this is offered as an excuse for the supposed 'banality' of the poetry.[8] But we should not characterise the poetry as necessarily spontaneous or banal. The poems were not scratched into the stone by the poet in the act of composition, but were inscribed some time later—how much later we cannot know. Poem 4 has two dates attached to it—it is not clear whether they record the day of the visit and then the day of the inscription, or the dates of two visits on which the statue was heard. That the author did not inscribe her own poetry is clear from the misspelling of her name in the title to poem 1—a mistake she surely could not have made herself![9] Indeed, poem 1, lines 9-12 suggest that Hadrian commissioned Balbilla to record his visit, according her some literary status as court poet. While there are some technical imperfections, the poems display good use of literary devices such as metaphor, and verbal and sound echoes. She displays erudition in mythology and history, but what is perhaps most striking about her poetry is the language which she uses, including archaic and rare words, forms of words reserved for poetry, and an artificial Aeolian dialect, which gives the poetry a Homeric tone. There is wit here too—Balbilla finds an amusing excuse for Memnon not addressing the party on the first day which flatters both Sabina and the majesty of Hadrian.[10]

Julia Balbilla

1.
When the August Hadrian heard Memnon.
By Julia Balbilla.[11]

Memnon the Egyptian, I learnt, when warmed by the rays of the sun,
Speaks from Theban stone.
When he saw Hadrian, the king of all, before the rays of the sun
He greeted him—as far as he was able.
But when the Titan driving through the heavens with his steeds of white   5
Brought into shadow the second measure of hours,
Like ringing bronze Memnon again sent out his voice
Sharp-toned; he sent out his greeting and for a third time a mighty-roar.
The Emperor Hadrian then himself bid welcome to
Memnon and left on stone for generations to come   10
this inscription recounting all that he saw and all that he heard.
It was clear to all that the gods love him.

2.
When with the August Sabina I stood before Memnon.

Memnon, son of Aurora and holy Tithon,
seated before Thebes, city of Zeus,
Or Amenoth, Egyptian King, as learned
Priests recount from ancient stories,
Greetings, and singing, welcome her kindly,   5
The august wife of the Emperor Hadrian.
A barbarian man cut off your tongue and ears,
Impious Cambyses; but he paid the penalty,
With a wretched death struck by the same sword point
With which pitiless he slew the divine Apis.   10
But I do not believe that this statue of yours will perish,
I saved your immortal spirit forever with my mind.
For my parents were noble, and my grandfathers,
The wise Balbillus and Antiochus the king,

Balbillus the father of our royal mother,   15
And Antiochus the king, father of my father.
From their race I too was given noble blood,
and these verses are mine, Balbilla, the pious.

3.
When on the first day we did not hear Memnon.

Yesterday Memnon met his wife in silence,
So the beautiful Sabina would come back again.
For you enjoy the beloved beauty of our queen.
But when she returns, send out your divine roar,
Lest the king grow angry with you. Too long without fear   5
you hold up his august wedded wife.
And Memnon trembling at the mighty power of Hadrian
Suddenly sang, which she heard and enjoyed.

4.
I, Balbilla, heard, when he sang from the stone,
The divine voice of Memnon or Phamenoth.
I had come here with my beloved queen Sabina;
The sun was holding its course for the first hour.
In the fifteenth year of Emperor Hadrian,   5
When Hathyr was in his twenty-fourth day.
On the twenty-fifth day of the month of Hathyr.

Notes

1. See poem 2. Her paternal grandfather was probably King Antiochis IV of Commagne in Syria (king AD 38–72), her maternal grandfather Tiberius Claudius Balbillus, Prefect of Egypt under Nero: see A. Bernard and E. Bernard, *Les Inscriptions Grecques et Latines du Colosse de Memnon* (Cairo: Institut français archéologie orientale, 1960), 92.
2. Ibid, 15, 33.
3. King Amenhotep III (c. 1468–1438 BC) was a lavish builder. For a translation of the stele from his mortuary temple that records his building achievements, see M. Lichtheim, *Ancient Egyptian Literature*, II (Berkeley: University of California Press, 1976), 43-47. The Greeks called Amenhotep both Amenoth and Phamenoth: see poems 2 and 4.
4. Balbilla's claim that Cambyses defaced the colossal statue is repeated by other graffiti (see Caecilia Trebulla 3 [=Bernard 94]) and Paus. 1.42.3; see Strab. 17.1.46 for the earthquake.
5. For other women who inscribed poetry on the statue, see Caecilia Trebulla, Demo and Dionysia. The statue continued to sing until it was repaired under the Roman emperor Septimius Severus at the start of the third century AD.
6. Bernard and Bernard, *Les Inscriptions Grecques et Latines du Colosse de Memnon*, numbers 32 and 33.
7. As ibid, 84.
8. Argued by J. Balmer, *Classical Women Poets* (Newcastle: Bloodaxe Books, 1996), 108, who defends the poetry against the charge of banality.
9. See Bernard and Bernard, *Les Inscriptions Grecques et Latines du Colosse de Memnon*, 81, for the text.

10. For further discussion on the text see M.L. West, 'Balbilla did not save Memnon's soul', *Zeitschrift für Papyrologie und Epigraphik* 25 (1977), 120; and more generally 'Die griechischen Dichterinnen der Kaiserzeit', in H.G. Beck *et al.* (eds), *Kyklos: Griechisches und Byzantinisches. Festschrift für R. Keydell* (Berlin: De Gruyter, 1978), 101-115; also E.L. Bowie, 'Greek poetry in the Antonine age', in D.A. Russell (ed.), *Antonine Literature* (Oxford: Clarendon Press, 1990), 61-63.

11. The headings which accompany three of the poems are by Balbilla herself.

44. Terentia (*lived about 1st–2nd centuries* AD)

Introduction

Terentia was a Roman visitor to Egypt whose only known work is a poem which she composed as an epitaph for her brother, Decimus Terentius Gentianus, and had inscribed on the pyramid of Cheops. The poem was discovered and recorded in 1335 by a German pilgrim, Wilhelm von Boldensele. Since then all the limestone facing on the pyramid has been removed and the inscription itself has been lost. Terentia's poem, as we have it, consists of six hexameters, but may originally have been longer.[1]

We do know a little about her brother. Decimus Terentius Gentianus was *consul suffectus* under the Emperor Trajan in AD 116, and governor of Macedonia under Hadrian as a *censitor* in AD 120.[2] This helps us to date Terentia's visit to Egypt and her poem. Still in mourning for her brother, she chose the pyramid for her epitaph to provide a suitably grand and everlasting site for her tribute to him.[3] She was proud of her brother's political achievements at such a young age (under thirty), and the status and position in the imperial court that this reflected. Traditionally a man could not attain the rank of consul before he turned forty, though this Republican practice, codified in the *Lex Vibia Annalis* in 180 BC, was disregarded by the emperors who promoted themselves, family members and favourites without regard to the age limit. There is no other record of Terentius reaching the rank of *censor*; Terentia may have elevated her brother's appointment as *censitor* in her poem to exaggerate his achievements.[4]

It has been suggested that Terentia visited Egypt as a member of Hadrian's touring party in AD 130.[5] This may be so but there is no evidence for it, and Terentia's epitaph must have been written after AD 130 as the *Historia Augusta* (23) records that Terentius did not die until after Hadrian's tour.

Terentius had been popular in the senate and at one time considered a possible successor by Hadrian.[6] Terentia's poem is all the more remarkable for her boldness in lauding a politician who had fallen out of favour with the reigning emperor. Terentia looks back to the success of her brother under Trajan, whom she addresses, but does not mention Hadrian at all. Perhaps Egypt was far enough away from Rome for such political graffiti to pass unnoticed. Terentia did not need to travel to Egypt with the Emperor: evidence from the graffiti on the statue of Memnon shows that there was considerable Roman tourism in Egypt by both men and women.[7]

Terentia's poem can be compared with the epigrams by Caecilia Trebulla and Julia Balbilla, inscribed in the time of Hadrian on the Colossus of Memnon, as examples of occasional poetry. They show that at this time women of the Roman elite were literate— Terentia adapts a verse of Horace in line three[8]—and could express themselves well in verse.

Terentia

Epitaph for her brother

I have seen the pyramids without you, dearest brother,
And mourning here I have poured forth my tears, as far as I
was able, for you,
And I carve this plaintive song as a memory of our mourning.
Here on this high pyramid may it remain: the name of
Decimus Gentianus, priest, companion, Trajan, in your triumphs,   5
and within six lustra,[9] censor and consul.

Notes

1. See E.A. Hemelrijk, *Matrona Docta: Educated Women in the Roman Elite from Cornelia to Julia Domna* (London and New York: Routledge, 1999), 171-74, 335 n. 112.
2. R. Syme, 'Hadrian and the Senate', *Athenaeum* 62 (1984), 31-60 (50); *CIL* III 1463; see Hemelrijk, *Matrona Docta*, 335 n. 114.
3. For other inscriptions on the pyramids, now lost, see Herodotus 2.124-25; Diodorus Siculus 1.64; E. Graefe, 'Der Pyramidenbesuch des Wilhelm von Boldensele aus dem Jahre 1335', in H. Altenmuller and D. Wildung (eds), *Festschrift Wolfgang Helk zu seinem 70. Geburtstag* (Hamburg: H. Busker, 1984), 569-84; and 'A propos der Pyramidenbeschreibung des Wilhelm von Boldensele aus dem Jahre 1335', in E. Hornung (ed.), *Zum Bild Aegyptens in Mittelalter und in der Renaissance* (Göttingen: Vandenhoeck and Ruprecht, 1990), 9-28.
4. The censorship had been a prestigious and important public office in the republic, assigning citizens to the appropriate rank and overseeing moral conduct. The office lost authority under the emperors: Domitian made himself censor for life, after which the censor's functions passed to other officials. A censitor fulfilled the duties of a censor in the provinces.
5. Syme, 'Hadrian and the Senate', 50-51.
6. *Augustan History* 23. Not all historians believe the *Augustan History*: see Hemelrijk, *Matrona Docta*, 335 n. 114.
7. See Dionysia, Caecilia Trebulla and Julia Balbilla, and A. Bernard and E. Bernard, *Les Inscriptions Grecques et Latines du Colosse de Memnon* (Cairo: Institut français d'archéologie orientale, 1960).
8. Horace, *Odes* 3.11.51-52; Hemelrijk, *Matrona Docta*, 336 n. 118.
9. A *lustrum* was a Roman purification sacrifice; the word was also used to indicate a period of five years.

45. Demo (fl. c. AD 200)

Introduction

Demo was the author of one short epigram which she composed at the Colossus of Memnon and had inscribed on the statue.[1] Her name indicates that she was Greek, but hers was not a rare name in the Hellenistic world, being attested both in Egypt and elsewhere, and so she cannot be further identified.[2] The date of her visit to the Colossus cannot be determined with any certainty, except to note that her epigram was inscribed high on the left leg after the two inscriptions which frame it and so must be dated after them.[3] One of these is dated, and so we can determine Demo's visit to Memnon was on 25th February AD 196, or some time later. The relative height of the inscription (the final line is 3.3 metres from the base) also suggests a late date, as lower, more easily accessible areas of the foot and leg were for the most part inscribed with graffiti before the higher areas.

Demo, like Julia Balbilla, adopts an Aeolic dialect for her verse and includes Homeric allusion, demonstrating that she too has had the traditional Greek education of the wealthy class. She calls herself a protégé of the Muses and a lover of song, traditional self-images for lyric poets. The persona the author adopts, that of a poet, hints at a vocation, and of other work no longer extant.

Demo begins in traditional fashion by greeting the hero. The invocation to Memnon as the son of Aurora (Dawn) is found in Julia Balbilla's poem 2, and regularly elsewhere on the statue too. By alluding to the Muses, the poet marks her poetry as divinely favoured, explaining the special respect Memnon has shown towards her. Demo offers something in return—her poetry—as a gift to the hero, recalling Balbilla's desire to confer immortality on the statue through her verse. The poet both begins and ends by addressing Memnon, highlighting his divine status in recalling both his strength and holiness. The language reflects a knowledge of Homer, a feature typical of epigrammatic poetry—'bearing a pleasant gift' for example, is a phrase found regularly in the *Iliad* and *Odyssey*.[4] Demo displays further erudition in using an artificial poetic (Aeolic) dialect and a metonymy: naming the Muses from their haunt on Mount Pierus in Thessaly. Demo balances praise of Memnon with pride in her own accomplishments. She neatly recalls her own epithet, 'song-loving', in describing the nature of her act of devotion to the hero, a device which suggests sincerity, as well as lauding her own literary and musical achievements.

Demo

Son of Aurora, I greet you. For you addressed me kindly,
Memnon, for the sake of the Pierides, who care for me,
song-loving Demo. And bearing a pleasant gift,
my lyre will always sing of your strength, holy one.

Notes

1. For further discussion of the statue and the graffiti on it, see Julia Balbilla, Dionysia, and Caecilia Trebulla.
2. The text perhaps reads Damo rather than Demo (the inscription was never deep and is difficult to read), the author adopting an Aeolic form of her name: as A. Bernard and E. Bernard, *Les Inscriptions Grecques et Latines du Colosse de Memnon* (Cairo: Institut français d'archéologie orientale, 1960), 179-80.
3. Ibid, 57: G4 and 84: G6.
4. *Iliad* 1.572, 578; 14.132; *Odyssey* 3.164; 16.375; 18.56. Ibid, 180, identifies the Homeric features and Aeolicisms.

46. Fabulla (before AD 210)

Introduction

Galen cites two passages from Fabulla (13.250) repeating the same two passages soon after (13.341).[1] He describes her as a Libyan (i.e. African), though her name marks her out as Roman. She uses a Roman weight system to measure her ingredients and this suggests that her text may have been written originally in Latin, and translated into Greek by Galen (or an unknown intermediary source). She was probably a *medica*, a female doctor.

Fabulla herself attributed the first of these two medicines to Antiochis, a Greek *medica* who lived in the first century AD and is known from an inscription from her home town of Tlos in Lycia. There Antiochis set up a statue of herself, with the approval of the council and people of Tlos. This was a great honour, awarded for her expertise in healing.[2] As work by her was read by Fabulla, Antiochis must have also published medicines.

The Roman weight Fabulla uses, the libra, was the Roman pound, which weighed about 325g (see notes to Cleopatra 6 ii); the unica was one twelfth of a libra. Galen omits the oak mistletoe (*Loranthus europaeus*) when he first cites Antiochis' remedy at 13.250, but includes it the second time (13.341); this is the only significant difference between the two citations of this remedy. Aromatic acorns were from the *Balanites aegyptiaca*. Asian stone was a mineral; henna oil was from *Lawsonia inermis*. Myrrh is an aromatic gum from the Arabian tree *Balsamo dendron*; Bdellion is similar, thought to be an aromatic gum from *Balsamodendron africanum* and *B. mukul*. Onycha was another aromatic substance (cf. Exodus 30.34), Hercules' woundwort is *Opoponax hispidus*; all-heal is *Ferula galbaniflora*.

The introductions below are from Galen.

Fabulla

1.
Antiochis' soap prepared by Fabulla the Libyan: for those with disease of the spleen, dropsy, sciatica, gout.

Three librae of wax, 3 librae of turpentine resin, 3 librae of oak mistletoe, 1 libra of aromatic acorns, 1 libra of sodium carbonate, powder of Asian stone, and gum ammoniacum incense, 3 librae of henna oil, and sufficient vinegar to dissolve the ammoniacum.

2.
Another medicine put together by Fabulla, excellent for the same problems.

Two librae each of myrrh oil, bdellion, onycha, stag-marrow, gum ammoniacum incense, and dried iris, one libra each of Hercules' woundwort, juice of all-heal, mastich, powder of Asian stone, storax, sycamore-fig juice, fruit of rosemary frankincense, six unciae of white pepper, five librae each of wax and turpentine. The medicine should be chopped finely. Apply the chopped ingredients with the sediment of the iris unguent until the medicine becomes most soft, for it becomes most soft after application.

Notes

1. The two passages are virtually identical.
2. See E. Kalinka (ed.), *Tituli Lyciae: Tituli Asiae Minores*, II (Vienna: Hoelder-Pichler-Tempsky, 1901–), 223, no. 595; A.F. Pauly and G. Wissowa (eds), *Paulys Real-Ecyclopädie der Classischen Alterumswissenschaft. Supplement* XIV (Stuttgart: J.B. Metzler 1974), 48-9.

47. Maia (*before* AD 210)

Introduction

Maia's remedy for cracks or chaps of the skin comes to us from Galen, but indirectly, appearing in a passage in which Galen is citing Andromachus Junior, and it was apparently he who attributed the recipe to a female author whom he called Maia (Galen 13.840 cf. 13.837). Although Maia was the name of Hermes' mother, the word generally denoted a title rather than a woman's name. It was used as a form of address to old women, meaning 'mother' (eg. Homer, *Odyssey* 19.482) and metaphorically of the 'mother' earth (Aeschylus, *Libation Bearers* 44). It was also used to mean 'midwife' (cf. *IG* II^2 6873) and to denote a profession rather than a personal name; this is the sense it carries here. The remedy Galen cites therefore comes from a work attributed to an anonymous midwife.[1]

Maia's recipe uses well known ingredients and most can be readily identified. Oak apple, also known as 'gall' was used to make a dye (Dioscorides 27.10, 43) and an ink (Eustathius 955.64). Myrrh would provide fragrance, and is in one of Cleopatra's recipes. White lead was a lead acetate made by pouring vinegar on lead shavings; it was used as a pigment in cosmetics, as white was considered the proper and most attractive colour for a woman's face (as Ar., *Ecclesiazusae* 878, 929). It was also used in salves (see Samithra). Molybdaena was a sulphurate of lead ('galena') and a common plant (*Plumbago europae,* the 'plumbago' or 'leadwort'), and both were used in medicines. Pliny tells us that the plant was thought to be effective in salves (25.155), and the plant could be meant here, though galena seems to be the preferred reading.[2] For the weights used see Cleopatra.

Maia

Maia's ointment: good for calluses and cracked skin.
Eight drachmae of oak apple, eight drachmae of molybdaena, four drachmae of myrrh and four drachmae of white lead; use ground up.

Notes

1. Pliny cites the 'better midwives' (28.67, 70, 255), naming some of them: see Salpe.
2. R.J. Durling, *A Dictionary of Medical Terms in Galen* (Leiden: Brill, 1993) reads molybdaena here as galena.

48. Samithra (*before* AD *210*)

Introduction

Galen cites one remedy by this otherwise unknown medical writer (13.310). The heading is from Galen. The remedy comes from a section in which Galen is discussing medicines for anal problems. He cites a remedy by Xanite for the same condition. His evidence shows that there were medical texts published by women and in use as reference works. The key ingredients used are found in other medicines: litharge is lead monoxide, formed after heating lead and silver; turpentine was used by Fabulla and Xanite. For the weights and measures used, see Cleopatra.

Samithra

Samithra's medicine. It is very effective.

Twelve drachmae of litharge, 2 drachmae of white lead, 2 drachmae of rock alum, 1 drachma of copperas, 6 drachmae of turpentine, 4 cotylae of oil and water.

49. Xanite (before AD 210)

Introduction

Galen cites just one remedy by this otherwise unknown medical writer (13.311) when he deals with topical treatments for anal complaints. Samithra published a remedy for a similar condition. Pliny the Elder testifies to the effectiveness of oesypum when mixed with butter in treating such ailments too (29.37). Another remedy for complaints of the anus used by the Romans included fats, oesypum and rose oil. Thus there is evidence for some consistency in medical knowledge and treatments (Plin. 30.69). For the Roman method of preparing butter, which was considered something which foreigners, rather than Greeks and Romans, enjoyed, see Plin. 28.133-134.

Xanite

Xanite's medicine. It is very effective.

Sixteen drachmae of wax, ten drachmae of butter, ten drachmae of oesypum, eight drachmae of goose fat, eight drachmae of turpentine, four drachmae of stag marrow, a little rose-oil.[1]

Notes

1. The heading is from Galen (13.311). For turpentine, see Fabulla. For oesypum, grease from sheep's wool, see Olympias 1 (and notes). For the weights referred to here, see Cleopatra.

50. Perpetua (AD 181–203)

Introduction

In nearly every case, stories of Christian martyrs are fictional. Some are wholly fictional, and some have been so greatly embellished by later writers that they can no longer be taken as historical. The martyrdom of Perpetua, however, is generally taken to be an exception to this rule. Not only is the account of the martyrdom accepted as historical, but many readers believe that part of the story, a first-hand account of the events leading up to her death, were written by Perpetua herself.[1]

According to *The Martyrdom of Saints Perpetua and Felicitas*, Vibia Perpetua was arrested in Carthage during a persecution of Christians by Septimius Severus in AD 202–203. The reasons for the persecution are not clear. The *Augustan History* tells us that Severus prohibited conversion to Christianity (and Judaism), which may have been to encourage correct (pagan) religious observance as well as to force political obedience to the emperor.[2] During her confinement, she was visited by family, including her pagan father. Despite the demands of her father, and her concerns for her baby, whom she was still nursing, Perpetua would not deny her Christianity nor make a sacrifice for the emperor's health.[3] She received visions which prepared her for her coming martyrdom, which is graphically described. She and Felicitas (her slave, who had been arrested with her) were attacked by a mad cow, but this failed to kill them, so they were executed with a sword.

The complete work is divided into 21 sections. There is an introduction in the third person by an unknown author or editor (*The Martyrdom* 1–2), an account in the first person of Perpetua's trials, time in prison and visions (*The Martyrdom* 3–10),[4] a first person account of Saturus' vision (*The Martyrdom* 11–13), and the editor's conclusion, with an eye-witness account of the martyrdom (*The Martyrdom* 14–21).

The editor tells us that Perpetua was a young married woman, about 22 years old, of good family and upbringing. When arrested, she was a catechumen, still taking instruction in the beliefs and teachings of the Christian faith prior to baptism, which she received while in prison. The account mentions her father—a pagan who repeatedly tried to persuade her to comply with the wishes of the Roman authorities—her mother, and two brothers, one of whom was a catechumen too.[5] The editor tells us that Perpetua was newly married (*The Martyrdom* 2) and it is strange that the account does not mention her husband at all; that her father takes her baby and refuses to return him (Perpetua 4) suggests that her husband was not alive.[6] Her independence in refusing to comply with the wishes of her father and the state (in the person of the governor, Hilarion) is remarkable, and highlighted her belief that her duty was to God and not earthly powers. Her disobedience to the norms of state, society and family were a form of revolution against her earthly life.[7]

While *The Martyrdom* is generally believed to give us a reliable account of the persecution in Carthage at this time, scholars are more hesitant about the attribution of the authorship of the first person sections of the text. The style of the 'framework' passages is quite different from that of the first person narratives,[8] though this in itself does not prove that more than one author worked on the text. What is clear is that the text adopts a Christian woman's point-of-view. Indeed, the details she gives about her nursing of her child, for example, and the concern she expresses as a mother, suggest that the author was a woman. Perpetua grieves for the pain her decision causes her father, and is especially anxious for her child. Her own illness coincides with anxiety for her family, but as she regains health she also gains a peace of mind that allows her to take strength from her faith. The focus of the account on her experiences, rather than those of her four male companions (who were also executed and died as martyrs), suggests a female author.[9]

Acceptance of female authorship makes this text particularly significant as it would stand as the earliest extant Christian literature written by a woman.[10] The account is also significant as an early portrayal of martyrdom, and for the information it provides about the beliefs and experiences of the early Christians in North Africa.[11]

The Christian community in Carthage seems to have supported her and her fellow prisoners with material as well as spiritual comfort. Indeed, their Christian instructor, Saturus, voluntarily joined the catechumens in jail (Perpetua 2) and died with them.[12] After their deaths, *The Martyrdom* was widely read and circulated in both Greek and Latin. A basilica was dedicated to her in Carthage by the fourth century, and inscriptions demonstrate her early popularity.[13] The anniversary of her death was included in the official calendar of the church at Rome,[14] and marked by a church festival in Carthage; Augustine gave sermons in her honour.[15] In about AD 500 her portrait was created for a mosaic in the Archiepiscopal Chapel in Ravenna.[16]

Perpetua

The Martyrdom of Perpetua

(1) While we were under arrest (she said), my father wanted to change my mind with his pleas and through his affection for me tried to dissuade me. 'Father,' I said, 'do you see this vase sitting here, for example, or little pitcher or whatever?' 'Yes I do.' And I said to him, 'Could it be called by any name other than what it is?' And he said, 'No.' 'So like this I cannot be called anything except what I am, a Christian.' Then my father was so disturbed by this word he came at me to pluck out my eyes, but he was merely angry and left, defeated along with his diabolical arguments.

Then, for a few days, I thanked the Lord that I was free of my father, and I was relieved by his absence. During this interval of a few days I was baptised, and the Spirit told me not to seek anything after the water except the enduring of the flesh. A few days later we were brought back to the prison; and I was very much afraid, because I had never been in such darkness. O desperate day! Thanks to the crowd the heat was stifling, and there was the extortion of the soldiers. Finally, I was tormented with worry for my baby there.

Then Tertius and Pomponius, blessed deacons who tried to look after us, arranged with a bribe for us to be sent to a better part of the prison for a few hours to get some relief. Then everyone came out of that prison and were free to attend to themselves. I nursed my baby who was now faint from hunger; worried, I spoke to my mother about him and comforted my brother, and I gave them my son to look after. I began to waste away because I saw that they were wasting away for my sake. Such worries I endured for many days. I got permission for my baby to stay in prison with me, and at once I got better and was relieved from the distress and worry about my baby, and suddenly my prison became a palace, so that I preferred to be there rather than anywhere else.

(2) Then my brother said to me, 'Dear sister, you are now greatly respected, so that you might ask for a vision and be shown whether you will suffer or be released.' And as I knew that I could talk with the

Lord, whose great blessings I had experienced, I promised faithfully to do so, saying to him, 'Tomorrow I will tell you.' And I did ask, and this was revealed to me. I saw a bronze ladder of amazing height reaching up to heaven. It was narrow, so that only one person at a time could climb it, and on the sides of the ladder was attached every type of iron weapon. There were swords, spears, hooks, daggers and spikes, so if anyone climbed up carelessly or without paying attention, he would be lacerated and his flesh stick to the iron weapons. And beneath the ladder itself lay a dragon of amazing size, which would reveal itself to those climbing up and try to frighten them into not climbing. But Saturus climbed up first. He later voluntarily handed himself in for our sake (because he had instructed us), although he had not been present when we were arrested. And he arrived at the top of the ladder and turned back and said to me, 'Perpetua, I am supporting you, but take care that dragon does not bite you.' And I said to him, 'He will not harm me, in the name of Jesus Christ.' And as if it were afraid of me, the dragon slowly put its head out from underneath that ladder. And as if it were the first step, I trod on its head and climbed up. And I saw a garden of immense size, and sitting in the middle a grey-haired man dressed as a shepherd. He was tall, and milking sheep. Many thousands of people were standing around him, wearing white. He raised his head and looked at me and said to me, 'I am pleased you have come, my child.' And he called me and gave me a small mouthful from the milk which he was drawing, and I took it with my hands joined and consumed it. And everyone who was standing around said, 'Amen.' At the sound of this word I woke up, still chewing something sweet, what I do not know. I immediately told this to my brother, and we understood that I was going to suffer, and then we began to have no hope in this lifetime.

(3) A few days later there came a rumour that we were going to be given a hearing. My father arrived from the city, tired out with worry, and he came up to see me to dissuade me, saying, 'Pity my grey-hair, my daughter. Pity you father, if I deserve to be called father by you, if I have raised you with these hands to this the prime of your life, if I have preferred you to all your brothers. Don't disgrace me in public. Look at your brothers, look at your mother and aunt, look at your son, who will not be able to live after you. Give up your arrogance, or you will destroy us all. For none of us will speak freely if something happens to you.' My father spoke like this because of his compassion for me, kissing my hands and throwing himself to my feet. Crying he called me not his daughter, but as a Lady. I grieved for my father's sake, because of my entire family, he alone would not be delighted at my suffering. I comforted him, saying, 'What will happen on that dock is what God wills. For you should know we are not placed our own power, but under God's power.' And saddened, he left me.

(4) Another day, when we were eating breakfast, we were suddenly dragged off to a hearing. We arrived at the forum, and at once a report spread through the neighbourhood of the forum and a huge crowd gathered. We climbed up into the dock. The others, when questioned, confessed. When it came to me, my father appeared with my son and dragged me from the step, saying, 'Sacrifice! Pity your baby!' Hilarianus the governor, who had received the judicial power of life or death in place of the late proconsul Minucius Timinianus, said to me, 'Spare your father's grey-hair, spare your baby boy. Perform the sacrifice for the health of the emperors.' And I replied, 'I am not doing it.' Hilarianus said, 'Are you a Christian?' And I replied, 'I am a Christian.' And when my father continued trying to dissuade me, Hilarianus ordered him to be thrown to the ground and beaten with a stick. I was saddened for my father's sake, as if I had been beaten. I was saddened for his miserable old age. Then he sentenced us all and he condemned us all to the beasts. We went down into the prison happy. Then because my baby was used to being nursed at the breast in the prison, I immediately sent Pomponius the deacon to my father to ask for my baby. But my father did not want to give him back. And as God willed, the baby no longer wanted the breast nor did my breasts produce any fever, so I was not tormented with worry for my baby nor with pain from my breasts.

(5) A few days later, while we were all praying, suddenly in the middle of a prayer, my voice spoke up and named Dinocrates. I was astounded, because until then it had not entered my mind at all, and I was saddened to remember him. I realised immediately that I was worthy to and ought to pray for him. I began a prayer for him and to sigh deeply for him to the Lord. At once, that very night, I had a vision. I saw Dinocrates coming out from a dark place where there were many other people, very hot and thirsty and pale, his clothes filthy, and on his face the wound which he had when he died. This Dinocrates had been my brother according to the flesh, and at seven years of age through cancer of the face he had died so horribly that his death had been hateful to everyone. So I made my prayer for him, and between him and me there was a great abyss so neither of us could approach the other. There, where Dinocrates was, was a pool full of water, with its edge higher than the height of the boy. Dinocrates was stretching up to drink. I was saddened because that pool had water and yet because of the height of the edge he could not drink. And I woke up, and I realised that my brother was suffering. But I had faith that I could help him in his suffering. And I began to pray for him every day until we were transferred to the military prison. For we were going to fight at the military games, on the birthday of Geta the Caesar. And I said a prayer for him day and night groaning and crying that it might be granted for me.

(6) On the day we remained in the prison, this vision was revealed to me. I saw the same place I had seen before and Dinocrates, who was clean, well dressed and refreshed. And where his wound had been I saw a scar, and that pool, which I had seen before, had its edge at the height of the boy's waist. And he was drinking water from it constantly. And above the edge was a golden bowl full of water, and Dinocrates went up and began to drink from it, yet the bowl was not emptied. And when he had had enough he went up to the water to play like a child, full of joy. I woke up and then I realised that he had been delivered from his suffering.

(7) A few days later a soldier named Pudens, the optio who was in charge of the prison, began to honour us, realising that we had great virtue within us, and he began to admit many people to see us, so that both we and they might be comforted. But the day of the games was growing near, and my father came in to see me completely overcome with sorrow, and he began ripping at his beard and throwing the hair on the ground, and he threw himself face down on the ground, and cursed his years and said such words as would move the whole of creation. I was saddened for his unhappy old age.

(8) The day before we were to fight, I saw this in a vision: Pomponius the deacon came to the gates of the prison and knocked loudly. I went out to him and opened them for him. He was wearing a white tunic without a belt and sandals with many windings. He said to me, 'Perpetua, we are waiting for you, come.' And he took my hand and we began to go through a place which was uneven and winding. At last and with much difficulty, we came to the amphitheatre out of breath, and he led me into the centre of the arena and said to me, 'Don't be afraid. I am here with you and I am suffering with you.' And he left. I looked at the huge crowd which was astonished. And because I knew that I had been condemned to the beasts, I was amazed that the beasts had not been let loose on me. And then opposite me out came a certain Egyptian, ugly in appearance, along with his supporters, to fight me. Handsome young men came up to me, my supporters and assistants. I was smoothed off and I became a man. And my supporters began to rub me down with oil, as is the custom for bouts. I saw that Egyptian opposite me rolling in the dust. Then out came a certain man of such great size that he rose above the pediment of the amphitheatre, dressed in a belt-less tunic, purple between two stripes down the centre of his chest, and complicated sandals made from gold and silver, and carrying a stick like a gladiator-trainer, and a green branch on which there were golden apples. He asked for silence and said, 'If he defeats her, this Egyptian will kill her with a sword; if she defeats him, she will receive this branch.' Then he left. And we came forward towards each other and began punching. He wanted

to get hold of my feet, but I kept kicking him in the face. Then suddenly I was lifted up into the air and I began to hit him as I would if I were not touching the ground. Then, when I saw there was a pause, I joined my hands, locking my fingers together, and grabbed his head. He fell face-down and I stood on his head. The crowd began to shout and my supporters sang psalms. I went up to the gladiator-trainer and I took the branch. He kissed me and said to me, 'Peace be with you, my daughter.' I began to make my way in glory to the Gate of Life and Health. And I woke up. And I realised that I was going to fight against the devil, not wild animals, but I knew that I would be victorious. This is what I did up until the day before the games; let whoever wants to write about what happened in the games themselves.

Notes

1. There is a full discussion of life and historical context of the martyrdom of Perpetua by J.E. Salisbury, *Perpetua's Passion: The Death and Memory of a Young Roman Woman* (London and New York: Routledge, 1997). She accepts the account as Perpetua's own, deriving from her diaries (p. 2); see also J.A. Robinson, *Passio Perpetua: Texts and Studies*, I.2 (Cambridge: Cambridge University Press, 1981), 47.
2. *Augustan History* 409; unfortunately this is not a reliable source.
3. Perpetua 4; cf. the procedure described by Pliny the Younger, and the reply by the emperor Trajan: *Letters* 10.96, 97.
4. It is this section of the work that I have translated and refer to by the short title Perpetua.
5. See *The Martyrdom* 2, Perpetua 3. A third brother, Dinocrates, had already died (Perpetua 5–6).
6. A Roman woman could remain under the authority of her father, even after marriage: see Salisbury, *Perpetua's Passion*, 8. For possible reasons for the absence of her husband from the text, see P. Dronke, *Women Writers of the Middle Ages: A Critical Study of Texts from Perpetua to Marguerite Porete* (Cambridge: Cambridge University Press, 1984), 282-83.
7. R. Rader, 'The Martyrdom of Perpetua: a protest account of third-century Christianity', in P. Wilson-Kastner *et al.* (eds), *A Lost Tradition: Women Writers of the Early Church* (Lanham: University Press of America, 1981), 3-4; for discussion of the context see also P. Habermehl, *Perpetua und der Ägypter oder Bilder des Bösen im frühen afrikanischen Christentum: ein Versuch zur Passio sanctarum Perpetuae et Felicitatis* (Berlin: Akademie Verlag, 1992).
8. H. Musurillo, *The Acts of the Christian Martyrs* (Oxford: Clarendon Press, 1972), lvii.
9. See M.R. Lefkowitz and M.B. Fant, *Women's Lives in Greece and Rome* (Baltimore: John Hopkins University Press, 1982), 214-19.
10. Rader, 'The Martyrdom of Perpetua', 3.
11. For discussion of the theological ideas raised by the text, see Salisbury, *Perpetua's Passion*, and Rader, 'The Martyrdom of Perpetua'.
12. G.D. Schlegel argues Tertullian wrote his *To the Martyrs* to encourage Perpetua's group: 'The *Ad Martyras* of Tertullian and the circumstances of its composition', *Downside Review* 63 (1945), 125-128; T. Barnes, *Tertullian: A Historical and Literary Study* (Oxford: Clarendon Press, 1971), 55, argues for an earlier date (AD 197). Tertullian's work does seem to have influenced the author of *Perpetua*: Salisbury, *Perpetua's Passion*, 86-87.
13. E. Diehl, *Inscriptiones Latinae Christianae Veterae* (Berlin: Weidmann, 1961), 2040a-41, 403; cf. 1959a, 1062c, 3138.
14. H.A. Wilson (ed.), *Gelasian Sacramentary* (Oxford: Clarendon Press, 1894), 168.
15. Augustine, *Sermons* 280-82.
16. Salisbury, *Perpetua's Passions*, uses the portrait for her cover illustration.

51. Theosebeia (*date uncertain: 3rd–6th centuries* AD)

Introduction

One epitaph attributed to Theosebeia has survived in the *Greek Anthology* (7.559). It is the only evidence we have for her and her work. The poem must postdate the death of Galen (about AD 207), and so a third or fourth century date for the poet is possible. We do know of a Theosebeia who wrote at about this time: Zosimus collaborated with his sister, Theosebeia, in composing an alchemical work. However the coincidence of the name and approximate date are not sufficient to identify the poet as the alchemist. The inclusion of the poem in the collection compiled by Agathias in the time of Justinian, means that Theosebeia may have lived as late as the sixth century AD.[1] Her name means 'religiousness'.

In Greek mythology, Acestoria (who was also called Aceso) was a daughter of Asclepius, the god of medicine. Here the poet describes her lamenting for Ablabius (who is otherwise unknown), ranking him alongside the two great men of Greek medicine, Hippocrates and Galen. Theosebeia evokes the traditional image of a mourning woman to express sorrow at the death of Ablabius, while using a mythical figure close to the god of medicine to elevate the dead man's importance in this profession.

Theosebeia

Acestoria saw three sorrows: first she
shaved her hair for Hippocrates, second for Galen,
and now she lies on the mournful tomb of Ablabius,
ashamed to appear among people bereft of him.

Notes

1. See W.R. Paton, *The Greek Anthology*, II (Cambridge, MA: Harvard University Press, 1917), 1.

52. Proba (*about* AD *322–70*)

Introduction

The author of a Christian Virgilian cento of over 690 lines, Proba is a significant author from the fourth century AD. She was the first writer to compose a substantial Christian cento, one of the first to use Virgil for a Christian purpose,[1] and the first Christian writer that we know for sure was a woman.[2]

She identifies herself simply as 'Proba' (line 12). Scholars have disagreed about which Proba she is: some thought that she was Anicia Faltonia Proba, who lived at the beginning of the fifth century AD, and is known in early Christian circles through the letters of Augustine, John Chrysostom, and Jerome.[3] Karl Schenkl, however, has argued persuasively that we should accept the ancient testimony of Isidore of Seville, a seventh century bishop who knew Proba's work well and identified her as Faltonia Betitia Proba (the grandmother of Anicia).[4] Isidore's identification was supported by a scholiast who noted in the margin of a tenth century manuscript (from the Benedictine abbey near Modena) that Proba was the wife of Adelphius, the grandfather of Anicia.[5]

We know a little about Faltonia Betitia Proba's family, and this helps to date her and her work. She was a member of an important and wealthy Roman family.[6] Her husband, Clodius Celsinus Adelphius, was city prefect of Rome in AD 351, and later proconsul; her grandfather, Probus, was consul in 310; her father, Petronius Probianus, in 322; and her son, Olybrius, in 379. Her granddaughter Anicia Faltonia Proba married Sextus Petronius Probus, one of the richest business men of his day, and Prefect of Illyricum, Italy and Africa in the 380s. As her son should have been at least 41 in AD 379 (to become consul), Proba herself would have been born by about AD 320.[7]

We can further date her cento itself by Proba's reference to an earlier work she composed 'long ago' on a civil war (lines 1-8). The scholiast tells us that this work was on Constantius' war against Magnentius (AD 350–52).[8] That poem is no longer extant, but if we accept the scholiast's opinion, we should date Proba's work 'long' after AD 352; line 46 implies that she is no longer young, as does the reference to grandchildren (line 694). Her work was known to Damasus, who imitated Proba. He died in 384, so publication must have been before then.[9]

Proba's remarks about her earlier martial poetry and her rejection of the Muses have been taken as evidence of a pagan past, her renunciation of those themes as a sign of her conversion to Christianity.[10] She does introduce the Holy Spirit as a source of inspiration instead of the Muses, but still sees herself as 'soaked by the Castalian spring' (line 20); references to literary motifs, however, are not good evidence for biography. The argument that her husband was a pagan, but was converted to Christianity by Proba, is also speculative.[11] The work is, however, an early example of confessional literature. Proba apologises for earlier work late in life (see line 335), confessing her errors as she turns to a Christian theme.

The cento (or 'patchwork') was an artistic response to a literary education grounded in a canon of the classics. In Greek centones were written from Homer—Eudocia's is a good example—in Latin they were written from Virgil from at least the second century AD.[12] Originally written just for fun, 'rules' were established for the proper composition of a cento: each line of the new poem had to be formed from a line or two half lines from the source; the repetition of two or more whole lines in succession was frowned upon as being very weak, and of course the centoist had to pay proper attention to the retention of an appropriate poetic metre. Some grammatical changes might need to be made, but otherwise the cento should be true to the verse of the original.[13] Proba is successful in this and has produced a work which is recognised for the poetic skill with which she has adapted the original to its new purpose and is a fine example of the cento.[14]

Her cento opens with an introduction in which Proba rejects martial themes (the usual stuff of epic poetry) and instead takes up a Christian theme, inspired by the spirit of God (lines 1-55). She then retells episodes from Genesis and other Old Testament stories (lines 56-332), before offering a second introduction and turning to the New Testament and the story of Christ (lines 333ff.). Proba was the first Christian poet to focus attention on Genesis 1–8, but she was followed by many others, including Cyprian of Gaul, Avitus, Marius Victor, Hilary of Arles, Dracontius and Sedulius, an indication of the significance of her work.[15] A further indication of the popularity of her work comes in a preface which includes a dedication to the Roman emperor Arcadius (AD 383–408) who had himself requested a copy of the text.[16]

In 362 the emperor Julian issued a decree forbidding Christian teachers from teaching pagan texts to their pupils, an attempt to deprive Christian children of an education based upon learning the classics, especially Virgil. Amatucci suggests that this decree prompted Proba to adapt Virgil for use in the class room: through her cento his poetry would remain the basis of a child's education, but with a new Christian plot and no paganism.[17] While we cannot rule out a didactic objective, we should not assume that Proba composed her cento to teach children, despite its apparent later use for that purpose,[18] just as we would not assume that that was the purpose Virgil imagined for his poetry.

There were critics of the cento. Jerome in a letter to Paulinus of Nola (*Letter* 53.7) belittles them as pieces of literature; he refers to a 'garrulous old woman' as a typical author, singling out a passage in Proba to demonstrate his point. Yet the cento was popular as a literary form in the fourth century. Originality was not as highly prized then as it is now: Virgil himself drew heavily on Homer in composing his epic. It is not until the poetry of Ambrose, Paulinus of Nola and Prudentius that original Christian poetry was written.[19]

Proba

Long ago, I confess, I wrote of leaders
who had violated sacred vows of peace,
—wretched men caught by a dreadful desire to rule—
and various killings, kings' cruel wars
and families in battle-lines, the illustrious shields
stained by parents' blood and trophies taken from no enemy,   5
triumphs splattered with blood which fame had brought,
cities widowed so often of countless citizens;
it is enough to remember these evils.

Now, almighty god, receive my sacred song, I pray,
unlock the mouths of your eternal sevenfold   10
spirit and unlock the interior of my heart,
so that I, Proba, prophet, can recall all mysteries.
No more am I anxious to seek ambrosial nectar,
nor do I like to lead the Muses from the Aonian peak,
nor should an idle error persuade me that rocks speak   15
and follow tripods crowned with laurel and empty prayers
and quarrelling gods of noblemen and defeated Penates.
For it is not my task to enhance my reputation with words
and to look for some small praise from people's enjoyment,
but soaked by the Castalian spring, imitating the blessed,   20
I who thirsting have drunk from the offerings of the holy light,
here I will begin to sing.

God be present, direct my mind;
may I say that Virgil sang of the holy gifts of Christ;
and repeating a theme obscure to no one I will proceed from the beginning,
if there is any faith in my heart, if flowing through my joints   25
the true mind moves my effort and the spirit mixes itself
with my whole body and harmful elements do not slow me down
and earthbound joints and mortal limbs not grow dull.
O Father, O eternal power over people and all things
give an easy course and flow into my spirit,   30
and you be at hand so that together we may hurry through the work begun,
O Son, you are the energy of the highest Father and heavenly beginning,
whom we first worship and renew due honours,
offspring now new, in whom every age believed.
For I remember, reflecting on the records of ancient men   35
that before all your Musaeus sang through the world
of things that were, things that had been, and things that soon were going to be.
And the young circle of the world itself will have taken shape completely.
Happy is he who could know the explanations for things,
where the race of people comes from and sheep and the lives of flying animals 40
and what marvels the sea bears beneath the marbled water
and at the same time fire and the fickle moisture of the liquid sky.
Not otherwise first at the beginning of the growing world
would I believe that the day became light or had another
course. A greater arrangement of the universe is born to me   45
if great age will bring truth to such a work.
For, I will confess, I used to sing of spectacles of trivial things,
always horses, arms of men and battles,
and in vain I eagerly wanted to labour at my work.
When I tried all those themes, a better purpose seemed to be   50
to disclose profound themes buried in earth and mist.
Day upon day, my mind moved me to seize something important
nor was it content with peaceful quiet.
Keep silent and all give me your cheerful attention,
mothers and men, boys and unmarried girls.   55

In the beginning, heaven and earth and the watery plains
and the bright globe of the moon and the sun's works
the Father himself set up, and you, O clearest lights of the world,
who lead the year as it sinks from heaven.
For neither the fires of the stars nor the clear sky existed   60
but black night drawn by a chariot held the pole,
and empty-space held as much in sheer descent to the shadows,
as looking up to the sky's heavenly Olympus.
Then the almighty Father, who holds supreme power over the universe,
moved apart the dark air and dispelled the shadows   65
and then divided the world, half to light, and half to shadows.
All the constellations he marked out sinking in the silent sky
turning watchful eyes, in which part he set the southern heat,
and which has its back turned to the pole.
When he saw everything was set up in a peaceful sky,   70
almighty, he numbered and named the stars
and made the year equal to four different seasons,
heat, and rains and winds that bring the cold.
And so that we could learn them by sure signs
the earth swells with spring and demands fruitful seed   75
and in mid-summer the threshing floor rubs the scorched fruits of the earth
and autumn lays out its various fruits and black
winter comes; Sicyonian olives are pressed in the olive-press;
and the year turns back on its own footprints.
Now from that time great heaven mixed with the   80
great body feeds with fertile rain its fruits.

And then the first dawn began to sprinkle the earth with new light
and lead in the day after the stars had fled.
Then he began to harden the land and to separate Nereus with his sea
and gradually to choose the shapes of things,   85
and various figures from the sea, monstrous whales,
began to sweep the level sea with their tails and cut the surf.
In addition all around the huge sea's water species,
now when the sun spreads through, now when things are uncovered by light,
in joy it scattered the bitter salt-spray far and wide.   90

Then at first dawn the day arose.
The earth poured out flowers and unfurled all its leaves
and wild haunts for birds blushed with blood-red berries,
not enslaved to hoes nor to any human care.

The third light removed the chilly shadow from the sky.   95
Then pathless copses sang with melodious birds
and ravens gave liquid cries from their tightened throats
nor did the dove cease cooing from its airy elm.

On the fourth day out of the woods and through the grass
suddenly the earth led marvellous animals of different kinds,   100

and all the flocks, with no shepherd, a miracle to see.
Then at last the lion roused his arms, then the tiger so dangerous
and the scaly snake and the lioness tawny-necked
began to vent her fury and the bodies of massive wolves began to howl.
Other oxen graze through the green grasses,   105
neither springs of water nor plants are in short supply for the herds.

Then a day advanced and another day, and as the Father
looked over all this work of excellence and draft of the divine mind
when everything was completed in succession
he was unable to satisfy his mind and he was inflamed by watching   110
the lands and expanse of the sea and depth of the sky,
the species of birds and flocks, and he turned over in his mind,
who would hold the sea, who the land with full sovereignty,
nor should the wheatfield lands lie neglected. He enjoyed delaying all the time.
While reflecting on these matters, suddenly a decision was settled upon   115
and he drew up lucky clay and moulded by kneading
straightway the fertile soil from the first months of the year.
And then unexpectedly the image of such holiness
the new and most beautiful form of man first went forth,
his face and shoulders resembling god, whose mind and soul   120
a greater god drives and turns to greater works.
Another is sought for him; but no one from such a large crowd
dared approach man and be called his ally in the kingdom.
Without delay immediately he gave quiet rest through the limbs
of the young man and his eyes closed in sweet sleep.   125
And then in the mid-time of shady night
the almighty Father laid bare his ribs and entrails.
He plucked out one of these from well-knit joints
of the young man's side and suddenly a wonderful gift arose
—substantial proof— and shone in the bright light,   130
a virgin, conspicuous in her face and beautiful breast,
now ready for a husband, now marriageable in age.
A mighty terror breaks his sleep; he calls his bones and limbs
his wife and amazed by the divine favour he squeezed her
and took hold of her by the hand and folded his arms around
her in embrace.   135

When he had done this, at length he puzzled over who created
the stars of heaven; as he was saying this the sea smoothed its tranquil surface
and the foundation of the earth trembled, the lofty sky grew quiet.
'Live happily among the splendid fields
and happy seats of blessed open woods.   140
This is your home, this is your native land, a sure rest from work.
I place no finishing post for this, no limit of time.
I have given rule without limit, and the ground
will not suffer the hoe for many years, nor vineyard the sickle.
But your species will stay immortal, nor will slow old age   145
enfeeble men's minds nor change their strength.

But now pay attention to what I say.
There is a tree in full view with fruitful branches;
divine law forbids you to level with fire or iron,
by holy religious scruple it is never allowed to be disturbed.   150
And whoever steals the holy fruit from this tree,
will pay the penalty of death deservedly; no argument has changed my mind.
Let no authority, however sensible, persuade you
to pollute your hands; you should be warned by a word—
woman, do not let the impetuosity of another defeat you,   155
if the proper glory of the divine fields awaits you.'

After the Father, whom the stars of heaven obey set out
everything, he gave laws and from above displayed
the shining plains, the glory of such a great world.
But look, at the rising of the first sun beneath its lintel   160
they came to a place where soft marjoram breathed upon them
and wrapped them with flowers and sweet shade.
Here spring is purple and summer in other months,
here there are springs of water, here at the time chosen by heaven
sweet honey squeezes out, here white poplar hangs over   165
the cave and supple vines weave together shady places.
Gardens breathing with saffron-coloured flowers attract
amid an open wood scented of laurel, and earth herself
kept bearing all freely without being asked.
Blessed pair, if the mind of the unspeakable wife had not been   170
stupid; afterwards the mighty exodus taught.
And now the unspeakable day was at hand; through the fields of flowers
look, a snake, abominable, hostile, with immeasurable circles,
seven huge coils, twisting with seven rolls
not easily seen nor courteous in speech to anyone,   175
it hung with hidden hatred from sprouting branch
breathing a viper's breath, in its heart sad wars
and anger and treachery and harmful crimes.
The Father himself hated it; it changed itself so many times in its face
and it bristled with its steep scales and, so as not to leave   180
neither wickedness nor trickery undared nor untried,
first it approached like this with words and showed itself of its own accord.
It said, 'Tell me, maiden –I live in the dark woods
and river banks and dwell in meadows refreshed by streams—
what great cowardice has come upon your courage?   185
Fruits lie scattered everywhere, each beneath its own tree
the cups are springs of water. It is wicked to touch
the heavenly gifts. That one thing the world lacks.
What prevents you testing reasons hidden far away?
It is empty superstition. The other part of the world has
been withdrawn.   190
Why did he give eternal life? Why have the arrangements for death
been withdrawn? If you think that what I said was not futile,
I the author of what should be dared annul the sacred laws.

You are his wife, it is right for you to test his soul by pleading.
I shall be your leader. If your choice of me is sure,   195
we will heap up the couches and feast on sumptuous banquets.'
It said this, and quicker than its speech, what was prohibited by law,
the once hallowed tree they submitted to their banquets
and began the meal, and defiled everything with their contact.
The especially unlucky woman, devoted to future ruin,   200
admired the new leaves and fruit that was not hers,
the cause of such great wrong-doing, she touched with her lips.
After venturing upon a very great crime, she rose to an even greater madness,
alas, the wife pushed the fruit from the tree that was not theirs
on the wretched man and moved his soul with sudden sweetness.   205
At once a new light shone from their eyes; but
they were frightened by their sudden vision and without delay
they shaded their bodies beneath the spreading of leafy branches;
they fastened together a covering. No hope of help was given.
But the creator of the humankind and of the world watched
these events   210
with his eyes and foresaw murders and the tyrant's actions,
and recognised what a woman in her madness could do.
Immediately he attacked them, 'Far away, be far away you
impious creatures',
cried he who supports heaven and earth with his divine power.
And they, when they saw him pacing far off and shouting   215
dreadful things, turned in fear and rushing back
fled off and searched for woods and hollow rocks anywhere
in secret. They regretted the coming of the light, nor did they
look upon the breezes; they hated to look upon the vault of heaven.
It was not long after that the repeated sound of feet seemed
to their ears   220
to be present and on the winds the Father addressed him,
hardly recognising him mournful in the shadows,
with words like these, and he rebuked him besides.
'Unhappy man, what mighty madness has taken your mind?
What new madness is this? Where, where are you aiming
to go now', he said.   225
'Forgetting your kingdom, what insanity changes your minds?
Tell me, what desire so dreadful for light, you wretched people?
Hurry your flight and be gone from this whole place;
nor is it lawful to recall your steps, even when misfortunes
call upon you. A river encircles it with scorching flames,   230
hissing through the middle and twists the roaring rocks
and throws up balls of flames and licks the stars.'
After this he said, 'Your sad image, Father, your image
...me...
(they) have put me in this place. I deserve it nor do I pray to avert it.
Almighty, I tremble at the sound of your feet and your voice   235
knowing the guilt of my rash deed. And with bad advice
the woman brought the bitter juice and slow taste.

She considered trickery and dreadful sin beneath her breast
and a girl who in her madness is going to die, by unspeakable evidence,
she destroyed an innocent and careless man with cruel death.   240
For she persuaded me, you know, for nothing escapes your notice.
As I saw, how I was destroyed, how a bad mistake mislead me,
and we touched with our hands what the tree itself does not produce.'
The almighty Father begins from his high throne,
'So take to heart and fix there these my words: 245
you first, your crime is larger than all others ,
you whom neither long days nor any pity will soften,
advisor of crimes, snake, feeding on bad grasses,
dishonoured, dragging your belly wide with idleness,
leave this place yourself, without the compulsion of people,   250
where clay is shallow and thorny fields have stones.
But your crime,' he said, 'for such great rashness
your whole life is worn away by iron, and you will be first with the skill,
alas wretched boy, to attack the earth with hoes
and frighten birds with noise. In the fields   255
the thistle will prickle and Christ's-thorn will rise up with sharp spikes,
and goose-grass and star-thistles and grass deceptive with poison.
But if you cultivate the ground for a wheat harvest
and stout spelt, you will look at the heap in vain
and be accustomed to hunger in the woods with a shaken oak.   260
In addition to this, sad old age will befall you with illness
and work and the severity of a hard death will carry you away.
This will always be your lot, and you, most cruel wife,
not unaware of wrong, the head and cause of these wrongs,
you will atone for your great crimes. Alas, lost woman,
you do not know   265
nor do you notice the dangers which will now stand around you.
Now die, as you have deserved, because you sought it with your mind.
My judgment is not now changed and does not yield.'
At first cruel dread surrounded the young man.
His eyes stiffened, nor did he hide himself in the shade   270
any longer nor hear familiar voices nor reply.
Without delay they hurried as they had been ordered and
carried themselves off
on quick feet, and walking together through the shadows of the way
they sped along the middle course and left the threshold
weeping and fixed their steps with equal trouble.   275
Then the branches gave them sustenance in the woods, berries
and stony cherries and the plants fed them with roots pulled out.

Meanwhile the sun turned the great year around.
Ten months brought a long-term nausea to the mother,
from whom people are born, a hard species. From that time
through skill   280
grasses grew on the plain or leaves on the tree,
and grains dared to trust themselves to new suns safely.

And they began to hang the vine from pliant branches
and teach it to grow in humid bark.
Then, when twin brothers were burning offerings on altar-top
with torches   285
one envied the offering presented by the other—
I shudder to tell it – he caught his incautious relation,
who shared his blood, and cut him down at his father's altar
staining with his blood the fire which he himself had consecrated.
Then the Father added venom to dark snakes   290
and struck honey from the leaves and took away fire
and ordered wolves to prey and the sea to roll
and everywhere he stopped the streams of flowing wine.
Soon a disease was added to the grain, so that there would be
an evil blight
on the stalks and sick crops would not provide the means of life.   295
Then snares to catch wild animals were invented, and birdlime
to trick them, and the poverty which pinches when times are hard
moved the fields, sharpening mortal hearts with cares,
until gradually an inferior and discoloured, age
offspring of iron, lifted its head from the hard fields   300
and the madness of war and love of having followed.
Justice made her footprints as she left the earth.
Not long after, madness and anger removed reason.
Soaked with the blood of their brothers they rejoiced.
Another man hid his wealth and used to sit on his buried gold   305
and with no pity for the poor he did not feel sorry nor offer
his right hand.
Then the almighty father was deeply angered and hurled himself
from the upper sky. He poured the earth into the waves
mixing in a flood, and loosed heaven into Tartarus.
He levelled the fields, he levelled the joyful crops and washed away   310
the oxen's work. The ditches were filled and the hollow river grew.
He gave every kind of flock death, every kind of wild animal.
Then the man respected for his piety and kindness
—marvellous to relate—
who on earth was most mindful of fairness,
he snatched away from death when the waves were rising up
to such great heights,   315
to have the race from which a new lineage would be recalled.
From out of that flood the Almighty gave laws to the elders
who had been summoned; they lived their lives under the great laws.
Why the memory of unspeakable murders, why the deeds of tyrants
and the ignorant hearts tamed by people's prayers,   320
the strength of Egypt and the distant wars of the east
and leaders brave with respect to the rank of the whole race,
by which direction he sought the deserts and the great race and tribe
of men, not ever forgetting such great service,
every holy priest next to the altars,   325
every pious prophet falling for freedom,

the kings who were roused to war, the battlelines
which filled the plains with red shore, with which arms
a king, his lineage outstanding, burned with great burning madness,
leading the column of cavalry and troops shining in bronze,   330
other deeds and wars of our forefathers fought in succession
I omit, and I leave to others after me what should be recorded.

Now I return to you and your great decrees, Father.
I begin my greater work. I take up the predictions of the
older prophets,
although the end of a slender life awaits,   335
I have to attempt the path by which I too could lift me
from the ground and carry your name in fame through countless years,
because your son came down from high heaven,
the age brought to us as we prayed for something
the help and advent of God, whom a woman first   340
wearing the face and clothing of a virgin—marvellous to relate—
gave birth to a boy not of our race nor blood.
And alarming prophets sang the late omens
that a magnificent man was coming to the people and to the earth
from heavenly seed, who would seize the world by his might.   345
And then the promised day was at hand, when for the first time
the source of divine progeny revealed his holy face.
He was sent for rule and came as virtue in body
mixed with god. The image of his dear father came down.
Without delay, in the peaceful area of heaven at once   350
a star leading a flame of great light rushed.
The princes recognised a god and suddenly with every
gift they increased and worshipped the holy star.
Then indeed faith was clear and the name of his
father's virtue distinguished. And they themselves recognised the face   355
and the signs of the divine beauty of brilliant God.
Forthwith rushing with great passion the news flew
to the king and sharpened his anger with the great rumour
and inflamed his soul and also fell upon his mother's ears.
She was not unaware of what was happening and foresaw his trickery   360
and dreadful wickedness and she first caught his future impulses.
With foreknowledge of what would come she ordered that he
be reared in secret,
while his cares were in doubt, while his mind was boiling with anger.
But the worried king ordered them to throw away the offspring
and all the future race and to light flames beneath and burn him.   365
He set many things in motion, sending out men to report the facts.
They did as they had been ordered, and carried on swift feet
they filled the city with great terror.
Immediately sounds were heard and mighty crying
and the breath of babies sobbing. Before their parents' faces   370
the bodies of their sons were strewn in the doorways.
But the mother terrified at such great sobbing, and rightly so,

carrying her baby before her in her bosom, during the confused uproar
she fled and returned to the full mangers.
Here under the scanty sloping roof she began to nurse her son   375
milking her breasts with his delicate lips.
Here, boy, your cradle first will pour out flowers,
and everywhere earth mixed with laughing cyclamen
and little by little caladium will pour out tender acanthus.
And at that time the cycle of time was completed and came to an end.   380
As soon as his raving ceased and his raging lips became quiet,
displaying a spirit beyond his years the heavenly source
walked through the middle of the cities and the neighbouring peoples.
All the young people poured out from the houses and fields
and watched him as he went by, gaping with spirits inspired.   385
A crowd of mothers were amazed, 'What spirit he has,
what a face, and the sound of his voice or step as he goes past.'
At once a prophet—and he was a most reliable authority—
when he saw the Mystery at a distance by a cool river
he said, 'It is the time. Look, God, God; our greatest faith in deed   390
or word rests with him. You now will be second to him,
lucky boy, whom the stars of heaven obey.
Indeed I used to think like this and suppose what would happen.
You, the one awaited, do come, our hope and our comfort.'
When he had said this, he took him come to dip in the
health-giving river   395
and drew him from the soft waves.
The waters rejoiced and suddenly excited a dove
flew down and stopped above his head. From there it suddenly
swiftly skimmed the liquid way, nor did it move its wings.
Here the whole crowd pouring to the banks began to rush   400
splashing copious water from their shoulders in contest.
Then the Father addressed his son with friendly words,
'Son, my strength, my great power alone
and most sweet glory, you who will return to your father
the beginning is from you, and will end with you. Listen,
I am testifying,   405
my son: wherever the sun catches sight of the Ocean
and returns, joyful at the glory completed
you will see everything turned and ruled beneath your feet.
Rule your people with authority, mothers and men,
their spirits idle long ago and hearts unused,   410
and pitying with me the indolent who are unaware of the way
go out and become used to being called in prayer now.'
He had spoken. He began to prepare to obey his great Father's
authority, pressing on with the work and the kingdom to come.
Alas for piety! Alas for old-fashioned faith! What thanks   415
am I to begin to speak, if I may compare small things with great?
Then I had no hope of seeing my ancient fatherland
nor any hope of freedom nor care for salvation.
Here he first gave an answer to me when I sought one,

he removed the set stain and left pure 420
heavenly understanding and sent me back into my kingdom.
So I would follow him through flames, if I were to spend time
as an exile in Sidra,
through various reasons, through a thousand approaching missiles,
where and whenever things may fall, the one, for his so great name,
and I would pile high his altars with his own gifts. 425
For his coming, for the rewards of such great glory
the unshaven mountains themselves toss their voices
to the joyful stars; the valleys echo everything.

At this time—a great and memorable story—
it is necessary to remember the fearful evil of the snake. 430
Indeed the snake even dared—the story is rather obscured by time—
to address the man and ask the reasons for his coming.
When it saw him making for him through the grass
the stricken snake stayed and fiercely growled and
with proud speech addressed the powerful lord: 435
'Is your appearance true? Do you bring news to me as a true messenger?
What is your birth? What home do you come from, you who make
your way to our threshold?
Come on now, tell me why you come. For they say you give laws.
Or who, most presumptuous young man, told you to come
to our home and impose the custom of peace? 440
Of course, I do not envy, I am all the more amazed. In turn, hear
what doubt and what thought now rises in my mind.
There is a high home. Call the west winds and glide with wings
and seek the steep roof, daring to trust yourself to heaven,
if whom you recall is really your Father, whom the stars obey.' 445
Smiling with heart calm he spoke to him
not unaware of the prophets and knowing of the age to come:
'Did you expect to deceive me, treacherous snake?
Do not doubt. For you will see the truth. Choose to follow
the high stars with wings and hide yourself shut in the hollow earth. 450
Where do you fall, doomed creature, and do you dare things
greater than your strength?
Yield to God, after you have thrown your whole body to the earth.'
No more than this. It was amazed at the respected gift
and pressed its forehead to the earth and forced bloody froth
from its mouth
and set on flight it mixed itself with the invisible shadows. 455

Meanwhile the story flew as it went through the great cities.
Men came together. They were all of one mind, to follow him
to whichever lands he wanted to lead them by sea.
Many moreover, whom dark fame hid away,
ran with great noise and crowded around pressing together 460
and rejoiced in their hearts. For the massive crowd
held him in its midst and they admired the width of his high shoulders.

When he reached the high mountains, the eternal power
began to give justice and laws to men, mysteries of his Father,
and he gave hope to doubtful minds and freed them of their cares.   465
Look, he saw others crowding left and right.
When he saw they were crowded together and were venturing to fight
he began and breathed with words a divine love.
'Be advised: learn justice. Help the tired,
each for his own sake, men, whatever wealth you each have,   470
and joyful call your universal God. Let us follow what is best
and whatever way the journey calls let us turn. The first road
of salvation
is pure faith and a mind aware of right.
Your share will be rest when the cycle of time is completed.
For who sit alone upon their wealth procured   475
and did not share a part with his family, while life remains,
or a parent is beaten and fraud contrived against a client,
then, when cold death has divided limb from soul,
they await the penalty imprisoned—the crowd of them is the largest—
and call out from dark underworld and suffer punishments   480
for old evils. For others beneath a vast abyss
the tainted crime is washed away or burned out by fire.
Here muddy with filth an abyss of vast depth
boils and throws up sand from its deepest chasm.
From here a groaning is heard and with cruel sound   485
floggings, then the clanking of iron and dragging chains,
and always the shadows are thickened by night drawn over.
Meanwhile, turn to what I say with your souls.
May I hear that in the future you are not still guarding sanctuaries with bullocks
duly slaughtered according to ancestral ceremony,   490
and a statue made from trunks and oak by mortal hand.
And I will warn you, repeating this again and again.
But to die once is sufficient, and it will benefit you more
to remember son and father, if it is worthwhile to believe.
But meanwhile time flees, flees irretrievable,   495
and the day of flames and enemy power approaches.'
They were at a loss, their courage terrified. Delaying no longer
he sang another greater judgment for the poor weak
mortals, and he gave them notice saddened with anger.
It would come to destruction and everything destroyed   500
by a huge disaster, then both the stars wandering from the axis
and the downfall of heaven would be equally mixed with red fire.
Then indeed terror slipped new terrors into the trembling
hearts of all, and they saw what was going to come in silence.
When he was warning about the coming of these many terrors,   505
a boy whose face was unshaven marked with the first down of youth,
rich in wealth, flourishing with enthusiasm for low-born idleness,
(five bleating flocks returned to him, and five herds, and
he loaded his table with feasts unbought)
immediately he eagerly held out both hands   510

52. Proba

'O virtue, O part most deserved of our reputation,
I flee for help to you and a suppliant I beg your divine favour.
I have anticipated everything, I have passed through everything with my soul.
Take me from these sins, unconquerable. What now remains,   515
or following what am I able to overcome such great labours?
Accept and return my faith. It is right for me to seize on
your commands.'
And with this brief response the hero replied:
'O young man outstanding in your soul, cease your praying,
and do not be sorry. My friend, there is nothing left for you to do.   520
I will even add to these prayers, if your goodwill towards me is sure.
Learn, boy, to despise wealth and also make yourself worthy
of God, and you will be able to understand what virtue is.
Give your right arm to the poor and as a brother do not desert
your brother.
If he is eager to join in friendship, join willingly.   525
Let a chaste home keep its chastity. Come on, interrupt
your lazy delays and come not bitter to the affairs of the destitute.'
He said this. And at these words, sadder, he turned his footsteps
lifting his face pale by a wondrous amount,
groaning deeply he turned himself from his eyes and took
himself away.   530

From the time when there was first confidence in the sea,
over the tranquil deep
allies launched their ships and with a master's skill
while one man transfixed the broad stream with his net
seeking the deep, another dragged his wet line in the sea.
When the boats held the deep and no longer met any land,   535
the air flickered with frequent fire,
suddenly the clouds snatched away the sky and the day,
the winds rose up and raised the waves to the stars.
But companions' blood grew stiff with sudden fear, frozen;
their spirits fell, and all suddenly began   540
to watch the sea weeping—one voice to them all—
vacillating between hope and fear, whether they could believe they were alive
or suffering the final moment, the thin line which separates off death:
many events like these the sailors suffer in the deep.

Look! God perceived that sea was mixed up with mighty rumbling   545
and a storm of very great power had been sent.
Like light winds and swifter than winged lightning
he sought the curling sea and hastened across the open sea.
He was not separated by far from a passing keel.
From afar the exposed companions recognised the king   550
and his strong right arm and greeted him with a great shouting.
When he touched the high waves and came to the sea-surface,
it was reported that it was indeed dreadful and an amazing sight.

The waves subsided, so there was no struggling with an oar,
and he caused the gathered clouds to fly away and then
walked through   555
the middle of the sea-surface, and yet it did not wet the high sides of his body.
But coming aboard amidships among the companions themselves
he took over the helm as pilot himself, himself the master.
The mast shook, the skiff groaned beneath the weight,
the sails fell, and god sat down in the high stern,   560
and at last the joyful men turned towards the well-known sands.

Then too the driver sat, shining from his cloud, on the ribs
of a little slow donkey. For him a crowd all around,
mothers, men and boys, threw down their customary garments
and rejoiced to take the rope with their hands.   565
And now they approached the gates; and the aged temple
of ancient cedar, lofty with one hundred columns,
he entered in the midst of a large accompanying troop.
This temple, dreaded with its woods, was the senate-house,
this the sacred seat, which they used to care for with
astonishing respect.   570
For while he was examining every single thing beneath
the huge temple,
he suddenly shuddered at the sight and cracked a whip
and gestured with his hand while he thundered with his great voice:
'What forms of sin, what shining bronze and name of Caesar,
do I see? What madness changes your mind?   575
This is our own seat; here at the time appointed
they have been accustomed to sit at their ancestors' unbroken tables.'
They were paralysed in their souls and a cold trembling ran
through their innermost bones, and the forefathers left the tables in fear.

Meanwhile the evening star came closer to steep Olympus.   580
Then men recovered with food and spread out on the grass
they burdened the tables with a banquet and put down the cups.
After the first rest from feasting and the removal of the tables,
he himself with the leaders celebrated honours to the Father,
looking up at heaven. Then silence came upon their tongues.   585
He put in their hands fruits of the earth and sweet water from springs
and filled a dish with wine and taught the rites of worship
and mixed in prayers and said things like this:
'Listen noble men,' he said, 'and learn your hopes.
No one from this number will leave me unrewarded,   590
and because of your Father's promises,' he said, 'definite rewards
wait for you, boys, and no one moves the victory-prize from
its set-place.
And when tomorrow's light first returns to the earth
there will be one man who sets himself so greatly against me, for the destruction
of my people, while in the midst of our body and for peace.   595
Now unless I err the day is here. Shut off your cares.

That labour will be mine, unless my judgment deceives me.
One head will be given for many.' When he had said this
he fell silent and gave his limbs to late rest.

Meanwhile the dawn rose up and left the ocean.   600
And now the priest along with the people filled the elders
far and wide with complaints, and the mumbling was passed
along the line.
What was the ancestry of the man, and what homeland is so barbaric
that it allows such a custom? They demanded he pay the
penalty with blood
and from all sides they gathered and with great shouting follow   605
the innocent man, and the crowd of insignificants are ferocious
in their souls.
The fiery sun had climbed to the mid-circle of the heaven,
when suddenly everyone, elders and the people, demanded
that he be summoned and ordered him to say from whose blood he was fathered,
what he was seeking and what he was offering himself. Deceit
mixed with   610
stupidity drove the lazy men who watched his famous deeds
—the mind of man is ignorant—and they competed to ridicule
the prisoner.
Then indeed they took their weapons and charged from all sides.
The shouting rose to heaven and suddenly they all
seized the holy image and with blood-stained hands   615
they positioned a huge oak after cutting off its branches on all sides
and tied him up with huge twisted bands,
and they stretched out his hands and pressed his feet together, one on the other
—a sad service—those whom the other young men followed,
all dared a savage sin and mastered what they dared.   620
But fearless he said, 'Why do you fasten bonds?
Has such great confidence in your race got hold of you?
Later you will atone with a punishment unlike the one inflicted on me.'
He mentioned these things and stood fast and remained affixed.
Meanwhile the heaven began to be confused with a great rumbling   625
and a black night took colour from the world
and impious generations feared an eternal night.
The earth shook, wild animals fled and low terror
threw to the ground mortal hearts, family by family. After that
the earth suddenly gave a groan and the whole heaven rang with noise.   630
Immediately excited the thin shades began to go from the deepest
seats of Erebus. The earth too and the surface of the sea
gave signs; the streams stopped and the lands yawned open.
Then Tartarus itself, home and intimate of Death, was stunned
and shadowy caves were opened deep within.   635
The sun too as it rose—all said that they knew this—
then covered its shining head with dark gloom.
The companions dispersed and were hidden by dark night
and turned in their sad hearts many hard facts.

What were they to do? His face and words stayed stamped   640
in their hearts; care gave limbs no quiet rest.
Then an older man reported such words with his heart,
thinking greatly: 'Where now for us is God, that master?
Whom do we follow? Where do you order us to go, where to place our home?
O sorrow and honour, glory of such great deeds!   645
Now, now there is no delay. Seize us, we pray, in everyway
and don't take yourself from our sight.'
During this emotion and in the midst of such words
the light had dispersed from heaven cold shadow,
and now retracing its step it was going up to the winds,   650
when suddenly before their eyes was the massive tomb
where lifeless his body had been placed—neither the bars nor the guards themselves
were strong enough to endure—and they saw
rocks from rocks pulled apart, the tight joins of the sides loosened.
There was a sound; the earth was struck by its huge weight.   655
Everywhere souls had terror and the silence itself was frightening.
But look—the first singing of birds beneath the roofs!
He walks, leaving the cave, proud of its spoils and rejoicing
he began to go, and the earth, encouraged, trembled at the striking
of his feet.
Wearing those wounds he took himself to the high entrance.   660
And here, amazed, he found a huge number of new
companions had flowed in, and unexpected, suddenly
to them all he said, 'I am here, the one whom you seek, in person.
Piety has defeated the hard journey and lively virtue.
Men, throw yourselves into keeping watch; let all fear be gone.   665
This is my return and triumph awaited,
this is my great faith. O three and four times blessed,
what rewards, what rewards are worthy, am I to suppose,
to be able to pay back your glories, what gifts to be provided?
So take this to your souls; earth, who first bore you from   670
your parents' stock, she will receive you with joyful breast.
Recall your spirit and send away gloomy fear
and save yourselves for the future to come.
For what is left, joyful at the things accomplished well and in order,
pray with your hands for peace, praise peace while you sit,   675
great men; your pledge of peace alone is inviolable.'
While he said this he showed his visage and face,
his face and hands both and chest ravaged by iron.
And they joined hand in hand and rejoiced in seeing him.
Nor was it enough to have seen him once; they enjoyed both delaying   680
and walking beside him and holding his hand with theirs.
When at last he completed his work, he parted the breathing winds.
Carried through the thin air and open heaven
he left mortal sight in mid-speech,
and the kingdom of starry heaven received him to his throne   685
and keeps his name eternal through the ages.
From that day his honour has been celebrated, and joyful

younger generations
have kept the day as year after year has slipped away.

Go, O our virtue, go, the glory of such great events,
and come to us favourable and to your annual holy rites,   690
which it is sinful to delay, with favourable step. Support
and celebrate this custom of holy rites, companions; keep it yourself,
O sweet husband, and if we deserve it through piety,
may our pure grandchildren stay in the religion.

Notes

1. See E.A. Clark and D.F. Hatch, *The Golden Bough, The Oaken Cross: The Virgilian Cento of Faltonia Betitia Proba* (Chicago: Scholars Press, 1981), 103; C. Schenkl (ed.), *Cento Vergilianus de laudibus Christi: Poetae Christiani Minores*, I. Corpus Scriptorum Ecclesiasticorum Latinorum 16 (Vienna: F. Tempsky, 1888), 609-27.
2. The authorship of the *Martyrdom of Perpetua* is in some doubt (see the text above), while the suggestion that the Epistle to the Hebrews had a female author is fanciful: see R. Hopkins, *Priscilla, Author of the Epistle to the Hebrews* (New York: Exposition Press, 1969).
3. Augustine, *Letters* 130, 131; John Chrysostom, *Letters* 168; Jerome, *Letters* 130.
4. *De Viris Illustribus* 22.18 (J.-P. Migne, *Patrologie cursus completus. Series Latina* [Paris: Garnier Frères, 1844–64], 83.1093); *Etymologiarum (De Originibus)* 1.39.26 (Migne, *Patrologie cursus completus*, 82.121).
5. Schenkl, *Cento Virgilianus de laudibus Christi*; the manuscript was reported by B. de Montfaucon, *Diarium Italicum* (Paris: J. Arisson, 1702), but is now lost: see Schenkl, 13. For discussion of Proba's life, see Clark and Hatch, *The Golden Bough, The Oaken Cross*, 97-102; and G.R. Kastner and A. Millin, 'Proba', in P. Wilson-Kastner *et al.* (eds), *A Lost Tradition: Women Writers of the Early Church* (Lanham: University Press of America, 1981), 33-35.
6. For her wealthy aristocratic status, see the advice to the rich, lines 469-81.
7. The minimum age for a consul was fixed in the second century BC, but this was often disregarded in the imperial period. For Proba's family see A.H.M. Jones *et al.*, *The Prosopography of the Later Roman Empire*, I (Cambridge: Cambridge University Press, 1971), 1144; M.T.W. Arnheim, *The Senatorial Aristocracy in the Later Roman Empire* (Oxford: Clarendon Press, 1972), 113-14.
8. Schenkl, *Cento Virgilianus de laudibus Christi*, 13; for the civil war, see Zosimus, 2.45-53.
9. For recent discussion of the cento's date, see R.P.H. Green, 'Proba's cento: its date, purpose, and reception', *Classical Quarterly* 45 (1995), 551-63. We do not know the date of Proba's death; her husband inscribed a dedication on her tomb, see E. Borman (ed.), *CIL* 6.1712.
10. See J. Balmer, *Classical Women Poets* (Newcastle: Bloodaxe Books, 1996), 111; Clark and Hatch, *The Golden Bough, The Oaken Cross*, 98.
11. The identification of Adelphius as a pagan rests upon the determination that Clodius Hermogenianus Caesarius (a pagan) was his son (ibid, 101), but this is not securely established; see *CIL* 6.499.
12. Tertullian, *On the Prescription of Heretics* 39.3-4; see F. Ermini, *Il Centone di Proba e la Poesia Centonaria Latina* (Rome, 1909), 42.
13. Ausonius, *Wedding Cento*: see H.G. Evelyn-White (trans.), *Ausonius*, I (Cambridge, MA and London: Harvard University Press, 1919), 373-75. Schenkl, *Cento Virgilianus de laudibus Christi*, established where each line of Proba comes from in Virgil; Clark and Hatch, *The Golden Bough, The Oaken Cross*, conveniently repeat this information with their text.

14. See R. Herzog, *Die Bibelepik der Lateinischen Spätanike*, I (Munich: Fink, 1975), xlix-li, 3-51; Clark and Hatch, *The Golden Bough, The Oaken Cross*, 97-181.

15. See ibid, 6.

16. The preface was not written by Proba; for text and translation see ibid, 12-13.

17. A.G. Amatucci, *Storia della Letteratura Latina Cristiana* (Bari: G. Laterza and Figli, 1955), 131; see also Green, 'Proba's cento', 554-60.

18. For its later use as a school text, see Kastner and Millin, 'Proba', 37.

19. Clark and Hatch, *The Golden Bough, The Oaken Cross*, 104-105.

53. Egeria (*fl. early 5th century* AD)

Introduction

Egeria's *Itinerarium*, a journal of her pilgrimage and an account of the liturgy of Jerusalem, was only rediscovered in 1884. Found in the library of the Brotherhood of St Mary in Arezzo, the manuscript came originally from the monastery of Monte Cassino where it was copied in the eleventh century.[1] The manuscript is incomplete and the author's name is missing, leading to considerable speculation about who she might be. St Silvia of Aquitaine was the initial suggestion, though the evidence for her existence is unreliable and for her authorship speculative.[2] A letter written by Valerius, a Spanish monk, in about AD 650 referred to an Aetheria, a pilgrim from Galicia in western Spain, who had published the story of a pilgrimage she had made many years earlier.[3] However, this letter did not settle the question of the author's name, as manuscripts of Valerius' letter variously gave her name as Echeria, Eiheria, or Egeria instead of Aetheria (or Etheria). A thirteenth-century catalogue from the library of St Martial in Limoges refers three times to an 'Itinerarium Egeria' ('Egeria's Journal'). Further references to her with a short quotation of her work in the *Liber Glossarum* (made about AD 750) and linguistic arguments support Egeria as the best reading of her name.[4]

Valerius calls Egeria 'beatissima sanctimonialis', the 'blessed nun', and the Limoges catalogue refers to her as an abbess. The nature of her pilgrimage, her devotional acts, her emphasis on meeting monks and other religious people, and her familiarity with liturgical life in Jerusalem, including services attended by monks and virgins (Chapter 24), suggest that Valerius was right. In her *Journal* she addresses her readers as 'sisters' (Chapters 3, 46), which is best interpreted to mean fellow religious.[5] The only contemporary she names in her text is her friend Marthana, a Deaconess who governed monastic cells at the shrine of St Thecla (Chapter 23). Her high social status is clear from the way she is received by the most important of the local clergy and monks, particularly the local bishops.[6] They readily provide her with guides and even a military escort (Chapter 9). The very fact that she makes such a long pilgrimage, apparently untroubled by the cost, indicates that she was wealthy. The freedom she has to pursue her own interests is a mark of her class, wealth and unmarried state.[7]

The date of Egeria's pilgrimage has been disputed, with arguments made for dates ranging from the late fourth to the early sixth centuries AD. Egeria quotes from Jerome's Latin translation of Eusebius' *Onomasticon*, which was published after AD 390, refers to the relics of St Thomas which were moved to the basilica dedicated to him in Edessa in AD 394, and she seems to quote Rufinus' Latin translation of Origen's *Homilies* published in AD 404. Evidence suggests that her friend Marthana died before AD 448, giving us the early fifth century as the best date for her work.[8]

In the first 23 chapters of her *Journal*, Egeria provides a first-person account of four journeys she made on a pilgrimage through the holy land. The text begins with her approaching Mt Sinai—the earlier part of her journey is lost, though she later describes the journey as beginning in Constantinople (Chapter 23) and this is where her account probably began.

Peter the Deacon, librarian of Monte Cassino in the twelfth century, compiled a digest of travelogues, including Egeria's. His descriptions of places in Egypt and the route from the Red Sea to Mt Sinai have been identified as extracts taken from the lost part of Egeria's work.[9] She describes her ascent of Mt Sinai, journey to Egypt, retracing the route of Exodus, and return to Jerusalem (Chapters 1–9). Along the way, she visited biblical sites, churches and monasteries, staying in hospices maintained by bishops, laymen and monks especially for the reception of pilgrims.[10] After staying in Jerusalem for 'some time', she set out on a second journey to Mount Nebo, from where she viewed places described in the books of Moses, returning by way of Jericho (Chapters 10–12). Some time later, she went to Carneas to visit the tomb of Job, along the river Jordan, and back to Jerusalem (Chapters 14–16). Her fourth journey was taken three years after she first came to Jerusalem, and took her through Antioch, into Mesopotamia, across the Euphrates to Edessa, the house of Abraham in Carrhae, and back to Constantinople via Tarsus, Cappadocia, Galatia, Bythinia and Chalcedon. Here she wrote up her *Journal*, mentioning that she hoped to be reunited with her readers but that she had another trip to Ephesus planned (Chapters 17–23).[11]

At this point in the text, Egeria closes her account of her travels. She refers to this work as a letter, and addresses it to readers she calls 'Your Charity'[12] and 'revered ladies…my sisters' (Chapter 23). The text was probably not intended for general publication, and this may explain its rough and repetitive style.[13]

Egeria opens a new work at Chapter 24, addressing her reader again as 'Your Charity'. This text is an account of the liturgical year and liturgy in Jerusalem (Chapters 24–49). She begins by describing the daily ceremonies, those performed every Sunday,[14] then the annual feasts and the seasonal cycle of the liturgy.

Egeria's work is of great significance. No other journal like hers had been written: Jerome's *Onomasticon*, and the *Journal of the Bordeaux Pilgrim* offer lists of places and information. Hers is a much more personal work, as she describes her journey and the people she meets. Her description of the liturgy and religious observances in fifth-century Jerusalem is valuable for the picture it gives us of the life of the Christian community there. She also adds to our knowledge of the biblical sites and religious buildings in her day. The testament of her faith, the religious objectives of her journeys, her faith in the physical reality of the Old and New Testament stories, provide insight into the beliefs and objectives of the Christian pilgrim.[15]

Due to the length of the text, only the first nine chapters, her first journey, are translated here.[16]

Egeria

Journal (The First Journey)

Chapter 1

(1) …were shown according to the Scriptures. As we made our way, we came to a certain place where the mountains we were travelling through opened up and made an endless, vast very flat and extremely beautiful valley, and across the valley appeared Mount Sinai, God's holy mountain. This place, where the mountains opened up, is joined to the place where the Graves of Lust are. (2) When you get there, as the holy men (who were used as our guides and advised us) said, 'The custom is for those who are approaching to say a prayer from here, when God's mountain is first seen from this

place.' And so that is what we did too. From there to God's mountain was in total about four miles across the valley, which, as I said, is vast.

Chapter 2
(1) This valley is extremely vast, lies beneath the side of the mountain of God, and is about sixteen miles long (as they said and as far as we could estimate by sight) and they said that it was four miles wide. So we had to cross this valley to be able to climb the mountain. (2) This is the vast and very flat valley where the sons of Israel waited during those days when holy Moses climbed the mountain of the Lord, and he was there for forty days and forty nights. This is the valley where the calf was made, and to this day its location is pointed out: for a large stone set up there stands on the very place. So this is the valley in which, at its head, is the place where holy Moses, as he was grazing his father-in-law's flocks, was addressed twice by God from the burning bush. (3) And so this was our route: first we would climb the mountain of God (because on this side, from which we were approaching, the ascent was easier) and then from there we would descend to the head of the valley where the burning bush was (because the descent from the mountain of God was easier from there). It was agreed that when we had seen everything we wanted to, we would come down from the mountain of god where the burning bush was, and from there continue our journey down the length of the valley, all the way down through the centre, with the men of god who would show us each place in the valley mentioned in Scripture. And this is what we did. (4) So we left from the place where we had prayed after arriving from Pharan, and so made our journey, crossing the middle of the head of the valley, and approached the mountain of God. (5) This mountain seems to be a single one all around, but when you get into the vicinity, there are many, but the whole lot is called the mountain of God. But that particular one, on the summit of which is the place where the Glory of God descended, as it is written in Scripture, is in the middle of them all. (6) And although all of them, which are all around, are as high as any I think I have seen, that one in the middle, where the Glory of God descended, is so much higher that all the others that when we had climbed it, all the other mountains which we had thought were high, were as far below us as if they were very small hillocks. (7) This is very wonderful and I think it would not be without the grace of God: although higher then the others the middle mountain, which in particular is called Sinai, the one on which the Glory of God descended, nevertheless cannot be seen until you get to its very base, before you climb it. When you have completed what you want to do and climb down from there, you see it in the distance, which it was not possible to do before you climbed up. Before we arrived at the mountain of God I knew this (as the brothers had described it), but after I had arrived there I knew that it manifestly was so.

Chapter 3
(1) On the evening of the Sabbath we entered the mountains and came to monastic cells, where the monks who lived there received us very hospitably and offered us every kindness. There was also a church there with a priest. So we stayed there for the night and early on the Lord's day, with the priest and the monks who lived there, we began to climb the mountains one by one. These mountains are climbed with great difficulty, since you do not ascend them slowly by a spiral route, in a snail-path as we say, but you ascend straight up like a wall, and you have to come down each of these mountains, until you get to the very foot of the central mountain, which in particular is Sinai. (2) By the will of Christ our God, and helped by the prayers of the holy men who were accompanying me, and with a great deal of difficulty (because I had to climb up on foot, since it was not possible to get up by saddle) I made the climb. But the labour itself was not felt (and the labour was not felt, because I saw the desire which I had being fulfilled by the will of God): and so at the fourth hour we arrived at the summit of the mountain of God, holy Sinai, where the law was given, that is, at the place where the Glory of the Lord came down on the day when the mountain smoked. (3) Now in that place there is a church, not a large one, as the place itself, that is, the summit of the mountain, is not large, yet the

church has a full-sized charm all of its own. (4) When by the will of God we came up onto the summit itself and arrived at the door of that church, there was a priest (who was appointed to that church) who come from the church and met us. He was an old man, pure, and a monk from a very early age, and (as they say here) an ascetic; in short, he was the sort of man who was worthy of being in such a place. The other priests met us too, and all the monks who lived there beside that mountain (that is, those who were not prevented by age or weakness). (5) In fact, no one lives on the summit itself of that mountain; there is nothing there except the church alone and the cave where holy Moses was. (6) All of the appropriate passage from the book of Moses was read, and the sacrifice was offered in the proper way. We received communion and as we were about to leave the church, the priests gave us gifts from that place, that is, from fruit trees which grow on the mountain. Since the mountain, holy Sinai itself, is completely rocky, and does not produce any bushes, yet down at the foot of these mountains, both around this one in the middle and around those which surround it, there is a small piece of ground; there the holy monks through their careful work put bushes and lay out small orchards or ploughed fields, and next to them their cells, and they take the fruit, which they seem to have worked so hard over with their own hands, as if from the earth of the mountain itself. (7) So after we had received communion and the holy men had given us their gifts and we had come out of the church door, then I began to ask them to show us each place. Then the holy men were kind enough to show us each one. They showed us the cave where holy Moses was when he ascended the mountain of god for the second time to receive again the tablets, after he had broken the first ones when the people had sinned; and they also were kind enough to show us other places, whatever we wanted or which they themselves knew well. (8) I would like you to know this, reverend sisters, that from that place, where we were standing (that is in the surrounds of the church, on the summit of the central mountain), those mountains, which we had first climbed with great difficulty, seemed to us in comparison with the central mountain (on which we were standing) as if they were hillocks, yet they were so big that I do not think that I have seen any higher, except this central one which surpassed them by a great deal. From there we saw beneath us Egypt and Palestine and the Red Sea and the Parthenian Sea, which stretches to Alexandria, and the endless lands of the Saracens. Although it is hardly possible to believe this, the holy men pointed out to us each one of these things.

Chapter 4
(1) After we had fulfilled the desires for which he had hurried to ascend, we now began to descend from the summit of the mountain of God, which we had climbed, to another mountain which joins it, called In Choreb. There is a church there. (2) Choreb is the place where holy Elias the prophet used to be, where he fled from the face of king Achab, where God spoke to him, saying,' What are you doing here, Elias?' (as is written in the books of Kings). Today the cave where holy Elias hid is on display, in front of the door of the church which is there. In addition, on display there is an altar stone which holy Elias himself set up to offer sacrifice to God, and the holy men were kind enough to show us each place. (3) We also offered sacrifice there and a most earnest prayer, and the appropriate passage was read from the book of Kings. For I had always wanted this very much, that when we came somewhere to always have the appropriate passage from the Bible read out. (4) After we had offered the sacrifice there, we set out again, for another place not far off from there which had been shown to us by the priests and monks: that is, the place where holy Aaron had stood with the 70 elders, when holy Moses was receiving the law for the children of Israel from the Lord. There is in this place, although it is not mentioned in Scripture, a huge rock, round in shape and flat on top, on which the holy men themselves are said to have stood. In the centre there is a sort of altar made of stone. There the appropriate passage from the book of Moses was read, and a Psalm suitable for the place was sung. We left after saying a prayer. (5) It was now getting on for the eighth hour, and there were still three miles to go before we would leave these mountains, which we had entered the previous evening. But we were not leaving on the same side as we had entered, as I said before, because we had to travel to

every holy place and see whatever monastic cells there were there, and so we had to leave the head of that valley, as I said before (that is, the valley which lies beneath the mountain of God). (6) We had to leave at the head of the valley because there were many monastic cells of holy men there and a church where the bush is. The bush is still alive today and produces shoots. (7) And so we came down from the mountain of God and arrived at the bush at about the tenth hour. This is the bush, as I said before, from which the Lord spoke in the fire to Moses. The bush is in a place where there are many monastic cells and a church at the head of the valley. In front of the church there is a very pleasing garden with good water in abundance; in this garden is the bush itself. (8) A place next to this is pointed out, where holy Moses stood when God said to him, 'Untie the strap of your shoe,' and so on. And when we arrived at the place it was about the tenth hour, and since it was already evening we were not able to offer sacrifice there. But we said prayers in the church and in the garden by the bush. Also, the appropriate passage from the book of Moses was read, as is our custom. And because it was evening, we ate with these holy men in the garden in front of the bush, and we stayed the night there. On the following day we got up early and asked the priests to make the sacrifice there, and this was done.

Chapter 5
(1) And now our route was as follows: we would go through that valley down its length (that is, the valley, as I said before, where the children of Israel camped while Moses climbed and then down the mountain of God). The holy men pointed out each place to us all the time, one by one, as we made our way through the valley. (2) For at the very head of that valley, where we had stayed and seen that bush from which God spoke to holy Moses in the fire, we had also seen the place where holy Moses had stood in front of the bush when God said to him, 'Untie the strap of your shoe, for the place on which you are standing is holy ground.' (3) And as we set out from the bush, they began to point out to us other places all the time. They pointed out the place where the camp of the children of Israel had been on the days when Moses was on the mountain. They also pointed out the place where the calf was made, for today there is a large stone set up there. (4) As we were going, we saw at a distance the summit of a mountain which looks down upon the whole valley and from which holy Moses saw the sons of Israel dancing in the days when they made their calf. They pointed out a huge rock in the place where holy Moses came down with Jesus, son of Nave. He broke the tablets which he was carrying on this rock. (5) They also pointed out how each of them had their own dwellings throughout the valley, the foundations of which are still visible today, and how they had been built circular in shape and of stone. They also pointed out the place where holy Moses ordered the children of Israel to run from door to door, on his return from the mountain. (6) Next they pointed out to us the place where the calf which Aaron had made was burnt on the order of holy Moses. Next they pointed out the torrent from which holy Moses made the sons of Israel drink, as is written in Exodus. (7) They also pointed out to us the place where the 70 men received from the spirit of Moses. Next they pointed out the place where the sons of Israel had lust for food. They even showed us the place which is called the Burning, because part of the camp was burnt there, but then the fire stopped because of the prayers of holy Moses. (8) They also pointed out the place where manna and quails had rained on them. And so we were shown every single thing which, according to the holy books of Moses, happened in there (that is, in the valley which lies beneath the mountain of God, holy Sinai, as I said). It was too much to write down everything one by one, because so much could not be remembered. But when Your Charity reads the holy books of Moses, she will see, most carefully recorded, everything which was done there. (9) This is the valley where the Passover was celebrated one year after the children of Israel had left the land of Egypt, and dwelt in that valley for a long time, while holy Moses climbed up and down the mountain of God for the first and second times. In addition, they stayed there long enough for the tabernacle to be made and for everything which was revealed on the mountain of God to happen. So we were shown the place where the tabernacle was

first put up by Moses and each thing which God had ordered Moses to do on the mountain was accomplished. (10) We also saw at the end of the valley the Graves of Lust, at the place where we returned to our route. Here is where we came out of the great valley and set off again on the road on which we had come through the mountains, which I mentioned earlier. On that same day we visited other, very holy monks, who were not able to go onto the mountain of God to offer sacrifice either because of age or weakness. Nevertheless, when we arrived they were kind enough to receive us very hospitably in their monastic cells. (11) When we had seen all the holy places we wanted to, especially all the places which the sons of Israel touched when going to and coming back from the mountain of God, and after we had seen the holy men who lived there, we returned to Pharan, in the name of God. (12) And although I should always thank God for everything, I shall not describe the many great favours which he deigned to bestow upon me, unworthy and undeserving as I am, so that I could travel through all these places, which I did not deserve. Nevertheless I cannot thank too much all the holy men who deigned to receive me, insignificant as I am, with such good will in their monastic cells and particularly to guide me through all the places for which I was always searching, following holy Scripture. Many of the holy men who lived on and around the mountain of God (those who were stronger in body) were kind enough to guide us as far as Pharan.

Chapter 6
(1) When we had arrived at Pharan, which is 35 miles from the mountain of God, we had to stay there for two days to recover. On the third day we left early in the morning and came again to the inn which is in the desert of Pharan, where we had also stayed on the way out, as I described before. On the next day, after taking on water, we went from there again a little way through the mountains and came to an inn which was right on the sea. This is the place where you come out of the mountains and again begin to walk close by the sea, so close that sometimes a wave touches the feet of the animals, and yet sometimes the route walked is through the desert, 100 or 200, or even more than 500 feet from the sea. There is absolutely no road at all, and the sands of the desert are all there is. (2) The Pharanites, who are used to travelling there with their camels, put up signs for themselves here and there. They aim for these signs and so travel by day. By night the camels follow the signs. In short, from habit the Pharanites travel about here at night more carefully and safely than other people can travel where there is an open road. (3) It was there that we came out of the mountains on our return, the same place where we had entered them on our journey into the mountains, and once again we approached the sea. The children of Israel also returned from Sinai, the mountain of God, and came back to the same place by the same route which they took going to the mountain. This is the same place where we also came out of the mountains and once again joined the Red Sea, and from where we reversed the route on which we had come. The children of Israel made their journey on by their own route, as is written in the books of holy Moses. (4) But we returned to Clysma by the same route and the same inns by which we had come. When we arrived in Clysma, once again we had to rest there, because we had made our journey through the very sandy desert.

Chapter 7
(1) Although of course I knew the land of Gessen very well, from the first time I had gone to Egypt, nevertheless I wanted to see all the places which the children of Israel had touched when they came away from Rameses, travelling until they arrived at the Red Sea, at a place which is now called Clysma from a fort there. For we wanted to travel from Clysma to the land of Gessen, to the city which is called Arabia. This city is in the land of Gessen and the territory itself is named after it, that is, the land of Arabia, the land of Gessen, which nevertheless is part of the land of Egypt, but better by far than all the rest of Egypt. (2) From Clysma (that is, from the Red Sea) to the city of Arabia there are four inns across the desert, and although it is a desert, each inn has a military post, with soldiers and officers, who always guided us from fort to fort. The holy men who accompanied us on this journey

(that is the priests and monks) showed us each place which I kept searching for, according to the Scriptures. Some were on the left, some on the right of our route, some were far from the road, some were nearby. (3) So I want Your Charity to believe that, as far as I was able to see, the children of Israel travelled in this way, going so far to the right, then turning back as far to the left, and in this way they made their journey until they came to the Red Sea. (4) We were shown Epauleum, but only from a distance, and we went to Magdalum. There is a fort there now with an officer and garrison, which now presides over the area for the authority of Rome. As is customary here, they guided us all the way to another fort and there we were shown Beelsephon (indeed we were at the very place). There is a plain above the Red Sea next to the side of the mountain which I mentioned earlier, where the children of Israel cried out when they saw the Egyptians coming after them. (5) They also showed us Etham, which is situated beside the desert, just as in Scripture, and even Soccoth. Soccoth is a small hill in the middle of a valley, and the children of Israel established their camp next to this hillock. This is the place where the law of the Passover was received. (6) We were also shown the city of Pithom, which the children of Israel built, on the same route, and here we crossed the Egyptian border, leaving the lands of the Saracens. The same Pithom is now a fort. (7) The city of Heroopolis, which existed at the time when Joseph went out to meet his father Jacob as he was coming, as is written in the book of Genesis, is now a hamlet, but a large one, which we would call a village. For the village has a church and martyr-shrines and many monastic cells of holy monks. We had to dismount to look at each one of these, following our normal custom. (8) The village itself is now called Hero, and Hero is sixteen miles from the land of Gessen, and is within the borders of Egypt. The place itself is fairly pleasant, and part of the river Nile runs through here. (9) We left Hero and arrived at the city which is called Arabia, which is in the land of Gessen, because of which it is written that Pharaoh said to Joseph, 'Bring your father and brothers together in the best land of Egypt, in the land of Gessen, in the land of Arabia.'

Chapter 8
(1) Ramesses is four miles from the city of Arabia. We crossed through the centre of Ramesses to get to the inn of Arabia. Today the city of Ramesses is a flat plain, with not a single dwelling. It is very clear that it was once huge in circumference and had many buildings, for its ruins, just as they fell, appear extensive today. (2) But now there is nothing except one huge Theban stone on which are two huge carved figures, which are said to be of the holy men, that is Moses and Aaron. For they say that the children of Israel set them there in their honour. (3) In addition there is a sycamore tree there. It is said to have been put there by the Patriarchs. It is now very old and so fairly small, yet it still bears fruit. Anyone who is ill visits it and takes away twigs, and this is helpful for them. (4) We learnt this when we were told about it by the holy Bishop of Arabia. He told us the name of the tree, that in Greek they call it 'dendros alethiae', or as we would say, 'tree of truth'. This holy bishop was kind enough to come to meet us at Ramesses. He is an old man, truly very devout, a former monk and a courteous man who received visitors very hospitably. He was also very learned in the Scriptures of God. (5) Since he had been kind enough to trouble himself to meet us, he pointed out each thing there and told the story of the carved figures, which I mentioned, as well as the sycamore tree. This holy bishop also told this story: that the Pharaoh, when he saw that the children of Israel had deserted him, before he attacked them, entered Ramesses with his whole army and burnt it to the ground, although it was very large, and then set out after the children of Israel.

Chapter 9
(1) By chance something very nice happened to us, as the day when we arrived at the inn of Arabia was the day before the most blessed day of the Epiphany, and on that very day the Vigil was to be held in the church. And so the holy bishop kept us there for about two days. He was truly a holy man of God, and I knew him from the time when I went to Thebes. (2) The holy bishop is a former monk.

He was raised from a child in a monastic cell, and was as learned in the Scriptures as he was pure in his whole life, as I said before. (3) At that time we sent back the soldiers who (through the authority of Rome) had provided us with help, when we were travelling through suspect areas. There was a public road through Egypt which crossed through the city of Arabia, and runs from Thebes to Pelusium. So it was no longer necessary to trouble the soldiers. (4) Setting out from there we journeyed through the whole land of Gessen, all the time through vineyards which produce wine, and fields which produce balsam, and we kept to a route through orchards and well-cultivated fields and fine gardens, along the bank of the river Nile through numerous estates which once belonged to the children of Israel. In short, I think that I have never seen a more beautiful area than the land of Gessen. (5) We made a journey of two whole days from the city of Arabia through the land of Gessen and came to Tanis, the city in which holy Moses was born. This is the same Tanis which was once the capital of the Pharaohs. (6) And although I already knew these places, as I said before, from when I visited Alexandria and the Thebaid, I wanted to learn more about the places where the children of Israel travelled when they left Ramesses and went to the mountain of God, holy Sinai. And so I had to return once more to the land of Gessen and from there to Tanis. We set out from Tanis and I travelled by a road I knew until I came to Pelusium. I set out from there again, made my way by each of the inns of Egypt by which we had come, and arrived at the border of Palestine. And from there, in the name of Christ our God, stopping again at a few inns I returned through Palestine to Aelia (that is, to Jerusalem).

Notes

1. G.F. Gamurrini, 'I misteri e gl' inni di s. Ilario vescovo di Poitiers ed una peregrinazione ai luoghi santi nel quarto secolo scoperti in un antichissimo codice', *Studii e documenti di storia e diritto* 5 (1884), 81-107, and 'Della inedita peregrinazione ai luoghi santi nel quarto secolo', *Studii e documenti di storia e diritto* 6 (1885), 145-67. For a review of the history of the manuscript and the arguments over the author's name, see G.E. Gingras, *Egeria: Diary of a Pilgrimage* (New York: Newman Press, 1970), 1-7.
2. See ibid, 2-4.
3. For a text of the letter, see J.P. Migne, *Patrologia cursus completus. Series Latina* (Paris: Garnier Frères, 1857–64), 87.421-26; also M.C. Diaz y Diaz, 'Valerius du Bierzo: Lettre sur la Bse Égérie', in P. Maraval (ed.), *Égérie: Journal de Voyage* (Paris: du Cerf, 1982), 323-49.
4. See J.F. Mountford, 'Silvia, Aetheria, or Egeria?' *Classical Quarterly* 17 (1923), 40-41. Egeria is the most common form of the name in the manuscripts of the Valerius letter, and the independent evidence from Limoges and the *Liber Glossarum* suggest that Egeria is the most appropriate form of the name to use. Echeria and Eiheria have been explained as attempts to reproduce the way the g in the name Egeria came to be pronounced in Spain; Aetheria, Etheria as scribal errors: A. Lambert, 'Egeria: Notes critiques sur la tradition de son nom et celle de l'Itinerarium', *Revue Mabillon* 26 (1936), 71-94; see also D.C. Swanson, 'A formal analysis of Egeria's (Silvia's) vocabulary', *Glotta* 44 (1966–67), 177-254.
5. For arguments against this reading see Gingras, *Egeria*, 172.
6. Chapters 9, 12, 14, 16, 19, 20, 23.
7. See further, H. Sivan, 'Who was Egeria? Piety and pilgrimage in the age of Gratian', *Harvard Theological Review* 81.1 (1988), 59-72.
8. This follows Gingras' argument and evidence, *Egeria*, 12-15.
9. Peter the Deacon, *Liber de locis sanctis*, in P. Geyer (ed.), *S. Silviae, quae fertur, peregrinatio ad loca sancta*, Corpus Scriptorum Ecclesiasticorum Latinorum 39 (1898), 105-21; and E. Franceschini

and R. Weber (eds), *Itinerarium Egeriae*, Corpus Christianorum, Series Latina 175 (Turnholti: Brepols, 1965), 93-103; Valerius also mentions that Egeria visited other parts of Egypt, Judea and Galilee: see Gingras, *Egeria*, 15-16, 147.

10. Ibid, 167-68.

11. For notes on the topographical, archaeological and biblical issues raised by Egeria's *Journal*, see J. Wilkinson, *Egeria's Travels* (London: SPCK, 1971; 2nd edn; Warminster: Aris and Phillips, 1998) and Gingras, *Egeria*.

12. Best read as a reference to a religious superior, but P. Wilson-Kastner, 'Introduction: The Pilgrimage of Egeria' in P. Wilson-Kastner *et al.* (eds), *A Lost Tradition: Women Writers of The Early Church* (Lanham: University Press of America, 1981), 83, suggests that it is a collective noun referring to the whole community; cf. Gingras, *Egeria*, 8. On her readers, see H. Sivan, 'Holy Land pilgrimage and western audiences: some reflections on Egeria and her circle', *Classical Quarterly* 38.2 (1988), 528-35.

13. The text has been much studied by philologists as an example of post-Classical Vulgar Latin. Its style has been defended by L. Spitzer, 'The epic style of the pilgrim Aetheria', *Comparative Literature* 1 (1949), 225-58. See also Maraval, *Égérie*.

14. There is a break in the text at this point; she probably reported other weekly ceremonies (Gingras, *Egeria*, 27).

15. On pilgrimages see R. Ousterhout (ed.), *The Blessings of Pilgrimage* (Urbana: The University of Illinois Press, 1990); E.D. Hunt, *Holy Land Pilgrimage in the Later Roman Empire AD 312-460* (Oxford: Clarendon Press, 1982); J. Wilkinson, *Jerusalem Pilgrims before the Crusades* (2nd edn; Warminster: Aris and Phillips, 1998).

16. For a translation of the whole text, see Gingras, *Egeria*, 49-128; Wilson-Kastner, *A Lost Tradition*, 85-132; or Wilkinson, *Egeria's Travels*.

54. Eudocia (c. AD 400–460)

Introduction

Eudocia is one of the best attested women writers from antiquity. She was born in Athens about AD 400, the daughter of the pagan philosopher Leontius, who named her Athenaïs after the place of her birth. She was educated by her father in Athens as a pagan.[1] She was both eloquent and beautiful.[2] In AD 420, after the death of her father, she moved to Constantinople to plead for a share of her father's estate, which had been claimed by her two brothers, Valerius and Gessius. There she met Pulcheria, the older sister of the Emperor Theodosius II, and Paulinus, one of his advisors. Pulcheria introduced her to her brother, and they were married in AD 421. Athenaïs converted to Christianity before her marriage and took the name Aelia Eudocia after baptism.[3]

She bore three children, Licinia Eudoxia (in 422), Flacilla (who died in 431), and Arcadius.[4] In 423 her husband honoured her with the title 'Augusta'.[5] In 438 Eudocia went on a pilgrimage to Jerusalem, visiting Antioch on the way, and returning with holy relics (the remains of St Stephen) in 439. Eudocia went back to Jerusalem shortly afterwards. There she became an active Christian patron, supporting the construction of churches and monasteries and other charities until her death in 460. There is a story that she was banished from Constantinople by Theodosius who suspected her of infidelity with Paulinus (apparently after Paulinus passed back to Theodosius a huge apple which he had received from Eudocia, not knowing that Theodosius had given it to her in the first place).[6] There was a political upheaval in Constantinople around 440, and Paulinus was executed. It is possible that Eudocia fell out of favour at court then, but it has also been argued that she chose to move to Jerusalem to pursue her religious activities.[7]

Eudocia wrote in hexameters (the verse of epic poetry) on Christian themes. She composed a poem on the Roman victories of her husband over the Persians in AD 421 and 422 (Socrates, *History of the Church* 7.21); a verse paraphrase of the Octateuch (the first eight books of the Old Testament) (Photius, *Library* 183); a paraphrase of the books of the prophets Zacharia and Daniel (Photius, *Library* 184; Tzetzes, *Thousands* 10.65); an epic poem on the martyrdom of St Cyprian, of which nearly 800 lines survive as well as a paraphrase by Photius (*Library* 184); and an Homeric cento of about 2,400 lines which has survived complete (Tzetzes 10.92). She also wrote an encomium in praise of Antioch, delivered there in AD 438 to great acclaim. Part of the encomium was also an Homeric cento (*Paschal Chronicle* 585.7; Evagrius Scholasticus, *Ecclesiastical History* 1.20; Nicephorus Callistus, *History of the Church* 14.50).[8] Recent excavations at the ruins of the baths at Hammat Gader in Israel (the ancient Greek city of Gadara) have uncovered another hexameter poem by Eudocia inscribed on a plaque, still mounted in its original position for visitors to the baths to read as they made their way in to the large pool.[9]

Given the amount of her extant work, I am only able here to include in this anthology one book of the *Martyrdom*, the preface to and opening of the cento, and the Baths inscription.

A cento is a patchwork quilt; cento poems are compilations, put together from verses taken from another poet's work. Homer seems to have been a popular choice as a source, and there are three short centos in the *Greek Anthology* (9.361, 381, 382). Eudocia's cento, at 2,344 lines, is the longest extant Homeric cento. The poem includes Old Testament stories from Genesis and the life of Christ.[10] Eudocia tells us that this cento is not wholly her own: she edited an earlier work by Patricius (who is otherwise unknown), completing and revising his half-finished cento (lines 2-14). As a genre, centos probably developed from the traditional literary education which consisted of reading and learning the Homeric poems (and later Virgil). Later 'rules' were established for the proper composition of a cento: each line of the new poem had to be formed from a line or two half lines from the source; the repetition of two or more whole lines in succession was frowned upon as being very weak, and of course the centonist had to pay proper attention to the retention of an appropriate poetic metre. Grammatical changes were allowed, as necessary, but otherwise the cento should reproduce the original verse.[11] Eudocia apologises for using double lines, but otherwise claims to have succeeded in a difficult exercise, given the differences in subject matter between Homer and her work. Until recently, her work had been largely ignored by modern scholars, and the only modern edition of her text was incomplete.[12] Usher, however, has now published a new edition of the text, and an extended study of it which re-evaluates it as a piece of literature.[13] In particular, he finds Eudocia exploiting the meaning of the verses in their original context to contrast them with their meaning in the new context, arguing that she should be recognised as a poet for this skill.

Book 1 of *The Martyrdom of St Cyprian* is the story of how Justa, the Christian virgin, defeated the magician Cyprian through her faith in God. Cyprian had been hired by Aglaïdas to force Justa to love him. The opening of Book 1 has been lost, but from Photius, we learn that it covered Justa's conversion to Christianity and explained how Aglaïdas fell in love with her. It ends with the conversion of Cyprian, his swift rise to Bishop, and Justa becoming a deaconess, with the new name, Justina.

Book 2 is very different. It is a monologue by Cyprian in which he confesses his pagan past, his work for Satan, and his attempts to seduce Justa. It also described the help Eusebius gave to Cyprian, and how Cyprian was able to convert Aglaïdas to Christianity. In Book 3 (known only from Photius) the martyrdoms of Justa and Cyprian under Diocletian and Maximian were described: they were tortured then beheaded, but their remains were secretly taken to Rome for burial in a temple built by Rufina, who traced her family back to the Emperor Claudian.[14] Eudocia took the story from three different prose works, using a different source for each book. This has led to some inconsistencies in plot, which Eudocia does not seem to have tried to assimilate.[15] There are a number of stories about Cyprian, bishop of Antioch, who was a fictional character, though perhaps in origin derived from Cyprian, Bishop of Carthage (AD 249–58).[16]

Eudocia

1. The Martyrdom of St Cyprian

Book 1: Justa and the Conversion of Cyprian
[17]...

[Justa] sadly sent away all the young men
as she set Christ as her only husband and lord.

Aglaïdas, after gathering a crowd in front of the official courts,
wanted to dishonour the glorious young girl by force.
But all the men who charged into her, suddenly shouted out,   5
and they all rushed out of her rooms with their weapons,
and immediately they made Aglaïdas' newcomers vanish.
But he, bearing desire within in his heart,
not noticing he had been smitten, blinded, tried to embrace the girl.
But she at once completed the strong sign of Christ,   10
and immediately threw the shameless man on his back, and with her hands
tore away at the body of Aglaïdas, his curly hair and cheeks,
and she ripped his lovely clothing. She laughed at everything,
following the example of godlike Thecla.
After doing this, she went back into the house of God.   15

But the angry Agaïdas begged a wicked man,
an impious magician named Cyprian, for advice,
and promised him two talents of gold
and shining silver, if he would persuade by force
the virgin who did not want to consent to his love.   20
Neither of them feared the power of the untiring Christ.

The magician pitied the miserable mortal and with an incantation
swiftly summoned a dangerous wicked demon.
He arrived instantly and said, 'Why do you summon me? Speak.'
And he replied, ' Love for a Galilean girl has completely tamed   25
my heart. Tell me, whether you are strong enough
to deliver her to my bed, for I long for her terribly.'
And the witless champion agreed to deliver what was beyond hope.
Cyprian again addressed his blood-avenger,
'Tell me your accomplishments, so I might have confidence in you.'   30
And he replied, 'I was the bravest of the companies of angels, before,
but persuaded by my father I abandoned the highest Lord
of the seven spheres of heaven. And what I have done,
you will know: I will tell you. By my evil I threw
the foundation of the pure axis into disorder and divided it in two   35
and I threw a company of heavenly inhabitants to earth.
I forcibly cajoled Eve, the mother of the race endowed with speech,
and I robbed Adam of much-cheering paradise.
And I myself moved the brother-slaying hand of Cain.
I soaked the earth with blood. Thorns sprouted   40
shameful fruit for the race endowed with speech because of me.
I gathered together sights hateful to God, and I perfected
the art of stealing into beds. I cajoled mortal minds
to worship ephemeral idols, and I revealed to humans
how to offer sacrifices with a burly bull.   45
I even roused the Hebrews to stretch angrily on a stake
the powerful Word of God, his Eternal Son.
I crashed together cities and threw down high walls,
and I have danced in celebration, after shaking

many marriage-beds with strife. After accomplishing all these evils,
and countless others,   50
how will I not succeed with this arrogant young girl?'

Cyprian was delighted with the baneful demon, who said,
'Take this herb and sprinkle it round the room
of that respectable girl, and in the end I will reach her myself
and put into her heart the mind of my father.   55
She will be persuaded in her dream to desire you badly.'

The young maiden, who was a great beauty upon the earth,
was singing about the good God at the third hour of the evening.
But when the girl was shaken to her very core,
she recognised in her heart the blind folly of the demon,   60
she was burnt with a fire, her kidneys cut in two. Quickly
she thought of the Lord, and prayed to him. With her hand she quickly made
the sign of the cross over her whole body, and calling out loudly she said,
'Master of all, glorious God, Father of the immaculate child
Jesus Christ, who hurled the monstrous snake   65
sent into hell and imprison it in dark halls, most glorious one,
 you who save those whom it captures whole in its fetters,
who stretch out your hand to the starry axis of heaven
and support the earth with its wet surfaces in the middle of the void.
You who gave as companion to the horses of Titan fiery torches,   70
and perfected the silver moon as a partner yoked to the night.
You who made your form exactly like a mortal man,
whom you commanded to be satisfied with the abundance of paradise,
and recoiling from the advice of the most terrible beast,
the snake of the well-forested earth, you yourself   75
sought to save, Lord, by your merciful spirit,
and heal completely our wound by your stake,
purifying all pains by the name of Christ,
for the whole earth appears rich in people,
heaven is stretched out, earth is sustained,   80
waters pour forth, and the whole course knows
that you are the only lord who is all-ruling. Come, save
your servant by your mighty will, in case some terrible
shame defeats me. For by your grace, immortal worker,
I want to stay continually a holy virgin.   85
Most powerful Jesus, I loved you deeply with all my heart,
my much-praised master. For you light a burning torch
of desire for you, and place it in my heart.
Now you will never tame your servant by the hand
of a hostile, hateful, lawless, enemy of god,   90
nor according to your word will you allow anything to happen to me
blessed one, but ward off this sinful, fearful argument.'
After declaring these things, she immediately
armed her body with the sign of God, and at once

she drove away the horrible demon through the name of Christ.   95
And she sent away the creature which had no honour at all.

It went into the presence of the magician with great shame.
and Cyprian said to the demon, 'Where is she,
the girl whom I told you to bring here as quickly as possible?'
And his champion said, 'Don't question me about all the details.   100
For I saw a fearful sign and I am terrified.'
The magician smiled, persuaded of the difficulty of the task,
and again summoned another, the evil Belial.
He addressed Cyprian, 'Tell me your evil
command. Your father sent me   105
as a helper for your troubles.' And at once the magician
was delighted and said, 'This is it, demon. Give the holy virgin
this whole drink filled with a drug. I will follow you.
I think she will be persuaded at once.' He went, and the most holy
virgin was reverently sending up a prayer to the lord   110
in the middle of the night, and sent forth this from her lips,
'In the middle of the night I leapt from my bed,
Glorious One, to tell you of the sins which I have committed,
before your righteousness, judgement and truth.
O merciful immortal Lord of mighty fathers,   115
Lawgiver to the atmosphere and protector of the heavens,
at whom the earth quakes with fear; you who destroy
the most disgraceful power of a deadly enemy of God,
and received the sacrifice of father Abraham as if it were a great hecatomb;
you who threw down Baal and the serpent which slays,   120
and through the service of holy Daniel
you taught all the tribes of the Persians your divinity;
you who through your dear son Christ, your son,
you provided order and kindled a light on the earth;
you who lead the dead after their destiny back to the light;   125
I pray to you, Lord, don't allow me to be lead into evils,
but keep my body safe and always, Lord,
and furnish me with the burning torch of virginity,
so I might see my wedding with our bridegroom,
Christ, and I might be rewarded for the covenants, which I promised.   130
For the power and the glory and the honour are his. Amen.'

After she had prayed like this, at once the demon
fled with shame, disgraced because of her courage.
He came and stood before the magician, and Cyprian
asked, 'Demon, where is she, the virgin whom I told you   135
to bring to me?' And he replied, 'She defeated me
with a mighty sign, which, when I looked upon it,
made me shudder completely, was overwhelming and would not yield.'

Cyprian summoned another more powerful demon,
who was lord of them all and was of the black-eyed race.   140

He said to him, 'Withdraw if you too are worthless, weak one.'
But he bravely replied, 'I am even now bringing
that virgin to you, be prepared.'
Cyprian replied, 'Give me a sign
that you will finish with a victory.'   145
And he said, 'First I will confuse her limbs with fevers,
then after six days I will amaze her
and at night produce her prepared for you.'

And the fool left, and stood before the holy maiden
in the image of another virgin, and similarly clothed.   150
He sat on her bed and spoke with cunning.
'I came from this dawn with you
enjoying my lovely virginity, since
Christ the lord sent me so that he might thus complete me.
But, my dear, tell me this: what is the prize   155
for your lovely virginity and what is the price paid?
For I see you are like a corpse,
a life dried up and a table with no water.'
But the respectable maiden answered, 'An immediate prize
is worthless, and a greater reward attends me.'   160
But the cunning evil one said, ' Was Eve a virgin
in the garden of paradise with Adam?
When in the fullness of time she slept in the bed
of Adam the first-born, a mother of children was revealed.
She produced the entire race of mortals   165
and learnt all good things.' At that moment Justa was about
to go out of the doors, obeying the demon,
and the dreadful one rejoiced and went out with the child.

But she recognised the trick of the baleful enemy,
and at once turned her mind to prayer, and immediately   170
made the sign of the cross on her body. And from her lips she sent
a blast and drove the disgraceful luckless one from the house.
After regaining her composure a little she said,
'I know the grace of the Immortal, and a fiery disease quenched me.'
And as she prayed she said, 'Christ, your gift of power,   175
pin it through my body: may I fear you, Most Glorious One,
and you pity me in your righteousness. And grant me
to bear the glory, your name.' The enemy of god came before
the magician mute in sorrow, mourning dreadfully.

Cyprian cast words of rebuke at him.   180
'Did you too not fear the eyes of the young shining-eyed girl?
But at least tell me, when you saw the girl, what sort of power is there within her?'
The enemy replied, 'Don't ask me nor search for anything more.
I cannot describe the sign I saw.
Wretched, I trembled, I stepped back and quickly fled.   185
If you want to learn something, she swore a mighty oath.'

Cyprian answered him and said, 'How might I swear
the oath?' And he replied, 'By my power over everything,
which I have and by which I rule.' When he heard this, at once he swore
never to abandon the haughty one. And then he bravely said,   190
'When I peeped at the sign of Christ stretched out
on the cross, I fled trembling.' And he said,
'Tell me then, is he more powerful than you?'
And the adversary answered, 'Listen to me, and I will tell the truth.
The things we release here by wretched sinfulness   195
leading mortals to deceit,
are everlasting for all. But in this life
the smith takes care of the bent tool, and it is placed
in the middle of the fire. So if anyone were to sin,
either angel or mortal, it would be announced to him   200
Christ hanging on the cross.'

Cyprian spoke. 'Come on, start; for I make friends
quickly, and enjoy speed. And I long for
the pleasures of the cross, so that I might not suffer the same things again.'
The ugly one replied, 'After swearing a mighty oath,   205
are you troubled by your transgression?' And he replied, 'Speak,
accursed wretch, what sort of oath did I just swear to you?' And he said,
'To my strong power.' And the magician replied,
'I do not fear you nor your works, hateful one.
This night I have learnt the whole truth   210
because of the holy prayers and worship of a young girl
and the powerful cross. For you are very weak.
Now I shall place on my limbs the powerful mark of the cross,
which you said has very great power.
I despise your friendship, and renounce your commands.'   215
As he said this, he straightway rendered honour to Christ,
and drove away the evil demon, saying, 'Go far away,
for I seek Christ.' And the evil one went swiftly away.

Cyprian took his magic books and put them
on the strong shoulders of some young men to take them to   220
the house of immaculate god, and he followed them.
He fell before the feet of the holy priest,
Anthimus, and as he met him he said this,
'A comrade in the army of immortal heavenly Christ, I want
to inscribe my heart in the Book.' But he was angry   225
and said to him, 'Keep far away from your evil ways.
Can you not be relied on to do what is against us
in what you desire? Keep out of the Lord's affairs.
For the strength of the Lord of all is invincible.'
And Cyprian replied, ' I too know   230
that the power of Christ is mighty and the greatest.
For this night I sent against an august girl
demons inimical to god to hunt the mind of the

strong-willed young girl in chains of deceit.
But she knew what to do, and won a mighty victory   235
through prayer and the sign of Christ. Now suffer and pity me.
Show compassion for your suppliant, best of men, and receive
these books from which I as a sinner created countless evils,
and with fire turn them to ashes, and pity my soul.'
The priest was persuaded and he took the books and burnt them all.   240
He also praised him and used gentle words,
persuading him to enter God's fold.

Cyprian went back to his home
and turned to dust the shapes of his powerless wooden idols,
and he struck his body for the whole of the gloomy night   245
and said, ' How could I appear in the sight of Christ
after doing so much evil? How could I praise God
with my lips, through which I slighted others;
with my lips I summoned destructive demons.'
He scattered the dust and pleaded silently for God's mercy   250
to come to earth, trembling when he spoke.
But when silver and rosy-armed Dawn of the great Sabbath
came, then everyone was full of rejoicing.
And as a newcomer he went to the august gathering
of the great God, and as a frequent visitor he prayed like this: 255
'Master, if you think I am worthy to be your servant,
grant that I may hear a word coming from your sanctuary
out of your written books, with good, very good news.'
And when he came to the threshold of the temple, David spoke,
the holy son of Jesse, 'Look, O glorious one, do not be silent,   260
do not be far from me, unknown to me.'[18]
And in turn the great prophet Hosea spoke these inspired
words, 'If he leaves he will not be my slave.'[19] But again
David spoke, 'My eyes look towards the dawn
and my bright eyes at the chariot driver of gloomy night   265
so that I might always follow your holy words.'[20]
And elsewhere Isaiah said, 'Fear of you does not trouble my
heart, Jacob my child, whom I love,
whom I chose first of all my neighbours.'[21]
Inspired by God, Paul said, 'Christ the Lord   270
himself redeems us from the previous law
of harsh destruction.'[22] And again David, the interpreter,
the finest lyre-player, said, 'Who could tell of the
power of the immortal God and describe to all ears
hymns of the invincible?'[23] Then a prayer of the Lord   275
with very holy words, and after the priest's
homily; then a human word was sounded,
'Leave the temple of God, half-perfected mortals.'
Gentle Cyprian took a seat in silence.
But Asterius, a deacon, said to him,   280
'Leave the Lord's hall.' And he replied,

'I am a servant of the crucified Christ, and you
drive me away?' And the deacon said to him, 'But you
are not yet perfected as a slave of the mighty God.'
And in turn he said, 'God is alive for ever,   285
who revealed the worst demons,
and saved a virgin, and pitied my heart.
It is not right for me to leave this building
until I have come into the faith of Christ.'

When he learnt this the temple-servant of god went quickly   290
to the angels' priest. He summoned him, and as was seemly
said many strong words to Cyprian,
and asked him what he had done. As he had prayed for such an event
he was excited at the works which God accomplished in the universe.
And then he made him holy with the holy rites.   295

On the eighth dawn he became a proclaimer of the most
holy books of Christ. On the twenty-fifth he was
humbler and accomplished in the duties of service
and became a keeper of the doors of the holy mysteries.
When twenty-five more days had passed, he was worthy   300
to become a deacon. And he tamed powerfully
the phalanxes of the shameless, lawless and inimical to god,
and he drove away the hateful minds of miserable people.
He led many into the flock of Christ,
who had rejected blind faith in idols.   305
When a year had been completed, he obtained the chair
of a priest. For sixteen years
he waited, managing the couch of his elder.
Then the blessed good bishop Anthimus
summoned all the priests dwelling nearby.   310
He spoke about the fate of the assembly of Christ,
and while he still saw heaven he handed on his chair to Cyprian.
Shortly after Athimus went to heaven,
laying down the flock of which he was champion for the glorious light.

Cyprian, managing the glorious house of god,   315
welcomed the virgin, honouring her with a deaconship.
And she was no longer called Justa, but he named her
Justinia the blameless, and he appointed her mother of all
tender girls, handmaidens of the great Christ.
And he saved many from disobedience and shameful worship,   320
advising them to long for Christ, although suffering he gathered them
into the flock of the guardian, who has glory for ever. Amen.

2. Homeric Cento

Preface
This is the history of a song pleasing to God.
Patricius, who composed this book cleverly,

is for ever worthy of praise everlasting,
because he first of all contrived a glorious work.
But even so he did not say everything very accurately. 5
Neither did he keep all the harmony of the verses,
nor when he sang did he remember only the verses
spoken by the bronze heart of blameless Homer.
But I, when I saw the half-finished most-famous work
of Patricius, took the holy columns of text with my hand, 10
and whatever verses in his books were not in order
I drew out from his wise book all together,
and whatever he left out, I wrote back
into the columns of text, and I gave harmony to the holy verses.

If anyone criticises us and drags us into blame, 15
because there are many double-lines through the conspicuous book
and of the Homeric verses a great deal that is not customary,
let him known this, that they are all the assistants of necessity.
And if anyone listens to the beauty of wise Tatian
the minstrel and enjoys what he hears, 20
because that poet never mixed up double-lines
from Homeric books and included them in his writing-tablets,
nor anything from someone else, but he made his epic poem
from Homeric song and from his own verses.
His epic sings of evil Trojans and Argives, 25
and how the sons of the Achaeans sacked the city of Priam,
Troy itself holding out, and in the grievous din of battle
men and gods fighting, the same men
whom Homer once sang, a man with a voice of bronze.

But Patricius, who composed this wise writing-tablet, 30
instead of the army of the Argives spoke of the race of Hebrews,
and instead of a miraculous and godlike phalanx
he sang of the immortals, both Son and Father.
Yet the labour was common to both of us,
Patricius and me, although I am a woman. 35
He alone among men carried off a great prize,
who first of all planted firmly the renowned seat of its home,
and brought forth the beautiful word of the mortal race.

Hear me, countless tribes of neighbouring men,
all who now are mortal and eat food on the earth 40
and all who dwell towards the east and the sunrise,
and all who dwell down towards the murky darkness,
when I say what my spirit in my breast tells me,
so you may know well both God and man.

3. The Baths

I have seen many wonders in my life, countless,
But who, noble Clibanus, however many his mouths, could proclaim

Your might, when born a worthless mortal? But rather
It is right for you to be called a new fiery ocean,
Paean and parent, provider of sweet streams.   5
From you the thousandfold swell is born, one here, one there,
On this side boiling-hot, on that side in turn icy-cold and tepid.
Into fountains four-fold four you pour out your beauty.

Indian and Matrona, Repentinus, holy Elijah,
Antoninus the Good, Dewy Galatia, and   10
Hygieia herself, warm baths both large and small,
Pearl, ancient Clibanus, Indian and other
Matrona, Strong, Nun, and the Patriarch's.
For those in pain your powerful might is always everlasting.
But I will sing of a god, renowned for wisdom [...]   15
For the benefit of speaking mortals [...].

Notes

1. Socrates, *History of the Church* 7.21; John Malalas, *Chronographia* 353; *Paschal Chronicle* s.a. 420; Theophanes, *Chronicle* 5911; Cedrenus, *Compendium of History* 1.590; Zonaras, *Epitome of History* 13.22.
2. Evagrius, *Ecclesiastical History* 1.20; Theophanes, *Chronicle* 5911.
3. John Malalas, *Chronographia* 353, 355; *Paschal Chronicle* s.a. 420; Cedrenus, *Compendium of History* 1.590; Zonaras, *Epitome of History* 13.22. For the Coin evidence see J. Sabatier, *Descriptions Générales des Monnaies Byzantines* (Paris: Rollin et Feuardent, 1862), 1.120-22.
4. Marcellus, s.a. 422, 431; Agnellus 42 (=*CIL* xi 276).
5. *Paschal Chronicle* s.a. 423; Leo, *Letters* 123; John Malalas, *Chronographia* 355, and coins.
6. John Malalas, *Chronographia*, 356-58.
7. On possible political machinations, see A. Cameron, 'The Empress and the poet: paganism and politics at the court of Theodosius II', in J.J. Winkler and G. Williams (eds), *Yale Classical Studies* 27 (1982), 217-91; and G.R. Kastner, 'Introduction to Eudocia's "Martyrdom of St. Cyprian"', in P. Wilson-Kastner *et al.* (eds), *A Lost Tradition: Women Writers of the Early Church* (Lanham: University Press of America, 1981), 136-39. We do know she was active politically in the Church. She supported the Monophysite heresy in Jerusalem, and Pope Leo himself was forced to write to her in 453, appealing to her to support orthodoxy in the area (Leo, *Letters* 123); she did return to orthodoxy in 455.
8. For the testimonia and texts see A. Ludwich, *Eudocia Augustae, Procli Lycii, Claudiani carminum graecorum reliquiae* (Leipzig: Teubner, 1897), 3-114.
9. J. Green and Y. Tsafrir, 'Greek inscriptions from Hammat Gader: a poem by the Empress Eudocia and two building inscriptions', *Israel Exploration Journal* 32:2-3 (1982), 77-96 (77-78). The stone itself, and the baths, are illustrated on H. Geva, 'Archaeological sites in Israel' 4 (2002). Internet edition: http://www.mfa.gov.il/mfa/go.asp?MFAH0g6w0.
10. Cf. Proba's Virgilian cento.
11. Ausonius, *Wedding Cento*: see H.G. Evelyn-White (trans.), *Ausonius*, I (Cambridge, MA and London: Harvard University Press, 1919), 373-75. M.D. Usher, *Homerocentones Eudociae Augustae* (Stuttgart and Leipzig: Teubner, 1999), lists the source of each line. For further discussion of the cento, see the introduction to Proba below.

12. Ludwich, *Eudocia Augustae*.

13. M.D. Usher, *Homerocentones Eudociae Augustae*, and *Homeric Stitchings: The Homeric Centos of the Empress Eudocia* (Lanham: University Press of America, 1998).

14. Photius, *Library* 184. Diocletian was emperor AD 284–305. He ruled with Maximian from AD 286. Claudian was emperor AD 268–70.

15. Kastner, 'Introduction to Eudokia's "Martyrdom of St Cyprian"', 141-42.

16. See T.A. Sabbatini, 'S. Cipriano nella tradizione agiographica', *Rivista de Studi Classici* 21 (1973), 183-204.

17. The beginning of the poem is lost. For a summary of the whole work, see Photius, *Library* 184, available in translation in N.G. Wilson, *The Bibliotheca: a selection* (London: Duckworth, 1994). For a translation of Books 1 and 2, see Kastner, 'Introduction to Eudokia's "Martyrdom of St Cyprian"', 149-69.

18. Psalm 35.22; this and the following biblical references are identified by Ludwich, *Eudocia Augustae*, 42-43.

19. Not Hosea, but Isaiah 52.13.

20. Psalm 119.148.

21. Isaiah 44.2.

22. Galatians 3.13.

23. Psalm 106.2

55. Eucheria (fl. late 5th or 6th centuries AD)

Introduction

Eucheria is known to us from one poem which has survived in her name. The Latin vocabulary she uses suggests that the poem was composed in Aquitania in the late fifth or sixth centuries AD. The text implies that its author is a well born woman who despises a man of lower class who has sought to marry her. While she is described as a woman of truly 'Amazon' spirit, well suited to the court in Aquitainia,[1] we should remember that the persona of the author is a literary creation. Indeed, the attribution of the poem to Eucheria may have arisen from the reference to her in line 32. While Eucheria cannot be identified with any certainty, her family name is well attested among the Roman nobility in Gaul: a Eucherius of senatorial rank was bishop of Lyons in the early to mid-fifth century AD.[2] She has been identified as the wife of Dynamius, who was governor of Provence and made rector of the papal patrimony in Gaul about AD 593.[3] This Eucheria died in AD 605, was buried in the same tomb as her husband in the church of the martyr Hippolytus in Massilia (modern Marseilles), and remembered by their grandson (also called Dynamius) who composed their epitaph.[4] Identification of Eucheria the poet with this Eucheria remains speculative.

This poem is a satirical epigram in which the author pokes fun at the notion that an uncouth 'slave' might seek her hand. Eucheria offers a series of incompatible matches, one creature or thing of beauty, grace, power or wealth, matched with an opposite. The pairing of incompatible couples against their nature echoes Virgil (*Eclogues* 8.26-36), but here the perspective is changed: Virgil's lowly goatherd complains that the object of his love despises him; Eucheria offers the woman's point-of-view in the voice of a well born woman who ridicules a low born man for thinking he might marry her. [5] The final line of the poem may well give us the name of Eucheria's admirer. For Rusticus (an adjective which means 'of the country' or as it is rendered here, 'Mr Country-bumkin') was a Roman family name which was not uncommon, nor restricted to a lower-class; indeed, the bishop of Lyons in the late fifth and early sixth centuries was a Rusticus.[6] On this reading, the poet plays upon the meaning of his name to belittle Rusticus, who is most likely to have been of the same class of the woman whose hand he sought, or at least in a position to aspire to such a class.[7] Class definition was particularly important for the Roman aristocrats of late fifth century Gaul, as they had to adapt to the loss of Roman political power there, first to the Visigoths, then in AD 486 to the Franks. The pursuit of literary culture was one way in which they maintained their identity as an elite.[8] Satire is regarded as a genre little used by women writers, though Sulpicia and Eucheria provide notable exceptions.

Eucheria

I want to join golden threads of shining
harmonious metal with a pile of hair;

a silk cover, sparkling fabrics of Laconia
I say are the equivalent of goats' skins;
may a noble's purple be joined with ignoble homespun,   5
may a flashing gem be set in heavy lead;
now may a pearl of great beauty be imprisoned
and shine locked in dull steel;
may an emerald equally be locked in the base metal of the Leucones,
now may a sapphire be the equal of pebbles;   10
may jasper be said to be the same as rocks and blocks,
now may the moon choose the immeasurable infernal darkness;
now may we even command lilies to be united with nettles,
and may dreadful hemlock humble the purple rose;
now at the same time with choice fish let us choose   15
to despise delights from the great sea;
may a toad love a golden-bream, a rock-dweller a serpent,
equally may a trout now desire a snail;
may a high lioness be joined with the worthless fox,
may an ape be satisfied with a bright lynx;   20
now may a hind be joined with an donkey, now a tiger with an ass,
may a fleet deer be joined with weary ox;
now may foul juice spoil sweet rose-wine,
and may honey-water be mixed with evil poisons;
let us unite sparkling water with mud from the infernal depths,   25
may a spring be well supplied with water mixed with dung;
may a swift swallow play with a deadly vulture,
now may a nightingale sing with a grave owl;
may a sad night-owl be with a bright partridge
and may a beautiful dove lie united with a crow—   30
may these monstrous prodigies change the present state of things
and the fickle laws of nature:
so may a servile Mr Country-bumkin seek the hand of Eucheria!

Notes

1. E. Raynaud, *Poetae Minores* (Paris: Garnier Frères, 1931), 339.
2. Eucherius 3: J.R. Martindale, *The Prosopography of the Later Roman Empire*, II (Cambridge: Cambridge University Press, 1980), 405. Sidonius Apollinaris addressed a letter to a Eucherius who was a candidate for the bishopric of Bourges in AD 470.
3. K.F. Stroheker, *Der Senatorische Adel im Spätantiken Gallien* (Darmstadt: Wissenschaftliche Buchgesellschaft, 1970), 167.
4. Dynamius 1, Dynamius 5, Eucheria: J.R. Martindale, *The Prosopography of the Later Roman Empire*, IIIA (Cambridge: Cambridge University Press, 1992), 429-31, 455.
5. As Raynaud, *Poetae Minores*, 340-41.
6. Martindale, *The Prosopography of the Later Roman Empire* II, 693-95 lists 10 Rustici, including the Bishop of Lyons (Rusticus 5). It is not clear from the poem whether Rusticus is to be taken as the

name of a person, or is simply an adjective describing Eucheria's admirer: see R.W. Mathisen, 'PLRE II: suggested addenda and corrigenda', Historia 31 (1982), 383.

7. There is a letter extant from a Rusticus to Eucherius, Bishop of Lyons, adding a further coincidence of family names: see ibid, 383.

8. See R.W. Mathisen, Roman Aristocrats in Barbarian Gaul: Strategies for Survival in an Age of Transition (Austin: University of Texas Press, 1993).

Bibliography

Abraham, L., *Dictionary of Alchemical Imagery* (Cambridge and New York: Cambridge University Press, 1998).

Ackermann, H.C. *et al.* (eds), *Lexicon Iconographicum Mythologiae Classicae* (Zurich: Artemis Verlag, 1981–99).

Adler, A. (ed.), *Suidae Lexicon* (Stuttgart: Teubner, 1928–38; 1967–71).

Amatucci, A.G., *Storia della Letteratura Latina Cristiana* (2nd edn; Bari: G. Laterza and Figli, 1955).

Anderson, L., *Studies in Oracular Voice: Concordance to Delphic Responses in Hexameter* (Copenhagen: Scientiarum Danica Regia Academia, 1987)

André, J., *Les Noms de Plantes dans la Rome Antique* (Paris: Belle Lettres, 1985).

Andronikos, M.A., 'Vergina', *Ergon* (1982), 19.

—*Vergina: The Royal Tombs and the Ancient City* (Athens: Ekdotike Athenon S.A., 1984).

—'Vergina', *Ergon* (1990), 83.

Arnheim, M.T.W., *The Senatorial Aristocracy in the Later Roman Empire* (Oxford: Clarendon Press, 1972).

Baehrens, A., *Poetae Latini Minores*, V (Leipzig: Teubner, 1883; New York: Garland Pub., 1979).

Bain, D., 'Salpe's *ΠΑΙΓΝΙΑ*: Athenaeus 322A and Plin. *H.N.* 28.38', *Classical Quarterly* 48.2 (1997), 262-68.

Balmer, J., *Sappho: Poems and Fragments* (Newcastle: Bloodaxe Books, 1992).

—*Classical Women Poets* (Newcastle: Bloodaxe Books, 1996).

Barker, A., *Greek Musical Writings* (2 vols; Oxford: Clarendon Press, 1984, 1989).

—*Greek Musical Theory* (Oxford: Clarendon Press, 1997).

Barnard, S., 'Hellenistic Women Poets', *Classical Journal* 73 (1978), 204-13.

Barnes, T., *Tertullian: A Historical and Literary Study* (Oxford: Clarendon Press, 1971).

Bataille, A. *et al.*, *Les Papyrus fouad* (Cairo: Institut français d'archéologie orientale, 1939).

Bauman, R.A., *Women and Politics in Ancient Rome* (London and New York: Routledge, 1992).

Becher, I., *Das Bild der Kleopatra in der Griechischen und Lateinischen Literatur* (Berlin: Akademie Verlag, 1966).

Berkowitz, L., and K.A. Squiter, *Thesaurus Linguae Graecae: Canon of Greek Authors and Works* (Oxford and New York: Oxford University Press, 1990).

Bernard, A., and E. Bernard, *Les Inscriptions Grecques et Latines du Colosse de Memnon* (Cairo: Institut français d'archéologie orientale, 1960).

Berthelot, M. (ed.), *Collection des Alchemistes Grecs* (Paris, 1888; repr. Osnabrück: Otto Zeller, 1967).

Betz, H.D., *The Greek Magical Papyri in Translation*, I (Chicago: University of Chicago Press, 1986).

Bicknell, P.J., 'Axiochos Alkibiadou, Aspasia and Aspasios', *L' Antiquité Classique* 51 (1982), 240-50.

Bowie, E.L., 'Greek Poetry in the Antonine Age', in D.A. Russell (ed.), *Antonine Literature* (Oxford: Clarendon Press, 1990), 61-63.

Bowman, A.K., and J.D. Thomas, *The Vindolanda Writing-Tablets* (London: British Museum Press, 1994).

Bowra, C.M., 'The date of Corinna', *Classical Review* 45 (1931), 4-5.

—*Greek Poetry and Life: Essays Presented to Gilbert Murray* (Oxford: Clarendon Press, 1936).

—'Melinno's hymn to Rome', *Journal of Roman Studies* 47 (1957), 21-28.

—*Greek Lyric Poetry* (2nd edn; Oxford: Clarendon Press, 1961).

—*On Greek Margins* (Oxford: Clarendon Press, 1970).

Bradley, J.R., 'The elegies of Sulpicia: an introduction and commentary', *New England Classical Journal* 22.4 (1995), 159-64.

Butler, H.E., *Post-Augustan Poetry: From Seneca to Juvenal* (Oxford: Clarendon Press, 1909).

Butrica, J.L., 'Sulpicia's complaint: on the state of the nation and the age of Domitian', *Diotima* (2000): http:/www.stoa.org/diotima/anthology/complaint.shtml.

Cameron, A., 'The Empress and the poet: paganism and politics at the court of Theodosius II', in J.J. Winkler and G. Williams (eds), *Yale Classical Studies* 27 (1982), 217-91.

Campbell, D.A., *Greek Lyric*, I–IV (Cambridge, MA: Harvard University Press, 1982–93).

Clark, E.A., and D.F. Hatch, *The Golden Bough, The Oaken Cross: The Virgilian Cento of Faltonia Betitia Proba* (Chicago: Scholars Press, 1981).

Clayman, D.L., 'The meaning of Corinna's Geroia', *Classical Quarterly* 28 (1978), 396-97.

Cole, S.G., 'Could Greek women read and write', in H.P. Foley (ed.), *Reflections of Women in Antiquity* (New York: Gordon and Breach Scientific Publishers, 1981), 219-45.

Courtney, E., *The Fragmentary Latin Poets* (Oxford: Clarendon Press, 1993).

Cramer, F.H., *Astrology in Roman law and politics*, I (Philadelphia: The Americal Philological Association, 1954).

Cramer, J.A. (ed.), *Anecdota Graeca e Codd. Manuscriptis Bibliothecarum Oxoniensum*, III (Oxford: Clarendon Press, 1836; Amsterdam: A.M. Hakkert, 1963).

Currie, H. MacL., 'The Poems of Sulpicia', *Aufstieg und Niedergang der römischen Welt*, II.30.3 (Berlin: De Gruyter, 1983), 1751-64.

Davidson, J.N., 'Don't try this at home: Pliny's Salpe, Salpe's *Paignia* and magic', *Classical Quarterly* 45 (1995), 590-92.

Dean-Jones, L., 'The cultural construct of the female body in Classical Greek science', in S.B. Pomeroy (ed.), *Women's History and Ancient History* (Chapel Hill: University of North Carolina Press, 1991), 111-37.

Demand, N., 'Monuments, midwives and gynecology', in Ph. J. Van der Eijk *et al.* (eds), *Ancient Medicine in its Socio-Cultural Context*, I (Amsterdam and Atlanta: Rodopi, 1995), 279-90.

Dickie M., *Magic and Magicans in the Greco-Roman World* (London and New York: Routledge, 2001).

Diehl, E., *Inscriptiones Latinae Christianae Veterae* (Berlin: Weidmann, 1961) .

Diels, H., and W. Kranz, *Die Fragmente der Vorsokratiker* (3rd edn; Berlin: Weidmann, 1952).

Dronke, P., *Women Writers of the Middle Ages: A Critical Study of Texts from Perpetua to Marguerite Porete* (Cambridge: Cambridge University Press, 1984).

DuBois, P., *Sappho is Burning* (Chicago: University of Chicago Press, 1995).

Düring, I., *Porphyrios Kommentar zur Harmonielehre des Ptolemaios* (Göteborg: Elanders boktryckeri aktiebolag, 1932).

—*Herodicus the Cratetean: A Study in Anti-Platonic Tradition* (Stockholm: Wahlström and Widstrand, 1941).

Durling, R.J., *A Dictionary of Medical Terms in Galen* (Leiden: Brill, 1993).

Edmonds, J.M., *Greek Elegy and Iambus*, I (Cambridge, MA: Harvard University Press, 1931, 1982), 160-65.

Englemann, H., D Knibbe and R. Merkelbach, *Die Inschriften von Ephesos* (Bonn: Habelt, 1980).

Ermini, F., *Il Centone di Proba e la Poesia Centonaria Latina* (Rome: Loescher, 1909).

Evelyn-White, H.G. (trans.), *Ausonius*, I (Cambridge, MA: Harvard University Press, 1919).

Fantham, E., 'Sex, status and survival in Hellenistic Athens: a study of women in new comedy', *Phoenix* 29 (1975), 44-74.

Faraone, C.A., and D. Obbink (eds), *Magika Hiera: Ancient Greek Magic and Religion* (Oxford and New York: Oxford University Press, 1991).

Fontenrose, J.E., *The Delphic Oracle: Its Responses and Operations, with a Catalogue of Responses* (Berkeley: University of California Press, 1981).

Franceschini, E., and R. Weber (eds), *Itinerarium Egeriae*, Corpus Christianorum, Series Latina 175 (Turnholti: Brepols, 1965).

Frazer, J.G., *Pausanias's Description of Greece*, III (New York: Macmillan, 1965).

Gamurrini, G.F., 'I misteri e gl' inni di s. Ilario vescovo di Poitiers et una peregrinazione ai luoghi santi nel quarto secolo scoperti in un antichissimo codice', *Studii e documenti di storia e diritto* 5 (1884), 81-107.

—'Della inedita peregrinazione ai luoghi santi nel quarto secolo', *Studii e documenti di storia e diritto* 6 (1885), 145-67.

Geoghegan, D. (ed.), *The Epigrams: Anyte* (Rome: Edizioni del'Ateneo and Bizarri, 1979).

Geva, H., 'Archaeological sites in Israel', 4 (2000). Internet edition: http://www.info.gov.il/mfa/go.asp?MFAHOb6w0

Geyer, P. (ed.), *S. Silviae, quae fertur, peregrinatio ad loca sancta*, Corpus Scriptorum Ecclesiasticorum Latinorum 39 (Vienna: F. Tempsky, 1898).

Gigante, M., 'Nosside', *La Parola del Passato* 29 (1974), 22-39.

Gingras, G.E., *Egeria: Diary of a Pilgrimage* (New York: Newman Press, 1970).

Giordano-Rampioni, A. (ed.), *Sulpiciae Conquestio* (Bologna: Pàtron, 1982).

Gow, A.S.F., and D.L. Page (eds), *The Greek Anthology: Hellenistic Epigrams* (Cambridge: Cambridge University Press, 1965).

—*Garland of Philip and Some Contemporary Epigrams* (Cambridge: Cambridge University Press, 1968).

Graefe, E., 'Der Pyramidenbesuch des Wilhelm von Boldensele aus dem Jahre 1335', in H. Altenmuller, and D. Wildung (eds), *Festschrift Wolfgang Helk zu seinem 70. Geburtstag* (Hamburg: H. Buske, 1984), 569-84.

—'A propos der Pyramidenbeschreibung des Wilhelm von Boldensele aus dem Jahre 1335', in E. Hornung (ed.), *Zum Bild Aegyptens in Mittelalter und in der Renaissance* (Freiburg: Universitäts-verlag; Göttingen: Vandenhoeck and Ruprecht, 1990), 9-28.

Gratwick, A.S., 'Prose Literature', in E.J. Kenney and W.V. Clausen (eds), *The Cambridge History of Classical Literature*, II. *Latin Literature* (Cambridge: Cambridge University Press, 1982).

Greene, E. (ed.), *Re-Reading Sappho: Reception and Transmission* (Berkeley: University of California Press, 1996).

Green, J., and Y. Tsafrir, 'Greek inscriptions from Hammat Gader: a poem by the Empress Eudocia and two building inscriptions', *Israel Exploration Journal* 32:2-3 (1982), 77-96.

Green, P., *Alexander to Actium: The Hellenistic Age* (London: Thames and Hudson; Berkeley: University of California Press, 1990).

Green, R.P.H., 'Proba's cento: its date, purpose, and reception', *Classical Quarterly* 45 (1995), 551-63.

Grenfell, B.P., and A.S. Hunt (eds), *The Amherst Papyri*, II (London: Henry Frowde, 1901).

Grenfell, B.P., *et al.* (eds), *The Oxyrhynchus Papyri* (London: Egypt Exploration Fund, 1896–).

Griffith, G.T., *Mercenaries in the Hellenistic World* (Cambridge: Cambridge University Press, 1935).

Grillet, B., *Les Femmes et les Fards dans l'Antiquité Grecque* (Lyon: Centre national de la recherche scientifique, 1975).

Gulik, C.B., *Athenaeus, 'The Deipnosophists'* (Cambridge, MA: Harvard University Press, 1927–43).

Guthrie, K.S., *The Pythagorean Sourcebook and Library* (Grand Rapids: Phanes Press, 1987).

Habermehl, P., *Perpetua und der Ägypter oder Bilder des Bösen im frühen afrikanischen Christentum: ein Versuch zur Passio Sanctarum Perpetuae et Felicitatis* (Berlin: Akademie Verlag, 1992).

Hallet, J.P., 'Martial's Sulpicia and Propertius' Cynthia', *Classical World* 86.2 (1992), 99-123.

Hallett, J.P., 'Martial's Sulpicia and Propertius' Cynthia', in M. DeForest (ed.), *Woman's Power, Man's Game: Essays in Honour of Joy King* (Wauconda: Bolchazy-Carducci, 1993), 322-52.

Halliday, W.R., *The Greek Questions of Plutarch* (Oxford: Clarendon Press, 1928).

Hammond, N.G.L., *Philip of Macedon*, II (London: Duckworth, 1994).

Hammond, N.G.L., and G.T. Griffith, *A History of Macedonia*, II (Oxford: Clarendon Press, 1979).

Heiberg, J.L. (ed.), *Paulus Aegineta* (Leipzig: Teubner, 1921).

Hemelrijk, E.A., *Matrona Docta: Educated Women in the Roman Élite from Cornelia to Julia Domna* (London and New York: Routledge, 1999).

Henrichs, A., 'Zum Text einiger Zauberpapyri', *Zeitschrift für Papyrologie und Epigraphik* 6 (1970), 204-209.

Henry, M.M., *Prisoner of History: Aspasia and her Biographical Tradition* (Oxford and New York: Oxford University Press, 1995).

Hense, O.P. (ed. and trans.), *Stobaeus: Eclogae Physicae Dialecticae et Ethicae*; *Florilegium* (Berlin: Weidmann, 1884–1912).

Hercher, R., *Epistolographi Graeci* (Paris: A. Firmin Didot, 1873; Amsterdam, 1965).

Herzog, R., *Die Bibelepik der Lateinischen Spätanike*, I (Munich: Fink, 1975).

Hinds, S., 'The poetess and the reader: further steps towards Sulpicia', *Hermathena* 143 (1987), 29-46.

Hopkins, R., *Priscilla, Author of the Epistle to the Hebrews* (New York: Exposition Press, 1969).

Hornblower, S., and A. Spawforth (eds), *Oxford Classical Dictionary* (Oxford: Clarendon Press, 1996).

Horsfall, N., 'The "Letter of Cornelia": yet more problems', *Athenaeum* 65 (1987), 231-34.

Hultsch, F., *Metrologicorum Scriptorum Reliquae*, I (Leipzig: Teubner, 1864; repr. 1971).

—*Griechische und Römische Metrologie* (Berlin: Weidmann, 1887).

Hunt, E.D., *Holy Land Pilgrimage in the Later Roman Empire AD 312–460* (Oxford: Clarendon Press, 1982).

Hussey, R., *An Essay on Ancient Weights and Money and the Roman and Greek Liquid Measures* (Oxford: Clarendon Press, 1836).

Instinsky, H.U., 'Zur Echtheitsfrage der Brieffragmente der Cornelia', *Chiron* 1 (1971), 177-89.

Irby-Massie, G.L., 'Women in Ancient Science', in M. DeForest (ed.), *Women's Power, Man's Game* (Wauconda: Bolchazy-Carducci, 1993), 354-72.

Jackson, R., *Doctors and Diseases in the Roman Empire* (London: British Museum Publications, 1988).

Jacoby, F., *Fragmente der griechischen Historiker* (Berlin: Weidmann, 1923–57).

Jay, P., *The Greek Anthology and Other Ancient Epigrams* (London: Allen Lane, 1973).

Jensen, A., *God's Self-Confident Daughters: Early Christianity and the Liberation of Women* (trans. O.C. Dean Jr.; Louisville: Westminster John Knox Press, 1996).

Jones, A.H.M. *et al.*, *The Prosopography of the Later Roman Empire*, I (Cambridge: Cambridge University Press, 1971).

Jones, W.H.S., *Pliny, Natural History* (Cambridge, MA: Harvard, Loeb, 1963).

Kalinka, E. (ed.), *Tituli Lyciae: Tituli Asiae Minores*, II (Vienna: Hoelder-Pichler-Tempsky, 1901–).

Kalkmann, A., 'Tatians Nachrichten über Kunstwerke', *Rheinisches Museum* 42 (1887), 489-524.

Kassel, R., and C. Austin (eds), *Poetae Comici Graeci* (Berlin and New York: De Gruyter, 1983).

Kastner, G.R., 'Introduction to Eudokia's "Martyrdom of St. Cyprian" ', in P. Wilson-Kastner *et al.* (eds), *A Lost Tradition: Women Writers of the Early Church* (Lanham: University Press of America, 1981), 135-58.

Kastner, G.R., and A. Millin, 'Proba' in P. Wilson-Kastner *et al.* (eds), *A Lost Tradition: Women Writers of the Early Church* (Lanham: University Press of America, 1981), 33-35.

Keyser, P.T., 'Alchemy in the ancient world: from science to magic', *Illinois Classical Studies* 15 (1990), 353-78.

Kisch, B., *Scales and Weights: A Historical Outline* (New Haven: Yale University Press, 1965).

Kühn, D.C.H., *Claudii Galeni Opera Omnia*, XII, XIX (Leipzig: Teubner, 1826, 1830; repr. Hildesheim: Olms, 1964).

Kyriakidis, S., 'Eve and Mary: Proba's technique in the creation of two different female figures', *Materiali e discussioni per l'analisi dei testi classici* 29 (1992), 121-53.

Lambert, A., 'Egeria: Notes critiques sur la tradition de son nom et celle de l'Itinerarium', *Revue Mabillon* 26 (1936), 71-94.

—'Keening Sappho: female speech and genres in Sappho's poetry', in A. Lardinois and L. McClure (eds), *Making Silence Speak* (Princeton: Princeton University Press, 2001), 75-92.

Lardinois, A., and L. McClure (eds), *Making Silence Speak: Women's Voices in Greek Literature and Society* (Princeton: Princeton University Press, 2001).

Lattimore, R., *Themes in Greek and Latin Epitaphs* (Urbana: The University of Illinois Press, 1942).

Lefkowitz, M.R., *The Lives of the Greek Poets* (Baltimore: John Hopkins University Press, 1981).

Lefkowitz, M.R., and M.B. Fant, *Women's Life in Greece and Rome: A Source Book in Translation* (Baltimore: John Hopkins University Press, 1st edn, 1982; 2nd edn, 1992).

Levi, P., *Pausanias: Guide to Greece*, I (Harmondsworth: Penguin, 1979).

Lichtheim, M., *Ancient Egyptian Literature*, II (Berkeley: University of California Press, 1976).

Lindsay, J., *The Origins of Alchemy in Graeco-Roman Egypt* (London: Muller, 1970).

Lloyd-Jones, H., and P. Parsons, *Supplementum Hellenisticum* (Berlin: De Gruyter, 1983).

Lobel, E., 'Corinna', *Hermes* 65 (1930), 356-65.

—*Oxyrhynchus Papyri* 39 (London: Egypt Exploration Society, 1972)

Lobel, E., and D.L. Page, *Poetarum Lesbiorum Fragmenta* (Oxford: Clarendon Press, 1963).

Lowe, N.J., 'Sulpicia's syntax', *Classical Quarterly* 38 (1988), 193-205.

Luck, G., 'Die Dichterinnen der griechischen Anthologie', *Museum Helveticum* 11 (1954), 170-87.

—*Arcana Mundi: Magic and the Occult in the Greek and Roman Worlds* (Baltimore: John Hopkins University Press, 1985).

Ludwich, A., *Eudocia Augustae, Procli Lycii, Claudiani carminum graecorum reliquiae* (Leipzig: Teubner, 1897).

Maas, P., 'The Philinna Papyrus', *Journal of Hellenic Studies* 62 (1942), 33-38.

Maraval, P., *Égérie: Journal de Voyage* (Paris: du Cerf, 1983).

Martin, R.P., 'Just like a woman: enigmas of the lyric voice', in A. Lardinois and L. McClure (eds), *Making Silence Speak* (Princeton: Princeton University Press, 2001), 55-75.

Martindale, J.R., *The Prosopography of the Later Roman Empire*, II (Cambridge: Cambridge University Press, 1980).

—*The Prosopography of the Later Roman Empire*, IIIA (Cambridge: Cambridge University Press, 1992).

Mathisen, R.W., '*PLRE* II: suggested addenda and corrigenda', *Historia* 31 (1982), 364-86.

—*Roman Aristocrats in Barbarian Gaul: Strategies for Survival in an Age of Transition* (Austin: University of Texas Press, 1993).

Matranga, C., *Anecdota Graeca* (Leipzig: Teubner, 1850).

Meineke, A. (ed.), *Stobaeus: Florilegium* (Leipzig: Teubner, 1855–57).

Mellor, R., *Thea Roma: The Worship of the Goddess Roma in the Greek World* (Göttingen: Vandenhoeck and Ruprecht, 1975).

Migne, J.-P., *Patrologiae cursus completus*. Series Latina (Paris: Garnier Frères, 1857–66).

—*Patrologiae cursus completus*. Series Graecae (Paris: Garnier Frères, 1857–86)

Milne, J.G., *A Catalogue of Alexandrian Coins* (Oxford: Clarendon Press, 1933).

Montfaucon, B. de, *Diarium Italicum* (Paris: J. Anisson, 1702).

Mountford, J.F., 'Silvia, Aetheria, or Egeria?', *Classical Quarterly* 17 (1923), 40-41.

Müller, C., *Fragmenta Historicorum Graecorum*, III (Paris: Didot, 1849).

Musurillo, H., *The Acts of the Christian Martyrs* (Oxford: Clarendon Press, 1972).

Nagy, B., 'The Naming of Athenian Girls', *Classical Journal* 74 (1979), 360-64.

O'Higgins, D.M., 'Women's cultic joking and mockery: some perspectives', in A. Lardinois and L. McClure (eds), *Making Silence Speak* (Princeton: Princeton University Press, 2001), 137-60.

Olivieri, A., *Aëtii Amideni libri medicinales i-iv*. Corpus Medicorum Graecorum VIII.2 (Leipzig: Teubner, 1935).

Ousterhout, R. (ed.), *The Blessings of Pilgrimage* (Urbana: The University of Illinois Press, 1990).

Pack, R.H., *The Greek and Latin Literary Texts from Greco-Roman Egypt* (Ann Arbor: University of Michigan Press, 1965).

Page, D.L., *Select Papyri*, III (Cambridge, MA: Harvard, Loeb, 1941), 486-89.

—*Corinna* (London: Society for Promotion of Hellenistic Studies, 1963).

—*Poetae Melici Graeci* (Oxford: Clarendon Press, 1962).

—*Epigrammata Graeca* (Oxford: Clarendon Press, 1975).

Page, T.E., *Lucius Annaeus Florus; Epitome of Roman History; Cornelius Nepos, fragments* (Cambridge, MA: Cambridge, MA: Harvard, Loeb, 1947).

Parke, H.W., and D.E. Wormell, *The Delphic Oracle* (Oxford: Blackwell, 1956).

Parker, H.N., 'Another go at the text of Philaenis (P. Oxy. 2891)', *Zeitschrift für Papyrologie und Epigraphik* 79 (1989), 49-50.

—'Other remarks on the other Sulpicia', *Classical World* 86.2 (1992), 89-95.

—'Sappho schoolmistress', *Transactions and Proceedings of the American Philological Association* 123 (1993), 309-51.

—'Sulpicia, The *Auctor de Sulpicia* and the Authorship of 3.9 and 3.11 of the *Corpus Tibullianum*', *Helios* 21.1 (1994), 39-62.

—'The myth of the heterosexual: anthropology and sexuality for classicists', *Arethusa* 34 (2001), 313-62.

Patai, R., 'Maria the Jewess: founding mother of alchemy', *Ambix* 29 (1982), 177-97.

Paton, W.R., *The Greek Anthology*, II (Cambridge, MA: Harvard University Press, 1917).

Pauly, A.F., and Wissowa, G. (eds), *Paulys Real-encyclopädie der classischen Alterumswissenschaft* (Stuttgart: J.B. Metzler, 1894–1962).

Pintaudi, R. (ed.), *Dai Papyri della Biblioteca Medicea Laurenziana*, III (Firenze: Gonnelli, 1979).

Pomeroy, S.B., *Goddesses, Whores, Wives and Slaves: Women in Classical Antiquity* (New York: Schocken Books, 1975).

—'*Technikai kai mousikai*: the education of women in the fourth century and in the Hellenistic period', *American Journal of History* 2 (1977), 51-68.

—'Plato and the female physician (*Republic* 454d2)', *American Journal of Philology* 99 (1978), 496-500.

—'Supplementary notes on Erinna', *Zeitschrift für Papyrologie und Epigraphik* 32 (1978), 17-22.

—*Women in Hellenistic Egypt: From Alexander to Cleopatra* (New York: Schocken Books, 1984).

Powell, J.U., *Collectanea Alexandrina* (Oxford: Clarendon Press, 1925).

Prinz, O., *Itinerarium Egeriae* (Heidelberg: Winter, 1960).

Rader, R., 'The Martyrdom of Perpetua: a protest account of third-century Christianity', in P. Wilson-Kastner *et al.* (eds), *A Lost Tradition: Women Writers of the Early Church* (Lanham: University Press of America, 1981), 1-32.

Raynaud, E., *Poetae Minores* (Paris: Garnier Frères, 1931).

Rayor, D.J., *Sappho's Lyre: Archaic Lyric and Women Poets of Ancient Greece* (Berkeley: University of California Press, 1991).

—'Korinna: gender and the narrative tradition', *Arethusa* 26.3 (1993), 219-31.

Reynolds, L.D., *Texts and Transmission* (Oxford: Clarendon Press, 1983).

—*Scribes and Scholars: A Guide to the Transmission of Greek and Latin Literature* (Oxford: Clarendon Press, 1991)

Richardson, W.F., *Numbering and Measuring in the Classical World* (Auckland: St Leonards Publications, 1985).

Richlin, A., 'Sulpicia the satirist', *Classical World* 86.2 (1992), 125-39.

Richlin, A. (ed.), *Pornography and Representation in Greece and Rome* (Oxford and New York: Oxford University Press, 1992).

Richter, G.M.A., *The Portraits of the Greeks*, I (London: Phaidon, 1965).

—*The Portraits of the Greeks*, abridged (ed. R.R.R. Smith; Oxford: Phaidon, 1984).

Riddle, J.M., 'High medicine and low medicine in the Roman Empire', *Aufstieg und Niedergang der römischen Welt* II, 37.1 (Berlin: De Gruyter, 1990), 102-20.

—'Oral contraceptives and early term abortifacients during Classical Antiquity and the Middle Ages', *Past and Present* 132 (1992), 3-32.

—*Contraception and Abortion from the Ancient World to the Renaissance* (Cambridge, MA: Harvard University Press, 1992).

Robeck, C.M., *Prophecy in Carthage: Perpetua, Tertullian, and Cyprian* (Cleveland: Pilgrim Press, 1992).

Robinson, J.A., *Passio Perpetua: Texts and Studies*, I.2 (Cambridge: Cambridge University Press, 1981).

Sabatier, J., *Descriptions Générales des Monnaies Byzantines* (Paris: Rollin et Feuardent, 1862).

Salisbury, J.E., *Perpetua's Passion: The Death and Memory of a Young Roman Woman* (London and New York: Routledge, 1997).

Santirocco, M., 'Sulpicia reconsidered', *Classical Journal* 74 (1979), 229-39.

Schachter, A., *Cults of Boeotia*, I (London: University of London, Institute of Classical Studies, 1981).

Schenkl, C., *Cento Vergilianus de laudibus Christi, Poetae Christiani Minores*, I. Corpus Scriptores Ecclesiasticorum Latinorum 16 (Vienna: F. Tempsky, 1888).

Schlegel, G.D., 'The *Ad Martyras* of Tertullian and the circumstances of its composition', *Downside Review* 63 (1945), 125.

Sivan, H., 'Holy Land pilgrimage and western audiences: some reflections on Egeria and her circle', *Classical Quarterly* 38.2 (1988), 528-35.

Sivan, H., 'Who was Egeria? Piety and pilgrimage in the age of Gratian', *Harvard Theological Review* 81.1 (1988), 59-72.

Skinner, M.B., 'Corinna of Tanagra and her audience', *Tulsa Studies in Women's Literature* 2.1 (1983), 9-20.

—'Sapphic Nossis', *Arethusa* 22 (1989), 5-18.

—'Nossis' *Thelyglossos*: the private text and the public book', in S.B. Pomeroy (ed.), *Women's History and Ancient History* (Chapel Hill: University of North Carolina Press, 1991), 20-47.

—'Ladies' day at the Art Institute: Theocritus, Herodas, and the gendered gaze', in A. Lardinois and L. McClure (eds), *Making Silence Speak* (Princeton: Princeton University Press, 2001), 201-22.

Smith, K.F., *The Elegies of Albius Tibullus* (New York, Cincinatti: American Book Co.,1913; Darmstadt: Wissenschaftliche Buchgesellschaft, 1979).

Snyder, J.McI., 'Korinna's "Glorious Songs of Heroes"', *Eranos* 82 (1984), 123-34.

—*The Woman and the Lyre: Women Writers in Classical Greece and Rome* (Carbondale: Southern Illinois University Press, 1989).

—*Lesbian Desire in the Lyrics of Sappho* (New York: Columbia University Press, 1997).

Spencer, W.G. (ed.), *Celsus De Medicina*, II (Cambridge MA: Harvard University Press, 1977).

Spitzer, L., 'The epic style of the pilgrim Aetheria', *Comparative Literature* 1 (1949), 225-58.

Stannard, J., 'Medical plants and folk remedies in Pliny, *Historia Naturalis*', *History and Philosophy of the Life Sciences* 4 (1982), 3-23.

Stehle, E., 'The good daughter: mothers' tutelage in Erinna's *Distaff* and fourth-century epitaphs', in A. Lardinois and L. McClure (eds), *Making Silence Speak* (Princeton: Princeton University Press, 2001), 179-200.

Stroheker, K.F., *Der Senatorische Adel im Spätantiken Gallien* (Darmstadt: Wissenschaftliche Buchgesellschaft, 1970).

Swanson, D.C., 'A formal analysis of Egeria's (Silvia's) vocabulary', *Glotta* 44 (1966–67), 177-254.

Syme, R., 'Hadrian and the Senate', *Athenaeum* 62 (1984), 31-60.

Tarn, W.W., *Hellenistic Civilisation* (Cleveland: World Publishing, 1961).

Taylor, F.S., 'A survey of Greek alchemy', *Journal of Hellenic Studies* 50 (1930), 109-39.

—'The origins of Greek alchemy', *Ambix* 1 (1937–38), 30-47.

—'The evolution of the still', *Annals of Science* 5:3 (1945), 185-202.

—*The Alchemists: Founders of Modern Chemistry* (London: Heineman, 1951).

Thesleff, H., 'An introduction to the Pythagorean writings of the Hellenistic Period', *Acta Academiae Aboensis, Humaniora* 24.3 (Abo: To akademi, 1961).

—'Pythagorean texts of the Hellenistic Period', *Acta Academiae Aboensis, Humaniora* A, 30.1 (Abo: To akademi, 1965).

Tomlinson, R.A., *Argos and the Argolid* (London: Routledge and Kegan Paul, 1972).

Tränkle, H., *Appendix Tibullianum* (Berlin: De Gruyter, 1990).

Tsantsanoglou, K., 'The memoirs of a lady from Samos', *Zeitschrift für Papyrologie und Epigraphik* 12 (1973), 183-95.

Usher, M.D., *Homeric Stitchings: The Homeric Centos of the Empress Eudocia* (Lanham: Rauman and Littlefield, 1998).

—*Homerocentones Eudociae Augustae* (Stuttgart and Leipzig: Teubner, 1998).

Waithe, M.E., *A History of Women Philosophers*, I (Dodrecht, Boston, Lancaster: M. Nijhoff, 1987).

Webster, T.B.L., *Hellenistic Poetry and Art* (New York: Barnes and Noble, 1964).

West, M.L., 'Corinna', *Classical Quarterly* 20 (1970), 277-87.

—'Erinna', *Zeitschrift für Papyrologie und Epigraphik* 25 (1977), 95-119.

—'Balbilla did not save Memnon's soul', *Zeitschrift für Papyrologie und Epigraphik* 25 (1977), 120.

—'Die griechischen Dichterinnen der Kaiserzeit', in H.G. Beck *et al.* (eds), *Kyklos: Griechisches und Byzantinisches. Festschrift für R. Keydell* (Berlin: De Gruyter, 1978), 101-15.

West, M.L., *Greek Metre* (Oxford: Clarendon Press, 1982).

Whitehorne, J.G.E., *Cleopatras* (London, New York: De Gruyter, 1994).

Wilamowitz-Moellendorff, U. von, *Sappho und Simonides* (Berlin: Weidmann, 1913).

—'Lesefrüchte CLXIX', *Hermes* 54 (1919), 71-72.

Wilkinson, J., *Egeria's Travels* (London: SPCK, 1971).

—*Jerusalem Pilgrims before the Crusades* (2nd edn; Warminster: Aris and Phillips, 1998).

Williamson, M., *Sappho's Immortal Daughters* (Cambridge, MA: Harvard University Press, 1995).

Wilson, H.A. (ed.), *Gelasian Sacramentary* (Oxford: Clarendon Press, 1894).

Wilson, L.H., *Sappho's Sweet Bitter Songs: Configurations of Female and Male in Ancient Greek Lyric* (London and New York: Routledge, 1996).

Wilson, N.G., *The Bibliotheca: a selection* (London: Duckworth, 1994).

Wilson-Kastner, P., G.R. Kastner, A. Millin, R. Rader, J. Reedy (eds), *A Lost Tradition: Women Writers of the Early Church* (Lanham: University Press of America, 1981).

Wilson-Kastner, P., 'Introduction: the pilgrimage of Egeria', in Wilson-Kastner, P. *et al.* (eds), *A Lost Tradition: Women Writers of the Early Church* (1981), 71-83.

Zeller, E., *Philosophie der Griechen*, III.2 (Leipzig: O.R. Reisland, 1903).

Editions Used and Sources of Fragments

AESARA

Edition: H. Thesleff, 'Pythagorean texts of the Hellenistic Period', *Acta Academiae Aboensis, Humaniora* A, 30.1 (Abo: To akademi, 1965), 48-50.

Source: Stob. 1.49.27.

ANYTE

Edition: D.L. Page, *Epigrammata Graeca* (Oxford, Clarendon, 1975), pp. 676-769.

Sources: 1: *Anth. Pal.* 6.123; 2: *Anth. Pal.* 6.153; 3: *Anth. Plan.* 291; 4: *Anth. Pal.* 7.724; 5: *Anth. Pal.* 7.486; 6: *Anth. Pal.* 7.490; 7: *Anth. Pal.* 7.646; 8: *Anth. Pal.* 7.649; 9: *Anth. Pal.* 7.208; 10: Pollux 5.48; 11: *Anth. Pal.* 7.202; 12: *Anth. Pal.* 7.215; 13: *Anth. Pal.* 6.312; 14: *Anth. Pal.* 9.745; 15: *Anth. Pal.* 9.144; 16: *Anth. Pal.* 9.313; 17: *Anth. Pal.* 9.314; 18: *Anth. Plan.* 228; 19: *Anth. Plan.* 231; 20: *Anth. Pal.* 7.190; 21: *Anth. Pal.* 7.232; 22: *Anth. Pal.* 7.236; 23: *Anth. Pal.* 7.492; 24: *Anth. Pal.* 7.538; 25: *Anth Pal.* 1.189.

ASPASIA

Edition: C.B. Gulick, *Athenaeus*, II (Cambridge, MA; Harvard: Loeb, 1928).

Sources: 1: Athen. 5.219c; 2: Athen. 5.219e.

BOEO

Edition: J.D. Powell, *Collectanea Alexandrina: Reliquiae minores Poetarum Graecorum Aetatis Ptolemaicae* (Oxford, 1925), 23-24.

Source: Paus. 10.5.8.

CAECILIA TREBULLA

Edition: A. Bernard and E. Bernard, *Les Inscriptions Grecques et Latines du Colosse de Memnon* (Cairo: Institut français d'archéologie orientale, 1960), 92-94.

Source: Inscriptions on Colossus of Memnon.

CLEOBULINA

Edition: J.M. Edmonds, *Elegy and Iambus* (Cambridge, MA; Harvard, Loeb, 1931, 1982), 164.

Sources: 1: Athen. 10.452B and Plut. *Moralia* 154 B; 2: Anonymous, *Dialexeis* (Diels-Kranz) 2.410 s; 3: Plut. *Moralia* 150E = *Seven Sages* 5.

CLEOPATRA

Editions: D.C.H. Kühn, *Claudii Galeni Opera Omnia*, vols. 12, 19 (Leipzig, Knobloch 1826, 1830; Repr. Hildesheim, Olms, 1964) (fragments 1-3, 6);
A. Olivieri, *Aëtii Amideni libri medicales i-iv. Corpus Medicorum Graecorum* 8.2 (Berlin, Teubner, 1935) (fragment 4);
J.L. Heiberg (ed.), *Paulus Aegineta* (Leipzig: Teubner, 1921) (fragment 5).

Sources: 1: Galen 12.403-405; 2: Galen 12.432-34; 3: Galen 12. 492-93; 4: Aëtius, *CMG* 8.2, 408; 5: Paulus of Aegina 3.2.1; 6: Pseudo-Galen 19.767-71.

CLEOPATRA the Alchemist

Edition: M. Berthelot (ed.), *Collection des Alchemistes Grecs* (Paris, 1888; repr. Osnabrück: Otto Zeller, 1967), fig. 11, 132.

Source: ms. Saint-Marc fol. 188, verso.

CORINNA

Edition: D.L. Page, *Poetae Melici Graeci* (Oxford: Clarendon Press, 1962), 654-89, 325-45.

Sources: 1, 2: *P.Berol.* 284 (Hermopolis, 2nd c. AD); 3: *P. Oxy.* 2370 (c. 200 AD); 4: Heph. 2.3; 5: Ap. Dysc., *Pronouns* 98bc; 6: Ap. Dysc., *Pronouns* 105b; 7, 8: Ap. Dysc., *Pronouns* 64b–65a; 9: Anonymous grammarian, ed. Egenolff, *Philol.* 59 (1900), 249; 10, 11: *PSI* 1174 (1st c. AD).

CORNELIA

Edition: T.E. Page, *Lucius Annaeus Florus, Epitome of Roman History; Cornelius Nepos, Fragments* (Cambridge, MA: Harvard, Loeb, 1947), 693-96.

Sources: 1: Cornelius Nepos, *Fr.* 1.1; 2: Cornelius Nepos, *Fr.* 1.2

DEMO

Edition: A. Bernard and E. Bernard, *Les Inscriptions Grecques et Latines du Colosse de Memnon* (Cairo: Institut français d'archéologie orientale, 1960), 83.

Source: Inscription on Colossus of Memnon.

DIONYSIA

Edition: A. Bernard and E. Bernard, *Les Inscriptions Grecques et Latines du Colosse de Memnon* (Cairo: Institut français d'archéologie orientale, 1960), 66.

Source: Inscription on Colossus of Memnon.

EGERIA

Edition: O. Prinz, *Itinerarium Egeriae* (Heidelberg: Winter, 1960).

ELEPHANTIS

Edition: W.H. Jones, *Pliny Natural History*, VIII (Cambridge, MA; Harvard, Loeb, 1963).

Source: Plin. 28.81.

ERINNA

Edition: H. Lloyd-Jones and P. Parsons, *Supplementum Hellenisticum* (Berlin: De Gruyter, 1983), 401-402, 404 (Poems 1-3);
A.S.F. Gow and D.L. Page (eds), *The Greek Anthology: Hellenistic Epigrams* (Cambridge: Cambridge University Press, 1965), 1781, 1797 (Poems 4-6);
M.L. West, 'Erinna', *Zeitschrift für Papyrologie und Epigraphik* 25 (1977), 95-119 (poem 1);
J.U. Powell, *Collectanea Alexandrina* (Oxford: Clarendon Press, 1925), 186 (Poem 7).

Sources: 1: *Papiri Greci e Latini* ix (1929), 1090; 2: Stob. 4.51.4; 3: ; Athen. 7.283.D; 4: *Anth. Pal.* 6.352; 5: *Anth. Pal.* 7.710; 6: *Anth. Pal.* 7.712; 7: *P. Oxy.* 1.8.

EUCHERIA
Edition: A. Baehrens, *Poetae Latini Minores* V (Leipzig: Teubner, 1883; New York: Garland Pub., 1979), 61-62.

EUDOCIA
Editions: A. Ludwich, *Eudociae Augustae, Procli Lycii, Claudiani carminum graecarum reliquiae* (Leipzig: Teubner, 1897); M.D. Usher, *Homerocentones Eudociae Augustae* (Stuttgart and Leipzig: Teubner, 1999).
J. Green and Y. Tsafir, 'Greek inscriptions from Hammat Gader: a poem by the Empress Eudocia and two building inscriptions', *Israel Exploration Journal* 32 (1982), 78-91.

EURYDICE
Edition: W.R. Paton and I. Wegehaupt, *Plutarchi Moralia* 1 (Leipzig: Teubner, 1925), 27.
Source: Plut., *On the Education of Children* 20.20-23 (= *Mor.* 14b-c).

FABULLA
Edition: D.C.H. Kühn, *Claudii Galeni Opera Omnia*, XIII (Leipzig: Knobloch, 1826; repr. Hildesheim: Olms, 1964).
Source: 1: Galen 13.250; 2: Galen 13.341.

HEDYLE
Edition: H. Lloyd-Jones and P. Parsons, *Supplementum Hellenisticum* (Berlin: De Gruyter, 1983), 456.
Source: Athen. 7.297A-C.

HORTENSIA
Edition: G.P. Goold, *Appian's Roman History*, IV (Cambridge, MA: Harvard University Press, 1979), 194-96.
Source: Appian, *Civil Wars* 4.32-33.

JULIA BALBILLA
Edition: A. Bernard and E. Bernard, *Les Inscriptions Grecques et Latines du Colosse de Memnon* (Cairo: Institut français d'archéologie orientale, 1960), 28-31.
Texts: Inscriptions on Colossus of Memnon.

LAÏS
Edition: W.H. Jones, *Pliny Natural History*, VIII (Cambridge, MA; Harvard, Loeb, 1963).
Source: Plin. 28.81.

MAIA
Edition: D.C.H. Kühn, *Claudii Galeni Opera Omnia*, XIII (Leipzig: Knobloch 1826; repr. Hildesheim: Olms, 1964).
Source: Galen 13.840.

MARIA
Edition: M. Berthelot (ed.), *Collection des Alchemistes Grecs* (Paris, 1888; repr. Osnabrück:

Otto Zeller, 1967); *Theatrum Chemicum* 6 (Strasbourg, 1661; repr. Torino, 1981), 479-80.

Sources: 1: Zos. 3.28.9 (*CAG* II.196-7); 2: Zos. 3.11.1 (*CAG* II .146); 3: Zos. 3.12.3 (*CAG* II.149); 4. Zos. 3.24.3 (*CAG* II.182); 5: Olympiodorus 2.4.54 (*CAG* II.103); 6: *Theatrum Chemicum* 6, 479-80; 7: Zos. 3.15.2-3 (*CAG* II.157); 8: Zos. 3.50.1 (*CAG* III.236), ms. Saint-Marc, fol. 194 verso (*CAG* I.139 fig. 15); 9: ms. Saint-Marc, fol. 195 verso (*CAG* I.146, fig. 22).

MELINNO

Edition: H. Lloyd-Jones and P. Parsons, *Supplementum Hellenisticum* (Berlin: De Gruyter, 1983), 541.

Source: Stob. 3.7.12.

MELISSA

Edition: H. Thesleff, 'Pythagorean texts of the Hellenistic Period', *Acta Academiae Aboensis, Humaniora* A, 30.1 (Abo: To akademi, 1965), 115-16.

Source: R. Hercher, *Epistolographi Graeci* (Paris: A. Firmin Didot, 1873), 607-608.

MOERO

Edition: A.S.F. Gow and D.L. Page (eds), *The Greek Anthology: Hellenistic Epigrams* (Cambridge: Cambridge University Press, 1965), 2675, 2679 (Poems 1,2); C.B. Gulick, *Athenaeus*, IV (Cambridge, MA; Harvard, Loeb, 1930).

Sources: 1: *Anth. Pal.* 6.119; 2: *Anth. Pal.* 6.189; 3: Athen. 11.491a-b.

MYIA

Edition: H. Thesleff, 'Pythagorean texts of the Hellenistic Period', *Acta Academiae Aboensis, Humaniora* A, 30.1 (Abo: To akademi, 1965), 123-24.

Source: R. Hercher, *Epistolographi Graeci* (Paris: A. Firmin Didot, 1873), 608.

MYRTIS

Edition: D.L. Page, *Poetae Melici Graeci* (Oxford: Clarendon Press, 1962), 716, 371.

Source: Plut. *Moralia* 300D–F, =*Greek Questions* 40.

NICOBULE

Edition: C.B. Gulick, *Athenaeus*, IV, V (Cambridge, MA; Harvard, Loeb, 1930, 1933).

Sources: 1: Athen. 10.434c; 2: Athen. 12.537d.

NOSSIS

Edition: D.L. Page, *Epigrammata Graeca* (Oxford: Clarendon Press, 1975), 786-833.

Sources: 1: *Anth. Pal.* 5.170: 2: *Anth. Pal.* 6.132; 3: *Anth. Pal.* 6.265; 4: *Anth. Pal.* 9.332; 5: *Anth. Pal.* 6.275; 6: *Anth. Pal.* 9.605; 7: *Anth. Pal.* 9.604; 8: *Anth. Pal.* 6.353; 9: *Anth. Pal.* 6.354; 10: *Anth. Pal.* 7.414; 11: *Anth. Pal.* 7.718; 12: *Anth. Pal.* 6.273.

OLYMPIAS

Edition: W.H. Jones, *Pliny Natural History*, VIII (Cambridge, MA; Harvard, Loeb, 1963).

Source: Plin. 1: 20.226; 2: 28.246; 3: 28.253.

PAMPHILA

Edition: C. Müller, *Fragmenta Historicorum Graecorum* (Paris: Didot, 1849; repr. Frankfurt/Main: Minerva, 1975).

Sources: 1: Diog. L. 1.24; 2: Diog. L. 1.63; 3: Diog. L. 1.76; 4: Diog. L. 1.90; 5: Diog. L. 1.98; 6: Diog. L. 2.24; 7: Gell. 15.23; 8: Diog. L. 3.23; 9: Gell. 15.17; 10: Diog. L. 5.36.

PERICTIONE

Edition: H. Thesleff, 'Pythagorean texts of the Hellenistic Period', *Acta Academiae Aboensis, Humaniora* A, 30.1 (Abo: To akademi, 1965), 142-46.

Sources: 1: Stob. 4.28.19; 2: Stob. 4.25.50; 3: Stob. 3.1.120; 4: Stob. 3.1.121.

PERPETUA

Edition: C.J.M.J. Van Beek, *Passio Sanctarum Perpetuae et Felicitatis* (Nijmegen: Dekker and Van de Vegt, 1936), 8-28.

Source: Anon., *The Martyrdom of Saints Perpetua and Felicitas*, 3-10.

PHILAENIS

Edition: K. Tsantsanoglou, 'The memoirs of a lady from Samos', *Zeitschrift für Papyrologie und Epigraphik* 12 (1973), 183-95.

Source: *P.Oxy.* 2891, E. Lobel, *Oxyrhynchus Papyri* 39 (1972), 51-54.

PHILINNA

Edition: H. Lloyd-Jones and P. Parsons, *Supplementum Hellenisticum* (Berlin: De Gruyter, 1983), 900, 399.

Source: B.P. Grenfell and A.S. Hunt, *The Amherst Papyri*, II (London: Henry Frowde, 1901); *P. Amh.* 11.

PHINTYS

Edition: H. Thesleff, 'Pythagorean texts of the Hellenistic Period', *Acta Academiae Aboensis, Humaniora* A, 30.1 (Abo: To akademi, 1965), 151-53.

Sources: 1: Stob. 4.23.61; 2: Stob. 4.23.61a.

PRAXILLA

Edition: D.L. Page, *Poetae Melici Graeci* (Oxford: Clarendon Press, 1962), 747-54, 903, 386-90, 477 (1-7); D.A. Campbell, *Greek Lyric*, IV (Cambridge, MA: Harvard University Press, 1992) 753, 378.

Sources: 1: Zenobius, *Proverbs* 4.21; 2: Heph. 2.3; 3: Ar., *Wasps* 1238, Schol. *ad loc.*; 4: Ar., *Thesmophoriazusae* 528-31; Schol. *ad loc.*; 5: Heph. 7.8; 6: Athen. 13.603a; 7: Paus. 3.13.5; 8: Schol. Theocritus 5.38.

PROBA

Edition: C. Schenkl, *Corpus Scriptorum Ecclesiasticorum Latinorum*, XVI. *Poetae Christiani Minores* (Vienna: Tempsky, 1888).

PTOLEMAÏS

Edition: I. During, *Porphyrios Kommentar zur Harmonielehre des Ptolemaios* (Göteborg: Elanders boktryckeri aktiebolag, 1932), 22-26.

Sources: 1: Porphyry, *Commentary on Ptolemaeus* 22.25–23.9; 2: Porphyry, *Comm.* 23.9-
                      22; 3: Porphyry, *Comm.* 23.25–24.6; 4: Porphyry, *Comm.* 25.9–26.5.

SALPE

Edition: W.H. Jones, *Pliny Natural History*, VIII (Cambridge, MA: Harvard, Loeb,
                      1963).
Source: Plin. 1: 28.38; 2: 28.66; 3: 28.82; 4: 28.262; 5: 32.135; 6: 32.140.

SAMITHRA

Edition: D.C.H. Kühn, *Claudii Galeni Opera Omnia* (Leipzig: Knobloch, 1826; repr.
                      Hildesheim: Olms, 1964).
Source: Galen 13.310.

SAPPHO

Edition :   E. Lobel and D.L. Page, *Poetarum Lesbiorum Fragmenta* (Oxford: Clarendon
                      Press, 1963), with D.A. Campbell, *Greek Lyric*, I: *Sappho and Alcaeus* (Cam-
                      bridge, MA: Harvard University Press, 1990).
Sources: 1: Dion. Hal. 23; 2: Ostracon (3rd century BC) (prim. ed. M. Norsa, Ann. R.
                      Scuola di Pisa 6 [1937] 8ff.); 3: *P. Oxy.* 7 + 2289.6 (3rd century); 4: *P. Oxy.*
                      1231 fr. 1 col. i 1-12 + fr. 3 (2nd century); 5: *P. Oxy.* 1231 fr. 1 col. i 13-34,
                      col. ii 1 + 2166 (a) 2 + *PSI* 123.1-2; 6: *PSI* ii 123.3-12 + *P. Oxy.* 1231 fr. 1
                      col. ii 2-21 + 2166 (a) 3 + 2289 fr. 9; 7: *P. Oxy.* 1231 fr. 56 + 2166(a) 6A;
                      8: Longinus, *On the Sublime* 10.1-3; 9: Ap. Dysc., *Pronouns* 144 a; 10: Ap.
                      Dysc., *Syntax* 3.247; 11: Eust., *Iliad* 8.555; 12: Strab. 1.2.33; 13: *Et. Gen.*, 31;
                      14: *Et. Gen.*, 25, 36; 15: Schol. Ar., *Peace* 1174; 16: Ap. Dysc., *Pronouns*
                      124c; 17: *P. Oxy.* 1232 fr. 1 coll. ii , iii, fr. 2 (3rd century)+ 2076 col. ii; 18:
                      P. Fouad 239; 19: Max. Tyr. 18.9; 20: Julian, *Letter to Iamblichus* 183; 21:
                      Heph. 7.7, Plut., *Dialogue on Love* 251d; 22: Galen 8.16; 23: Chrysipp. 23; 24:
                      Hdn. 7; 25: Schol. to Theocritus 28; 26: Pollux 10.124; 27: Stob. 3.4.12; 28:
                      Chrysipp. 13; 29: Athen. 21 bc; 30: Athen. 15.674e + *P. Oxy.* 1787 fr. 33;
                      31: Heph.11.5; 32: Heph. 11.5; 33: *P. Berol.* 9722 fol. 1 (6th century) +
                      ALG 1.4 p. 57; 34: *P. Berol.* 9722 fol. 4; 35: *P. Berol.* 9722 fol. 5; 36: *P.
                      Haun.* 301 (3rd century BC), P. Mediol.; 37: Pollux 7.73; 38: Heph. 10.5; 39:
                      P. Oxy. 2294 (2nd century); 40: Demmetr. 141, Himmer. 46.8; 41: Syrian in
                      Hermog. 1.1, Himmer. 9.16, Demmetr. 106; 42: Demmetr. 146; 43: Ap.
                      Dysc., *Conjunctions* 490; 44: Himmer. 9.19; 45: *Anecd. Oxon.* 1.190; 46: Heph.
                      7.6; 47: Heph., *Poem.* 7.1; 48: Heph. 15.26; 49: Dion. Hal. 25; 50:
                      Demmetr. 140; 51: Heph. 7.6; 52: Servius on Virgil, *Georgics* 1.31; 53: Heph.
                      4.2; 54: Hermog. 2.4; 55: *Et. Mag.* 2.43; 56: Stob. 4.22.112; 57: Athen.
                      12.554b; 58: Ammonius, *On Similar but Different Words* 75; 59: Heph. 15.4;
                      60: *Et. Gen.*, 22; 61: Heph. 15.25; 62: Heph. 9.2; 63: Ap. Dysc., *Pronouns*
                      83bc; 64: Heph. 7.7; 65: Heph. 15.18; 66: Heph. 14.7; 67: Heph. 12.4; 68:
                      Heph. 12.2; 69: Schol. Sophocles, *Electra* 149; 70: Arist., *Rhetoric* 1367a; 71:
                      Heph. 10.4; 72: Athen. 10.425d; 73: Athen. 13.571d; 74: Athen. 2.54f; 75:
                      Herodian, *On the Declension of Nouns*; 76: Tryphon, *Figures of Speech* 25; 77: Dio
                      Chrys. 37.47; 78: Schol. Pindar, *Olympian* 2.96f.; 79: Max. Tyr. 18.9; 80: *Et.
                      Gen.*, 19; 81: Schol. Ap. Rhod. 1.727; 82: Atilius Fortunatianus, *Art* 28; 83:
                      Heph. 11.3; 84: Max. Tyr. 18.9d; 85: Demmetr. 161s; 86: *Et. Gen.*, 18; 87:
                      Plut., *On Restraining Anger* 456e; 88: Max. Tyr. 18.9g; 89: Athen. 13.571d;

90: Athen. 2.57d; 91: Marius Plotius Sacerdos, *Grammar* 3.3; 92: Heph. 11.5; 93: Demmetr. 164; 94: Heph. 11.3, 5; 95: Philodemus, *Piety* (T. Gomperza [ed.], *Philodem über Frömmigkeit* [Leipzig: Teubner, 1866], 42); 96: Schol. Theocritus 1.55b; 97: Eust., *Iliad* 2.713; 98: *Anth. Pal.* 6.269; 99: *Anth. Pal.* 7.489; 100: *Anth. Pal.* 7.505.

SOTIRA

Edition: W.H. Jones, *Pliny Natural History*, VIII (Cambridge, MA: Harvard, Loeb, 1963).

Source: Plin. 28.83.

SULPICIA

Edition: G. Luck, *Tibullus* (Stuttgart: Teubner, 1988).

Source: 1-6: [Tibullus] 4.7-12 (3.13-18); 7: [Tib.] 4.3 (3.9); 8 [Tib.] 4.5 (3.11); 9-11: [Tib.] 4.2, .4, .6 (3.8, .10, .12).

SULPICIA II

Editions: 1: H. Parker, 'Other remarks on the other Sulpicia', *Classical World* 86.2 (1992), 89-95; 2: A. Baehrens, *Poetae Latini Minores*, V (Leipzig: Teubner, 1883; New York: Garland Pub., 1979), 93-97.

Sources: 1: Probus, Schol. on *Satires* 6.537, cited by Valla of Piacenza, *Satires of Juvenal* (Venice, 1486); 2: *Epigrammata Bobiensia* 70.

SYRA

Edition: H. Lloyd-Jones and P. Parsons, *Supplementum Hellenisticum* (Berlin: De Gruyter, 1983), 900, 399.

Source: B.P. Grenfell and A.S. Hunt, *The Amherst Papyri*, II (London: Henry Frowde, 1901); *P. Amh.* 11.

TELESILLA

Edition: D.L. Page, *Poetae Melici Graeci* (Oxford: Clarendon Press, 1962), 717-25, 372-4.

Sources: 1: Heph. 11.2; 2: Athen. 14.619b; 3: Paus. 2.35.2; 4: Paus. 2.82.2; 5: Apollodorus 3.46; 6: Hesychius s.v.; 7: Athen. 11.567; 8: Pollux 2.23; 9: Schol. A Homer, *Odyssey* 13.289.

TERENTIA

Edition: F. Bücheler, *Carmina Latina Epigraphica* (Leipzig: Teubner, 1894–1926; repr. Amsterdam, 1972), 270.

Source: Inscription on Pyramid of Cheops, now lost: *CIL* III 21, *ILS* 1046a.

THEANO

Editions: H. Thesleff, 'Pythagorean texts of the Hellenistic Period', *Acta Academiae Aboensis, Humaniora* A, 30.1 (Abo: To akademi, 1965), 193-95.
F. Hultsh, *Censorinus* (Leipzig: Teubner, 1867) (frg. 2).
R.D. Hicks, *Diogenes Laertius* (Cambridge, MA: Harvard, Loeb, 1925) (frg. 7).
C. Wachsmuth and O. Hense (eds), *Stobaeus Eclogae Physicae Dialecticae et Ethicae* (Berlin, 1884–1912).
R. Hercher, *Epistolographi Graeci* (Paris: A. Firmin Didot, 1873) (frg. 9-16).

Sources: 1: Stob. 1.10.13; 2: Censorinus, *De Die Natali Volumen Illustre* 7.5; 3: Stob.
                              4.580.15; 4: Plut., *Mor.* 142c=Stob. 4.585.1; 5: Stob. 4.586.20; 6: Stob.
                              4.587.8; 7: Diog. L. 8.43; 8: Clem., *Stromata* 4.7; 9: *Epist. Gr.* 603 n. 4; 10:
                              Epist. Gr., 607 n. 9; 11: *Epist. Gr.*, 606 n. 7; 12: *Epist. Gr.*, 605 n. 6; 13: *Epist.
                              Gr.*, 604 n. 5; 14: *Epist. Gr.*, 607 n. 10; 15: Pollux, *Onomasticon* 10.21; 16:
                              Epist. Gr., 606 n. 8.

THEOSEBEIA
Edition: W.R. Paton, *The Greek Anthology* (Cambridge, MA: Harvard, Loeb, 1917),
                              7.559.
Source: *Anth. Pal.* 7.559.

TIMARIS
Edition: H. Lloyd-Jones and P. Parsons, *Supplementum Hellenisticum* (Berlin: De Gruyter,
                              1983), 774, 368.
Source: Plin. 37.178.

XANITE
Edition: D.C.H. Kühn, *Claudii Galeni Opera Omnia* (Leipzig: Knobloch, 1826; repr.
                              Hildesheim: Olms, 1964).
Source: Galen 13.311.

Glossary

Achaea	In historical times this referred to an area of South-East Thessaly; in Homer the Greeks are called Achaeans.
Acheron	A river in Greece (in southern Epirus) which disappeared underground and was reputed to lead to Hades.
Acraephen	A mythological prophet, one of the fifty sons of Orion. There was a town in Boeotia called Acraephnia, and Acraephnius was an epithet of the god Apollo.
Admetus	In Greek mythology the king of Pherae, whose wife Alcestis selflessly agreed to die on his behalf after the Fates allowed him to live if he could find a substitute to die in his place.
Adonis	In Greek mythology he was the son of Cinyras, the king of Crete, and his daughter Myrrha or Smyrna. He was loved by Aphrodite, who, after his death, restored him to life, but had to share him with Persephone in the underworld. He has been identified as a male fertility and vegetation god.
Adonia	An annual Greek festival, popular among women, dedicated to the cult worship of Adonis.
Aegina	In Greek mythology she was a daughter of Asopus, but was changed by Zeus into the island in the Saronic Gulf named after her.
Aelia	The Roman emperor Titus razed Jerusalem in AD 70 during the first Jewish War. The Emperor Hadrian (Publius Aelius Hadrianus) rebuilt it in AD 135, and renamed it Aelia after himself.
Aelian	A Roman who wrote (in Greek) moralizing works on animals, people and history, c. AD 170–235.
Aeolic	A dialect of Greek which came from Boeotia and Thessaly, and was taken by emigrants to Lesbos.
Aeschrion	A Greek lyric poet from Samos, c. 3rd century BC; fragments of his work survive in the *Greek Anthology*.
Aëtius	A Greek from Amida (in Mesopotamia), who wrote on philosophy in the mid-sixth century AD in Alexandria.
Agrippina	Sometimes known as Agrippina Minor, Julia Agrippina (AD 15–59) was the eldest daughter of Germanicus and Agrippina (Major). She was the sister of the emperor Caligula (Gaius), married her uncle, the emperor Claudius, and was the mother of the emperor Nero (who was said to have murdered her). She was granted the title 'Augusta'. She wrote a family history.
Alcaeus	A Greek lyric poet from Mytilene; he lived in the late seventh century BC and was contemporary with Sappho.
Alcibiades	The son of Cleinias was an Athenian general and politician, c. 450–404 BC.
Alciphron	An Athenian sophist of the second century AD; he wrote fictitious letters.
Alcman	A lyric poet of Sparta, about 654–611BC.
Alexander	King Alexander III (the Great) of Macedonia, son of Philip II and Olympias. He lived 356–323 BC. Most famous for his invasion of Asia Minor and conquering of the Persian empire.
Alexandria	An important Greek city founded by Alexander the Great in the Nile Delta; it became the literary centre of the Greek world between about 300–330 BC.
Alexis	Athenian comic playwright, c. 372–270 BC, originally from Thurii.

Alpheus	The largest river in the Peloponnese. In mythology a river god; in Telesilla's version of the myth, Alphaeus pursues Artemis. The more familiar version is in Ovid, *Metamorphoses* 5, where he pursues the nymph Arethusa.
Alyattes	King of Lydia, c. 610–560BC.
Amazon	In mythology, a race of female warriors from the borders of the known world, fated to be defeated by Greek heroes.
Amphion	In mythology, he was a Boeotian hero, the son of Antiope and Zeus, and the husband of Niobe.
Amyclas	Son of Niobe, traditionally slain by Apollo and Artemis.
Ambrosia	The food of the gods, it made whoever tasted it immortal.
Anacreon	A Greek lyric poet, c. 575–510BC.
Andromeda	In Greek mythology she was the daughter of King Cephus of Ethiopia and Queen Cassiopia; she was rescued from a sea monster by the hero Perseus. Euripides' lost play *Andromeda* was produced in 412 BC.
Antipater	A poet from Thessalonica, who lived first century BC–first century AD. There are about eighty of his epigrams in the *Greek Anthology*.
Antony	Marcus Antonius, c. 82–30 BC. A supporter of Julius Caesar, Mark Antony shared power with Caesar's heir Octavian (Augustus) before their rivalry led to civil war in which Antony was defeated. Cleopatra bore him three children.
Aonia	Ancient and poetic name for Boeotia.
Aphrodite	In mythology, Aphrodite was born from the foam of the sea touched by the severed phallus of Uranus (though in an alternative version, she is the daughter of Zeus and a minor deity, Dione). She was the goddess of love.
Apis	A sacred bull, worshipped initially at Memphis in Egypt; later under Ptolemaic and Roman rule it was recognised with a national cult in Egypt.
Apollo	An important Greek god, adopted by the Romans. In mythology he was the son of Leto and Zeus, twin brother of Artemis. He was the god of music, medicine and prophecy.
Appian	A Greek historian from Alexandria, born c. AD 95. He wrote a history of Rome between c. AD 145–165.
Aquitania	The name of a Roman province in South Western Gaul. It came under Visigoth rule from about AD 413, and the Franks from AD 486. Its major city was Burdigala (modern Bordeaux).
Arcadia	The mountainous region of the central Peloponnese. It included the city of Tegea. The dialect was not Doric, but closely related to the eastern Greek dialects.
Ares	The Greek war god, in mythology the son of Zeus and Hera.
Argos	An important Greek polis in the Peloponnese. In legend, King Agamemnon of Argos led the Greeks in the Trojan War. In epic poetry the Greeks are sometimes called 'Argives'.
Aristophanes	Athenian comic playwright, c. 450–385 BC.
Aristotle	A Greek philosopher; born in Stagirus, he founded a famous school in Athens. He lived 384–322 BC.
Aristoxenus	A Greek philosopher and musical theorist from Tarentum (in southern Italy), born about 375 BC.
Arrentine	From the Etruscan city of Aretium (or Arretium), now Arezzo in Tuscany, Italy.
Artemis	In mythology, daughter of Leto and Zeus, sister of Apollo, a virgin goddess with concern for the hunt and childbirth.

Asclepius	A Greek hero and god of healing; in mythology he is the son of Apollo and Coronis: Epidaurus claimed to be his birthplace.
Asclepiades	An influential Hellenistic poet of c. 270 BC; there are about forty of his poems in the *Greek Anthology*.
Asia	The Greeks divided the world into three continents: Europe, Africa and Asia. Asia stretched (roughly) east from the Suez in the south to the river Don in the north.
Asopus	A Boeotian river which separated Thebes from Plataea.
Athena	Daughter of Zeus and Metis (Intelligence) but born by Zeus himself after he swallowed Metis. A warrior goddess of wisdom, war and crafts.
Athenaeus	From Naucratis in Egypt, his only extant work *Deipnosophistai* ('The Sophists at Dinner') was written about AD 200.
Attic	Of Athens or Attica: the land that made up the Athenian polis. Also used to refer to the Athenian dialect of Greek.
Augustan	The period from 31 BC to AD 14 when Augustus ruled Rome.
Augustus	A title adopted by Gaius Octavius in 27 BC, and used thereafter by the Roman emperors.
Aulos	A Greek wind instrument, similar to a clarinet or oboe.
Aurora	Roman name for Eos, goddess of the dawn.
Ausonia	A Greek name for Italy.
Autolycus	In Homer he is he father of Anticleia, and so grandfather of Odysseus.
Bacchylides	A lyric poet from Iulis in Ceos, he was born c. 518 BC.
Bromius	An epithet of Bacchus or Dionysus, god of wine and fertility.
Bruttians	Inhabitants of the south-west peninsula of Italy.
Byzantium	A Greek city on the Bosporus, renamed Constantinople in AD 330 (and later Istanbul).
Caesar	Surname of the Julian family, particularly associated with Julius Caesar. It became a title used by Roman emperors (later still a title for a junior co-emperor who ranked below an Augustus).
Cain	In Jewish mythology Cain was the elder son of Adam and Eve. He murdered his younger brother Abel.
Callimachus	An important Hellenistic poet, c. 305–240 BC. He also wrote prose, including a catalogue of the library in Alexandria.
Calliope	The Muse of epic poetry.
Cambyses	King of Persia, 529–521 BC: he conquered Egypt in 525 BC.
Camillus	According to Roman legend, Marcus Furius Camillus was elected dictator five times in the early fourth century BC and on each occasion led the Romans to a great military victory. One of his victories was against the Gauls, who were besieging the Capitol.
Carneius	Also known as Carnus, in Praxilla's mythology he was the son of Zeus and Europa. He may have once been considered a god. An important Doric festival to Apollo (the Carneia) and a month in most Doric calendars was named after him.
Carneia	A Doric festival to Apollo; see Carneius.
Carthage	A Tyrian colony in North Africa, this important city was destroyed by Rome in 146 BC. The city was later recolonised by Julius Caesar and Augustus.
Castalian Spring	A spring on Mt Parnassus, sacred to the Muses.
Catullus	A popular Roman lyric, erotic and epigrammatic poet, c. 84–54 BC.
Cato	Marcus Porcius Cato was a Roman politician (234–149 BC), who also wrote history (*Orignes*) and on agriculture (*De Agri Cultura*). He was surnamed the

	Censor, Sapiens, Priscus, or Elder (to distinguish him from his great-grandson). He was a conservative moralist.
Censor	The Romans elected two censors and under the republic it was a prestigious office. Censors registered citizens, their property and age for military, political and taxation purposes. They had other financial duties too. The office lost authority under the emperors. The censitor fulfilled the duties of the censor in the provinces.
Cento	A poem composed entirely of lines (or half-lines) taken from another poet's work and reordered. Virgil and Homer were popular sources.
Celts	A people originally from northern Europe, who settled in areas that are now part of modern France, Britain and north-western Spain. In the fourth century BC Celts invaded Italy and sacked Rome. In the third century they ventured further east, invading Greece and even areas across the Hellespont, where some of them settled (Galatia).
Cephisus	A Greek river that flows through Boeotia to lake Copais.
Cheops	The Greek name for the Egyptian king Khufu who reigned in the fourth dynasty of the Old Kingdom (c. 2560–2537 BC). He built the largest of the Great Pyramids at Giza.
Chilon	One of the 'seven wise men' of ancient Greece. He was reputed to have written poetry and to have been the Spartan Ephor who first proposed that Ephors be appointed as auxiliaries to the kings. He lived c. 560 BC.
Christodorus	A poet from Coptus in Egypt, fifth–sixth centuries AD.
Chrysippus	In mythology, the son of Pelops and his concubine, Astyoche, killed by Pelops' wife Hippodamia, but saved and carried off by Zeus.
Chrysippus	An important stoic philosopher and author. He lived c. 280–207 BC.
Cicero	Marcus Tullius Cicero, an important Roman politician and writer, 106-43 BC.
Clazomenae	A Greek city in Ionia.
Clement	Titus Flavius Clemens wrote on the superiority of Christianity in Alexandria in the mid-second century AD.
Cleobulus	From Lindus and conventionally dated to the early sixth century BC, the father of Cleobulina was remembered as the one of the 'seven wise men' of ancient Greece and author of songs and riddles.
Clymenus	A euphemistic title of Hades.
Constantius	Constantius II was the son of Constantine. Roman emperor in the West, AD 337–40, in the East 337–61.
Consul	The highest ranking civil and military elected office in the Roman government. Under the empire, the elections disappeared as the emperors took the consulship themselves or nominated and appointed the candidates. The *consul suffectus* (substitute consul) was originally appointed only when the consul was unable to finish his term of office. However, under the empire, the consulship was regularly held for only two months and the appointment of substitute consuls became common.
Corcyra	A Greek island in the north of the Ionian Sea; modern Corfu.
Cornelius Nepos	A Roman author, c. 100–25 BC. He wrote biographies of famous men, among other work.
Crates	An Athenian comic playwright who worked in the period c. 450–421 BC.
Cratinus	An Athenian comic playwright, c. 484–c. 419 BC.
Crito	Titus Statilius Crito was a Greek physician who worked at Trajan's court c. 100 AD; Galen quotes his work.

Cronus	In Greek mythology he was the son of Uranus and Gaea (Heaven and Earth) and by his sister Rhea, father of the older Olympian gods (Hestia, Demeter, Hera, Hades, Poseidon and Zeus).
Croton	A Greek colony situated in the 'toe' of Italy, settled by Achaeans
Ctesias	A Greek doctor from Cnidus, born late in the fifth century BC, who worked at the Persian court and wrote histories of Persia and India.
Cumae	The earliest Greek colony in Italy, founded on the coast near Naples in the eighth century BC.
Curetes	Demigods on Crete who rescued Zeus as an infant from his father, Cronus, who had eaten all of his siblings.
Cybele	The mother-goddess, originally worshipped in Anatolia. Her orgiastic cult later spread to Greece and Rome. She was primarily a goddess of fertility.
Cynic	Cynic philosophers followed the principles of Diogenes, who advocated living simply and cheaply, and rejected social conventions not deemed natural.
Cyprian	A fictional Christian bishop of Antioch, who was said to have been martyred in the reign of the Roman emperor Diocletian (AD 84–305). There was a bishop of Carthage named Cyprian (AD 249–58).
Cypris	An epithet of Aphrodite, who was said to have been born from the foam on the sea at Paphos on Cyprus.
Cyrene	A Greek colony on the coast of north Africa, east of Alexandria.
Damasus	Bishop of Rome, AD 366–84, and poet.
Deinomache	Mother of Alcibiades and wife of Cleinias; she was born about 450 BC.
Delia	An epithet of the goddess Artemis who was born on Delos.
Delos	A small island in the Cyclades, regarded as the birthplace of the gods Artemis and Apollo.
Delphi	Situated on the southern slopes of Mount Parnassus, this was the site of the most important sanctuary and oracle of Apollo.
Demeter	Greek goddess of wheat and the harvest; in mythology she was the sister of Zeus.
Demetrius	A politician and writer from Phalerum in Athens, who was born c. 350 BC.
Diana	A Roman virgin goddess of the hunt and childbirth, identified with the Greek goddess Artemis.
Diocletian	Roman emperor, AD 284–305.
Diogenes Laertius	Author of a work on ancient philosophers; lived c. AD 225–50.
Dionysus	The son of Zeus and Semele, the functions of this Greek god included the cultivation of wine, vegetation, fertility and patronage of poetry, drama and song.
Dioscorides	A Greek poet of about the third century BC, whose epigrams are in the *Greek Anthology*.
Doric	Of the Dorians (the Greeks of Megara and the Peloponnese), used especially of their dialect of Greek.
Dithyramb	A choral song in honour of Dionysus. Competitions for dithyrambs were held at festivals.
Egeria	In Roman mythology she was a goddess or nymph of fountains and springs. The lover and adviser of King Numa, she was also identified with the cult of Diana and worshipped as a goddess of childbirth.
Elegiac	Verse composed in couplets, with a variation of the hexameter of epic poetry. It begins with a dactylic hexameter followed by a dactylic pentameter. Some elegiac couplets were probably sung, accompanied by the aulos.

Eos	The Greek goddess of dawn, daughter of Hyperion and Theia and sister of Helios (Sun) and Selene (Moon). Her name means 'dawn' or 'east'.
Epicurean	A follower of the Athenian philosopher, Epicurus (342–271 BC). He was the first philosopher to admit women to his school.
Epidaurus	A small Greek city-state on the Saronic Gulf, famous for its sanctuary of Aesculapius.
Epigram	Originally an inscription, in practice a poetic inscription. In the Hellenistic period the epigram became a literary genre in its own right, epideictic (for display) rather than for inscription.
Epitaphios	A funeral speech, especially one delivered in Athens in a public funeral for those killed in battle.
Epithalamium	A Greek marriage song, sung by a chorus of young men and women outside the bridal chamber.
Erastes	The older partner in male homosexual relations which were pederastic.
Eromenos	The younger partner in male homosexual relations which were pederastic.
Eros	The Greek word for love; personified as the god of love.
Erythraean	Meaning 'Red', this was the Greeks' name for the Indian Ocean off the coast of Arabia.
Euboea	A long island off the east coast of the Greek mainland.
Europa	In Greek mythology, Zeus turned himself into a bull to carry Europa away to Crete, where she bore him three children, Minos, Rhadamanthys and Sarpedon. Praxilla states that Carneius was also her son.
Eusebius	From Caesarea in Palestine, he wrote an epitome of universal history and a history of the Christian Church in the fourth century AD.
Eustathius	A Greek scholar of the twelfth century AD. He wrote a commentary on Pindar, amongst other works.
Evagrius	A Syrian ecclesiastical historian, (AD c. 536–c. 600) prominent in Antioch and Constantinople. His *Ecclesiastical History* (AD 431–594) is written in excellent Greek and provides a good source for the history of Monophysitism and Nestorianism.
Gadara	A city in Palestine (originally Greek), about 7 km east of the sea of Galilee in the Yarmuk River valley. Hot and cold springs there led to the building of popular baths. The modern name for the Israeli side of the valley is Hammat Gader. The archaeological site of ancient Gadara runs through the Jordanian village of Um-Qeis.
Galicia	A Roman province in north-west Spain.
Galen	A physician from Pergamum c. AD 129–99, who became court physician to the Roman Emperor Marcus Aurelius. He wrote philosophy and, later, medical texts.
Gellius, Aulus	A Roman writer who compiled an eclectic work on a wide variety of topics c. AD 125–65.
Geta	Lucius Septimius Severus Geta, son of Septimius Severus. He became Caesar in AD 198.
Glaucus	Glaucus was a sea deity (and the name of a fish); Athenaeus tells various stories about him 7.296-97c
Glyconic	A metre of Greek lyric poetry, first found in Sappho, Alcaeus and Anacreon.
Gracchi	Tiberius Gracchus, tribune 133 BC, introduced a controversial land ownership reform bill. He was killed during a riot the following year when he presented himself for re-election. His younger brother Gaius, tribune 123 and 122 BC, continued his brother's reforms. He too was killed in riots.

Greek Anthology	An anthology of Greek lyric poetry, this is an important source for women writers. It was composed of the anthologies of Constantine Cephalas (tenth century, known as the *Anthologia Palatina*) and Maximus Planudes (twelfth or thirteenth centuries, known as the *Anthologia Planudea*). Cephalas' anthology was compiled from three older anthologies: the *Stephanus* (Wreath) of Meleager (beginning of the first century BC); the *Stephanus* of Philippus (Augustan period: first century AD); and the *Cycle* of Agathias (from the reign of Justinian: sixth century AD).
Hades	The brother of Zeus and god of the underworld; the dead travel to Hades.
Hadrian	Roman Emperor AD 117–38.
Hammat Gader	See Gadara.
Hathyr	The third Egyptian month of the year.
Heaven	*Ouranos* in Greek means 'heaven'; anthropomorphised as the father of Cronus, grandfather of Zeus, and the first supreme deity.
Hecatomb	A large sacrifice made to a god or gods. In theory, an offering of one hundred oxen.
Hedylus	A Hellenistic poet who lived around the second half of the fourth century BC, he came from Athens or Samos. He was the son and grandson of women poets (Hedyle and Moschine).
Hellanicus	Born in Mytilene early in the fifth century BC, he wrote history and mythology.
Hellenistic	A modern term to define the period from the death of Alexander (323 BC) to the defeat of Cleopatra, Queen of Egypt, and Antony by Octavian at the battle of Actium (31 BC). It was a period in which Greek art and literature flourished.
Hephaestion	Wrote a treatise on poetic metre in the mid-second century AD.
Hera	In mythology the sister of Zeus, she was the goddess of marriage and the life of women.
Heraclides	A Greek philosopher and writer, who came to Athens from Heraclea; he lived c. 390–310 BC.
Hermes	A major Greek god; the son of Zeus and Maia, he was patron of messengers, merchants, travellers and thieves.
Hermonthis	An Egyptian town on the Nile in the district of Thebais.
Hero	Greek heroes and heroines were dead men and women who were recognised for their extraordinary achievements (in reality or in myth) and offered cult worship. They were thought to have superhuman powers, and possibly a divine parent, and acted to protect their local community.
Herodas	Author of literary mimes (i.e. imitative plays) in the third century BC.
Herodicus	A Greek grammarian from Babylon, second century BC.
Herodotus	A Greek historian from Halicarnassus, c. 485–c. 430.
Hesiod	A Greek poet who lived in Boeotia c. 700 BC.
Hesperus	The evening star.
Hexameter	A line of verse with six feet; the dactylic hexameter was used by epic, pastoral and didactic poets.
Hetaera	Greek term for a courtesan or prostitute.
Homer	A Greek poet who lived in Ionia in c. 725 BC.
Humours	In Greek medical doctrine, the human body was composed of four fluids (humours): blood, phlegm, yellow bile and black bile. When the humours were in harmony the body was healthy. Sickness was a product of their disharmony.

Hyccara	A town on the north-west coast of Sicily.
Hymen	A personified marriage song or chant; later tradition invented Apollo and one of the Muses as his parents.
Hyperboreans	A legendary race of worshippers of Apollo who lived in the far north.
Hyrieus	In mythology he was the king of Tanagra and a son of Poseidon. Because of his hospitality to Zeus, Poseidon and Hermes, he was given a child, Orion. Hyria is an region of Boeotia.
Iambic	The main metre of Greek dramatic dialogue, also used in lyric verse.
Iamblichus	A Neoplatonist philosopher from Chalcis who lived c. AD 250–325.
Illyrians	A non-Greek people who inhabited the Adriatic coast to the west and north-west of Macedonia.
Inopus	A river on Delos; Artemis and Apollo were thought to have been born near it.
Ionic	Of the Ionians, Greek colonists of the west coast of Asia Minor: Athens claimed to be their metropolis.
Isidore	Bishop of Seville, AD 602-36. An important scholar of the early Middle Ages.
Jerome	A Christian writer of biographies and commentaries on the scriptures, c. AD 340–420. He wrote the Latin translation of the Bible that came to be called the Vulgate.
Julius Caesar	The famous Roman politician, general and author who lived 100–44 BC.
Juno	An important Roman goddess, worshipped on the Capitol; as queen of the Olympian gods, she protected marriage. She was the wife and sister of Jupiter; identified with the Greek goddess Hera.
Jupiter	The Italian sky god, Jupiter was the most powerful Roman god. He came to be identified with the Greek god Zeus.
Juvenal	Roman satirical poet, AD 60–117.
Laconia	The area of land in the south-east of the Peloponnese which formed the territory of the Spartans and in which the city of Sparta was situated. The Spartans were commonly called Lacedaemonians.
Latopolis	An Egyptian nomes.
Lesbos	A large Greek island off the coast of Asia Minor which supported five independent cities, including Mytilene. Its population were mostly Aeolian. Its famous writers included the poets Sappho, Alcaeus and Arion, and later the philosopher Theophrastus.
Leto	A Titan, the daughter of Coeus and Phoebe; by Zeus mother of the twin gods Apollo and Artemis.
Leucas	A Greek island in the Ionian sea, and the city on that island, famous for the headland called Leucate where disappointed lovers were said to throw themselves into the sea.
Leucones	A people in Gaul.
Library of Alexandria	The library founded by Ptolemy I and II in the third century BC which became the centre of literary and scholarly activity in the Hellenistic world.
Libya	The Greek name for the continent of Africa.
Lindus	A Dorian Greek polis on Rhodes.
Locris	Locris was split into two parts: Eastern Locris (Opuntian Locris) was on the east coast of central Greece, Western Locris (Ozolian Locris) comprised the valley of Larissa and part of the northern coast of the Corinthian Gulf. Opuntian Locris founded a third Locris (Locri Epizephyrii) in the 'toe' of Italy, about 700 BC.
Lucania	A region of southern Italy.

Lucian	A Greek author from Samosata, particularly famous for his satiric dialogues, c. AD 120–80.
Lycia	An area of south-west Asia Minor, mostly under Persian rule until Alexander the Great. In the third century BC, under the Ptolemies, the Lycians adopted Greek language and script.
Lydia	An important kingdom in the west of Asia Minor until 550 BC when it was conquered by the Persians. Its capital was Sardis.
Lygdamus	A Roman poet of the first century BC. He is only known through his elegies, which survive along with Sulpicia's in the body of work attributed to Tibullus (*Corpus Tibullianum*).
Lyncestis	An upper Macedonian canton, whose king was nominally under the suzerainty of the Macedonian king. Philip II of Macedon defeated the Illyrians who had been holding Lyncestis and incorporated it into his kingdom, c. 359 BC.
Lyric poetry	The term 'lyric' is used to cover wide variety of types of poetry. Perhaps more properly it refers to songs composed to be accompanied by a musical instrument (especially the lyre). Some of these were designed to be sung by a chorus, some by an individual. Elegiac and iambic verses were also performed solo, but were not normally set to music (though some elegiacs were probably accompanied by an aulos).
Lysippus	A famous Greek sculptor from Sicyon in the second half of the fourth century BC.
Maia	In Greek mythology she was one of the Pleiades, and the mother of Hermes. Her name means 'mother' or 'nurse'.
Magnentius	Revolted in AD 350, murdering the Roman emperor Constans. He was defeated by Constantius II at Nursa in AD 352.
Magnesia	An Ionian city on a tributary of the Maeander river, subject to Lydia, then Persia. In the fifth century BC it was given to the Athenian Themistocles by the Persian king.
Malalas	John Malalas was a Byzantine chronicler of the sixth century AD.
Mars	The Roman war god, identifed with the Greek Ares. He was the son of Juno, and in Roman mythology, the father of the founder of Rome, Romulus.
Matinus	A mountain in Apulia, a region in south-eastern Italy on the Adriatic.
Maximian	Roman emperor, AD 286–305. He ruled with Diocletian.
Maximus	Maximus of Tyre was a sophist, lecturer and author, c. AD 125–85.
Medea	In mythology the daughter of Aeetes and Eidyia of Colchis, granddaughter of Helios and Circe. She was a powerful witch who enabled Jason to complete his quest for the Golden Fleece. She used her powers to carry out horrific murders.
Megalopolis	A Greek city founded between 370–362 BC by the Theban Epaminondas to be the main city of the Arcadians.
Meleager	A poet and philosopher who lived in Tyre and Cos, about 140–70 BC. He published the first critical anthology of epigrams, called the *Stephanus* (Wreath), which formed the core of the later anthology by Constantine Cephalas and the *Greek Anthology*.
Meliboea	Daughter of Niobe, traditionally slain by Apollo and Artemis.
Memnon	In Greek mythology, the son of Eos or Aurora (dawn) and Tithon (the brother of King Priam of Troy). He was king of Eithiopia and made immortal by Zeus after being slain by Achilles.
Menander	Athenian comic playwright, c. 342–291BC.
Messalla	Marcus Valerius Messalla Corvinus, a Roman politician and patron of the arts, 64 BC–AD 8. His literary circle included Tibullus, Lygdamus and Sulpicia.

Metapontum	A Greek colony in southern Italy, settled by Achaeans.
Miletus	An important Ionian polis in Asia Minor.
Mnemosyne	In mythology, she was one of the titans, a daughter of Gaea (Earth) and Uranus (heaven). She bore to Zeus the nine Muses. Her name means 'Memory'.
Mormo	A female monster of Greek folklore, invoked to frighten children.
Musaeus	A mythical Greek singer, the archetypal musician.
Museum	A place for the Muses and especially the arts inspired by them. The most famous museum in antiquity was in Alexandria, founded by Ptolemy I in about 280 BC.
Muses	The nine daughters of Mnemonysne (Memory) and Zeus were Greek deities of poetry, literature, music and dance. In late Roman times the Muses were allocated individual responsibilities: Calliope was Muse of epic, Clio of history, Euterpe of flutes, Terpsichore of lyric poetry and dance, Erato of lyric and love poetry, Melpomene of tragedy, Thalia of comedy, Polyhymnia of sacred song, and Urania of astronomy (though the names and functions of the Muses vary).
Mytilene	(or Mitylene) The largest polis on the Greek island of Lesbos.
Naiad	A minor Greek water deity of rivers, springs, wells and fountains. They were personified as young girls.
Neanthes	A Greek historian and biographer from Cyzicus, who lived in the third century BC.
Nomos	A Greek term for an administrative district or town in Egypt (plural = *nomoi*).
Numa	Numa Pompilius was the legendary second king of Rome. He introduced most of the Roman cults and sacred institutions, in some versions of the legend through the guidance of the nymph Egeria.
Nymph	The Greek word *numphē* means both a 'nymph' (i.e. a female nature-deity) and a 'bride'.
Odysseus	In mythology, the son of Laertes king of Ithaca, husband of Penelope, and eponymous hero of the *Odyssey*.
Olen	A legendary Greek poet who was said to have brought the worship of Apollo and Artemis to Delos.
Olympus	In Greek mythology, the home of the gods, sometimes identified with Mt Olympus in Thessaly.
Optio	Latin for 'assistant'. In the Roman military, the optio was second-in-command to the centurion.
Ortygia	An alternative name for the island of Delos; Artemis was sometimes called 'Ortygia', as she was born there.
Ouranos	See Uranus.
Ouroborus	The alchemical symbol of a snake or dragon devouring its tail. It represented the idea of the process of alchemy in a closed system. Also spelt Uroborus.
Ovid	A famous Roman poet, who lived 43 BC–AD 17.
Oxyrhynchus	An Egyptian town, famous for the discovery there of ancient papyri texts.
Pan	A minor Greek god, half-goat in shape, originally perhaps from Arcadia. He frequented lonely places, often playing his pipes.
Panacea	Goddess of healing, in Greek mythology she was the daughter of Aesculapius. Her name means 'All-Healer'.
Parcae	Three Roman goddesses of destiny. They were originally attendant spirits of childbirth.
Parian Marble	A stele inscribed with a summary of Greek history down to 264/3 BC.
Parmenides	A Greek philosopher from Elea, who lived in the middle of the fifth century BC.

Parthenian Sea	The eastern end of the Mediterranean Sea.
Parthenius	A Greek elegiac poet of the first century BC.
Paulus	Of Aegina, lived in the mid-seventh century AD. He was a Greek physician who wrote a medical history; his treatise on surgery influenced both European and Arabic surgery in the Middle Ages.
Pausanias	A Greek geographer and writer, perhaps originally from Magnesia in Asia Minor. He wrote a guide to Greece for Romans in the period AD 150–70.
Penates	Roman gods who guarded the home and hearth. Each Roman home had its own Penates. They were represented by two statues of seated youths.
Periander	Tyrant of Corinth, c. 625–585 BC. He was considered one of the seven wise men (sages) of Greece.
Pericles	An important Athenian statesman who lived c. 495–429 BC.
Persephone	In mythology, the daughter of Demeter, carried off by Hades to the underworld to be his bride; she was also known as Kore and (in Latin) Proserpina.
Phamenoth	A rendering of Amenoth, the name the Greeks gave to the Egyptian king Amenhotep III.
Philochorus	An Athenian who wrote on the myths and history of Attica, a type of literature called *Atthis* and its writers Atthidographers. He was executed shortly after 260 BC by Antigonus Gonatas.
Philodemus	A Greek poet and philosopher of the first century BC.
Philostratus	Flavius Philostratus, AD 170–c. 249, wrote on philosophers. His patrons were Julia Domna and the emperor Septimius Severus.
Photius	Patriarch of Constantinople, AD 858–67 and 878–86, and a scholar. He wrote the *Bibliotheca*, a critical survey of 280 prose works for his brother Tarasius.
Phrygia	A country in the centre of Asia Minor, east of Lydia.
Pierides	A poetic name for the Muses, from their haunt on Mount Pierus in Thessaly.
Pindar	Famous Greek Lyric poet from Boeotia, c. 518–438 BC.
Pittacus	A statesman of Mytilene, c. 650–570 BC remembered as one of the seven wise men of Greece.
Planudes	Maximus Planudes was a monk who edited the *Greek Anthology* in 1301.
Plato	An important Athenian philosopher, son of Perictione and Ariston, who lived c. 429–347.
Pliny	Gaius Plinius Secundus lived AD 23–79. He wrote history and an encyclopaedic *Natural History*; known as 'The Elder' to distinguish him from his younger nephew, the epistolographer.
Pliny the Younger	Gaius Plinius Caecilius Secundus, lived AD 61–c. 114, consul AD 100. He published a panegyric of Trajan, and ten books of letters.
Plutarch	A Greek philosopher and biographer from Chaeronea in Boeotia, who lived c. AD 46–c. 120.
Polis	A Greek city-state.
Pollux	A Roman scholar and rhetorician of the second century AD.
Polycrates	An Athenian sophist and writer, fourth century BC.
Porphyry	A philosopher and scholar, AD 232–305. Among many other works, he wrote a biography of Pythagoras.
Poseidon	The Greek god of water, especially the sea, and earthquakes. He was the brother of Zeus.
Prometheus	In Greek mythology he was a titan. He came to be regarded as a master craftsman who created people from clay.

Propertius	A Roman elegiac poet, c. 47–16 BC.
Ptolemy	The name of the Macedonian kings of Egypt, after Ptolemy I (c. 367–282 BC).
Ptolemy Alorites	Regent or perhaps king of Macedonia, c. 369–365 BC. He married Eurynome, the daughter of Amyntas III and Eurydice.
Ptolemy Philometor	The sixth Macedonian king of Egypt, c. 186–145 BC.
Pythagoras	An influential Greek philosopher, originally from Samos, who emigrated to Croton, c. 531 BC. He later moved to Metapontum, where he died.
Pythia	The priestess of Apollo at Delphi, his most important shrine. Inspired by the god, she pronounced his oracles.
Quintilian	A famous teacher of rhetoric, AD 35–c. 95. Wrote on the training of an orator and the education of children, with a useful review of Latin literature.
Rhea	In Greek mythology she was the daughter of Uranus and Gaea (Heaven and Earth) and by her brother Cronus, mother of the older Olympians (Hestia, Demeter, Hera, Hades, Poseidon and Zeus). Cronus ate all his children except Zeus, whom Rhea hid.
Rhinthon	Writer of a type of farce (Phylax play) popular in southern Italy and Alexandria. He lived in the early third century BC.
Romulus	The eponymous founder of Rome and its first king. He was said to be the son of the god Mars.
Sabine	The Sabines were an ancient people of central Italy, neighbours of Rome. In Roman legend they provided the first women for Rome.
Scylla	A monster of Greek mythology who would swoop down and devour sailors passing her cave.
Samos	A Greek island off the coast of Asia Minor.
Scipio Numantius	Publius Cornelius Scipio Aemilianus Africanus Numantinus (c. 185–129 BC), the Roman general who destroyed Numantia in Spain and Carthage. He married Sempronia, the sister of the Gracchi, but lead the political faction opposed to them. He was associated in Rome with a Stoic philosopher from Rhodes named Panaetius.
Seneca the Elder	Lucius or Marcus Annaeus Seneca (c. 60 BC–c. AD 37) was Roman rhetorician and writer. The *Controversies* was a collection of imaginary legal cases.
Seneca the Younger	Lucius Annaeus Seneca (c. 3 BC–AD 65), son of Seneca the Elder, was a Roman philosopher, dramatist, and politician. An adviser to Nero, he was accused of a conspiracy against the emperor and forced to commit suicide.
Seven Sages	In Greek legend seven early Greek philosophers were said to have met to discuss philosophy. There was no agreed canon of the seven; Diogenes Laertius lists Thales, Solon, Periander, Cleobulus, Chilon, Bias and Pittacus, but notes that Anacharsis, Myson, Pherecydes, Epimenides and Pisistratus may be added (1.12-14).
Severus	Lucius Septimius Severus was Roman emperor, 193–211 AD.
Sicyon	A small Greek polis, situated to the west of Corinth.
Silanion	An Athenian sculptor of the fourth century BC. He made statues of both Corinna and Sappho.
Simonides	Lyric and elegiac poet from Ceos, c. 556–468 BC.
Sinis	In Greek mythology he was brigand who would kill his victims by making them hold down a bent pine tree which would fling them into the air; he was killed by the hero Theseus.
Sinope	A Greek colony on the south shore of the Black Sea.
Siren	Sirens were half-bird, half-women monsters of myth who lured men to their deaths with their beautiful singing. They were said to sing the songs of Hades,

and accompany the dead to Hades. They are depicted on tombs where they could be described as mourning for the dead.

Socrates	A famous Athenian philosopher, 469–399 BC.
Socrates Scholasticus	Wrote a church history from AD 309 to the death of Theodosius (AD 450).
Soranus	A Greek physician and author of medical texts from Ephesus, who practised in Rome in the time of Trajan and Hadrian (AD 98–138).
Sotion	Alexandrian Peripatetic philosopher, who wrote 200–170 BC.
Statius	A Roman poet, AD c. 40–96.
Stobaeus	Compiler of an anthology of Greek poetry and prose in the fifth century AD.
Strategos	The Greek word for 'general', used in Roman Hellenistic Egypt as the title of an official.
Suda	A Greek lexicon compiled in the tenth century AD. Sometimes referred to as Suidas or *Suidae Lexicon*.
Suetonius	Roman biographer, c. AD 69–c. 140.
Symposium	A Greek drinking party; the entertainment at the party might include music, singing, hired entertainers, impromptu poetry and riddles, as well as conversation.
Tanagra	A Greek polis in eastern Boeotia.
Tartarus	In Greek mythology Tartarus is the deepest region of the underworld, beneath Hades, and the place where the gods locked away their enemies.
Tatian	A Greek Christian writer, mid-second century AD.
Tegea	A Dorian polis in Arcadia.
Telos	A small Greek island of the eastern Aegean sea, near Rhodes.
Tenos	A Greek island in the Cyclades.
Teos	A Greek city in Ionia.
Terpsichore	One of the Muses; in Roman times associated with lyric poetry and dance.
Thales	A Greek philosopher from Miletus, considered one of the seven sages. He was said to have been the son of Cleobulina, and to have lived in the early sixth century BC.
Thebes	The most important polis in Boeotia; the subject of much early Greek mythology.
Thebes (2)	An important Egyptian city.
Themistocles	An Athenian politician, c. 528–462 BC. He is famous for his role in the Persian wars and in establishing Athens as a maritime power.
Theocritus	A Greek pastoral poet from Syracuse, who worked in Sicily and Egypt, c. 310–250 BC.
Theodosius II	Roman emperor in the east, AD 408–450.
Theophrastus	A Peripatetic philosopher from Eresus in Lesbos, who took over Aristotle's school in Athens in 323 BC.
Thespiae	A Greek polis in southern Boeotia.
Thessaly	A district of northern Greece.
Thucydides	Athenian historian, c. 460–395 BC.
Tiberius	Born in 42 BC, Roman Emperor AD 14–37.
Tibullus	A Roman elegiac poet, c. 60–19 BC.
Timaeus	A Greek historian from Tauromenium in Sicily, c. 356–260 BC.
Titans	The 12 children of Uranus (Heaven) and Gaea (Earth): Oceanus, Coeus, Crius, Hyperion, Iapetus, Theia, Rhea, Themis, Mnemosyne, Phoebe, Tethys, Cronus.
Tithon	In Greek mythology the brother of King Priam of Troy, he became the lover of Eos (Dawn) and was granted eternal life, but not eternal youth.

Tlos	A town in Lycia.
Tribunate	By the late republic, tribunes (tribuni plebis) were elected in Rome each year to protect the rights of the plebians. They had important powers, including the right to veto acts of the other magistrates, elections and laws.
Triumvir	A member of a commission of three men, especially the triumvirate of Antony, Lepidus and Octavian (later called Augustus) in 43 BC. These three supporters of Julius Caesar cooperated after his assassination to restore order to the state by eliminating his and their political enemies.
Tyre	A city of the Phoenicians; now Sour in Lebanon. In Roman legend, the Carthaginians came originally from Tyre. Tyre was famous for its purple dye and 'Tyrian' came to mean both purple and Carthaginian.
Tzetes, John	A Greek scholar who worked in Byzantium in the twelfth century AD.
Uranus	(Also Ouranos) Father of Cronus, grandfather of Zeus, the first supreme male deity in Greek mythology. See Heaven.
Valerius Maximus	Wrote a compilation of historical anecdotes with moralizing commentary dedicated to the emperor Tiberius, c. AD 30.
Venus	An ancient Latin Goddess, later identified by the Romans with the Greek goddess of love, Aphrodite.
Vertumnus	A Roman fertility god, originally Etruscan. He had the ability to change into any shape and personified the idea of change.
Virgil	Publius Vergilius Maro (70–19 BC), the most famous Latin poet. Author of the epic *Aeneid*.
Vulgar Latin	The form of Latin spoken by the 'uneducated' classes in Italy and the provinces, which emerged in fifth century AD in literary works.
Xenophon	An Athenian historian, c. 428–c. 354 BC.
Zenobius	A Greek writer of the mid-second century AD.
Zephyr	A personification of the west wind.
Zeus	Son of Cronus and Rhea, he was the most powerful of the Olympian gods, ruler of heaven and earth.
Zonaras	John Zonaras was a Byzantine chronicler who lived from the 11th–mid 12th centuries AD. He wrote a history from creation until the accession of John Comnenus in AD 1118.
Zosimus	A Greek writer on alchemy who probably dates to about AD 300. Said to have written a chemical encyclopedia with his sister, Theosebeia.

Attested Women Writers of the Graeco-Roman World

This is a list of Greek and Roman women writers (i.e. composers of Greek or Latin verse or prose) from the seventh century BC to the fifth century AD who are attested in ancient sources with brief notes on what is known about them and their work. Authors who are included in this anthology are in bold; for the other authors a source which attests to their work is given. I have not included authors of private correspondence in this list, except where the correspondence was discussed as a literary piece or published in antiquity. The list includes some legendary women and some whose designation as 'author' is doubtful or only conjectural.

Acanthis	Greek lyric poetry; place of origin unknown, before c. AD 50. No work extant; referred to by Titus Calpurnius Siculus (*Eclogues* 6.76).
Aelia Eudocia	(See Eudocia Augusta).
Aesara	Greek philosophy; Lucania, third century BC. Extant work: some Pythagorean (pseudonymous?) literature ascribed to her (Stob. 1.49.27).
Aetheria	(See Egeria).
Agallis	Greek prose (literary criticism); Corcyra, third century BC. No work extant; wrote on Homer (Athen. 1.14d, *Suda* s.v. Anagallis).
Agrippina	Latin prose (history); Rome, AD 15–59. No work extant, but her family history used as a source by Tacitus (Tacitus, *Annals* 4.53; Plin. 7.46).
Alcinoë	Greek erotic poetry; Thronion, third century BC. No work extant (*IG* XII.5.812).
Anagora	Greek lyric poet?; Miletus, sixth century BC. No work attributed to her, but she is listed as a pupil of Sappho (*Suda* s.v. Sappho).
Andromeda	Greek lyric poetry; Lesbos seventh–sixth centuries BC. No work extant, but named as a rival to Sappho (Maximus of Tyre, *Orations* 18.9).
Antiochis	Greek prose (medicines); Tlos, Lycia, first century AD. One of Fabulla's medicines attributed to her (Galen 13.250, 341); an honorary inscription by and to her is extant.
Anyte	Greek lyric poetry (epigrams); Tegea, c. 300 BC. Extant work: 21 of 24 extant epigrams attributed to her.
Arignote	Greek philosophy; Croton?, c. 500 BC. Extant work: some later Pythagorean (pseudonymous?) literature ascribed to her; wrote a history of Dionysius (Clement of Alexandria, *Stromata* 4.7).
Aristodama	Greek epic poetry; Smyrna, c. 220 BC. No work extant (*IG* IX.2.62).
Aristomache	Greek poetry; Erythrae, third century BC. No work extant.
Aspasia	Greek lyric poetry and prose (epigrams and rhetoric); Miletus and Athens, fifth century BC. No work extant, but some pseudonymous literature attributed to her (*Anth. Plan.* 4.17, 5.6; Plato, *Menexenus*).
Aspasia II	Greek prose (medicine); second century AD. No work extant. She wrote on gynaecology and obstetrics.
Astyanassa	Greek erotic prose; figure of legend—the maid of Helen and Menelaus. Name

	used for pseudonymous erotic literature. No work extant (*Suda* s.v.).
Athenaïs	(See Eudocia Augusta).
Boeo	Greek lyric poetry (epigrams); Delphi, third century BC? Extant work: two fragments of a Delphic hymn.
Caecilia Trebulla	Greek iambic poetry (epigrams); Roman, fl. c. 130 AD. Extant work: three poems inscribed as graffiti on the Colossus of Memnon at Thebes, Egypt.
Charixena	Greek lyric poetry; Athens?, c. fifth century BC. No work extant (*Suda* s.v., *Etymologicum Magnum* 36.7.21).
Claudia Trophime	Greek lyric poetry (epigrams); Ephesus, AD 92/93. Extant work: two inscriptions at Ephesus (*Inscr. Eph.* 1062 G).
Cleitagora	Greek lyric poetry (drinking songs?); Sparta (or perhaps Thessaly), fifth century BC. No work extant (*Suda* s.v., Schol. on Ar., *Lysistrata* 1237 and *Wasps* 1245).
Cleito	Greek lyric (?) poetry; origins unknown; fourth century BC or earlier. No work extant (Tatian, *Oration to the Greeks* 33).
Cleobulina	Greek lyric poetry (riddles); Rhodes?, c. sixth century BC? Extant work: 3 riddles. She was also known as Eumetis.
Cleopatra	Greek prose (medicines); Alexandria, first century AD. Incorrectly identified as Queen Cleopatra VII. Extant work: fragments preserved by Galen, Aëtius, Paulus Aegineta.
Cleopatra II	Greek prose (alchemy); Alexandria, first–third centuries AD? Pseudonym (?) for a Greek alchemical writer, cited by Olympiodorus and Zosimus.
Clodia	Latin poetry, plays; first century BC. No extant work. Cicero alludes to her work (Cicero, *For Marcus Caelius* 64).
Corinna	Greek lyric poetry; Tanagra, third century BC (though ancient sources place her in the fifth century BC). Extant work: about 42 fragments.
Cornelia	Latin prose (rhetoric); Rome, second century BC. Extant work: fragments of two letters (authenticity in doubt).
Cornificia	Latin poetry (epigrams); Rome, first century BC. No work extant (Jerome, *Chronicle*, Olympic Year 184.4).
Cynthia	Greek lyric poetry; Rome, first century BC. No work extant: Propertius praises her poetry (*Elegies* 2.3.21-2). Apuleius claims that her real name was Hostia (*Apology* 10), though she may be fictional.
Damo	(An alternative spelling of Demo).
Damophyla	Greek lyric poetry (love poetry and hymns); Pamphylia, sixth century BC (?). No work extant. Said to have been an associate of Sappho (Philostratus, *Life of Apollonius of Tyana* 1.30).
Demareta	Greek poetry; date and place of origin unknown (but before c. AD 200). Named by Athenaeus as the author of a poem entitled *Trefoil* (15.685B).
Demo	Greek lyric poetry (epigram); Greek, date uncertain, but probably early second century AD. Author of one poem extant on Colossus of Memnon at Thebes, Egypt, as graffiti. (Also known as Damo.)
Demo II	Greek prose (literary criticism); date uncertain (fifth century AD?). No work extant; said to have written an allegorical commentary on Homer (J. Cramer [ed.], *Anecdota Graeca* III, 189.19).
Dionysia	Greek lyric poetry (epigram); place of origin unknown, second century AD. Extant work: one short inscription as graffiti on the Colossus of Memnon at Thebes, Egypt.
Diophila	Greek poetry (astronomy); Alexandria, c. 300 BC. No work extant. Schol. on

	Callimachus frag.10.
Egeria	Latin prose (travel diary); Galicia (Western Spain), early fifth century AD. Extant work: travel journal and description of Christian liturgy in Jerusalem. She is also known as Aetheria and Silvia Aquitana.
Elephantis	Greek erotic prose and medicines; Greek, from Elephantis?, late first century BC. No work extant, but cited and paraphrased by Pliny (28.81).
Erinna	Greek lyric poetry; Rhodes or Telos, c. 350 BC. Extant work: 7 poems (some fragments).
Eriphanis	Greek lyric poetry (pastoral); probably a fictional character. Said by Clearchus in Book 1 of his *Love Stories* to have been the author of pastoral poetry (Athen. 14.619c).
Eucheria	Latin satirical poetry; Aquitania, c. AD 600. Extant work: one satirical poem.
Eudocia Augusta	Greek epic poetry (Christian); Byzantium and Jerusalem, c. AD 400–460. Extant work: epic (about 900 lines) and a papyrus fragment. Also known as Aelia Eudocia, Eudoxia Augusta and Athenaïs.
Eudoxia Augusta	Alternative name for Eudocia Augusta (see above).
Eumetis	Alternative name for Cleobulina (see above).
Eunica	Greek lyric poet?; Salamis, sixth century BC. No work attributed to her, but she is listed as a pupil of Sappho (*Suda* s.v. Sappho).
Eurydice	Greek lyric poetry (epigram); Macedonia, fourth century BC. One verse epigram extant (and two short dedicatory inscriptions).
Eustochium	See Paula (below).
Fabulla	Latin ? prose (medicines); Libya, before AD 210. Extant work: two medicines quoted by Galen.
Faltonia	See Proba (below).
Funisulana Vettulla	Latin prose (graffiti); Thebes, Egypt, AD 82; one inscription on the Colossus of Memnon (A. and E. Bernard, *Les Inscriptions Grecque et Latines du Colosse de Memnon*).
Glauce	Greek lyric poetry; Chios, c. 300 BC. No work extant (Theocritus, *Idyl* 4.30).
Gnathaena	Greek prose; Athens, second half of the fourth century BC. A prostitute, said to have written *Rules for Dining in Company* for her lovers in imitation of philosophers' rules, cited by Callimachus (in Athen. 13.585b).
Gongyla	Greek lyric poet?; Colophon, sixth century BC. No work attributed to her, but she is listed as a pupil of Sappho (*Suda* s.v. Sappho).
Gorgo	Greek lyric poetry; Lesbos, seventh–sixth centuries BC. No work extant, but named as a rival to Sappho (Maximus of Tyre, *Orations* 18.9).
Hedyle	Greek elegiac poetry; Athens, second half of the fourth century BC. Extant work: 1 fragment.
Hipparchia	Greek prose (philosophy); Thebes, fourth century BC. No work extant. A Cynic philosopher (*Suda* s. v. Hipparchia).
Histiaea	Greek prose (grammar, history and topography); Alexandra, c. 200 BC. No work extant (Str. 13.599). Her name was also spelt Hestiaea.
Hortensia	Latin prose (rhetoric); Rome, 42 BC. No work extant, but one speech reported by Appian (*Civil Wars* 4.32-4).
Hostia	Apuleius tells us this was the real name of Propertius' Cynthia (*Apology* 10). See Cynthia above.
Hypatia	Greek philosophy, mathematics and astronomy; Alexandria, died AD 415. No work extant, except her revised version of a commentary by Theon (Socrates Scholasticus, *Church History* 7.15, *Suda* s.v.).

Iambe
Greek iambic poetry; the mythical daughter of Pan and Echo, inventor of iambic poetry (Apollodorus 1.5.1; *Homeric Hymn to Demeter* 202; Diodorus Siculus 5.4).

Isis
Greek prose (alchemy); Greek Egyptian, c. first century AD? Pseudonym of alchemist. Extant work: an address to her son Horus (*CAG* II.28-33).

Julia Balbilla
Greek elegiac poetry (epigrams); Roman, second century AD. Extant work: four poems inscribed c. AD 130 as graffiti on the Colossus of Memnon at Thebes, Egypt.

Julia Domna
Greek prose (letter): native of Syria, the wife of Roman Emperor Septimius Severus; died AD 208. Extant work: a letter to the Ephesians, inscribed and published at Ephesus (*Inscr. Eph.* 212).

Julia Saturnina
Greek prose (graffiti); Roman, second century AD. Extant work: one short inscription as graffiti on the Colossus of Memnon at Thebes, Egypt.

Laïs
Greek prose (medicines); before AD 79 (cf. Laïs the famous *hetaera* from Hyccara, fl. 416 BC). No work extant, but cited and paraphrased by Pliny (28.81, 82).

Learchis
Greek lyric (?) poetry; origins unknown; fourth century BC or earlier. No work extant (Tatian, *Oration to the Greeks* 33).

Leontion
Greek prose (philosophy); Athenian fourth–third centuries BC. No work extant; she was an Epicurean (Cicero, *Nature of the Gods* 1.93, Diog. Laert. 10.4-7, .23, Athen. 13.588b; Plin. Preface 29 may refer to her).

Maia
Greek prose (medicines); origins unknown: name generic, used as a title by midwives; before AD 210. Extant work: one short fragment in Galen.

Maria
Greek prose (alchemy); Jewish, origins unknown, date uncertain: first century AD? Her name is generally thought to be a pseudonym. Extant work: numerous fragments in Olympiodorus and Zosimus.

Megalostrata
Greek lyric poetry; Sparta, late 7th century BC. No work extant, but referred to by Alcman (poem 6).

Melinno
Greek lyric poetry; Lesbos (?) c. 200-150 BC. Extant work: one hymn.

Melissa
Greek philosophy; Samos, c. third century BC. Extant work: some Pythagorean (pseudonymous?) literature ascribed to her.

Metrodora
Greek prose (medicine); second century AD. Extant work: treatise entitled *On the female suffering of the mother* (R. Pintaudi [ed.], *Dai papiri della Biblioteca Medicea Laurenziana*, III [Firenze: Gonnelli, 1979] 75.3f.4-33).

Mnesiarchis
Greek lyric (?) poetry; Euboea, fourth century BC (or earlier). No work extant (Tatian, *Oration to the Greeks* 33).

Moero
Greek lyric and epic poetry; Byzantium, c. 300 BC. Extant work: three poems. She was also known as Myro.

Moschine
Greek poetry; Athens, c. 320 BC (mother of Hedyle). No work extant (Athen. 7.297 A-B).

Myia
Greek philosophy; Croton?, c. 500 BC. No genuine work extant (some Pythagorean pseudonymous literature of the third century BC ascribed to her).

Myia II
Greek lyric poetry; Sparta, fifth or third century BC (?). No work extant. Wrote hymns to Apollo and Artemis (*Suda* s.v.).

Myia III
Greek lyric poetry; Thespia, date unknown. No work extant.

Mynna
Greek lyric poetry; Lesbos? Date unknown. No work extant—said to use the Aeolic dialect (John Grammaticus, *On the Aeolic Dialect* 1.22).

Myro
An alternative spelling of Moero (see above) (*Suda* s.v.).

Myrtis
Greek lyric poetry; Anthedon, fifth century BC. Extant work: a prose summary of one of her poems.

Mystis	Greek lyric (?) poetry; date and origins unknown (before AD 165). No work extant (Tatian, *Oration to the Greeks* 33).
Nicobule	Greek prose (history); perhaps 300 BC, origins unknown. Two fragments of her history of Alexander the Great extant (Athen. 10.434C, 12.537D; cf. *Scriptores Historiarum Alexandri Magni* 157, J.2B667; FGrH 127).
Nossis	Greek lyric poetry (epigrams); Locri, c. 300 BC. Extant work: 12 epigrams.
Olympias	Greek prose (medicines); Thebes, before AD 79. Extant work: cited and paraphrased by Pliny (*Natural History* 20–28).
Pamphila	Greek prose (history); Epidaurus, first century AD. Extant work: 10 fragments from original 33 books.
Pantaenis	Greek lyric poetry; Rome, first century AD or perhaps a contemporary of Sappho. No work extant (Martial 7.69).
Parthenis	Greek lyric poetry (epigrams); origins unknown, before 100 BC. No work extant (Meleanger, *Anth. Pal.* 4.1.31-2).
Paula	Latin prose (letter); Rome, late fourth century AD. Extant work: one private letter, written with her daughter Eustochium from Jerusalem to Marcella in Rome, published in the correspondence of Jerome (*Letters* 46).
Perictione	Greek prose (philosophy); Alexandria(?), fourth–third centuries BC. Extant work: some Pythagorean pseudonymous (?) literature ascribed to her.
Perictione II	Greek prose (philosophy); Alexandria(?), 3rd–2nd centuries BC. Extant work: some Pythagorean pseudonymous (?) literature ascribed to her.
Perilla	Latin poetry; Rome, early first century AD. No work extant. Ovid, probably her stepfather, mentions her work, but it is not known if she published any of it (Ovid, *Tristia* 3.7).
Perpetua	Latin prose (autobiography); Carthage, AD 181–203. Extant work: one work attributed to her, an account of her arrest and trial in AD 203, leading up to her martyrdom (*Acts of the Christian Martyrs* 8.2-10).
Phanothea	Greek poetry (hexameters); mythological figure, said to have invented the hexameter (Clement of Alexandria, *Miscellanies* 1.366; Stob., *Anthology* 21.26).
Phantasia	Greek epic poetry; Memphis, eighth century BC. Legendary figure, said to have predated Homer, and been his source for the *Iliad* and *Odyssey* (Ptolemaeus Chennus in Photius 190.151a-b).
Philaenis	Greek erotic prose; Leucas, fourth century BC. Extant work: one fragment on papyrus (*P. Oxy.* 2891; for testimonia see Athen. 220F, 335b-d, 457e; Polybius XII 13.1; *Anth. Pal.* VII 450).
Philinna	Greek poetry (enchantments in hexameters); Thessaly, first century BC or earlier. Extant work: one papyrus fragment.
Phintys	Greek philosophy; Sparta (?) third century BC (?). Extant work: some Pythagorean pseudonymous (?) literature ascribed to her.
Plotina Augusta	Greek and Latin prose (letters); wife of Roman emperor Trajan, she died about AD 121. Extant work: one letter to the Athenian Epicurians, and one petition to Hadrian, both inscribed on marble (*IG* II^2 1099, *ILS* 7784).
Praxigoris	Greek lyric (?) poetry; date and origins unknown (before AD 165). Her name should perhaps be Praxagoris. No work extant (Tatian, *Oration to the Greeks* 33).
Praxilla	Greek lyric poetry (dithyrambs, hymns and scolia); Sicyon, mid-fifth century BC. Extant work: 6 fragments.
Proba	Latin epic poetry (and cento); Rome, AD c. 322–c. 370. Extant work: 1 Christian Virgilian cento. Her full name was Faltonia Betitia Proba.

Ptolemaïs   Greek muscial theory; Cyrene and Alexandria, between fourth century BC and
                       first century AD, perhaps c. 250 BC. Extant work: three fragments quoted by
                       Porphyry.

Sabina Augusta   Greek prose inscription; Rome (wife of the Emperor Hadrian), second century
                       AD. Extant work: one inscription on the Colossus of Memnon at Thebes,
                       Egypt, now incomplete.

Salpe   Greek *paignia* (frivolous works), possibly pornography; Lesbos, date uncertain
                       (third century BC?). No work extant (*Athen.* 322 A, = Nymphodorus of
                       Syracuse, *FGrH* 572 F5 cf. Polybius 12.13 = Timaeus, *FGrH* 566 T2).

Salpe   Greek prose (medicines); before 79 AD. Extant work: cited and paraphrased by
                       Pliny.

Samithra   Greek prose (medicines); origin and date uncertain, before AD 210. Extant
                       work: one fragment quoted by Galen (13.310).

Sappho   Greek lyric poetry; Lesbos, seventh–sixth century BC; fl. c. 620–600 BC.
                       Extant work: 200+ fragments.

Sempronia   Latin poetry; Rome, first century BC. No work extant (Sallust, *Conspiracy of
                       Catiline* 25).

Silvia Aquitana   (See Egeria).

Sotira   Greek prose (medicines); origins unknown, before AD 79. Extant work: cited
                       and paraphrased by Pliny (28.83).

Sulpicia I   Latin elegiac poetry; Rome, late first century BC. Extant work: 11 (or only 8?)
                       elegies preserved in the corpus of Tibullus.

Sulpicia II   Latin poetry (satire); Rome, late first century AD. Extant work: 2 lines; a 70
                       line poem in her name is also extant.

Syra   (= the Syrian; name lost from manuscript) Greek poetry (enchantments in
                       hexameters); Syria, first century BC or earlier. Extant work: one papyrus
                       fragment.

Telesilla   Greek lyric poetry; Argos, early fifth century BC. Extant work: 5 short
                       fragments.

Terentia   Latin poetry; Rome/Egypt, second century AD. Extant work: one epitaph to
                       her brother, once inscribed on the pyramid of Cheops.

Thaliarchis   Greek lyric (?) poetry; Argos, fourth century BC (or earlier). No work extant
                       (Tatian, *Oration to the Greeks* 33).

Theano   Greek philosophy; Croton (?), c. 515 BC. Extant work: some Pythagorean
                       pseudonymous literature (mostly of the third century BC) ascribed to her.

Theano II   Greek lyric poetry; Locri, date unknown, but among the 'early writers'
                       (perhaps third century BC). No work extant (*Suda* s.v., Eustathius, *On the Iliad*
                       2.327.10, Clement of Alexandria, *Miscellanies* 1.80.3).

Theophila   Greek lyric poetry; Rome, first century AD. No work extant (Martial 7.69).

Theosebeia   Greek lyric poetry (epigram); date and place of origin unknown, third–sixth
                       centuries AD possible. Extant work: one epigram.

Theosebeia II   Greek prose (alchemy); third–fourth centuries AD. Extant work: collaborated
                       with her brother Zosimus in composing an alchemical encyclopaedia in 28
                       books, of which there are substantial fragments. (*Suda*; cf. *CAG* II.148, 153-
                       54, 156, etc).

Timaris   Greek poetry (hymns?); date and origins uncertain: first century AD or earlier;
                       a Hellenistic queen. No work extant, but Pliny refers to her *Hymn to Venus*
                       (37.178).

Timoxena   Greek prose (epistle); first century AD(?). No work extant (Plut., *Moralia*
                       145 A).

Unnamed I	(Daughter of Thucydides Greek prose (history); Athens, late fifth century BC. Some ancient readers attributed Book 8 of Thucydides' *Histories* to her (Marcellinus, *Life of Thucydides* 43).
Unnamed II	Greek prose (philosophy); name, origins and date unknown (between fourth century BC and first century AD). Author of a critical commentary on Theophrastus (Plin., preface 29); may be a reference to Leontion.
Unnamed III	(Wife of Pompeius Saturnius) Latin prose (epistles); second century AD. No work extant. Pliny the Younger discusses her work but does not give her name (*Epistles* 1.16.6).
Vestal	(An unnamed Vestal virgin) Latin verse; Rome, first century BC. One hexameter verse extant (Seneca the Elder, *Controversies* 6.8).
Vibia Perpetua	See Perpetua.
Xanite	Greek prose (medicines); origin and date uncertain, before AD 210. Extant work: one fragment (Galen 13.311).
Zenobia	Greek (?) prose (history); queen of Palmyra, late third century AD. Extant work: her history of Alexandria and the East is not extant (Trebellius Pollio, *Thirty Tyrants* 30.22); two pseudonymous fragments of correspondence purporting to be from her to the Roman emperor Aurelianus (*Augustan History*: Flavius Vopsicus, *Aurelian* 27; *FGrH* 3.664; Anon., *FGrH* 4.197).

Attested Verse Oracles

This is a list of attested givers of verse oracles. The oracle-givers were not regarded as the authors of the verses.[1]

Aristonice   Greek poetry (Pythian oracles); Delphi, c. 480 BC. Extant work: two attested fragments (Herodotus 7.140-41).

Demo   Greek poetry (Sibylline oracles); Cumae, date uncertain (sixth–fifth centuries BC?). No work extant. Pausanias 10.12.8.

Herophile   Greek poetry (Sibylline oracles); Samos or Erythrae: a name given to all Sibyls (or Sibyllae) from Erythrae. Extant work: numerous fragments; two collections from antiquity (cf. Pausanias 10.12).

Perialla   Greek poetry (Pythian oracles); Delphi, c. 495 BC. No work extant (Herodotus 6.66).

Phaënnis   Greek poetry (oracles); Dodona, daughter of the king of the Chaonians, born c. 280 BC. Extant work: one fragment a verse prophecy (Pausanias 10.15.2; cf. 10.12.5).

Phemonoë   Greek poetry (Pythian oracles). Delphi, date uncertain—said to have been the first Pythian prophet and to have invented the hexameter. Extant work: one attested fragment (Pausanias 10.6.6, 5.4; Diog. L. 1.40; cf. also J. Cramer (ed.), *Anecdota Graeca* III, 189.19).

Pythia   Greek poetry (Pythian oracles); Delphi, throughout the Classical Period. A title held by the chief priestess, who gave verse or prose oracles from Apollo.

Sabbe   Greek poetry (Sibylline oracles); Palestine, Babylon of Egypt, date uncertain, but early. No work extant (Pausanias 10.12.9).

Sibylla   Greek poetry (hexameter oracles); figure of legend, said to have been the first woman to give oracles at Delphi (Pausanias 10.12.1).

Themistocleia   Greek poetry (Pythian oracles); Delphi, date uncertain, probably fictitious. No work extant; said to have been the source for Pythagoras' doctrine (Aristoxenus frg.2; Diog. L. 8.1.8, .21).

Xenocleia   Greek poetry (Pythian oracles); Delphi, date unknown, said to have been in the time of Heracles. Extant work: one attested fragment.

Notes

1. For collections of the Delphic oracles, see H.W. Parke and D.E.W. Wormell, *The Delphic Oracle* (Oxford: Blackwell, 1956), and J. Fontenrose, *The Delphic Oracle: Its Responses and Operations with a Catalogue of Responses* (Berkeley: University of California Press, 1978). The verse (hexameter) oracles have been collected by L. Anderson, *Studies in Oracular Voice: Concordance to Delphic Responses in Hexameter* (Copenhagen: Scientarium Danica Regia Academia, 1987).

Chronological Survey of Women Writers of the Ancient Word

The dates of many of the women writers are uncertain or unknown. This list suggests a century for each writer but should not be taken as definitive in each case. Women named as oracles are included.

Women writers centuries BC

Legendary	7th	6th	5th	4th	3rd	2nd	1st
Astyanassa	Andromeda	Anagora	Aristonice	Anyte	Aesara	Cornelia	Clodia
Iambe	Megalostrata	Arignote	Aspasia	Cleito	Agallis	Maria	Cornificia
Phanothea	Gorgo	Cleobulina	Charixena	Diophila	Alcinoë	Melinno	Cynthia (Hostia)
Phantasia	Sappho	Damophyla	Cleitagora	Erinna	Aristodama	Parthenis	Elephantis
Phemonoë		Eunica	Demo (Sibyl)	Eurydice	Aristomache	Perictione II	Hortensia
Sibylla		Gongyla	Myia II	Glauce	Boeo		Philinna
Themistocleia		Myia	Myrtis	Hedyle	Corinna		Sempronia
Xenocleia		Theano	Perialla	Hipparchia	Histiaea		Sulpicia I
			Praxilla	Learchis	Melissa		Syra
			Telesilla	Leontion	Perictione		Vestal
				Mnesiarchis	Phaënnis		
				Moero	Phintys		
				Moschine	Ptolemaïs		
				Nicobule	Salpe (Paignia)		
				Nossis	Theano		
				Philaenis			
				Gnathaena			

Other writers (especially those mentioned in this work) centuries BC

8th	7th	6th	5th	4th	3rd	2nd	1st
Homer	Alcaeus	Cleobulus	Aeschylus	Aristotle	Callimachus	Meleager	Antipater
Hesiod	Tyrtaeus		Aristophanes	Ctesias	Cato	Plautus	Catullus
	Solon		Crates	Heraclides	Dioscorides		Julius Caesar
			Cratinus	Plato	Philochorus		Cicero
			Euripides	Theophrastus	Theocritus		Livy
			Herodotus	Xenophon			Propertius
			Pindar				Tibullus
			Sophocles				Virgil
			Thucydides				Seneca (Elder)

Women writers centuries AD

1st	2nd	3rd	4th	5th	6th
Agrippina	Aspasia II	Julia Domna	Paula	Demo II	Eucheria
Acanthis	Cleopatra II	Perpetua	Proba	Egeria	
Antiochis	Caecilia Trebulla	Theosebeia		Eudocia Augusta	
Claudia Trophime	Demo	Theosebeia II		Hypatia	
Cleopatra	Dionysia	Zenobia			
Demareta	Fabulla				
Funisulana	Julia Balbilla				
Vettulla					
Isis	Julia Saturnina				
Laïs	Maia				
Maria	Metrodora				
Olympias	Plotina Augusta				
Pamphila	Sabina Augusta				
Pantaenis	Samithra				
Perilla	Terentia				
Salpe	Xanite				
Sotira					
Sulpicia II					
Theophila					
Timaris					
Timoxena					

Other writers (especially those mentioned in this work) centuries AD

1st	2nd	3rd	4th	5th
Lucian	Clement	Athenaeus	Eusebius	St Augustine
Martial	Galen	Diogenes Laertius	Iamblichus	Jerome
Ovid	Aulus Gellius	Porphyry		Stobaeus
Pliny	Juvenal	Tertullian		
Plutarch	Pausanias	Zosimus		
Quintilian	Pliny (Younger)			
Seneca (Younger)	Pollux			
Valerius Maximus	Suetonius			
	Tacitus			
	Tatian			
	Zenobius			

Select Tables of Comparative Numeration

I have supplied tables of comparative numeration with the standard editions for Corinna, Sappho and Sulpicia.

Corinna

Plant	PMG	
1	1i	654
2	1ii	654
3	2	655
4	4	657
5	9	662
6	10	663
7	11a	664a
8	11b	664b
9	21	674
10	37	690
11	37	690

Sulpicia

Plant	3 Book Text	4 Book Text
1	[Tib] 3.13	[Tib] 4.7
2	[Tib] 3.14	[Tib] 4.8
3	[Tib] 3.15	[Tib] 4.9
4	[Tib] 3.16	[Tib] 4.10
5	[Tib] 3.17	[Tib] 4.11
6	[Tib] 3.18	[Tib] 4.12
7	[Tib] 3.9	[Tib] 4.3
8	[Tib] 3.11	[Tib] 4.5
9	[Tib] 3.8	[Tib] 4.2
10	[Tib] 3.10	[Tib] 4.4
11	[Tib] 3.12	[Tib] 4.6

Sappho

Plant (P)	L-P	P	L-P	P	L-P	P	LP	P	L-P
1	1	21	49	41	105abc	61	127	81	152
2	2	22	50	42	106	62	128	82	153
3	5	23	51	43	107	63	129	83	154
4	15	24	52	44	108	64	130-1	84	155
5	16	25	53	45	109	65	132	85	156
6	17	26	54	46	110a	66	133	86	157
7	30	27	55	47	111	67	134	87	158
8	31	28	56	48	112	68	135	88	159
9	32	29	57	49	113	69	136	89	160
10	33	30	81	50	114	70	137	90	166, 167
11	34	31	82a	51	115	71	140a	91	168, 178
12	35	32	91	52	116	72	141	92	–
13	36	33	94	53	117	73	142	93	–
14	37	34	95	54	118	74	143	94	S/A 16
15	39	35	96	55	120	75	144	95	S/A 23
16	41	36	98a-b	56	121	76	146	96	S/A 25
17	44	37	100	57	122	77	147	97	S/A 25C
18	Alc.	38	102	58	123	78	148	98	157D
	304	39	103	59	124	79	150	99	158D
19	47	40	104a-b	60	126	80	151	100	159D
20	48								

PMG = D.L. Page, *Poetae Melici Graeci* (Oxford: Clarendon Press, 1962).
L-P = E. Lobel and D.L. Page, *Poetarum Lesbiorum Fragmenta* (Oxford: Clarendon Press, 1963).

Maps

Eurydice

MACEDONIA

By

Moero

Philinna

THESSALY

Boeo
Olympias LESBOS
Myrtis
Corinna

Melinno

Philaenis

Praxilla Le
Telesilla
Anyte

De
An
Th
Si

At

Hedyle
Eudocia

My AEOLIS

Sappho

IONIA

Melissa

SAMOS

Ar Ep
Te

Mi

Aspasia

Key to cities

An = Anthedon
Ar = Argos
At = Athens
By = Byzantium
De = Delphi
Ep = Epidauros
Le = Leucas
Li = Lindus
Mi = Miletus
My = Mytilene
Si = Sicyon
Sp = Sparta
T = Tanagra
Te = Tegea
Th = Thebes

Sp

Pamphila
Phintys

Erinna
Cleobulina

TELOS

RHODES

Li

N

CRETE

0   kms   250

Map 1. Greece. Places of birth (where known) of Greek women writers in this collection.

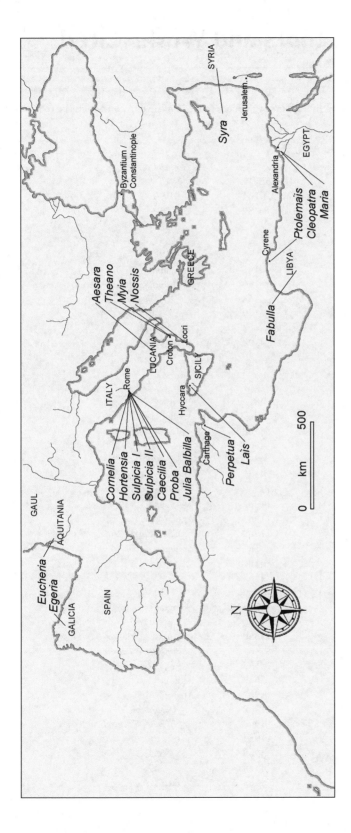

Map 2. The Mediterranean. Places of birth, citizenship or residence (where known) of women writers in this collection.

Index of Authors and Works Cited

In this index works cited within a footnote are referenced on the page on which the footnote marker appears.

General Index